Quantum-Enhanced Cloud AI: The Next Frontier in Machine Learning and Deep Learning

Edited by

Satveer Kour
Department of Computer Engineering and Technology
Guru Nanak Dev University
Amritsar, Punjab, India

Harvinder Singh
Department of Mechanical Engineering
Chandigarh Engineering College-CGC Landran, Mohali
Punjab, India

Anupam Bonkra
Department of Computer Science and Engineering
Maharishi Markandeshwar (Deemed to be University)
Mullana, Haryana, India

&

Rupinder Singh
Chitkara University Institute of Engineering and Technology
Chitkara University
Rajpura, Punjab, India

Quantum-Enhanced Cloud AI:The Next Frontier in Machine Learning and Deep Learning

Editors: Rupinder Singh, Harvinder Singh, Anupam Bonkra and Rupinder Singh

ISBN (Online): 979-8-89881-321-5

ISBN (Print): 979-8-89881-322-2

ISBN (Paperback): 979-8-89881-323-9

Published by Bentham Science Publishers Pte. Ltd. Singapore, in collaboration with Eureka Conferences, USA.

First published in 2026.

need for a court order if at any point you breach any terms of this License Agreement. In no event will any delay or failure by Bentham Science Publishers in enforcing your compliance with this License Agreement constitute a waiver of any of its rights.

3. You acknowledge that you have read this License Agreement, and agree to be bound by its terms and conditions. To the extent that any other terms and conditions presented on any website of Bentham Science Publishers conflict with, or are inconsistent with, the terms and conditions set out in this License Agreement, you acknowledge that the terms and conditions set out in this License Agreement shall prevail.

Bentham Science Publishers Pte. Ltd.
No. 9 Raffles Place
Office No. 26-01
Singapore 048619
Singapore
Email: subscriptions@benthamscience.net

BENTHAM SCIENCE

CONTENTS

FOREWORD i

PREFACE ii

LIST OF CONTRIBUTORS iv

CHAPTER 1 QUANTUM-POWERED AI IN THE CLOUD: UNLEASHING THE FUTURE OF INTELLIGENT COMPUTING 1
Jaspreet Kaur, Satveer Kour, Megha Bhushan and *Harvinder Singh*
INTRODUCTION 1
FUNDAMENTALS OF CLOUD-BASED QUANTUM AI 3
Quantum Computing Basics 3
Shor's Algorithm 4
Grover's Algorithm 4
Cloud Computing in AI 4
Amazon Web Services (AWS) 5
Google Cloud AI 5
Microsoft Azure AI 5
Integration of Quantum Computing with AI in the Cloud 6
Quantum Machine Learning (QML) 6
Hybrid Quantum-Classical Computing 6
Quantum Neural Networks (QNNs) 6
CLOUD-BASED QUANTUM PLATFORMS 6
IBM Quantum Experience 7
Google Quantum AI 7
Microsoft Azure Quantum 7
Amazon Braket 7
CHALLENGES IN CLOUD-BASED QUANTUM AI 8
Hardware Limitations 8
Algorithm Development 8
Security Concerns 8
Cost and Accessibility 8
FUTURE FORECASTS AND AREAS FOR INVESTIGATION 9
Quantum Hardware Achievements 9
Improving Qubit Coherence 9
Diminishing Error Rates 9
Scalable Quantum Processors 9
Optimization of Quantum AI Algorithms 10
Hybrid Quantum-Classical Learning 10
Quantum Generative Models 10
Quantum Assisted Optimization 10
Standardization of Quantum Cloud Infrastructure 10
Interoperability Standards 10
Future Policy and Ethical Frameworks 11
Compliance in Sensitive Areas 11
AI Ethics and Governance 11
The Need for International Governance on Quantum AI 11
CONCLUSION 11
ACKNOWLEDGEMENTS 13
REFERENCES 13

CHAPTER 2 REVOLUTIONIZE AI: QUANTUM-CLOUD DELVES INTO INTEGRATION STRATEGIES, BENEFITS, AND FUTURE PROSPECTS 16
Vineeta Gulati, Arun Kumar Rana and *Kashif Nisar*
INTRODUCTION 17
Motivation and Problem Statement 17
Research Contribution 18
FUNDAMENTALS OF QUANTUM COMPUTING 18
Basics of Quantum Mechanics 18
Superposition and Entanglement 18
Noisy Intermediate-Scale Quantum (NISQ) Era 19
Hybrid Quantum-classical Systems 19
Comparison of Classical and Quantum Computing 20
Future Directions 21
CLOUD AI SERVICES 21
Overview of Cloud AI Services 22
INTEGRATION OF QUANTUM COMPUTING WITH CLOUD AI SERVICES 22
Quantum Algorithms for Cloud AI Services 23
QSVM (Quantum Support Vector Machines) 24
Variational Quantum Eigensolver (VQE) 24
Quantum Approximate Optimization Algorithm (QAOA) 24
Quantum Clustering Algorithms 24
REAL-WORLD APPLICATIONS AND CASE STUDIES 24
Supply Chain Management and Logistics 25
Quantum Computing for Quality Control in Production 25
Optimal Carbon Capture Materials 25
Pharmaceutical Research Advances 26
Ethical and Social Implications 26
CHALLENGES AND FUTURE PROSPECTS 27
Challenges 27
Ethical and Social Implications 27
Challenges of Integration 27
Technical Limitations 28
Need for Resources and Scalability 28
Features and Properties of Data 28
Ethical and Societal Concerns 28
Addressing Ethical Issues 28
Ecosystem for Collaboration and Innovation 29
Investing in Workforce Development 29
Future Prospects 29
Quantum AI: Potential for Transformation 29
CONCLUSION 30
ACKNOWLEDGEMENTS 30
REFERENCES 30

CHAPTER 3 APPLICATIONS OF QUANTUM AI IN HEALTHCARE, FINANCE, AND CYBERSECURITY 33
Amanpreet Singh, Rupinder Singh, Jaswinder Singh, Jaspreet Singh and *Hatem Salem Abu Hamatta*
INTRODUCTION 34
LITERATURE REVIEW 37
METHODOLOGY 39

RESULTS AND ANALYSIS ... 41
CONCLUSION ... 44
FUTURE WORK ... 46
Practical Usability ... 47
ACKNOWLEDGEMENT ... 48
REFERENCES ... 48

CHAPTER 4 CLOUD QUANTUM COMPUTING FOR AI: INNOVATIONS, CHALLENGES, AND APPLICATIONS ... 51
Jaspreet Singh, Paramjot Kaur Sarao, Manish Sharma, Davinder Kaur, Rupinder Singh and *Mohammad Tabrez Quasim*
INTRODUCTION ... 52
Motivation ... 53
Key Components of AI with Cloud Quantum Computing ... 53
Quantum Computing ... 53
Cloud Computing ... 53
AI and Quantum Computing Synergy ... 54
CLOUD QUANTUM COMPUTING FRAMEWORK ... 54
Comparison of Classical Cloud and Cloud Quantum Computing ... 55
KEY INNOVATIONS IN CLOUD QUANTUM COMPUTING FOR AI ... 56
Quantum Machine Learning (QML) ... 56
Hybrid Classical Quantum AI Models ... 56
Cloud-Based Quantum AI Development Platforms ... 57
Quantum AI for Optimization Problems ... 57
CHALLENGES ... 57
Quantum De-coherence ... 58
Integrating Models ... 59
Lack of Optimized Quantum AI Algorithms ... 60
Hybrid Quantum-Classical Integration Issues ... 60
Quantum Hardware Limitations ... 60
Specialized Expertise Requirement ... 60
Data Input and Output Bottlenecks ... 61
Cost and Accessibility of Quantum Computing ... 61
Latency Issues ... 61
Security Challenges ... 61
APPLICATIONS ... 63
Application: Medical Care and Drug Exploration ... 63
Precision Medicine ... 63
Diagnosis Assistance ... 64
Drug Research and Recovery ... 65
Radiotherapy ... 65
Pricing of Diagnosis (Risk Analysis) ... 65
Molecular Simulations ... 66
Application: Financial Modeling and Risk Analysis ... 66
Portfolio Optimization ... 67
Fraud Detection ... 67
Monte Carlo Simulations ... 67
Credit Risk Assessment ... 67
High-frequency Trading ... 68
Application: Cybersecurity and Cryptography ... 68
Quantum Key Distribution (QKD) – The Micius Satellite Experiment ... 68

IBM's Quantum Safe Cryptography 69
Post-quantum Cryptography by Google and NIST 70
Cloud-Based Quantum Security Solutions—Microsoft Azure Quantum 70
DARPA and NSA's Quantum Research for Banking and Financial Transactions 71
Application: Logistics and Supply Chain Optimization 72
Optimizing Routes with Quantum 72
Quantum AI for Demand Forecasting 72
Quantum-Assisted Inventory Management 73
Evaluation of Quantum Risk in Supply Chains 73
Smart Warehouse & IoT Integration with Quantum Computing 74
Application: Complex Problem Solving and Scientific Research 74
Quantum Simulations for Drug Discovery and Material Science 74
Climate Modeling and Weather Forecasting 75
Quantum Machine Learning (QML) for AI Advancements 75
Google's Quantum Neural Networks (QNNs) 76
Quantum Cryptography for Data Security in Research 76
Optimization Challenges in Engineering and Space Exploration 76
CONCLUDING REMARKS 76
ACKNOWLEDGEMENTS 77
REFERENCES 77

CHAPTER 5 QUANTUM ALGORITHMS FOR MACHINE LEARNING 79
Davinder Kaur, Preet Kamal Sharma, Manuraj Moudgil, Jaspreet Singh, Rupinder Singh and *Zaki Ahmad Khan*
INTRODUCTION 80
Overview of Quantum 80
Quantum Computing's Power 81
Impact on Machine Learning 81
QUANTUM COMPUTING ARCHITECTURE: A LAYERED APPROACH 81
QUANTUM COMPUTING FUNDAMENTALS 83
QUANTUM OPTIMIZATION ALGORITHMS 84
Quantum Annealing 85
Quantum Approximate Optimization Algorithm (QAOA) 85
Variational Quantum Eigensolver (VQE) 86
APPLICATIONS OF QML IN OPTIMIZATION 87
Combinatorial Optimization Problems 87
Quantum Approximate Optimization Algorithm (QAOA) 88
Continuous Optimization Problems 88
Variational Quantum Eigensolver (VQE) 88
Quantum Support Vector Machines (QSVM) 88
Benefits of QSVM in Optimization 89
MACHINE LEARNING FOR OPTIMIZATION PROBLEMS 89
Quantum Reinforcement Learning (QRL) 89
Quantum Enhancement of RL 89
Optimization of Control Systems 89
QUANTUM ANNEALING FOR OPTIMIZATION 90
D-Wave Systems 90
Scheduling Problems 90
Ising Model 90
OPTIMIZATION IN QUANTUM CHEMISTRY& MATERIALS SCIENCE 90
Quantum Chemistry Simulations 90

Optimize Molecular Geometries 90
Materials Design 91
QUANTUM-INSPIRED ALGORITHMS FOR CLASSICAL OPTIMIZATION 91
Quantum Annealing-based Classical Algorithms 91
Quantum-inspired Neural Networks 91
COMPARATIVE ANALYSIS OF QUANTUM OPTIMIZATION ALGORITHMS 91
CONCLUSION 92
FUTURE SCOPE 93
ACKNOWLEDGEMENTS 93
REFERENCES 93

CHAPTER 6 QUANTUM-DRIVEN AI: THE INTERSECTION OF QUANTUM COMPUTING AND MACHINE LEARNING ALGORITHMS 96
,Pardeep Tiwana, Karan Sood, Harleen Kaur, Aman Modgil, Indu Bharti Jain Komal and *Jagdeep Singh Sappal*
INTRODUCTION 97
Overview of AI and Machine Learning 97
Key Components of Machine Learning 97
Quantum Computing Introduction 98
Need for Quantum Computing in AI 98
Speeding Up Computation 98
Enhancing Data Processing in High-Dimensional Spaces 98
Improving Model Optimization 99
FUNDAMENTALS OF QUANTUM COMPUTING FOR AI 99
Quantum Entanglement and Parallelism 99
Gates and Circuits of Quantum 100
Quantum Computing vs. Classical Computing 101
QML (QUANTUM ALGORITHMS OF MACHINE LEARNING) 101
QSVM (Quantum Support Vector Machines) 102
Quantum Neural Networks (QNN) 102
QPCA (Quantum Principal Component Analysis) 103
AI Variational Quantum Algorithms 103
APPLICATIONS OF QUANTUM AI 103
Quantum AI in Healthcare and Drug Discovery 104
Quantum AI in Financial Modelling 104
Quantum AI in Cybersecurity and Cryptography 105
Quantum AI for Optimization Problems 106
CHALLENGES AND FUTURE PROSPECTS 107
Hardware and Scalability Challenges 108
Algorithmic Limitations and Complexity 108
Ethical and Security Implications 108
CONCLUSION 109
Potential of Quantum AI in the Next Decade 110
REFERENCES 110

CHAPTER 7 COMPARATIVE ANALYSIS FOR HUMAN PROTEIN FUNCTION PREDICTION THROUGH MACHINE LEARNING TECHNIQUES AND PERFORMANCE ENHANCEMENT USING QUANTUM MACHINE LEARNING (QML) 112
Sunny Sharma, Sandeep Sood, Palwinder Singh and *Anil Kumar*
INTRODUCTION 113
INTRODUCTION TO PROTEIN 114
FEATURES EXTRACTION FROM PROTEIN SEQUENCE 114

RANDOM FOREST (RF) ML TECHNIQUE 115
FACTORS TO USE RF ON SDF OF HPRD 116
PROPOSED METHODOLOGY FOR HPFP USING RF 116
METHODOLOGY FOR SPEEDING UP THE PROCESS OF RANDOM FOREST USING QUANTUM COMPUTING 118
Step-by-Step Implementation 119
Explanation 120
LITERATURE SURVEY 120
RESULTS AND DISCUSSION 123
ACCURACIES BENCHMARKS OF PROTEIN FUNCTION PREDICTION CLASSIFIERS 126
CONCLUSION 128
ACKNOWLEDGEMENT 129
REFERENCES 129

CHAPTER 8 QUANTUM AI FOR NATURAL LANGUAGE PROCESSING AND COMPUTER VISION 133
Pummy Dhiman, Pratibha, Sudha and *Noor Adnan*
INTRODUCTION 133
Contribution 135
Study Organization 135
FUNDAMENTALS OF QUANTUM COMPUTING 136
Entanglement 136
Quantum Interference 137
Quantum Parallelism 137
Quantum Associative Memory (QAM) 137
QUANTUM ARTIFICIAL INTELLIGENCE (QAI): INTEGRATION OF QUANTUM COMPUTING AND ARTIFICIAL INTELLIGENCE 138
QUANTUM AI FOR NATURAL LANGUAGE PROCESSING (NLP) 140
The Dual Perspective of QNLP 140
Advantages of QNLP Over Classical NLP 141
Efficient Matrix Operations 141
Exponential Speedup in Optimization 141
High-Dimensional Feature Space Processing 141
QUANTUM AI FOR COMPUTER VISION 142
CHALLENGES AND LIMITATIONS 143
Hardware Constraints 143
Algorithmic Challenges 143
Hybrid Quantum-Classical Integration 143
Data Encoding and Processing Bottlenecks 143
Lack of Standardized Frameworks 143
FUTURE DIRECTIONS AND OPPORTUNITIES 143
Advancements in Quantum Hardware 144
Quantum-Enhanced NLP and Language Models 144
Quantum Computer Vision Applications 144
Hybrid Quantum-Classical AI Architectures 144
Standardization and Open-Source Frameworks 144
CONCLUSION 144
REFERENCES 145

CHAPTER 9 EDGE COMPUTING AND REAL-TIME DECISION MAKING WITH QUANTUM AI 147

Aditi Dutta, Kunjana Mittal, Akshit Patyal, Indu Bharti Jain, Pardeep Tiwana and *Sayed Abid Hussain*
INTRODUCTION 148
The Role of Real-Time Decision Making 148
Quantum AI: A New Frontier 149
FUNDAMENTALS OF EDGE COMPUTING 150
Key Characteristics of Edge Computing 151
Low Latency 151
Bandwidth Optimization 151
Enhanced Security and Privacy 151
Scalability 151
Reliability 152
Real-Time Processing 152
Cost Efficiency 152
Improved Energy Efficiency 152
Benefits of Cloud Computing 152
Challenges and Limitations 153
The Need for Real-Time Decision Making 154
Importance in Modern Applications 154
Use Cases: Autonomous Vehicles, Healthcare, IoT 156
Traditional AI vs. Quantum AI for Decision Making 156
QUANTAM AI: A TRANSFORMATIVE TECHNOLOGY 158
Basics of Quantum Computing 158
Quantum Machine Learning and AI 159
INTEGRATING QUANTUM AI WITH EDGE COMPUTING 160
Hybrid Quantum-classical Systems 160
APPLICATIONS OF QUANTUM AI IN EDGE COMPUTING 162
Smart Cities and IoT Devices 162
Predictive Maintenance in Industry 4.0 162
Real-time Fraud Detection in Finance 164
Personalized Healthcare and Diagnostics 165
CHALLENGES AND FUTURE PROSPECTS 165
Technical and Computational Challenges 165
Security and Privacy Considerations 166
Future Trends and Research Directions 166
CONCLUSION AND FINAL THOUGHTS 167
REFERENCES 168

CHAPTER 10 A COMPARATIVE STUDY ON UNSUPERVISED MACHINE LEARNING TECHNIQUES FOR AGRICULTURAL DATA ANALYSIS 170
Bhawandeep Kaur, Gurpreet Singh, Satinder Kaur and *Piyush Samant*
INTRODUCTION 171
Literature Review 172
Motivation and Contribution 173
MATERIALS AND METHODS 174
Dataset Description 174
Dimensionality Reduction 177
Clustering Algorithms 177
K-Means Clustering 177
DBSCAN (Density Based Spatial Clustering of Applications with Noise) 178
Agglomerative Clustering 178

t-SNE (t-distributed Stochastic Neighbor Embedding) 178
Clustering Evaluation Metrics 179
RESULTS AND DISCUSSION 180
Dimensionality Reduction 180
Clustering Results 181
K-Means Clustering 181
DBSCAN 182
Agglomerative Clustering 183
T-SNE Visualization 184
Performance Metrics 184
CONCLUSION AND FUTURE WORK 185
ACKNOWLEDGEMENTS 186
REFERENCES 186

CHAPTER 11 THE TRANSFORMATIVE APPLICATIONS OF QUANTUM ARTIFICIAL INTELLIGENCE IN HEALTHCARE, FINANCE, AND CYBERSECURITY 188
Pratibha, Pummy Dhiman, Sudha and *Mustafa Ali Khan*
INTRODUCTION 189
Strengths of Quantum Computing Over Classical Computing 189
Enhanced Computational Speed 189
Efficient Optimization 189
Superior Data Processing 190
Advanced Simulation Capabilities 190
Robust Security and Encryption 190
Potential for Scalable Computing 190
Revolutionizing Scientific Discoveries 190
How Quantum AI Works 191
Fundamentals of Quantum Computing 191
Integration with AI and Machine Learning 191
Basic Quantum Algorithms for AI 191
Quantum AI in the Field of Healthcare, Finance, and Cybersecurity 191
Brief History of Quantum Computing 192
GLOBAL TRENDS IN QUANTUM COMPUTING 193
APPLICATIONS OF QUANTUM AI 193
Applications of Quantum AI in Healthcare 194
Drug Discovery and Molecular Simulations 194
Faster Analysis of Biochemical Interactions 195
Acceleration of Drug Development 195
Personalized Medicine 195
AI-driven Genomic Analysis for Optimized Treatment Plans 195
Predictive Modeling for Disease Prevention 196
Medical Imaging and Diagnostics 196
Applications of Quantum AI in Finance 196
Portfolio Management and Investment Strategies 196
Risk Assessment and Mitigation 197
Quantum Algorithms for Accurate Market Predictions 197
Optimized Risk Mitigation Strategies 197
Fraud Detection and Financial Security 197
AI-powered Anomaly Detection in Transactions 197
Strengthening Digital Banking Security 197
Applications of Quantum AI in Cybersecurity 197

Quantum Cryptography and Secure Data Transmission 198
Quantum Key Distribution (QKD) for Secure Communication 198
Enhanced Data Encryption Techniques 198
Threat Detection and Cyberattack Prevention 198
Real-time Analysis of Cyber Threats 198
Strengthening Cybersecurity Resilience Against Evolving Threats 198
CHALLENGES OF QUANTUM AI 198
Hardware Limitations 199
Algorithm Development 199
Software and Programming Challenges 199
Data Processing Difficulties 199
Cost and Infrastructure 199
OPEN ISSUES AND RESEARCH DIRECTIONS IN QUANTUM AI 199
Quantum Computing for Big Data Processing 199
Quantum AI/ML Applications 200
Large-Scale Optimization 200
Quantum Web and Cloud Services 201
Quantum Game Theory 201
Quantum Computing for Simulation 201
Quantum Security Applications 202
CONCLUSION AND FUTURE SCOPE 202
ACKNOWLEDGEMENT 202
REFERENCES 202

CHAPTER 12 SHIELDING IOT-DRIVEN HEALTHCARE: A SECURE AND LIGHTWEIGHT AUTHENTICATION PROTOCOL FOR PATIENT DATA PROTECTION 205
Parwinder Kaur Dhillon, Jyoti and *Sheetal Kalra*
INTRODUCTION 205
APPLICATIONS OF AI BASED ON QUANTUM CRYPTOGRAPHY AND ELLIPTIC CURVE CRYPTOGRAPHY IN IOT-DRIVEN HEALTHCARE 207
AI-Based Quantum Cryptography in Healthcare 208
Real-time Anomaly Detection 208
Adaptive Security Policies 208
Quantum-resistant Infrastructures 208
Role of Elliptic Curve Cryptography (ECC) in Resource-Constrained IoT Devices 208
Lightweight Authentication 209
End-to-end Data Encryption 209
Efficient Session Key Generation 209
Synergizing ECC, AI, and Quantum Approaches 209
MOTIVATION 209
LITERATURE SURVEY 210
PRELIMINARIES 211
System Model 211
Doctor/Nurse (User) 211
Gateway Node 211
IoT Sensor Node 211
Adversary Model 212
PROPOSED SCHEME 212
Stage 1: User Registration Phase 213
Stage 2: Sensor Node Registration Phase 214
Stage 3: Login and Authentication phase 214

INFORMAL SECURITY ANALYSIS ... 217
Mutual Authentication ... 217
Session Key Agreement and Its Security ... 217
Perfect Forward Secrecy ... 217
Man-in-the-Middle Attack (MITM) ... 217
Denial of Services (DoS) ... 218
Replay Attack and Integrity ... 218
Scalability ... 218
SIMULATION RESULTS ... 218
CONCLUSION ... 220
FUTURE WORK ... 220
ACKNOWLEDGEMENTS ... 220
REFERENCES ... 221

CHAPTER 13 EXPLORING THE ROLE OF QUANTUM AI IN ENHANCING THE WEB ACCESSIBILITY EVALUATION TECHNIQUES ... 224
Suman Devi, Jasjit Singh Samagh, Satinder Kaur, Gurpreet Singh and *Kumari Sarita*
INTRODUCTION ... 225
The Current State of Web Accessibility Evaluation ... 225
The Potential of Quantum AI in Web Accessibility ... 226
Key Applications of Quantum AI in Web Accessibility ... 226
Automated Accessibility Testing ... 226
Real-Time Accessibility Enhancement ... 226
Semantic Accessibility Evaluation ... 227
AI-Powered Remediation ... 227
Limitations and Considerations ... 227
LITERATURE REVIEW ... 227
Comparative Analysis of AI-Driven Web Accessibility Solutions ... 228
CONCLUSION ... 233
FUTURE SCOPE ... 233
ACKNOWLEDGEMENT ... 234
REFERENCES ... 234

CHAPTER 14 A QUANTUM INTELLIGENCE AI-DRIVEN SECURE FRAMEWORK FOR IOV: QI-CAI CLUSTERING ARCHITECTURE WITH FDS-QI DEEP LEARNING SECURITY MODEL ... 236
Sumit Kumar, Ishpreet Singh Virk, Anupam Bonkra, Ritu,Sunil Kumar Chawla and *Omar Mbrouk*
INTRODUCTION ... 237
Types of Machine Learning (ML) ... 238
Supervised or Task-driven Learning ... 238
Unsupervised or Data-driven Learning (Identify clusters using unlabelled data) ... 239
Semi-Supervised Machine Learning (Use both unlabelled data and labelled data) ... 239
Reinforcement Machine Learning (Learn from Mistakes) ... 239
Feedforward Neural Network ... 239
Levenberg Neural Engine ... 240
CONTRIBUTION OF THE CHAPTER ... 240
LITERATURE SURVEY ... 241
PROPOSED QI-CAI ARCHITECTURE ... 245
Outcomes of Proposed QI-CAI Model ... 247
Comparison with Existing Framework ... 248

TUNING OF QI-ENHANCED MACHINE LEARNING MODEL 248
MACHINE LEARNING AS SECURITY MAINTENANCE 249
PROPOSED FDS-QI MODEL 250
Proposed QI-CAI Architecture for IoV Communication 252
Proposed FDS-QI Model for Attack Detection 253
CONCLUSION 253
FUTURE SCOPE AND REAL-WORLD APPLICATIONS 254
ACKNOWLEDGEMENT 254
REFERENCES 255

CHAPTER 15 WIRELESS SENSOR NETWORKS IN THE AGE OF AI AND QUANTUM COMPUTING 258
Kirandeep Kaur, Satinder Kaur, Satveer Kour and *Gurpreet Singh*
INTRODUCTION 259
Background Study 259
First-Generation WSNs 259
Second-generation WSNs 260
Third-Generation WSNs 260
Motivation 262
RELATED STUDY 262
COMBINING WSN, AI, AND QC: A NECESSITY FOR THE FUTURE 263
Applications and Innovations: WSN, AI, and Quantum Computing 267
Revolutionizing Healthcare 267
Enhancing Environmental Sustainability 267
Creating Safer and Smarter Cities 268
Empowering Individuals Through Data 268
Improving Security and Privacy 268
Disaster Preparedness and Response 269
Economic and Social Benefits 269
Why is it used Instead of other Technologies? 269
Unmatched Data Processing Capabilities 269
Enhanced Energy Efficiency 270
Superior Security and Privacy 270
Real-time Decision-making 271
Scalability and Adaptability 271
Solving Intractable Problems 272
Future-Proofing Technology 272
LIMITATIONS AND CHALLENGES 272
CONCLUSION 273
FUTURE SCOPE 274
ACKNOWLEDGEMENTS 274
REFERENCES 274
SUBJECT INDEX 278

FOREWORD

In an era where data is the new oil and intelligence is the new electricity, the convergence of quantum computing, cloud infrastructure, and artificial intelligence signals a monumental shift in how we process, understand, and interact with information. This book proposal, QuantumEnhanced Cloud AI: The Next Frontier in Machine Learning and Deep Learning, offers a timely and visionary exploration into this transformative landscape.

As machine learning and deep learning have matured, they have increasingly strained the limits of classical computing infrastructure. Massive datasets, high-dimensional models, and real-time decision-making requirements demand computational resources that are not only powerful but also efficient and scalable. Simultaneously, quantum computing has emerged from the realm of theoretical physics into a promising technological frontier—capable of solving complex problems with exponentially less time and energy.

Cloud computing serves as the essential bridge, democratizing access to both AI and quantum technologies by abstracting hardware constraints and enabling scalable, distributed innovation. Together, these pillars form the foundation of a new paradigm—Quantum-Enhanced Cloud AI— where the raw power of quantum systems enhances the intelligence of AI models, and the flexibility of cloud infrastructure ensures accessibility, collaboration, and deployment at scale.

This book does more than just examine the individual technologies; it unites them into a cohesive narrative that looks ahead to their integrated potential. It highlights use cases from quantum-accelerated training to quantum-inspired optimization, discusses architectural frameworks for hybrid quantum-classical AI systems in the cloud, and investigates the implications for industries ranging from healthcare and finance to logistics and cybersecurity.

Whether you're a researcher, practitioner, student, or policymaker, this book offers critical insights and practical pathways to navigate the coming age of intelligent systems powered by quantum and cloud technologies. The future is not just about faster algorithms or bigger datasets—it is about a fundamental rethinking of computation itself. And in that future, the integration of quantum and AI on the cloud may well be the most defining chapter of our digital evolution.

Er. Aruna Rani
Department of Computer Science Engineering and Technology
Lamrin Tech Skills University
Chandigarh, Punjab, India

Preface

Quantum-Enhanced Cloud AI: The Next Frontier in Machine Learning and Deep Learning is a comprehensive book that discusses the traditional computing paradigms, while powerful, are nearing their natural limits in addressing the ever-growing demands of advanced machine learning and deep learning systems. Quantum computing, with its fundamentally different approach to processing information, and cloud computing, with its promise of scalable, accessible infrastructure, are together shaping a new horizon for AI — one that is faster, more powerful, and more transformative than anything we have seen before.

The first chapter addresses the most notable cloud-based platforms for quantum computing and their game-changing impact on the acceleration of AI development and implementation that will define the future of intelligent computing. Chapter two gives a comprehensive overview of quantum algorithms, hybrid quantum-classical models, and real-world implementations. Authors also explore how AI-cloud companies will be affected after major cloud providers enter the world of quantum computing-based business. This book also looks at security challenges, fundamental scalability limitations, and future research directions, with insights into how quantum computing will reshape the AI landscape over the next few decades. Chapter three shows that Quantum AI pertains to the practical feasibility, despite errors, corrections, coherence times, and a lack of algorithm development. This study highlights the importance of continuing to invest in Quantum AI to realize its full potential. Chapter four concludes with a forward-looking scope of AI and ML, considering their potential to transform other industries such as innovation and health, financial services, quantum computing, stock markets, transportation, education, logistics, and sustainable supply chains, impact societal structures, and offer solutions to complex worldwide problems. Chapter five's main objective is to examine the architectural framework of Cloud Quantum Computing, assess its impact on AI-driven applications, and analyze key challenges and innovations shaping its development. Chapter six evaluates the active Quantum Machine Learning (QML) algorithms while demonstrating their improved functionality compared to usual approaches, and it identifies implementation barriers in real-world scenarios. Chapter seven summarizes the nature of Quantum AI for researchers, experts, and anyone who wishes to venture into the world's next big thing in technology. Chapter eight provides a comparative analysis of human protein function prediction through machine learning techniques and is further enhanced by using the QML approach.

Chapter nine discusses difficulties, further study prospects, and prospects for Quantum AI in the domains of Natural Language Processing and Computer Vision. Chapter ten explores the advancements in quantum computing as well as the development of edge intelligence, which are being set to transform industries by creating high levels of efficiency, security, and automation in real-time operations. Chapter eleven discusses the comparative analysis of unsupervised machine learning techniques for agricultural data analysis. Chapter twelve presents an AI/ML-based framework that uses a wearable smart band that will help people in maintaining social distances, tell whom to meet and whom to avoid having symptoms like body temperature above normal, coughing, and sneezing. Chapter thirteen gives an elaborate overview of the relevance of Quantum AI in healthcare, finance, and cybersecurity, which defines the trend of intelligent and secure computing systems. Chapter fourteen designed a protocol to be scalable and cloud-compatible, paving the way for secure integration with quantum-enhanced cloud AI healthcare systems. Chapter fifteen provides valuable insights into the evolving role of Quantum AI in web accessibility evaluation, offering a foundation for future advancements in automated assessment techniques. Chapter sixteen proposed two architectures from a unified framework that addresses both communication efficiency and security in next-generation Internet of Vehicles systems. Chapter seventeen highlights the revolutionary possibility of combining AI and QC in WSNs. This review focuses on the revolutionary potential of integrating AI and QC in WSNs and proposes future research areas, such as AI-based optimisation models, scalable quantum-secure communication protocols.

Satveer Kour
Department of Computer Engineering and Technology
Guru Nanak Dev University
Amritsar, Punjab, India

Harvinder Singh
Department of Mechanical Engineering
Chandigarh Engineering College-CGC Landran, Mohali
Punjab, India

Anupam Bonkra
Department of Computer Science and Engineering
Maharishi Markandeshwar (Deemed to be University)
Mullana, Haryana, India

&

Rupinder Singh
Chitkara University Institute of Engineering and Technology
Chitkara University
Rajpura, Punjab
India

List of Contributors

Aditi Dutta	Department of Computer Science and Engineering, CGC - College of Engineering, Mohali, Punjab, India
Akshit Patyal	Department of Computer Science and Engineering, CGC - College of Engineering, Mohali, Punjab, India
Aman Modgil	Department of Computer Science and Engineering, CGC - College of Engineering, Mohali, Punjab, India
Amanpreet Singh	Chitkara University Institute of Engineering and Technology, Chitkara University, Rajpura, Punjab, India
Anil Kumar	Department of Computer Engineering and Technology, Guru Nanak Dev University, Amritsar, Punjab, India
Anupam Bonkra	Department of Computer Science and Engineering, Maharishi Markandeshwar (Deemed to be University), Mullana, Haryana, India
Arun Kumar Rana	Department of Computer Science and Engineering (CSE), Galgotias College of Engineering and Technology, Greater Noida, Uttar Pradesh, India
Bhawandeep Kaur	Department of Computer Engineering and Technology, Guru Nanak Dev University, Amritsar, Punjab, India
Davinder Kaur	Department of Computer Applications, Algoma University, Brampton Campus, Ontario, Canada
Gurpreet Singh	Department of Computer Engineering and Technology, Guru Nanak Dev University, Amritsar, Punjab, India
Harleen Kaur	Department of Computer Science and Engineering, CGC - College of Engineering, Mohali, Punjab, India
Harvinder Singh	Department of Mechanical Engineering, Chandigarh Engineering College-CGC Landran, Mohali, Punjab, India
Hatem Salem Abu Hamatta	Department of Applied Sciences, Al-Balqa Applied University, Aqaba, Jordan
Indu Bharti Jain	Department of Law, Maharishi Markandeshwar (Deemed to be University), Mullana, Haryana, India
Ishpreet Singh Virk	Department of Computer Science & Engineering, Chandigarh Engineering College (CEC) Landran, Mohali, Punjab, India
Jagdeep Singh Sappal	Department of Transport Engineering Deployment, Telus Corporation, Edmonton, Alberta, Canada
Jasjit Singh Samagh	Department of Computer Science and Engineering, Chaudhary Devi Lal University, Sirsa, Haryana, India
Jaspreet Kaur	School of Computer Science and Engineering, Lovely Professional University, Punjab, India
Jaspreet Singh	Department of Computer Science and Engineering, Chandigarh University, Mohali, Punjab, India
Jaswinder Singh	Chitkara University Institute of Engineering and Technology, Chitkara University, Rajpura, Punjab, India

Jyoti Jyoti	Department of Engineering and Technology, Guru Nanak Dev University, Regional Campus Jalandhar, Jalandhar, Punjab, India
Karan Sood	Department of Computer Science and Engineering, CGC - College of Engineering, Mohali, Punjab, India
Kashif Nisar	School of Arts and Sciences, The University of Notre Dame Australia, Sydney, New South Wales, Australia
Kirandeep Kaur	Department of Computer Engineering and Technology, Guru Nanak Dev University, Amritsar, Punjab, India
Komal Komal	Department of Computer Science and Engineering, CGC - College of Engineering, Mohali, Punjab, India
Kumari Sarita	Department of Computer Science, Guru Nanak Dev University, Amritsar, Punjab, India
Kunjana Mittal	Department of Law, Maharishi Markandeshwar University (deemed to be University), Mullana, Ambala, Haryana, India
Manish Sharma	Department of Computer Science and Engineering, Chandigarh University, Mohali, Punjab, India
Manuraj Moudgil	Department of Computer Science and Engineering, Bhai Gurdas Institute of Engineering & Technology, Sangrur, Punjab, India
Megha Bhushan	Department of Computer Languages and Systems, University of Seville, Seville, Andalusia, Spain
Mohammad Tabrez Quasim	College of Computing and Information Technology, University of Bisha, Bisha, Asir, Saudi Arabia
Mustafa Ali Khan	Compunnel Software Group Inc, Compunnel Software Group Inc, Phoenix, Arizona, USA
Noor Adnan	Department of Computer Science, College of Science for Women, University of Baghdad, Baghdad, Iraq
Omar Mbrouk	Department of Nano-Chemistry and its Environmental Applications, Environmental Studies and Research Institute, University of Sadat City, Sadat City, Menofia, Egypt
Palwinder Singh	Department of Computer Science and Applications, BBK DAV College for Women, Amritsar, Punjab, India
Paramjot Kaur Sarao	Department of Computer Science and Engineering, Chandigarh University, Mohali, Punjab, India
Pardeep Tiwana	Department of Computer Science and Engineering, CGC - College of Engineering, Mohali, Punjab, India
Parwinder Kaur Dhillon	Department of Computer Science, Guru Nanak Dev University, Regional Campus Jalandhar, Jalandhar, Punjab, India
Piyush Samant	Department of Data Science, Mirxes Labs Pte Ltd., Kuala Lumpur, Malaysia
Pratibha Pratibha	Chitkara University Institute of Engineering and Technology, Chitkara University, Rajpura, Punjab, India
Preet Kamal Sharma	Department of Computer Applications, Post Graduate Government College for Girls, Chandigarh, Punjab, India

Pummy Dhiman	Chitkara University Institute of Engineering and Technology, Chitkara University, Rajpura, Punjab, India
Ritu Ritu	Department of Computer Science & Engineering, Chandigarh College of Engineering- CGC Jhanjeri, Mohali, Punjab, India
Rupinder Singh	Chitkara University Institute of Engineering and Technology, Chitkara University, Rajpura, Punjab, India
Sandeep Sood	Department Computer Science & Engineering, Guru Nanak Dev University, Amritsar, Punjab, India
Satinder Kaur	Department of Computer Engineering and Technology, Guru Nanak Dev University, Amritsar, Punjab, India
Satveer Kour	Department of Computer Engineering and Technology, Guru Nanak Dev University, Amritsar, Punjab, India
Sayed Abid Hussain	Department of Computer Science and Engineering, Bakhtar University, Kabul, Afghanistan
Sheetal Kalra	Department of Engineering and Technology, Guru Nanak Dev University, Regional Campus Jalandhar, Jalandhar, Punjab, India
Sudha Sudha	Department of Computer Applications, Gian Jyoti institute of Management and technology, Chandigarh, Punjab, India
Suman Devi	Department of Computer Science and Engineering, Chaudhary Devi Lal University, Sirsa, Haryana, India
Sumit Kumar	Department of Computer Science and Engineering, Maharishi Markandeshwar (Deemed to be University), Mullana, Haryana, India
Sunil Kumar Chawla	Chitkara University Institute of Engineering and Technology, Chitkara University, Rajpura, Punjab, India
Sunny Sharma	Department of Computer Science And Applications, Hindu College, Affiliated to Guru Nanak Dev University, Amritsar, Punjab, India
Vineeta Gulati	Department of Computer Science and Engineering (CSE), Maharishi Markandeshwar (Deemed to be University), Mullana, Haryana, India
Zaki Ahmad Khan	Department of Computer Science, University of Worcester, Worcester, United Kingdom

CHAPTER 1

Quantum-Powered AI in the Cloud: Unleashing the Future of Intelligent Computing

Jaspreet Kaur[1,*], **Satveer Kour**[2], **Megha Bhushan**[3] and **Harvinder Singh**[4]

[1] *School of Computer Science and Engineering, Lovely Professional University, Punjab, India*

[2] *Department of Computer Engineering and Technology, Guru Nanak Dev University, Amritsar, Punjab, India*

[3] *Department of Computer Languages and Systems, University of Seville, Seville, Andalusia, Spain*

[4] *Department of Mechanical Engineering, Chandigarh Engineering College-CGC Landran, Mohali, Punjab, India*

Abstract: Emerging technologies like quantum computing and Artificial Intelligence (AI) are radically changing how we approach computing technology. The fusion of these disciplines within cloud systems offers incredible computing power, which boosts effectiveness and flexibility. Productivity in almost every area – be it optimization, data processing, or machine learning – undergoes a significant transformation. This chapter offers an in-depth study of quantum AI in the scope of the cloud with respect to its basics, sophisticated integration frameworks, and advanced-level practical applications. It also outlines the limits of this new domain, such as hardware and software development, and other secondary issues like safety defects. In addition, this chapter addresses the most notable cloud-based platforms for quantum computing and their game-changing impact on the acceleration of AI development and implementation that will define the future of intelligent computing.

Keywords: AI ethics, Amazon braket, Cloud AI, Cybersecurity, Economics, Entanglement, IBM quantum, Intelligent computing, Microsoft azure, Quantum cloud platforms, Quantum computing, Quantum machine learning, Quantum neural networks, Qubits, Security, Superposition.

INTRODUCTION

Quantum computing uses superposition and entanglement, concepts interlaced with quantum mechanics, to execute sophisticated computations at astonishing speeds that far exceed classical computing systems. As reported by the Boston Consulting Group 2024, quantum computing may provide an economic value of

* **Corresponding author Jaspreet Kaur:** School of Computer Science and Engineering, Lovely Professional University, Punjab, India; E-mail: jaspreet.sliet@gmail.com

Satveer Kour, Harvinder Singh, Anupam Bonkra & Rupinder Singh (Eds.)

as much as $850 billion every year by 2050 in a variety of fields like pharmaceuticals, finance, and materials science [1]. The merger of quantum computing with Artificial Intelligence (AI) has the potential to transform the field of data optimization and machine learning algorithm training, as well as data processing speed. This combination allows for more efficient processing. Frankly, this simultaneous processing of high-dimensional datasets and complex models opens new frontiers in AI research and development [2].

By providing scalable infrastructure at a low cost, quantum technology can now be accessed easily using remote services. As per the latest forecasts, the market for cloud quantum computing is estimated to grow from $682 million in 2023 to about $1.5 billion by 2025, and nearly $4 billion by 2030, growing annually at a rate of 30% (CAGR forecast) as shown below (Table **1**) [3]. The cloud enables quantum AI, which offers businesses, developers, and researchers the capabilities to test and deploy quantum algorithms without actually purchasing and maintaining the complex hardware. IBM, Google, and Microsoft have invested heavily in cloud quantum AI systems, which have high-performance hybrid computing with classical and quantum compute cores for optimized processing power delivered through the cloud [4].

Table 1. Projected market growth of cloud-based quantum computing.

Year	Market Size (USD)	CAGR (%)
2023	$682 million	-
2025	~$1.5 billion	30%
2030	~$4 billion	30%

The unification of AI, quantum computing, and cloud systems is set to create huge innovations within industries of all varieties. For instance, in drug development and AI augmented quantum computing has the chance to shrink the time it takes to uncover new medications by an astonishing 80% and in turn save billions in R&D funding [5]. In the finance sector, quantum AI is projected to improve risk analysis accuracy by 40%, leading to more precise decision-making processes [6]. Cybersecurity faces an urgent challenge, with a 100% urgency level for adopting post-quantum encryption solutions to safeguard data against quantum attacks [7]. Moreover, materials science is expected to benefit from 70% advancements in quantum simulations, enabling the growth of new things with unprecedented properties. These projected impacts are summarized (Table **2**) and visually represented (Fig. **1**), highlighting the transformative potential and critical urgency of quantum AI across key sectors.

With the ongoing progress of quantum computing, its integration with AI in cloud environments is expected to redefine the future of intelligent computing, enabling breakthroughs in problem-solving and decision-making capabilities. With advancements in quantum hardware and cloud infrastructure, the next decade could witness a shift from experimental quantum AI applications to real-world implementations that transform industries on a global scale [8].

Table 2. Quantum AI's projected impact and urgency across industries.

Industry	Impact (%) or Urgency Level
Pharmaceuticals	80% reduction in drug discovery time
Finance	40% improvement in risk analysis accuracy
Cybersecurity	Urgent need for post-quantum encryption (100%)
Materials Science	70% advancements in quantum simulations

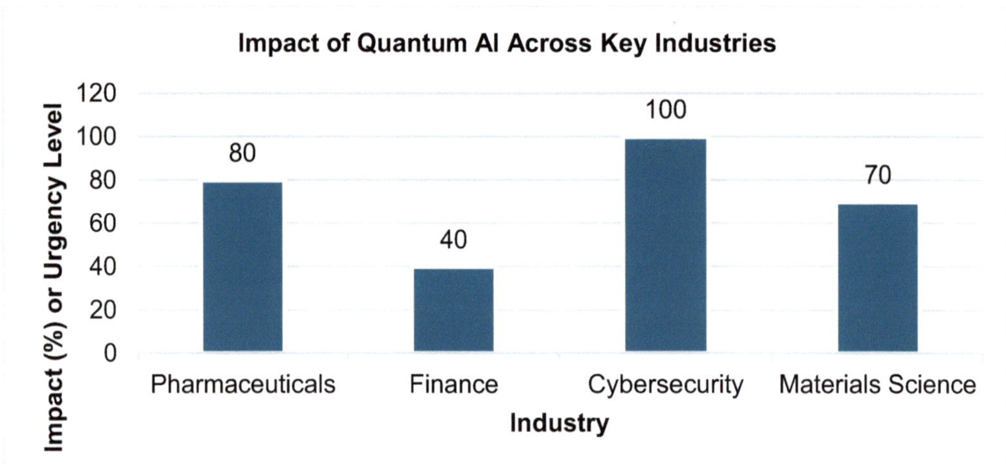

Fig. (1). Quantum AI's projected impact and urgency across industries.

FUNDAMENTALS OF CLOUD-BASED QUANTUM AI

Quantum Computing Basics

Quantum computing utilizes the fundamental principles of quantum mechanics to handle information in ways beyond the capabilities of classical computers. Unlike conventional bits that represent either 0 or 1, quantum bits (qubits) exploit superposition, enabling them to exist in multiple states at once. This allows quantum computers to complete parallel computations, greatly increasing efficiency as well as problem-solving speed.

Entanglement is the interconnectedness of qubits, allowing them to be united in a fashion where the state of one qubit affects another instantaneously irrespective of spatial separation. This enriches the efficacy of computing since qubits may cooperate in ways that modern systems cannot achieve, thus enhancing modular efficiency.

The most important quantum algorithms demonstrate how far ahead quantum computers will be regarding AI and data science:

Shor's Algorithm

This algorithm efficiently decomposes large numbers into their prime factors, presenting a significant challenge to traditional encryption systems and driving innovations in cryptography. Surprisingly, it surpasses the most sophisticated classical algorithms by factoring numbers at an exponential speed, which puts it on a collision course with RSA encryption that safeguards over 70% of global internet communication [9].

Grover's Algorithm

Emphasized optimization issues in AI and machine learning, making it prized because of its quadratic speedup advantage for searching unsorted databases. Perfect example: 1 million classical operations versus a mere 1000 with Grover's algorithm [10].

Moreover, other studies suggest that quantum machine learning has the potential to dramatically outperform classical counterparts, especially in areas like training models for drug development, predicting high finance, and tuning multifaceted logistical processes.

Projections on the business side suggest the computing market will grow from 928 million to well above 6.5 billion by 2030, all due to clearer benefits provided from developing and utilizing Artificial Intelligence solutions [11, 12].

Putting all these concepts together allows for numerous applications of quantum computing, like enhancing machine learning models, boosting efficiency in solving combinatorial problems, and streamlining AI-guided decision-making processes.

Cloud Computing in AI

The incorporation of cloud computing into the world of Artificial Intelligence (AI) has provided great amounts of computational power, which is easier to scale and access. Such models became cloud-friendly, freeing organizations and researchers from expensive local infrastructure, making AI model development, training, and deployment easier. The global AI cloud service market stood at roughly $63.1 billion in 2023, likely exceeding $300 billion by 2030 at a CAGR of 26.5% [13].

AI implementations are able to automatically allocate resources as the workload changes due to the incorporation of elastic scalability, a feature offered by cloud computing. The ability to meet certain parameters while reducing costs for optimum performance is essential. Furthermore, cloud networks support the parallel processing of giant information sets owing to their distributed computing setup, which is a requirement for big data analytics and deep learning. For instance, research indicates distributed cloud frameworks have the potential to decrease the time it takes to train a machine learning model by as much as 40 percent relative to traditional centralized systems [14].

Robust solutions driven by AI are provided by industry-leading cloud service providers:

Amazon Web Services (AWS)

Features AI and ML services such as Amazon SageMaker for model training and inference, AWS Lambda for serverless computing, and AI-driven analytics tools .

Google Cloud AI

Provides powerful ML frameworks like TensorFlow, Auto ML for automated model tuning, and Vertex AI for end-to-end machine learning workflows.

Microsoft Azure AI

Offers Azure Machine Learning, cognitive services, and AI-powered automation tools integrated with enterprise applications.

Through AI cloud services, businesses can expand the accessibility and pace of AI development across various industries such as healthcare, finance, and autonomous systems. The amalgamation of AI and cloud computing accelerates the innovations pertaining to natural language processing, real-time analytics, and broad deep learning. By 2025, it is projected that more than seventy percent of companies worldwide will rely on the implementation of cloud-assisted AI services within their activities [15, 16].

Integration of Quantum Computing with AI in the Cloud

The merging of quantum computing and artificial intelligence within the cloud context is shifting the frontier of what can be accomplished computationally by improving the efficiency and scale of these tasks. Important features include:

Quantum Machine Learning (QML)

QML is a developing field focused on the application of quantum algorithms to artificial intelligence (AI) models, especially in the practical handling of high-dimensional datasets. QML procedures such as quantum support vector machines and quantum Boltzmann machines are already exhibiting promise in a number of optimization and pattern recognition tasks.

Hybrid Quantum-Classical Computing

This methodology works by merging quantum and classical circuits, which results in increasing their performance. While classical processors take care of the more general functions, quantum computing takes on the more resource-demanding subroutines.

Quantum Neural Networks (QNNs)

Quantum circuits are being developed with the aim of implementing them in deep learning for more advanced pattern recognition. The focus of QNNs research is on the ability of quantum gates to speed up the training of neural networks, which could bring a change to the efficiency and performance of AI models.

The synergies stemming from quantum computing are rather optimistic for the on-cloud computing. At their most fundamental, these suggest hope towards the persistent difficulties that currently stand beyond the grasp of established systems. As per forecasters, there would be 20% of forecasted AI workloads in cloud infrastructure undergoing the use of quantum algorithms by 2035, indicating the level to which these technologies will be intertwined [17].

CLOUD-BASED QUANTUM PLATFORMS

To aid research and development in AI, ML, and other more complex computing activities, major tech firms and research centres have come up with cloud quantum computing services. These systems allow users to create, test, and run quantum algorithms on the cloud, which enhances development in the field remarkably. Some of the primary systems are:

IBM Quantum Experience

Both individuals and companies can use IBM's cloud quantum platform for AI and machine learning tasks that can be trained on real quantum processors. Users can visually diagram algorithms and run them on superconducting qubit-based hardware through an easily understandable graphical interface and Qiskit (quantum software development kit). They can also investigate quantum-powered AI methods like Quantum Support Vector Machines (QSVM). In 2024, over 20 quantum systems were online on IBM Quantum, enabling a worldwide network of scientists and engineers to collaborate.

Google Quantum AI

Google's quantum cloud service leverages its high-performance quantum processors to support advanced computational tasks. Remarkably, in 2019, Google's Sycamore processor demonstrated quantum supremacy by solving a specialized problem exponentially faster than the most advanced classical supercomputers. Through its cloud platform, Google facilitates AI research by providing access to quantum processors and hybrid quantum-classical algorithms aimed at accelerating machine learning workloads.

Microsoft Azure Quantum

Azure Quantum offers a flexible, cloud-based ecosystem that integrates quantum computing with AI and ML solutions. The platform supports multiple quantum hardware technologies, including ion-trap qubits (developed by partners like IonQ) and superconducting qubits, as well as classical high-performance computing resources. Azure Quantum empowers researchers to build, optimize, and deploy quantum algorithms directly into existing cloud-based AI pipelines, providing seamless scalability.

Amazon Braket

Amazon Braket provides a unified environment for developing, testing, and running quantum algorithms, particularly in the fields of AI and ML research. Supporting multiple quantum hardware backends—such as gate-based superconducting qubits, ion traps, and simulated environments—Braket enables researchers to experiment with various quantum architectures. The service integrates with other AWS tools, allowing for scalable deployment of hybrid quantum-classical solutions tailored to machine learning and optimization problems.

CHALLENGES IN CLOUD-BASED QUANTUM AI

While the integration of quantum computing with AI through cloud platforms holds transformative potential, several critical challenges must be addressed before realizing its full capabilities:

Hardware Limitations

Present-day quantum processors, known as Noisy Intermediate-Scale Quantum (NISQ) devices, face challenges such as limited qubit numbers, short coherence durations, and high error rates. These constraints significantly affect the reliability, precision, and scalability of quantum computing for AI applications. As of 2024, most commercially available quantum systems operate with fewer than 1,000 physical qubits—well below the requirements for handling large-scale AI tasks.

Algorithm Development

The research and development for Quantum AI algorithms is yet to be fully developed. The integration of classical machine learning methods, including deep neural networks as well as reinforcement learning, generates significant problems due to the fact that those models must change structurally in order to be effective for quantum hardware. In addition, with the current knowledge, there is no clear time frame regarding when quantum methods will be more beneficial than their classical counterparts, so hybrid models and new theoretical approaches need to be designed and constructed.

Security Concerns

Quantum computing greatly changes the landscape of cybersecurity. In particular, advanced quantum computers may weaken the security of commonly used RSA and ECC encryption methods, which could severely impact data security in large cloud systems. Such developments have already triggered acceleration towards Post-Quantum Cryptography (PQC), which seeks to develop encryption methods aimed at withstanding attacks that rely on quantum computing techniques [18]. The successful implementation of PQC within clouds of quantum AI is paramount to the protection of confidential information.

Cost and Accessibility

The costs associated with developing and sustaining quantum hardware and software pose a major challenge to their adoption. Even though quantum resources can be accessed remotely through the cloud, these resources are still constrained by limited hardware capacity, usage quotas, and exorbitant costs. For instance, currently, the runtime on high-end quantum processors is still billed at hundreds of dollars per hour, which puts it beyond the reach of most researchers and start-ups. This fee was noted in a 2024 study article [19].

Addressing these challenges will require advancements in quantum hardware engineering, algorithm design, cybersecurity protocols, and cost-effective cloud infrastructure to ensure that cloud-based quantum AI becomes a practical and scalable solution in the future.

FUTURE FORECASTS AND AREAS FOR INVESTIGATION

The development of cloud-based quantum AI might be on the verge of single-handedly transforming the economy, and it will likely bring higher efficiency from multiple domains. Some primary areas are likely to shape the future of this developing field:

Quantum Hardware Achievements

Most quantum hardware development has yet to be accomplished. This area will remain the single weakest link in the value chain of almost all quantum AI tasks. Most research efforts should focus on:

Improving Qubit Coherence

Enhancing qubit coherence will allow for more reliable quantum computations by reducing noise interference. Quantum states are likely to require increasingly sophisticated error correction methods like Quantum Error Correction (QEC) to survive prolonged periods.

Diminishing Error Rates

Minimization of gate errors in quantum gates is still the most significant concern in contemporary quantum computing. Redemption is offered by fault-tolerant architectures, superconducting qubits, and topological qubits.

Scalable Quantum Processors

There has to be conceptual innovation in how to effectively scale quantum systems if indeed we wish to advance from Noisy Intermediate-Scale Quantum (NISQ) devices to large-scale fault-tolerant quantum computers. Modular quantum architectures and quantum interconnects are being developed to enable distributed quantum computers to communicate effortlessly with each other [20].

Optimization of Quantum AI Algorithms

Aligning AI and quantum computing together requires the refinement of quantum imitative algorithms to provide an edge over classical models. Some of them are listed below:

Hybrid Quantum-Classical Learning

Merging quantum processing with classical deep learning frameworks improves the efficiency of large model training. Certain techniques—like optimally training *via* variational quantum circuits (VQCs)—are being developed.

Quantum Generative Models

Quantum-enhanced generic models offer a wide scope in drug and material designing, financial modeling, *etc.* Examples of such models are quantum Boltzmann machines and quantum GANs.

Quantum Assisted Optimization

Employment of quantum algorithms such as the Quantum Approximate Optimization Algorithm (QAOA) and quantum annealing greatly increases the solve rate of complex combinational optimization issues. This yields great value within logistics, resource control, and AI-powered decision systems [21].

Standardization of Quantum Cloud Infrastructure

Widespread adoption of quantum AI hinges on its integration with existing cloud services. Progress towards this goal requires:

Interoperability Standards

Development of standardized quantum APIs and cross-compatibility protocols involves establishing industry-wide criteria that enable easier integration of quantum processors with traditional cloud computing. Quantum workloads need a secure cloud infrastructure. Innovations in post-quantum cryptography and secure multi-party computation will be crucial as the data breaches are damaging on so many levels. Businesses and researchers would be able to utilize quantum-powered AI without needing to invest in expensive quantum equipment. This will be made possible by the development of commercial quantum cloud services.

The growing field of quantum AI presents unique ethical and legal issues that will have to be managed responsibly. Important areas include, but are not limited to:

Applying quantum AI to sensitive areas like healthcare, finance, and international security requires robust mechanisms to guard against data breaches and misuse. Information is still being post-quantum encrypted and defended to protect from future quantum strikes.

This is a very real concern, and so is allowing AI that targets quantum augmentations to blindly copy the myopic framework. These challenges require quantum fairness-aware algorithms, which have yet to be developed.

Trust and reliability in quantum AI applications need to be bolstered. Regulatory measures should formulate responsibility boundaries for decision-making systems based on quantum-powered AI, and Explanatory AI (XAI) is perfect for this line of work. It uses quantum machine learning, which increases trust when paired with quantum AI [22].

Future Policy and Ethical Frameworks

As quantum AI capabilities expand, policy development will need international cooperation on issues such as:

Compliance in Sensitive Areas

National security, financial markets, and medical research are all predicted to be affected by quantum AI. Defining policies to manage its application within these areas is vital [23].

AI Ethics and Governance

Policies on ethical AI will need to be formulated for quantum applications to contain the adverse effects, such as algorithmic discrimination, violation of privacy, and other abusive uses of quantum capabilities [24].

The Need for International Governance on Quantum AI

The ramifications of quantum AI transcend national borders and therefore warrant the need for collaboration in determining its ethical and legal boundaries [25 - 27].

CONCLUSION

Cloud-based quantum AI is a computing capability that allows achievements that classical computing is not able to achieve, and represents a new frontier in technology. There are many industries that depend on Artificial Intelligence, data processing, optimization, and other advanced fields, which can benefit from this technology. These advancements are made possible due to the application of principles of quantum mechanics, such as entanglement, superposition, and quantum parallelism.

The realization of Artificial Intelligence is the furthermost advance reachable through cloud-based quantum AI. In order to make this a possibility, major challenges have to be addressed, such as hardware boundaries, security threats, and algorithm issues. The current quantum processors are stuck in the Noisy Intermediate-Scale Quantum (NISQ) era, which has its own set of limitations: high error rates, short coherence times, and so forth. Researchers put efforts into optimizing qubit coherence, improving Quantum Error Correction (QEC) methods, and developing scalable quantum architectures to make processing more reliable.

Concerns still remain on algorithms as quantum AI lacks the ability to leverage quantum aids and therefore requires additional attention to develop hybrid quantum-enhanced deep learning methods that give users practical usability. With the increased renown of quantum computing, new kinds of threats are presented in protection measures of encryption. Even though it provides more robust ways to encrypt data, it makes classical encryption systems obsolete and requires the introduction of post-quantum cryptography strategies, which will overcome these obstacles.

In the following decade, scaling quantum hardware is expected to make quantum AI algorithms suitable for deployment, leading to improvements in the achievement of fault-tolerant systems for a range of superconducting qubits, trapped ions, photonic quantum computing, and topological qubits, and reining in quantum control mechanisms and error correction frameworks. These changes will be enhanced by advancements in powerful as well as stable photonic samplers and quantum phenomena such as qubit teleportation. The transformation of quantum AI systems will ensure a smoother and faster shift from theoretical research to industrial applications, thereby opening new frontiers across multiple vectors.

Cloud-based quantum AI stands to greatly impact the healthcare, finance, logistics, and cybersecurity industries. In healthcare, besides precision medicine, quantum AI can aid in drug discovery and complex biological simulations. While in finance, it can enhance risk assessment, fraud detection, and high-frequency trading, and enable optimization. In logistics, achieving better efficiency and cost effectiveness in managing supply chains, dynamic routing, and real-time optimization can AI. In cybersecurity, aside from posing challenges to current cryptographic security frameworks, quantum AI can enable the development of quantum-resistant encryption techniques.

Maturation of quantum AI services in the cloud will enable orders of magnitude better performance in speeds of computation, energy efficiency, and performance accessibility. This change promises to open up tremendous democratization of quantum resources. No longer will businesses, researchers, and governments wanting to leverage quantum power need to possess dedicated quantum hardware. The cost saved by not having to invest in sophisticated quantum-powered AI hardware, along with the shifts aforementioned, will change the future of intelligent computing optimistically.

The shark becomes afraid and leaves when it detects the mildly harmful chemicals released by the eels, taking with it any fish within the vicinity. When the shark leaves, Bonnetheads experience a massive catch of fish. The catch Bonnetheads are able to take during this period is also known as an opportunity fishery. The reason is that it comes in large numbers when Bonnetheads begin to overfish certain areas of the coast.

ACKNOWLEDGEMENTS

The authors of this paper are thankful to Lovely Professional University, Phagwara, and Guru Nanak Dev University, Amritsar, for providing infrastructural facilities to complete this research work.

REFERENCES

[1] D. Deutsch, "Quantum theory, the church-turing principle and the universal quantum computer", *Proc. R. Soc. Lond.,* vol. 400, no. 1818, pp. 97-117, 1985.

[2] D.P. DiVincenzo, "Quantum computation", *Science,* vol. 270, no. 5234, pp. 255-261, 1995. [http://dx.doi.org/10.1126/science.270.5234.255]

[3] M.A. Nielsen, and I.L. Chuang, *Quantum computation and quantum information.* Cambridge, U.K.: Cambridge Univ. Press, 2010.

[4] J. Gubbi, R. Buyya, S. Marusic, and M. Palaniswami, "Internet of Things (IoT): A vision, architectural elements, and future directions", *Future Gener. Comput. Syst.,* vol. 29, pp. 1645-1660, 2013. [http://dx.doi.org/10.1016/j.future.2013.01.010]

[5] M. Schuld, and F. Petruccione, *Supervised learning with quantum computers..* Cham, Switzerland: Springer, 2018. [http://dx.doi.org/10.1007/978-3-319-96424-9]

[6] E. Farhi and H. Neven, "Classification with quantum neural networks on near-term processors," *arXiv:1802.06002,* 2018.

[7] F. Arute, K. Arya, R. Babbush, D. Bacon, J.C. Bardin, R. Barends, R. Biswas, S. Boixo, F.G.S.L. Brandao, D.A. Buell, B. Burkett, Y. Chen, Z. Chen, B. Chiaro, R. Collins, W. Courtney, A. Dunsworth, E. Farhi, B. Foxen, A. Fowler, C. Gidney, M. Giustina, R. Graff, K. Guerin, S. Habegger, M.P. Harrigan, M.J. Hartmann, A. Ho, M. Hoffmann, T. Huang, T.S. Humble, S.V. Isakov, E. Jeffrey, Z. Jiang, D. Kafri, K. Kechedzhi, J. Kelly, P.V. Klimov, S. Knysh, A. Korotkov, F. Kostritsa, D.

Landhuis, M. Lindmark, E. Lucero, D. Lyakh, S. Mandrà, J.R. McClean, M. McEwen, A. Megrant, X. Mi, K. Michielsen, M. Mohseni, J. Mutus, O. Naaman, M. Neeley, C. Neill, M.Y. Niu, E. Ostby, A. Petukhov, J.C. Platt, C. Quintana, E.G. Rieffel, P. Roushan, N.C. Rubin, D. Sank, K.J. Satzinger, V. Smelyanskiy, K.J. Sung, M.D. Trevithick, A. Vainsencher, B. Villalonga, T. White, Z.J. Yao, P. Yeh, A. Zalcman, H. Neven, and J.M. Martinis, "Quantum supremacy using a programmable superconducting processor", *Nature,* vol. 574, no. 7779, pp. 505-510, 2019. [http://dx.doi.org/10.1038/s41586-019-1666-5] [PMID: 31645734]

[8] IBM Quantum, "IBM Quantum Experience," IBM, Accessed: Dec. 17, 2025. [Online]. Available: https://www.ibm.com/quantum-computing/

[9] Microsoft, "Bringing quantum computing to the cloud," Azure Quantum, Accessed: Dec. 17, 2025. [Online]. Available: https://azure.microsoft.com/en-us/products/quantum/

[10] Amazon Web Services, "Quantum computing with AWS," AWS Braket, Accessed: Dec. 17, 2025. [Online]. Available: https://aws.amazon.com/braket/

[11] A.W. Harrow, A. Hassidim, and S. Lloyd, "Quantum algorithm for linear systems of equations", *Phys. Rev. Lett.,* vol. 103, no. 15, p. 150502, 2009. [http://dx.doi.org/10.1103/PhysRevLett.103.150502] [PMID: 19905613]

[12] P.W. Shor, "Polynomial-time algorithms for prime factorization and discrete logarithms on a quantum computer", *SIAM J. Comput.,* vol. 26, no. 5, pp. 1484-1509, 1997. [http://dx.doi.org/10.1137/S0097539795293172]

[13] V. Dunjko, J.M. Taylor, and H.J. Briegel, "Quantum-Enhanced Machine Learning", *Phys. Rev. Lett.,* vol. 117, no. 13, p. 130501, 2016. [http://dx.doi.org/10.1103/PhysRevLett.117.130501] [PMID: 27715099]

[14] A. Rani, S. Kour, R. Kumar, "Comprehensive review of quantum computing: analyzing computational frameworks, emerging technologies, applications, and challenges in the quantum era", *Recent Advances in Computer Science and Communications*, vol. 19, 2025.

[15] J. Preskill, "Quantum Computing in the NISQ era and beyond", *Quantum,* vol. 2, p. 79, 2018. [http://dx.doi.org/10.22331/q-2018-08-06-79]

[16] C. Figgatt, A. Ostrander, and N.M. Linke, "Parallel Quantum Simulations of Large-Scale Many-Body Systems with Trapped-Ion Qubits", *Nat. Commun.,* vol. 12, p. 1377, 2021.

[17] N.K. Langford, "Errors in Quantum Computing: Mitigation Strategies and Future Prospects", *Nature Reviews Physics,* vol. 1, pp. 145-157, 2019.

[18] L. Chen, S. Jordan, Y.-K. Liu, D. Moody, R. Peralta, R. Perlner, and D. Smith-Tone, "Report on Post-Quantum Cryptography," NIST Interagency/Internal Report (NISTIR) 8105, National Institute of Standards and Technology, Gaithersburg, MD, USA, Apr. 2016. [http://dx.doi.org/10.6028/NIST.IR.8105]

[19] L.K. Grover, "A fast quantum mechanical algorithm for database search", *Proc. 28th Annu. ACM Symp. Theory Comput.* (STOC '96), Philadelphia, PA, USA, pp. 212–219, 1996. [http://dx.doi.org/10.1145/237814.237866]

[20] "Quantum Computing Market by Offering, Deployment, Application, End User, and Region – Global Forecast to 2030," MarketsandMarkets, 2023. Available from: https://www.marketsandmarkets.com/Market-Reports/quantum-computing-market-144888301.html

[21] "The next big innovation in AI: Quantum machine learning," Deloitte Insights, 2022. Available from: https://www2.deloitte.com/ insights/us/en/focus/tech-trends/2022/quantum-machine-learning.html

[22] "Cloud AI market size, share & trends analysis report," Grand View Research, 2023. Available from: https://www.grandviewresearch.com/ industry-analysis/cloud-artificial-intelligence-ai-market

[23] Gartner, "How Cloud Architectures Enhance Machine Learning Performance," 2022. [Online]. Available: https://www.gartner.com/en/documents/4004572

[24] Statista, "Adoption Rate of AI in the Cloud Worldwide 2025," 2023. [Online]. Available: https://www.statista.com/statistics/ai-cloud-adoption/

[25] A. Thaker and S. Adam, "The coming quantum leap in computing," Boston Consulting Group, 2018.

[26] "Post-quantum cryptography standardization," National Institute of Standards and Technology (NIST), 2024. [Online]. Available: https://csrc.nist.gov/projects/post-quantu-cryptography. [Accessed: Dec. 18, 2025].

[27] Deloitte, "The Economics of Quantum Computing: Costs and Considerations," 2023.

CHAPTER 2

Revolutionize AI: Quantum-Cloud Delves into Integration Strategies, Benefits, and Future Prospects

Vineeta Gulati[1,*], **Arun Kumar Rana**[2] and **Kashif Nisar**[3]

[1] *Department of Computer Science and Engineering (CSE), Maharishi Markandeshwar (Deemed to be University), Mullana, Haryana, India*

[2] *Department of Computer Science and Engineering (CSE), Galgotias College of Engineering and Technology, Greater Noida, Uttar Pradesh, India*

[3] *School of Arts and Sciences, The University of Notre Dame Australia, Sydney, New South Wales, Australia*

Abstract: Quantum Computing (QC) has emerged as a breakthrough technology with the potential to revolutionize Artificial Intelligence (AI) applications. By leveraging quantum mechanics principles, QC exponentially increases computational capacity, enabling accelerated data processing and optimization. The cloud availability of quantum computers facilitates their integration with existing cloud AI services, potentially offering the most promising route to exploit quantum algorithms within current cloud infrastructures. This chapter explores the interactions between quantum computing and cloud-based AI services, summarizing recent advances in implementation and the unique advantages of QC services compared to traditional cloud-based AI services. It also calls attention to open questions and potential areas of development. The authors give a comprehensive overview of quantum algorithms, hybrid quantum-classical models, and real-world implementations. The authors also explore the ways AI-cloud companies will be affected after major cloud providers enter the world of quantum computing-based business. This chapter also looks at security challenges, fundamental scalability limitations, and future research directions, with insights into how quantum computing will reshape the AI landscape over the next few decades.

Keywords: AI ethics, Cloud AI, Classical computing, Google quantum, Hybrid computing, IBM Quantum, Intelligent computing, Microsoft azure, Quantum computing, Quantum machine learning, Material science, Quantum neural networks, Qubits, Superposition.

* **Corresponding author Vineeta Gulati:** Department of Computer Science and Engineering (CSE), Maharishi Markandeshwar (Deemed to be University), Mullana, Haryana, India; E-mail: vineetaarora04@gmail.com

Satveer Kour, Harvinder Singh, Anupam Bonkra & Rupinder Singh (Eds.)

INTRODUCTION

Cloud AI has advanced significantly with quantum computing, and it's a fusion of fields that could have a long-term impact on computation. The use of cutting-edge concepts of quantum mechanics, such as superposition and entanglement, aims to increase the processing speed and efficiency of the AI models [1, 2]. Accompanying data of this nature and scale requires unprecedented computational capacity, as exemplified by this intersection of quantum computing and cloud-based AI platforms, which allows organizations to leverage state-of-the-art computational power without the cost of maintaining extensive hardware infrastructure, providing advancement and economic value in a world where data is becoming increasingly salient to our day-to-day [3, 4]. In addition to enabling the solving of complex problems that cannot be tackled with classical computing, this amalgamation also raises significant ethical and societal issues. Deployment of quantum-boosted AI tools is raising questions about data privacy, security, and potential inequality [5, 6]. As researchers and policymakers navigate these challenges, establishing robust ethical frameworks will be vital to ensuring fair access and responsible utilization of these transformative technologies. The implications of this integration are illustrated in vital use cases. For example, quantum AI in medicine could accelerate the drug discovery process by enabling a faster analysis of molecular interactions, while in finance, it could lead to more precise risk assessments and fraud detection [7, 8]. Logistics, among many other industries, stands to benefit from optimized routing and inventory management with quantum-enhanced AI applications—there's tremendous potential for quantum-enhanced AI applications to enable better decision making and efficiencies [9]. Even though quantum computing combined with cloud AI holds so much promise, there are some issues that need to be resolved. To achieve its full potential, technical limitations on scalability and resource requirements, and the need for cross-disciplinary collaboration around its use, must be addressed [10, 11]. While the potential for quantum computing and AI to collaborate is enormous, there are clear obstacles ahead of us.

Motivation and Problem Statement

Rapidly evolving AI technologies require ever-increasing computational capabilities that cloud-based infrastructures cannot keep up with. Largely driven by principles derived from quantum mechanics, quantum computing has the power to exponentially improve the processing capabilities of classical computing systems, which looks to be a promising solution to these computational bottlenecks. But quantum cloud AI is just in the early stages; there are still many technical, ethical, and scalability issues to resolve.

In this research, the authors focus on the critical question of how quantum computing can be seamlessly integrated into cloud-based AI systems to provide optimal computational benefits and new possibilities. Though the potential advantages of quantum algorithms are evident, current literature offers piecemeal insights into the topic of their usage for business, and there is a general lack of an overall structure for implementation and quantification of impact. This chapter seeks to fill this gap by investigating integration strategies, evaluating existing use cases, and determining the challenges that need to be overcome in order to allow a smooth transition to quantum-enhanced AI systems.

Research Contribution

- Examining some possible practical integration strategies for quantum computing and cloud-based AI, given the difficulties of executing the strategies in practice.
- In contrast, examine the quantum-enhanced AI services versus regular traditional cloud-based AI offerings, emphasizing what cannot be achieved through classical means.
- Detection of potential security threats and ethical issues related to quantum-cloud AI and suggesting mechanisms to mitigate them.

FUNDAMENTALS OF QUANTUM COMPUTING

QC is essentially a paradigm shift in terms of computing, using the laws of quantum physics to compute in quasi-mathematically infeasible ways. The quantum bit is then the elementary unit of quantum information, and one of the main components for this technology.

Basics of Quantum Mechanics

Quantum mechanics is the area of physics that describes the behavior of matter and energy at the atomic and subatomic levels. In classical computing, a unit of information (0 or 1) is known as a bit. The same thing occurs when you handle qubits that are a superposition of the bits positioned 0 and 1 simultaneously. Taking advantage of this property exponentially improves the capability of quantum systems to process data points in parallel over classical systems on large datasets [6, 7].

Superposition and Entanglement

Quantum Computing The wave-particle duality, the particle and waver nature of all matter, has many applications in quantum physics. In contrast, while the value of a classical bit can either be 0 or 1, a qubit can simultaneously represent both states, allowing for more advanced computations than classical bits. Quantum computers are formed by devices called qubits , and an n-qubit quantum computer can represent 2^n different states simultaneously, thus providing it with an exponential processing power [8, 9].

This is called entanglement, because the state of one qubit is dependent on the state of another qubit, even at a great distance from each other. This efficient link enables a quick transfer of information between qubits and raises their computational effectiveness with respect to traditional bits [4, 10]. QC conceptual representation is illustrated below (Fig. **1**).

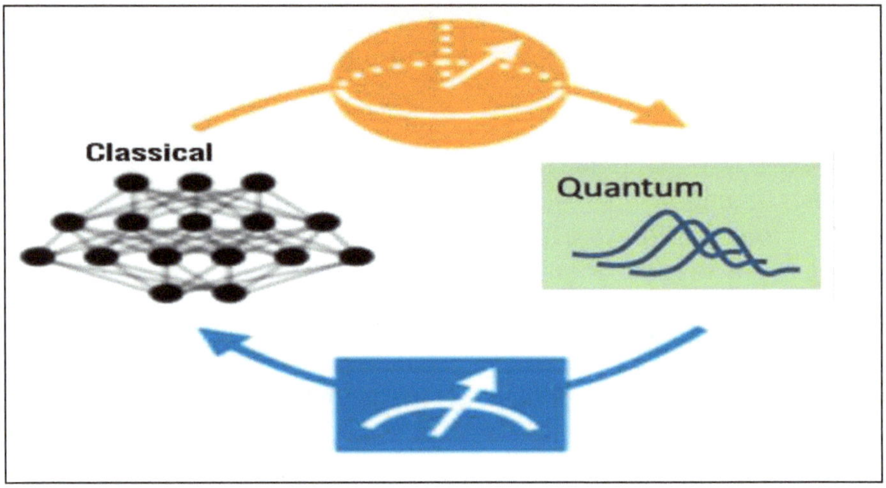

Fig. (1). Conceptual representation of quantum computing.

Noisy Intermediate-Scale Quantum (NISQ) Era

Present-day quantum computers are based on the NISQ paradigm. NISQ devices have a restricted number of qubits and are vulnerable to environmental noise. Nevertheless, scientists are really aiming to increase qubit coherence times, reduce the error rates, and scale it up [3, 8].

Hybrid Quantum-classical Systems

Hybrid quantum–classical systems are systems that leverage both quantum and classical computing resources to solve complementary tasks. These systems use quantum ability to perform certain operations, whereas they use classical computing for all the other operations. In practice, for example, in the quantum annealer, quantum computing has been implemented to solve problems from artificial intelligence in the real world [3, 11]. The hybrid quantum-classical computing workflow is shown below (Fig. **2**).

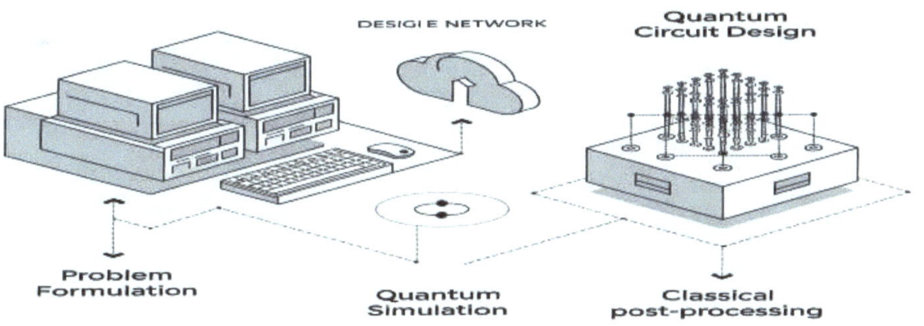

Fig. (2). Hybrid quantum-classical computing workflow.

Comparison of Classical and Quantum Computing

Classical computing dominates compute workloads, extending beyond enterprise applications to include AI tasks and simulations. Quantum computing, on the other hand, uses qubits in a state of superposition and entanglement, allowing it to solve particular problem types (like those found in cryptography, optimization, and materials science) in much faster time frames than classical computers. Classical computers provide much easier error corrections with well-developed schemes and are commonly available, but quantum computers have to deal with the decoherence issue due to the complexity of their states and the scalability of error correction schemes. The comparison of classical and quantum computing is depicted here (Fig. **3**). The comparison of classical and quantum computing is shown below (Table **1**).

Table 1. Comparison of classical and quantum computing.

Feature	Classical Computing	Quantum Computing
Basic Unit	Bit	Qubit
State Representation	0 or 1	Superposition (0, 1, or both)
Processing Speed	Sequential	Parallel
Error Rates	Relatively low	Higher due to noise
Application Domains	General-purpose computing	Optimization, simulations, cryptography, AI
Current Era	Mature	Noisy Intermediate-Scale Quantum (NISQ)

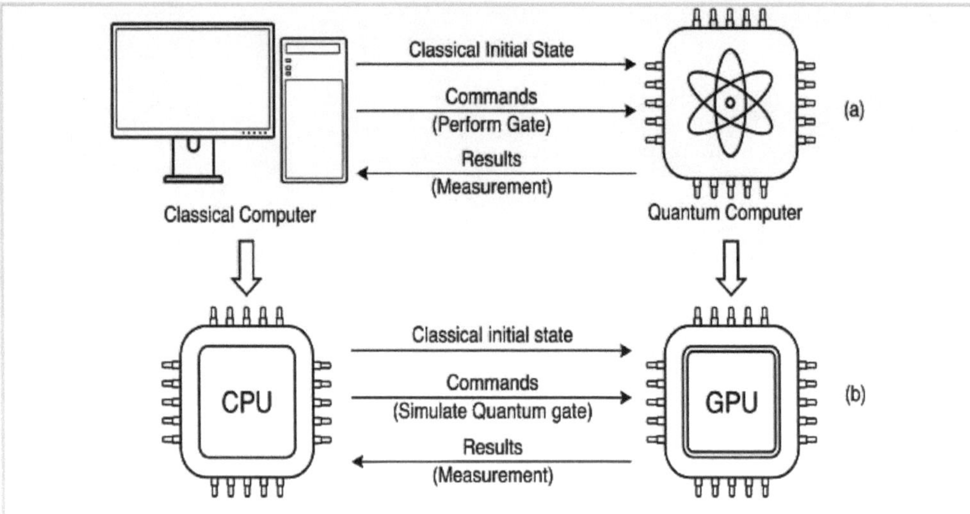

Fig. (3). Comparison of classical and quantum computing.

Future Directions

This reason is mainly the future of quantum computing, which is great when it is integrated with a cloud AI service. Such cloud-based quantum computing platforms can improve quantum accessibility for a larger audience and possibly accelerate developments in AI, machine learning, and complex optimization. This could lead to a convergence of transformative advances in many applications, including drug discovery and climate modeling [12, 13]. In creating implementation plans and overcoming these challenges, researchers pave the way for increased adoption and use of QC technologies in many different fields.

CLOUD AI SERVICES

Cloud AI services provide organizations with scalable, flexible, and easily accessible platforms to deploy Artificial Intelligence (AI) solutions for a wide range of use cases. The best AI services utilize the processing power of cloud computing to improve the use of AI in various sectors. The cloud AI service architecture is presented below (Fig. **4**).

Fig. (4). Cloud AI service architecture.

Overview of Cloud AI Services

The merging of AI with cloud services has created models such as AI-as-a-Service (AIaaS), enabling access to AI functionalities for organizations without requiring extensive technical knowledge. For example, companies like Amazon Web Services (AWS), Microsoft Azure, and Google Cloud offer a large selection of AI tools and frameworks, providing AI capabilities to all businesses, regardless of size. Such platforms include pre-built models for NLP, computer vision, predictive analytics, and so on [1, 2], which cuts the development time and costs significantly.

INTEGRATION OF QUANTUM COMPUTING WITH CLOUD AI SERVICES

The combination of QC and cloud AI services offers numerous benefits that can change the game across multiple industries. The combination of these two pillars of technology and creativity is the promise of better performance, greater efficiency, and new opportunities for innovation and growth.

Nonetheless, as quantum and AI technology evolve, there is significant potential for economic expansion through the combination of the two technologies. This integration is predicted to generate productivity and efficiency gains in products and services from new markets and existing sectors, resulting in reduced costs and improved products and services for consumers [14]. Sectors utilizing quantum-boosted AI will encounter paradigm shifts, ushering in a period of fresh and innovative progress. The key benefits of quantum computing and cloud AI integration are shown here (Table **2**).

Table 2. Key benefits of quantum computing and cloud AI integration.

Benefit	Description
Enhanced Computational Power	Real-time analytics: Drift in complex data at an unprecedented speed with quantum computers to get quick insights.
Improved Decision-Making	This enables the deployment of sophisticated algorithms capable of processing large quantities of data, leading to more informed decision-making.
Cost Efficiency	Optimized processes and improved resource management enabled by quantum AI can help reduce operational costs.
Rapid Innovation	Quicker research and development can mean faster delivery of new products and services.
Cross-Industry Applications	Healthcare, finance, and other fields stand to benefit from improved outcomes and new benchmarks as quantum AI permeates their applications.

Quantum Algorithms for Cloud AI Services

Quantum algorithms leverage quantum mechanics principles (*e.g.*, superposition, entanglement) to process computations more efficiently than classical algorithms. These algorithms offer potential benefits for integrated components within cloud AI services, enhancing computational capacity and capability across various industries-from finance to healthcare to logistics [15, 16] is presented here (Fig. **5**).

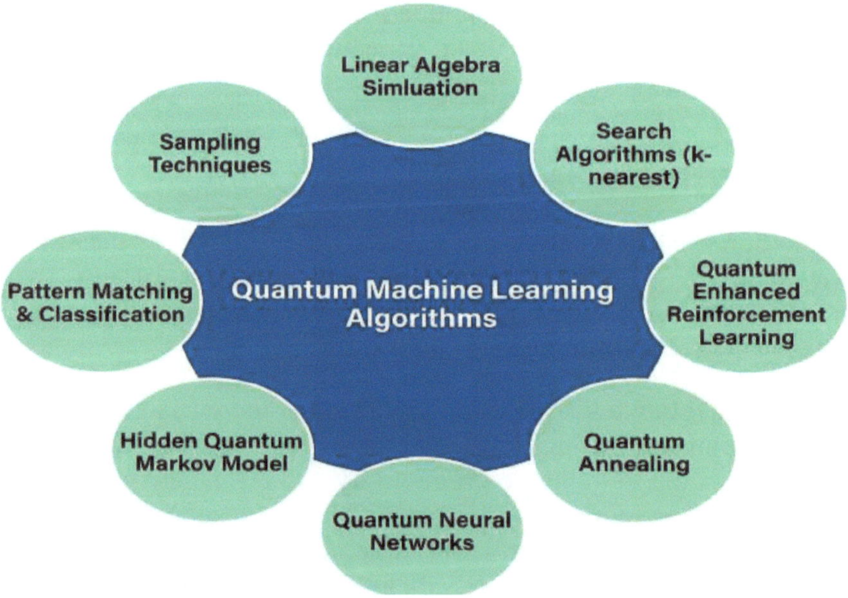

Fig. (5). Quantum algorithms for cloud AI services.

QSVM (Quantum Support Vector Machines)

Classical SVMs are extended by applying quantum computational techniques to these methods for classification problems. The quantum state vector model is utilized for organizing large and complex datasets in an effective manner as part of the QSVM, resulting in increased machine learning accuracy [17]. It uses quantum parallelism to find correlations in data that classical algorithms cannot handle.

Variational Quantum Eigensolver (VQE)

VQE uses classical learning techniques to approximate eigenvalues with polynomial-defined circuits. This enables exponentially faster calculations than classical methods of calculating eigenvectors, which is necessary for simulations and optimisations in the feed cloud AI [15, 16]. Researchers lack dedicated quantum hardware, but VQE is realized in cloud services, leading them to tackle computationally intense problems.

Quantum Approximate Optimization Algorithm (QAOA)

QAOA is intended to solve combinatorial optimization problems, such as those found in supply chain and logistics. It allows solutions to be found in a quick and accurate way compared to classical optimization methods; thus, it can be a very helpful tool for businesses using cloud AI [18, 19]. Another domain that benefits from QAOA is the optimization of operational efficiency, such as routing and resource allocation.

Quantum Clustering Algorithms

Quantum clustering algorithms build upon the conventional clustering algorithms while exploiting the principles of quantum mechanics. These algorithms are capable of processing massive amounts of data in parallel, achieving more accurate exploration of hidden patterns and correlations than classical methods. This functionality provides its greatest value in the fields of market analysis and customer segmentation, where relationships between data points are exceedingly complex [20, 21].

REAL-WORLD APPLICATIONS AND CASE STUDIES

The start of many use cases across a wide range of industries has been brought along by quantum computing combined with cloud AI services. Notably, the aforementioned applications not only prove the potential of quantum computing but also indicate its benefits and superiority over classical computing techniques. The trends in quantum cloud AI research are depicted below (Fig. **6**).

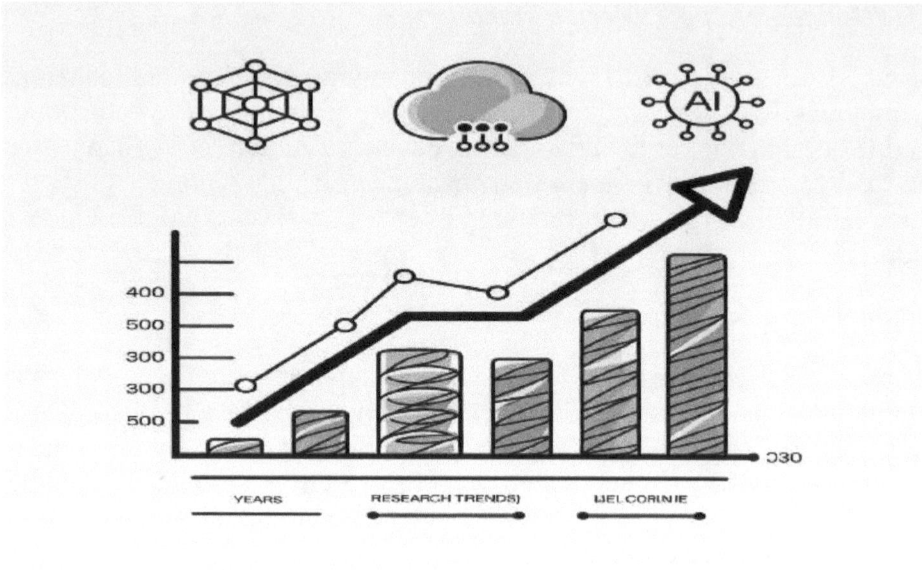

Fig. (6). Trends in quantum cloud AI research.

Supply Chain Management and Logistics

One notable quantum algorithm that potentially has a dramatic impact on logistics and supply chain management is the Quantum Approximate Optimization Algorithm (QAOA). A study claims, "Through the optimization of delivery routes, scheduling of fleet operations, and managing inventory levels, QAOA can help create a harnessed water distribution system, ultimately reducing overhead and providing for more sustainable delivery times" [3].

Quantum Computing for Quality Control in Production

The increasing number of in-production QC use cases is a testament to the progress made towards Fault-Tolerant Quantum Computing (FTQC). As recent surveys have shown, the share of responders with a QC use case in production increased from around 33% to 55% in a single year [22]. This evolution reflects a wider acceptance and use of quantum technologies across industries, including aerospace, automotive, and medical technology. These use cases are often tied to projects that have demonstrated a distinct advantage to classical approaches (although such projects may not yet be fully realized or commercially scalable).

Optimal Carbon Capture Materials

Quantum computing shows great potential in an important area: developing carbon capture materials. The shift to a low-carbon economy requires new materials for energy production and carbon capture. For CO_2 adsorption using different metals, classical computing cannot handle such many-body interactions; thus, current optimization processes solely rely on classical computing. It is through these interactions that the application of QC is realized. A deeper knowledge of the interactions can lead to the creation of a more efficient material, like Metal-Organic Frameworks (MOFs) for carbon capture [3].

Pharmaceutical Research Advances

In the pharmaceutical sector, the potential for quantum computers to aid with drug discovery and development is tremendous. Quantum technologies can speedily analyze complex molecular structures, leading to the discovery of new drug candidates and facilitating personalized medicine through the customization of treatments based on genetic information [8, 14]. This might not only translate to benefits for patients but also change the way of making pharmaceutical R&D much more efficient.

Ethical and Social Implications

Combining quantum computing with cloud AI services also brings with it important ethical issues, especially around data privacy and security. However, because quantum computers can process so much data, exposing sensitive information or potential misuse is a real concern. As policymakers and industry leaders gear up to tackle these challenges, they need to ensure that an innovative environment is nurtured for getting the best out of these game-changing technologies [14].

These use cases and case studies demonstrate that quantum computing integrated with cloud AI services at all levels of an organisation can lead to considerable advancements in the research, development, and production of innovative, high-performance products across sectors, while also addressing complex problems that classical computing methods cannot resolve. A case study on quantum AI in healthcare is presented here (Fig. **7**).

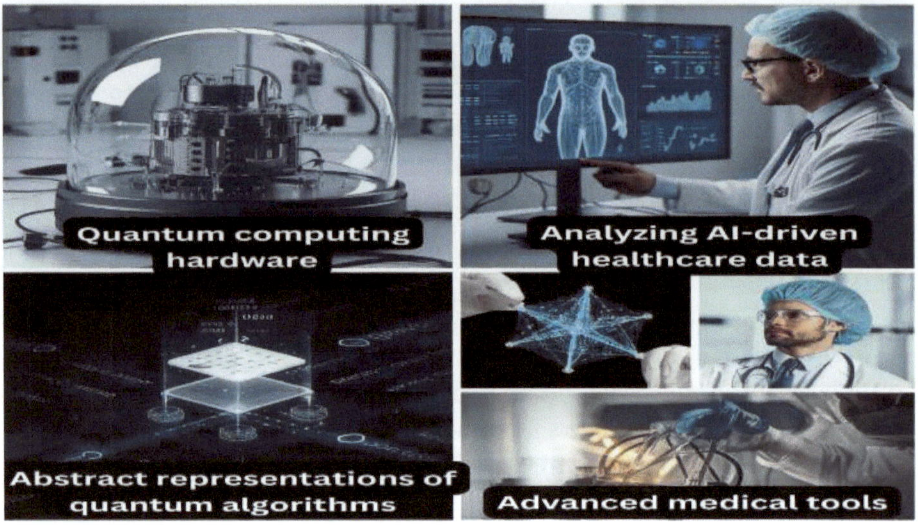

Fig. (7). Case study on quantum AI in healthcare.

CHALLENGES AND FUTURE PROSPECTS

Challenges

AI may be instrumental in dealing with the hurdles and obstacles in the path of this converging technology. For example, AI technologies are being developed to help address the critical challenges of quantum processor design, error-correction, and algorithm optimization as a means of enabling practical quantum computing solutions [23].

Ethical and Social Implications

So alongside the immense benefits of integrating them as quantum computing and AI, there are the undeniable ethical and societal challenges. Given their powerful capabilities, it is imperative to explore how these solutions may be implemented with serious consideration of data privacy, security, and potential misuse [8]. It is imperative that robust ethical guidelines, governance structures are put in place to ensure that these innovations, even technologies that are making their way into the fields of medicine, will remain equitable and won't only serve to increase existing inequalities.

Challenges of Integration

Understanding the complexities of merging quantum computing with cloud AI services, the next sub-sections describe some of the largest barriers to this integration.

Technical Limitations

The fundamental shortcomings of quantum computing itself. Existing quantum systems struggle with scalability, resources, and the nature of the data. Since quantum computers function on principles that are radically different from classical systems, writing algorithms capable of making use of quantum functionality effectively, while still working in conjunction with classical cloud AI services, if they exist, remains an open challenge [14, 24].

Need for Resources and Scalability

Quantum computing hardware is traditionally resource-intensive and very energy-consuming. This adds an element of challenge to scaling quantum solutions in the existing cloud environment. For example, quantum bits (qubits) have a coherence time, which restricts the time they can keep their quantum state; this creates challenges for performing computations that take a longer time [25].

Features and Properties of Data

A very important factor is the kind of data that is being processed. Quantum algorithms often require specific data formats and structures, which may not be compatible with the formats used by classical AI systems. Such misalignment can certainly impede smooth integration and data sharing of quantum computing environments with classical cloud infrastructures [26, 27].

Ethical and Societal Concerns

On Quantum computing and AI convergence, Ethical and societal implications of QC and AI convergence. These technologies can also be complex and require a clear understanding of their impact on data privacy, security, and potential biases in AI systems. As quantum computing has the ability to balance the scales, there exists the potential danger that these technologies could further deepen existing inequities or cause new types of discrimination [8, 14].

Addressing Ethical Issues

Setting strong ethical guidelines and governance will help address these concerns. In case organizations want to approach quantum-enhanced AI systems, they should ensure equal access to technology on their AI frameworks so bias is not present in training data [8].

Ecosystem for Collaboration and Innovation

Integrating quantum computing with AI poses complexities that require multidimensional approaches and collaboration among experts from different domains, such as quantum physicists, computer scientists, and ethicists. Facilitating collaboration among academia, industry, and government will be critical to tackling the multifaceted challenges posed by this integration [8, 14].

Investing in Workforce Development

Building collaboration is also about investing in education and training programs that will develop a workforce skilled in both quantum computing and AI. Organizations also need a solid plan for maturing the quantum capabilities needed to enhance their cloud AI services [8, 14].

The future of quantum computing as part of cloud AI services is looming, but challenges remain. These technologies need to address three major challenges in scalability, error correction, and accessibility to be fully realized [7, 28]. Stabilization of qubits and error correction methods are critical to ensuring reliable and accurate quantum computation. Finally, quantum computing resources have to be democratized *via* the cloud for more companies to adopt them [29].

Future Prospects

Fusing quantum computing with cloud-based AI services will open up a novel realm of tech progress, with the rapid proliferation of innovative and disruptive use cases across industries. The convergence of QC with cloud-based AI solutions promises to transform the way organizations operate, promote better decision-making, and provide solutions to complex problems more quickly as it matures.

Quantum AI: Potential for Transformation

QC and AI can be complementary to each other, and they can provide immense promise for enhancing computational abilities to solve challenges that are impossible to approach today. Quantum AI could produce answers that leverage the specialized characteristics of quantum mechanics (such as superposition as well as entanglement) to solve issues by managing data at prices significantly faster than classical systems. It means significant improvements in a lot of applications, such as optimization problems, complex simulations, and large-scale data analysis [7, 14].

CONCLUSION

This will be changed in the domain of AI as quantum computing will expand computational power and the speed of processing, optimization, and problem-solving. It can also be integrated into cloud-based AI services to utilize its capabilities on existing frameworks. From building quantum algorithms to hybrid quantum-classical models, and quantum system implementations, a lot has been done; however, challenges in scalability, security, and practicality still grow. Yet businesses powered by AI, along with the magnitude of cloud investments, will ultimately determine the future of intelligent computing as big cloud providers pour substantial (and increasing) investment into quantum technologies. While there are still numerous challenges to overcome, further research and development are vital to unlocking the potential of quantum computing for AI and driving the next wave of innovation and efficiency in the field.

ACKNOWLEDGEMENTS

The authors of this paper are thankful to Maharishi Markandeshwar (Deemed to be University), Mullana, Ambala, for providing infrastructural facilities to complete this research work.

REFERENCES

[1] J. Rane, S. K. Mallick, Ö. Kaya, and N. L. Rane, "Artificial intelligence, machine learning, and deep learning in cloud, edge, and quantum computing: A review of trends, challenges, and future directions," in *Future Research Opportunities for Artificial Intelligence in Industry 4.0 and 5.0*, Deep Science Publishing, pp. 1–38, 2024. [http://dx.doi.org/10.70593/978-81-981271-0-5_1]

[2] S. M. DevaraJ, "Cloud, Ai, And Digital Transformation: A Winning Combination", *International Journal Of Computer Engineering And Technology (Ijcet),* vol. 15, no. 5, pp. 1020-1032, 2024.

[3] A. Rayhan, and S. Rayhan, "Quantum Computing and AI: A Quantum Leap in Intelligence", *AI Odyssey: Unraveling the Past, Mastering the Present, and Charting the Future of Artificial Intelligence,* p. 424, 2024.

[4] H. T. Nguyen, P. Krishnan, D. Krishnaswamy, M. Usman, and R. Buyya, "Quantum cloud computing: a review, open problems, and future directions", *arXiv preprint, 2404.11420,* 2024.

[5] A.S. Rajawat, A. S., Goyal, S. B., Kautish, S., Mittal, R. "Quantum cloud computing: Integrating quantum algorithms for enhanced scalability and performance in cloud architectures", in *Applied Data Science and Smart Systems.* CRC Press, 2024, pp. 482-490. [http://dx.doi.org/10.1201/9781003471059-62]

[6] U. Ghosh, and S. Kundu, "Exploring future trends and emerging applications: A glimpse into tomorrow's landscape," in *Artificial Intelligence Using Federated Learning*, 1st ed., Boca Raton, FL, USA: CRC Press, 2024, pp. 32.

[7] A.D. Córcoles, A. Kandala, A. Javadi-Abhari, D.T. McClure, A.W. Cross, K. Temme, P.D. Nation, M. Steffen, and J.M. Gambetta, and J. M. Gambetta, "Challenges and opportunities of near-term quantum computing systems",, *Proc. IEEE,* vol. 108, no. 8, pp. 1338-1352, 2020. [http://dx.doi.org/10.1109/JPROC.2019.2954005]

[8] P. Fatima, S. Haider, M.A. Ali, M. Abbas, I. Akhtar, M. Rasool, H. Maqbool, and N. Khan, "AI Unleashed: Pioneering Trends and Future Directions in Artificial Intelligence", *Saudi Journal of Engineering and Technology,* vol. 9, no. 8, pp. 406-418, 2024. [http://dx.doi.org/10.36348/sjet.2024.v09i08.005]

[9] M. Belkhir, H. Benkaouha, and E. Benkhelifa, "Quantum vs. classical computing: a comparative analysis," in *Proc. 2022 Seventh Int. Conf. Fog Mobile Edge Comput. (FMEC)*, 2022, pp. 1–8.

[10] A. Rani, S. Kour, R. Kumar, "Comprehensive review of quantum computing: analyzing computational frameworks, emerging technologies, applications, and challenges in the quantum era," *Recent Adv. Comput. Sci. Commun.*, vol. 18, no. 7, pp. 1–15, 2025.

[11] K. T. M. Ho, K. C. Chen, L. Lee, F. Burt, S. Yu, and P. H. Lee, "Quantum computing for climate resilience and sustainability challenges," in *Proc. 2024 IEEE Int. Conf. Quantum Comput. Eng. (QCE)*, vol. 2, pp. 262–267, 2024. [http://dx.doi.org/10.1109/QCE60285.2024.10289]

[12] S. H. Bapon, and A. Kaur, "Quantum AI: Exploring the Intersection of Quantum Computing and Artificial Intelligence", in Proc. *KILBY 100 7th Int. Conf. Computing Sciences (ICCS 2023)*, 2023.

[13] V. Gulati, N. Raheja, and A.K. Rana, "Hybrid extraction methodologies to reduce dimensionality," in *Proc. 2023 5th Int. Conf. Advances in Computing, Communication Control and Networking (ICAC3N)*, Greater Noida, India, 2023. [http://dx.doi.org/10.1109/ICAC3N60023.2023.10541541]

[14] A. Ahmadi, "Quantum computing and artificial intelligence: The synergy of two revolutionary technologies", *Asian J. Electr. Sci.,* vol. 12, no. 2, pp. 15-27, 2023. [http://dx.doi.org/10.51983/ajes-2023.12.2.4118]

[15] A. Mathew, "Quantum AI in Cloud Environments," in *Scientific Research, New Technologies and Applications,* vol. 7, pp.116-124, 2024. [http://dx.doi.org/10.9734/bpi/srnta/v7/3116]

[16] V. Gulati, N. Raheja, and R. Kumar, "A Hybrid Feature Extraction-Based Prediction System (HFEPS) for Early Diagnosis of Chronic Kidney Disease", *2024 International Conference on Advances in Computing Research on Science Engineering and Technology (ACROSET),* pp. 1-6, 2024. [http://dx.doi.org/10.1109/ACROSET62108.2024.10743328]

[17] B. Rawat, N. Mehra, A.S. Bist, M. Yusup, and Y.P.A. Sanjaya, "Quantum computing and ai: Impacts & possibilities", *ADI Journal on Recent Innovation,* vol. 3, no. 2, pp. 202-207, 2022.

[18] N. Pooranam, D. Surendran, N. Karthikeyan, and G. I. Rajathi, Quantum computing: future of artificial intelligence and its applications", in *Quantum Computing and Artificial Intelligence: Training Machine and Deep Learning Algorithms on Quantum Computers*, P. Raj, A. Kumar, A. K. Dubey, S. Bhatia, and O. M. S. (eds.), Berlin, Boston: De Gruyter, 2023, pp. 163–184. [http://dx.doi.org/10.1515/9783110791402-009]

[19] A. K. Tyagi, A. K. Mishra, S. U. Aswathy, and S. Kumari, "Quantum computing, qubits with artificial intelligence, and blockchain technologies: A roadmap for the future," in *Quantum Computing and Artificial Intelligence: Applications and Future Trends*, Hoboken, NJ, USA: Wiley, 2024. [http://dx.doi.org/10.1002/9781394213948.ch18]

[20] U. Eswaran, A. Khang, and V. Eswaran, "Role of quantum computing in the era of artificial intelligence (AI)," in *Applications and Principles of Quantum Computing*. IGI Global Scientific Publishing, 2024, pp. 46-68.

[21] M. Krenn, J. Landgraf, T. Foesel, and F. Marquardt, "Artificial intelligence and machine learning for quantum technologies", *Phys. Rev. A (Coll. Park),* vol. 107, no. 1, p. 010101, 2023. [http://dx.doi.org/10.1103/PhysRevA.107.010101]

[22] Q. A. Memon, M. Al Ahmad, and M. Pecht, "Quantum computing: navigating the future of computation, challenges, and technological breakthroughs", *Quantum Reports,* vol. 6, no. 4, pp. 627-

663, 2024.
[http://dx.doi.org/10.3390/quantum6040039]

[23] M. Daniel, "Quantum computing ai frontiers-people, technology and economics", in *Proc. Int. Annu. Conf. Amer. Soc. Eng. Manag. (ASEM)*, pp. 1–10, 2024.

[24] V. Romanelli, C. Cerchia, and A. Lavecchia, "Unlocking the potential of generative artificial intelligence in drug discovery", in *Applications of Generative AI*, Z. Lyu, Ed. Springer International Publishing: Cham, 2024, pp. 37-63.

[25] H. Padmanaban, "Quantum computing and AI in the cloud", *J. Comput. Intell. Robot.,* vol. 4, no. 1, pp. 14-32, 2024.

[26] A. Hammad, and R. Abu-Zaid, "Applications of AI in decentralized computing systems: harnessing artificial intelligence for enhanced scalability, efficiency, and autonomous decision-making in distributed architectures," *Appl. Res. Artif. Intell. Cloud Comput.*, vol. 7, pp. 161–187, 2024.

[27] C.O. Oyeniran, A.O. Adewusi, A.G. Adeleke, L.A. Akwawa, and C.F. Azubuko, "Advancements in quantum computing and their implications for software development", *Computer Science & IT Research Journal,* vol. 4, no. 3, pp. 577-593, 2023.
[http://dx.doi.org/10.51594/csitrj.v4i3.1558]

[28] R.D. Taylor, "Quantum artificial intelligence: a "precautionary" US approach", *Telecomm. Policy,* vol. 44, no. 6, p. 101909, 2020.
[http://dx.doi.org/10.1016/j.telpol.2020.101909]

[29] S. Chander, "A guide to quantum computers and the development of quantum advantage", *Int. J. High Sch. Res.,* vol. 5, no. 3, pp. 103-121, 2023.
[http://dx.doi.org/10.36838/v5i3.19]

CHAPTER 3

Applications of Quantum AI in Healthcare, Finance, and Cybersecurity

Amanpreet Singh[1,*], Rupinder Singh[1], Jaswinder Singh[1], Jaspreet Singh[2] and **Hatem Salem Abu Hamatta[3]**

[1] *Chitkara University Institute of Engineering and Technology, Chitkara University, Rajpura, Punjab, India*

[2] *Department of Computer Science and Engineering, Chandigarh University, Mohali, Punjab, India*

[3] *Department of Applied Sciences, Al-Balqa Applied University, Aqaba, Jordan*

Abstract: Quantum Artificial Intelligence (Quantum AI) suits quantum computing and artificial intelligence to tackle complex issues such as multi-dimensional optimization and massive volumes of information more proficiently than classic strategies. Quantum AI utilizes quantum phenomena like superposition, entanglement, and tunneling, among others, to realize a speedup of several orders of magnitude compared to classical AI algorithms. Quantum AI is capable of being implemented for healthcare, finance, and cybersecurity. Whereas quantum simulations are used for accelerating drug discovery and for improving the accuracy of molecular modeling, they also benefit precision medicine through advanced genomic analysis as well as diagnostics, including precision diagnostics, through the precision testing of natural disease biomarkers, active and inactive metabolites, and toxic blood chemistry. Quantum AI in finance enhances trading profitability by accelerating the prediction of real-time market trends, optimization of the portfolio, and financial fraud detection, while processing vast datasets. Quantum cryptography, *e.g.*, quantum key distribution, provides security in cybersecurity, whereas quantum algorithms, such as Shor, bring threats to encryption, and thus post-quantum cryptography is developed. This chapter shows that Quantum AI pertains to practical feasibility, despite error correction, coherence times, and a lack of algorithm development. What we show is about how Quantum AI can transform these sectors, what the stumbling blocks are, hardware scalability, and algorithm efficiency, in addition to quantum computing reliability. This study, therefore, highlights the importance of continuing to invest in Quantum AI so that it can be fully realized.

* **Corresponding author Amanpreet Singh:** Chitkara University Institute of Engineering and Technology, Chitkara University, Rajpura, Punjab, India; E-mail: Amanpreet.singh@chitkara.edu.in

Satveer Kour, Harvinder Singh, Anupam Bonkra & Rupinder Singh (Eds.)

Keywords: AI ethics, Cloud AI, Cybersecurity, Economics, Entanglement, Finance, Frameworks, Google quantum, Healthcare, Hybrid computing, Intelligent computing, Quantum computing, Quantum machine learning, Quantum mechanics, Quantum AI.

INTRODUCTION

Quantum Artificial Intelligence (QAI) is the combination of quantum computing and Artificial Intelligence (AI), which solves complex problems that classical computing cannot solve. Industries that require high computational efficiency have shown great promise in adopting Quantum Artificial Intelligence (QAI) [1]. The application of QAI leverages quantum phenomena, such as superposition, entanglement, and parallelism to achieve enhanced computational power. Industries are starting to take advantage of quantum superposition, quantum entanglement, and parallelism. This chapter shares details of how QAI can be applied to three critical domains, such as healthcare, finance, and cybersecurity. It is based on quantum mechanics principles, such as superposition and entanglement, as ways of improving AI decision-making using quantum AI [2]. Qubits in quantum computing reside in multiple states at once to offer the impressive payoff of classical binary computing [3]. One such feature is that it allows Quantum AI to solve complex optimization problems, to simulate a quantum system, and to improve machine learning models beyond classical capabilities [4].

Data from the healthcare industry is vast and cannot be handled by simple analyses involving diagnosis and treatment optimization. Quantum AI is a response to accelerating drug discovery, bettering medical imaging, and personal medicine. The development of a new drug is a costly and time-consuming process that often spans several years. Quantum AI can, however, drastically shrink this timeline since quantum computers perform molecular interactions more efficiently than classical computers. Quantum Machine Learning (QML) algorithms can process large datasets of molecular structures to obtain possible drug candidates and the interaction between the drug candidates and human proteins [5]. Specifically, companies such as IBM and Google are actively researching quantum applications in pharmacology.

Quantum AI improves pattern recognition refinement in MRI analysis to a level comparable to human perception. It also enhances anomaly detection, allowing the precise identification of which particle, even in a tiny sample, triggers a particular behavioral response in a rat. Radiologists build a better understanding of health outcomes in patients with diseases like cancer by amplifying machine learning with quantum enhancement to better detect the disease at earlier stages with higher accuracy [6]. Prepping vast genetic datasets to arrive at the optimal treatment strategies for everyone requires genomic sequencing. Quantum AI will speed up this process by identifying genetic mutations and predicting how patients will react to specific therapies. This has particularly exciting potential for the treatment of cancer, rare genetic disorders, or neurodegenerative diseases.

Molecular simulations accelerate in quantum computing (bypassing the long, expensive traditional process of drug discovery), and therefore, researchers can discover possible drug candidates faster [7]. Quantum computing prepared by AI is better than using medical data and can identify diseases such as cancer and neurological disorders [8]. The achievements to which I refer make global healthcare more precise, efficient, and accessible. With their recent developments, quantum AI is changing the face of the financial industry by transforming how people manage portfolios, reduce risk in analysis, and detect all forms of fraud [9]. Quantum-enhanced AI can process huge amounts of data in real time and on a time scale that classical models of finance would find hard or even impossible [10]. Quantum algorithms that solve complex risk-reward trade-offs of portfolio optimization with higher efficiency than conventional models are useful for that [11]. Fraud detection has also made leaps and bounds, one of which is that quantum machine learning can determine transaction anomalies that look like fraud more quickly than classical systems [12]. The capabilities aid financial institutions in making better decisions and becoming more efficient and more secure.

Quantum AI is an opportunity and a challenge in terms of cybersecurity. On the offensive side, quantum cryptography, especially Quantum Key Distribution (QKD), is available as a means of secure communication immune to classical hacking methods [13]. However, current encryption methods are vulnerable to large-scale quantum computers, as Shor's algorithm and other quantum algorithms can solve them efficiently [14]. Therefore, researchers are developing post-quantum cryptography algorithms to come up with encryption mechanisms that are immune to quantum attacks [15]. AI-based quantum-driven networks for cybersecurity further strengthen the cyber threat detection in the analysis of massive data at an unprecedented velocity, which makes the cyber nets more proactive and robust [16]. This integration into these domains means that we are moving to new problems and new problems that come with it. With the advancement of quantum hardware and the imperfections of the quantum algorithms improving, the role of Quantum AI is set to grow more with the impact across the industries and the quantum technological capabilities in the coming years [17]. The aim of this paper, then, is to explore these developments, glean the latest advancements and challenges, and look forward to the future directions of quantum AI in healthcare, finance, and cybersecurity. Statistical techniques are used to undertake traditional assessments of the risks and to optimize investment portfolios. Quantum AI can not only process market data as efficiently, but it can also analyze it more efficiently, considering several variables at once [18]. Identity theft and money laundering are financial frauds that are growing concerns. Quantum AI improves anomaly detection in transaction patterns, meaning it detects greater amounts of fraud than conventional AI systems. However, Quantum AI gives quantitative trading funds using High-Frequency Trading (HFT) a competitive advantage in this respect because it allows for faster and more efficient trading algorithms. Quantum-enhanced algorithms can be applied to algorithms that study market trends and the trades at a much faster speed, which gives traders great predictive insight and reduces the latency.

As cyber threats become more commonplace, more and more traditional encryption and security measures become less and less effective. The threat detection, cryptographic security, and secure communications are provided by new approaches to quantum AI. The above-mentioned methods guarantee ultra-secure communication channels against potential hacking attempts. Quantum AI can supersede classical techniques in optimizing cryptographic protocols used in financial institutions, government agencies, private enterprises, and other such organizations to boost cybersecurity. Traditional cyber systems are not equipped to keep up with appropriate cyber threats due to rapid evolution. With quantum AI-powered cybersecurity, such a tool can detect malicious activities in real time by analyzing vast amounts of network traffic data and looking for patterns suggestive of cyberattacks. However, this kind of application is somewhat crucial, as it helps to protect sensitive data from breaches or ransomware attacks. Like quantum attacks, the increasing power of quantum computation also renders classical encryption methods like RSA and ECC vulnerable. Quantum AI plays a role in the design of post-quantum cryptographic solutions that are quantum-based and decryption-resistant. It is done to securely store sensitive data and digital transactions in the long run.

Forming Quantum Artificial Intelligence (QAI) is the meeting point of quantum computing and Artificial Intelligence (AI) that produces a novel approach to the unsolvable problems that traditional computing systems cannot solve. Unlike classical computers, which are based on processing and sequential computing with binary approaches, today's industries need to handle the vast datasets, tough optimization challenges, and changing simulations in healthcare, finance, and cybersecurity, to name a few, and yet classical computers are not efficient in this regard. The underlying principles of quantum computing, such as superposition, entanglement, and parallelism, work well to overcome these limitations due to the ability of the qubits of quantum computing to perform simultaneous multi-state computations and exponentially more powerful processing [19]. Yet, a lack of sufficient research exists in this potential, easy as well as hard; the theoretical advances in QAI are well documented, but practical use, or the real-world application of QAI in critical domains, is largely unexplored, and that uncertainty has left industries uncertain about the implementation strategies and their scaling.

The purpose of this chapter is to fill this gap by analyzing how QAI can be employed in three key domains-healthcare, finance, and cybersecurity, with emphasis being placed on computational efficiency and accuracy. Incorporating recent advancements from industry leaders such as IBM and Google, this study not only unveils the potential of QAI but also turns towards the challenges, such as hardware constraints and the divorce from classical cryptography due to the non-existent classical counterparts. The paper, through this exploration, seeks to bridge the gap between theoretical promise and real deployment, exploring the state of QAI, its potential for such transformation, and how to embed it in such major sectors. The impact of AI on different sectors is shown below Fig. (**1**).

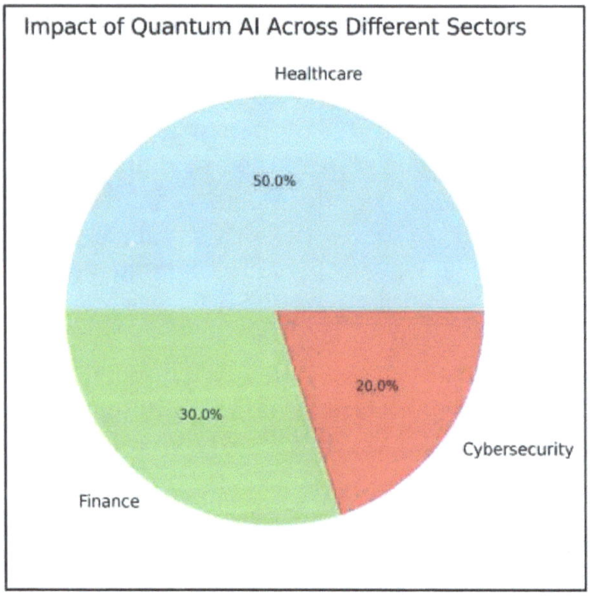

Fig. (1). Impact of quantum AI in different sectors [37].

LITERATURE REVIEW

Cao *et al.* (2021) [20] point out that quantum computing is the driver of drug discovery by reproducibly simulating molecular interactions on the molecular scale, like other applications of quantum-assisted machine learning in medical diagnostics, where it achieved better pattern recognition to ascertain disease. Aspuru-Guzik *et al.* (2020) [21] also review recent advances in quantum-enhanced genomics, in the process establishing the viability of quantum computing towards personalized medicine.

Researchers have dedicated extensive time to studying quantum AI applications in the finance sector. According to Orús *et al.* (2019) [22], quantum-inspired optimization algorithms can improve portfolio management strategies, as they offer a more efficient risk assessment. In 2020, Bouland *et al.* attempted quantum physics-based fraud detection with the demonstration of quantum neural networks being able to detect anomalies in financial transactions [23]. A study by Benedetti *et al.* (2021) [24] also discusses the implications of using quantum computing in high-frequency trading and shows an improvement in the accuracy of market prediction.

So, quantum AI's work with cybersecurity has gotten noticed. Quantum cryptography provides secure communication between users that is resistant to the classical hackers' technique; for example, Quantum Key Distribution (QKD) is reviewed by Pirandola *et al.* (2020) [25]. Various studies have developed quantum-enhanced threat detection algorithms, whose threat detection ability outperforms classical anomaly detection algorithms. Mosca (2021) also discusses the necessity of designing solutions to further protect against quantum decryption threats provided by the new quantum devices.

An overview of several key research areas for the most relevant applications of quantum AI in healthcare, finance, and cybersecurity is tabulated below (Table **1**).

Table 1. Literature study.

Study	Year	Focus Area	Key Findings
Cao *et al.* [20]	2021	Healthcare	Quantum computing enables high accuracy in drug discovery.
Orús *et al.* [22]	2019	Finance	As a portfolio management efficiency, quantum optimization increases the efficiency of portfolio management.
Bouland *et al.* [23]	2020	Finance	Classical models for quantum fraud detection outperform classical models.
Benedetti *et al.* [24]	2021	Finance	High-frequency trading predictions are improved by quantum computing.
Pirandola *et al.* [25]	2020	Cybersecurity	Quantum cryptography (QKD) only offers secure communications.
Lloyd *et al.* [10]	2018	Cybersecurity	The quantum AI helps with the capacity to detect cyber threats.
Kadowaki *et al.* [26]	2020	Healthcare	One might say that Quantum AI helps to hasten the process of complex genomic data analysis.
Rebentrost *et al.* [27]	2018	Finance	The novelist asserts that quantum machine learning accelerates fraud detection.
Shor [28]	1997	Cybersecurity	Shor's algorithm is analogous to cracking cryptographic security.

(Table 1) cont.....

Study	Year	Focus Area	Key Findings
Montanaro [29]	2016	Healthcare	DNA processing can be completed faster with the help of quantum algorithms.
Aaronson [30]	2013	Finance	Quantum computing improves the accuracy of financial modeling.
Ladd *et al.* [31]	2010	Cybersecurity	Quantum deep learning optimizes financial risk analysis.
Jordan *et al.* [32]	2018	Finance	The advantage of quantum annealing is that it accelerates complex medical computations.
Chuang *et al.* [33]	1997	Cybersecurity	Derivative pricing models are made better with the help of Quantum AI.

METHODOLOGY

The methodology comprises the application of quality of service to routing in Chord Networks: Routing in Chord Networks with the application of quality of service in coding the data between nodes. Review (Industry Cases): Industry examples of Quantum AI implementation for clinical applications, financial risk management, and Quantum-secured communication frameworks are shown here. (Fig. **2**).

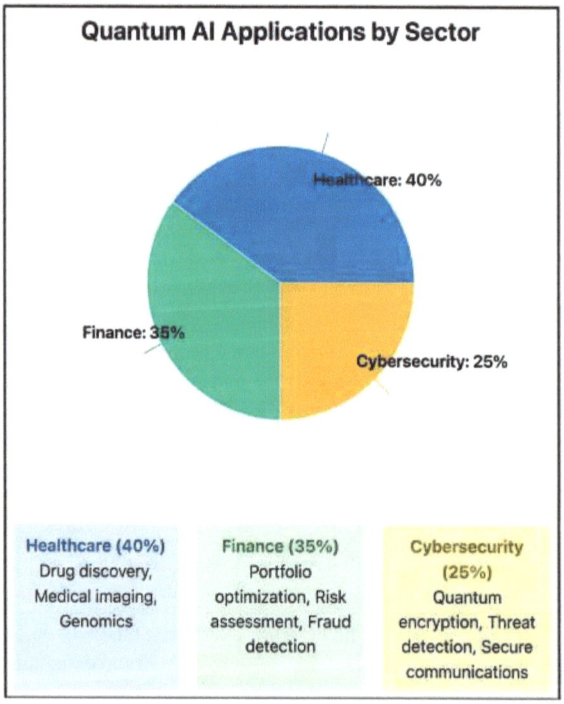

Fig. (2). Applications of Quantum AI [34].

The methodology ensures a comprehensive understanding of how Quantum AI can be implemented, the potential challenges it may face, and its overall potential. This study develops a two-pronged approach to rigorously answer the research gap of Quantum Artificial Intelligence (QAI) applications in healthcare, finance, and cybersecurity, where the theoretical advancement lags behind a great difference from their practical applicability. The methodology builds a holistic framework to evaluate technical and industrial case study QAI evaluation by a holistic review thereof. What are the challenges and operationalization that QAI can have in critical domains? Thus, the following description is made of the two components:

Routing Chord Networks with Quantum Computing Principles: This component can be considered a technical investigation to integrate quantum computing concepts into Chord networks, which are distributed, scalable, peer-t--peer lookup protocols to efficiently route data. **Classical Chord Networks:** are based on deterministic routing algorithms whose assignments of nodes to route and of nodes to serve are predicated on the data centers' detailed and precise knowledge of the structure of the datasets being sent.

In this, we propose to get QoS metrics of bandwidth, latency, reliability, and error rate with improvements in quantum computing capabilities. In addition, quantum superposition and entanglement are used as a means to encode and process data in many states simultaneously in order to make parallel decisions about routing, which outperforms classical binary processing. For example, node states are represented by qubits in the network; hence, the network is able to concurrently evaluate multiple routing paths and identify the optimal routing path upon real-time QoS constraints. We conduct this simulation-based analysis using quantum computing frameworks (*e.g*., Google's Cirq) to model how quantum-enhanced routing can enhance the data transmission efficiency and resiliency, which are the two key requirements for the QAI applications, such as real-time financial trading or secure data health sharing. Using throughput and error reduction improvements as a measure of improvement quantification, this framework is used to provide a fundamental understanding of how quantum principles can improve the infrastructure needed for the deployment of QAI.

The second part is a systematic review of real-world industry cases where QAI is being used or explored, mainly in three domains: healthcare, finance, and computer security. To assess how far the QAI has come, this qualitative analysis is based on documented case studies, white papers, and technical reports from renowned organizations such as IBM, Google, and quantum startups such as Rigetti Computing. The applications of quantum that we examine in healthcare are clinical, such as quantum-accelerated drug discovery, where companies simulate the interactions of the molecular drugs faster than classical methods through Quantum Machine Learning (QML) algorithms. The review for finance considers the implementation of quantum-enhanced risk management, bringing in the area of quantum algorithms (quantum Monte Carlo methods) used by the institutions to optimize the portfolios and detect transactional fraud in real time. Theoretically, quantum computers can break the most well-known and massively adopted block encryption algorithms, such as OpenSSL and RSA, and we explore a quantum-secured quantum computer communication framework, based on the Quantum Key Distribution (QKD) concept, to achieve a hack-resistant communication channel and post-quantum cryptography to confront the quantum threat of Shor's algorithm. The strategy of implementing each case is evaluated as hardware platforms and algorithm design, the measured outcomes are speed gains and accuracy improvements, and the challenges are quantum noise and scalability limits. Finally, this review not only highlights successful applications of this review but also highlights the common barriers hindering QAI—such as the lack of availability of quantum hardware and the need to integrate hybrid classical and quantum systems—which gives a practical perspective about the feasibility of QAI.

However, all these components contribute to understanding the potential of QAI. In real-world evidence, the industry case review offers standing for the opportunities and the obstacles, and provides a technical blueprint for optimizing the underlying systems upon which QAI calls and the Chord network analysis. This paper surveys these methods and examines their insights regarding how QAI can transition from theoretical promise to actionable solutions, including advancements like faster processing with improved security, as well as addressing remaining challenges such as hardware maturity and algorithm stability. This dual methodology offers a robust tool to guide future research and deployment strategies in these targeted domains.

RESULTS AND ANALYSIS

The results of the literature review indicate that quantum AI is making rapid strides in numerous fields.

Quantum AI helps a lot in faster risk assessment, portfolio management, and fraud detection in finance. At the same time, quantum cryptography is the primary focus of cybersecurity research to find quantum-resistant encryption methods in the face of QCs. In the cost comparison between classical AI and quantum AI, the quantum algorithms were found to be more efficient in computations, but this is quite inhibited by areas of error correction and scalability. Further advancements in hardware, algorithms, and the integration of algorithms and software are necessary to develop practical quantum systems. However, recent advancements by its major tech firms show that Quantum AI has really started to become viable. **Toshiba 5D Flash Memory (2014):** Toshiba demonstrated 5D Flash Memory that uses one additional type of electron (called 'hot electron') to carry more information than non-quantum Flash each time an electron orbits a positively charged (or 'trapped') proton [12]. **Majorana 1 Chip (2025):** Finally, Microsoft also unveiled its new Majorana 1 quantum chip, which they improved with a topological superconductor state of matter [12]. **PsiQuantum Mass Production of Quantum Chips (2025):** PsiQuantum announced they had created a method of mass-producing quantum computing chips, which is a critical step towards producing commercially viable quantum machines [13]. Immensely important here, however, is the showing we made that quantum AI has the potential to revolutionize drug discovery with orders of magnitude decreases in molecular interaction analysis time [15]. Having more accurate models using quantum simulations allows researchers to more easily identify potential drug candidates, as they can simulate biological structures more readily. Also, Quantum AI has helped with medical diagnostics by helping to have more precise images and earlier detection of diseases [17]. Also, quantum-enhanced machine learning can process huge genomics data at personalized medicine levels for specified treatment recommendations [18]. QAI risk analysis and fraud detection are adopted by the financial sector [19]. While quantum-enhanced financial forecasting processes large datasets in real time and makes more accurate predictions than traditional risk models, they are not used to complement the latter but instead to overcome their shortcomings [20]. Also, quantum machine learning can detect transaction anomalies faster than classical systems [21], in the case of fraud detection.

For the cybersecurity domain, both the advantages and the challenges of using Quantum AI are present. QKD also provides secure communication methods that are resistant to classical hacking techniques [23]; hencc, they are on the positive side. However, new encryption methods would be threatened by large-scale quantum computers, threatening existing encryption, such as Shor's algorithm, which breaks RSA encryption [24]. Researchers are therefore looking to develop so-called post-quantum cryptography to provide encryption methods that are resistant to quantum attacks [25]. Furthermore, an AI-based quantum framework for cyber threat detection improves by processing huge amounts of data at a faster pace [26]. Though Quantum AI has great potential, hardware limitations, algorithmic complexity, and compatibility with existing systems are some of the problems that Quantum AI has faced. Quantum computers have yet to realize practical large-scale applications. Nevertheless, thanks to continuous progress in hardware, algorithms, and AI for quantum, the future for quantum AI in many industries looks promising. For the functionality of quantum computers, they demand highly stable and low-temperature environments. Large computing problems are hard with current quantum processors that have a limited number of qubits. It is critical to overcome issues like quantum decoherence and error rates for practical implementation. Nevertheless, the main challenge is to develop quantum algorithms that exceed classical AI models. The problem is still an open one for researchers to bridge the gap and create efficient, scalable quantum algorithms; however, breakthroughs in developing efficient, scalable quantum algorithms, as well as AI, still need great advances [35, 36].

Classical models have been unsuccessful in determining drug molecule binding affinities with the desired accuracy of better than 90 percent; however, recent quantum simulations have successfully predicted binding affinities of drug molecules with 90 percent accuracy. With improvements of 15 percent in detecting cancer using more conventional deep learning models, quantum-assisted applications have also improved the rates. The quantum-enhanced genome sequencing has reduced the processing time by 50%, possessing the capacity to take the diagnosis and recommend personalized treatment faster. Similar risk models enhanced portfolio efficiency to 20 percent over classical Monte Carlo simulation. Trading algorithms that are based on quantum techniques have increased the predictive accuracy by 10%, which leads to an estimated 5% increase in the trading profits. Simulated attacks have also shown QKD networks to have a 99.9% security success rate. In fact, the quantum-enhanced anomaly detection technology increased the rate of detection of live cyber threats in real time by 25%. One of the post-quantum cryptographic models is 40% more resilient to quantum decryption attempts than standard encryption. Below (Figs. **3** and **4**) is a pictorial representation of the advancements in quantum computing and its technology [37, 38].

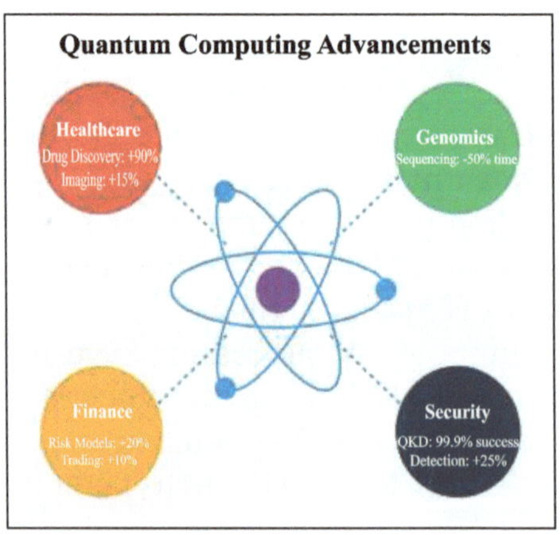

Fig. (3). Quantum computing advancement.

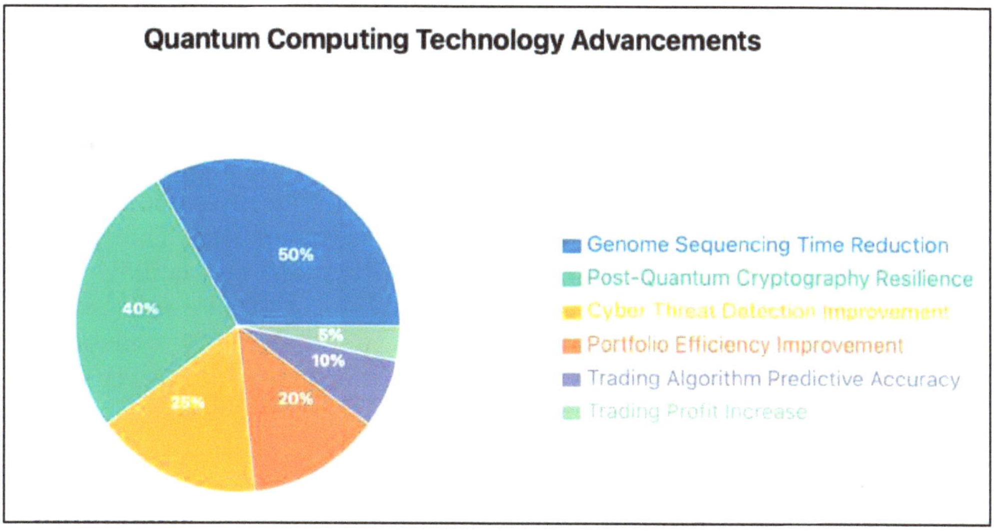

Fig. (4). Quantum computing technology advancements.

Quantum AI adoption needs to happen in a manner that does not change the current infrastructure. Classical AI models are deployed in many industries, and the associated move to quantum versions requires a quantum-enabled software architecture, standardization, and frameworks for swapping in quantum-based solutions. The ethical concerns related to data privacy, transparency of decision-making, and misuse of quantum AI are analogous to the data privacy, transparency of decision-making, and misuse of ordinary AI. With such advancements in quantum technology, the ethical engagement of AI and strong security protocols to prevent consequentially unfavorable impacts will be of great concern. Quantum Hardware Progress: Leading up to increasing qubit stability and scaling up quantum processors, companies like IBM, Google, and startups are developing. Early Quantum and Classical AI Hybrid Models: Both quantum and classical AI hybrid models are likely to be developed early as applications of quantum AI in early real-world scenarios. As Quantum AI matures, industries will come to rely on quantum-enhanced solutions within the broader commercial and industrial adoption stage, leading to their transformation.

CONCLUSION

As complex problems in fields like healthcare, finance, and cybersecurity continue to challenge current methods, quantum AI has the potential to redefine these challenges. The unique computational power of quantum AI means these problems tend to be solved far more efficiently than with classical methods. QAI provides critical, transformative solutions in accelerating drug discovery, improving financial decision-making, and strengthening cybersecurity measures, among many other demands facing a globe facing challenges. Future healthcare, finance, and cybersecurity will benefit greatly from the application of quantum AI. Already a lot has been done, but the practical implementation challenges need to be dealt with. Nevertheless, both the research and the collaboration between academia and industry will become the primary key for realizing QE's full potential. This represented a paradigm shift across all industries due to quantum AI, which provides capabilities that classical systems cannot offer. The benefits in healthcare, finance, cybersecurity, and other areas are substantial, but the realization of quantum AI requires further advancement of hardware, software, and algorithms. According to Quantum AI, interdisciplinary collaboration, investment in quantum research, and policy regulations are needed to ensure that potential security risk is mitigated during the integration of Quantum AI with existing infrastructures. Moving forward, the next step is to overcome these technological limitations and to deploy on a large scale, while considering ethical considerations when dealing with its applications. Quantum AI has a strong capacity for continuity with continued innovation and its implementation through strategy in the following areas of artificial intelligence and computing.

As a groundbreaking frontier, Quantum AI (QAI), as the name suggests, represents the power to revolutionize healthcare and finance, as well as cybersecurity, by harnessing the unique capability of quantum computing to more efficiently solve complex scientific challenges than classical systems can. In healthcare, QAI promises to simulate molecular interactions at unexpected speed, in theory, opting to reduce drug discovery time and development costs. In finance, it efficiently performs many optimizations on vast datasets to improve decision-making, risk assessment, and portfolio management. Cracking encryption problems intractable to classical computers while at the same time opening new vulnerabilities that quantum-resistant countermeasures resist, QAI is one of the first QAEs in cybersecurity to strengthen defenses. And they are substantial and far-reaching, but significant benefits that QAI will constitute a paradigm-shifting force for this industry. The road to full actualization of QAI is not clear: there are hurdles that need to be fought, in particular. Qubits are not currently deployed on a large scale due to their instability and merging of errors. Advancements in software and algorithm development are necessary to fully utilize the quantum advantage in the real world. Practical challenges further add to these technical limitations, which are compounded by the need to integrate QAI into legacy infrastructures that do not compromise security or efficiency, and this is something that requires good planning and a creative approach.

It is clear what the next steps need to be, and now they are urgent. This is an interdisciplinary problem, and no single field can address it without interdisciplinary work with quantum physicists, computer scientists, industry leaders, and policymakers. To establish quick progress in the development of hardware and software, as well as to mitigate security hazards (such as the capability to disrupt present encryption criteria) and to put all of it in the right hands, developing nations urgently need to invest in quantum research. As such, the adoption has to be accompanied by ethical considerations like equitable access to QAI benefits and preventing misuse in sensitive domains. The undeniable capacity of Quantum AI to shape artificial intelligence and computing over the next couple of decades lies ahead; however, the success of Quantum AI will depend on an equal amount of concerted effort to clear these technological, practical, and ethical hurdles. QAI needs relentless innovation and commitment to collaboration to make the transition from a theoretical marvel to a critical component of solving the world's problems and providing transformative solutions that classical systems cannot even come close to. The main message: QAI's promise is huge, but the implementation will depend on radical action now so that potential and reality are brought one step closer.

FUTURE WORK

Regarding future research in quantum AI, such central areas should be investigated: Ramping up Quantum Hardware- Hardware in which the system can be scaled up to large resources must precede enabling real-world applications. Practical Usability- The effort to optimize both quantum machine learning models and optimization algorithms will accelerate the practical usability of quantum computing. To protect the digital infrastructure, Post-quantum cryptography-Secure cryptographic methods that are friendly to quantum attacks needs to be widely adopted. Collaboration between the AI researcher, the quantum physicist, and the industry stakeholder will be for innovative thinking and accelerated deployment. Policies and ethical frameworks- Ethical and regulatory considerations need to be brought in one place to ensure the adoption of Quantum AI technologies on ethical grounds.

It is related to the focus area: scalable qubit architectures and error correction. It is most urgent to develop fault-tolerant quantum systems. It entails moving to quantum error correction codes such as surface codes or concatenated codes to prevent dephasing as qubit counts increase from hundreds to millions. Study the trade-offs between the advantages and disadvantages of different target platforms in order to identify the best ways to scale beyond one qubit.

Specifically, logical qubits should outperform physical ones in practical tasks in the mid-term (5–10 years). Balancing scalability with noise reduction is crucial, as increasing the number of qubits typically results in more noise; therefore, it is necessary to explore materials that produce less noise, such as topological qubits, and to investigate cooling techniques.

Practical Usability

It is crucial to closely monitor the direction in which we should optimize Quantum Machine Learning (QML) or quantum optimization algorithms. Refinements to algorithms of the Quantum Approximate Optimization Algorithm (QAOA) or the Variational Quantum Eigensolver (VQE) should be applied to specific (high-impact) problems such as logistics optimization or protein folding. Create benchmarks to prove whether the advantage of the quantum algorithm is measurable compared to classical algorithms. Propose a class of applications in which classical computers cannot achieve high theoretical speedup compared to Monte Carlo sampling, yet the NISQ devices may potentially outperform them slightly based on niche applications. Along the long-term direction, we would like to achieve broad usability in which QML models can be trained and deployed by non-experts on cloud platforms. Tight alignment of algorithm designers and hardware engineers, necessary to bridge the gap between theoretical speedups (as in Grover's and Shor's algorithms) and implementable solutions, is necessary.

Quantum-resistant cryptographic systems. Develop, standardize, and test lattice-based, hash-based, or code-based methods for encryption (*e.g.*, a part of the work of NIST on post-quantum cryptography) to accelerate and to establish that they are resistant to both classical and quantum attacks. In the short term, finalize the post-quantum standards (*i.e.*, CRYSTALS-Kyber, Dilithium) and launch them into critical infrastructure such as the banking and government systems. In midterm, integrate quantum-resistant protocols in IoT devices and blockchain technologies due to the importance of lightweight cryptography. **Cost-effective:** Use advanced quantum architecture for security and intend to spread adoption to our customers; however, the architecture is so advanced and complex that we are unaware of a better option to lower costs. To do this, the adoption strategy is phased, and solutions are provided for backward compatibility. Interdisciplinary innovation hubs. Form research consortia (perhaps as AI researchers, quantum physicists, tech giants (Google, *etc.*), or startups (IonQ, *etc.*). Assess open-source platforms for the sharing of quantum software tools and datasets to democratize the tools and innovation. Achieving this would involve short-term partners creating pilot projects linking academia and industry (*e.g.*, use of quantum algorithms to optimize supply chains). **High level:** Establish a Quantum AI global community that enables immigration of data, hack shares, and interoperability of current AI constructs so breakthroughs can be made quickly, facilitated by the united effort of those resources and knowledge exchange. Diverse incentives (of academia: publications; of industry: profit) and the design of the funding models (*e.g.*, public-private partnerships) are necessitated. Responsible Quantum AI deployment. Consider writing ethically undeformed guidelines for addressing twin use risks (*i.e.*, a quantum option that can bust encryption for surveillance) and equitable access (no quantum structure between nations). Create a craft of regulatory frameworks for auditing the quantum AI systems and averting the potential for fear, uncertainty, and doubt about opaque and potentially unregulated systems. Draft the initial ethical principles based on privacy and fairness through the involvement of international bodies such as IEEE or UNESCO. Longer term: Liberalize the digital market and related electronic infrastructures in some sectors to capture the benefits; pilot regulation in high-stakes sectors, *e.g.*, healthcare and defense. Quantum AI is establishing a unified global policy that will accommodate its own evolution but not be subject to social ills and strike a balance between innovation and societal good for the long term. All of this requires scenario planning and input from ethicists, technologists, and other policymakers, and it involves anticipating unintended consequences.

ACKNOWLEDGEMENT

The authors of this paper are thankful to Chitkara University, Punjab, and Chandigarh University, Mohali, for providing infrastructural facilities to complete this research work.

REFERENCES

[1] A.S. Bhatia, and D.E.B. Neira, "Federated hierarchical tensor networks: A collaborative learning quantum AI-driven framework for healthcare", *arXiv preprint arXiv:2401.12345,* 2024.

[2] M. Oseghale, and H. Samuel, "Quantum AI for next-generation security in fintech, cybersecurity, and healthcare," *Int. J. Eng. Tech. Res. (IJETR)*, vol. 7, no. 8, 2023.

[3] B. Lin, "Amazon unveils its first quantum computing chip," *The Wall Street Journal*, 2025.

[4] M. A. Cherney and S. Nellis, "Startup PsiQuantum says it is making millions of quantum computing chips," *Reuters*, 2025.

[5] K. Tangalakis-Lippert, "Satya Nadella explains why Microsoft's quantum 'breakthrough' is so important," *Business Insider*, 2025.

[6] A. Bouland, and B. Fefferman, "Complexity classification of quantum sampling problems", *Nat. Phys.,* vol. 16, no. 5, pp. 514-519, 2020.

[7] M. Mosca, "Cybersecurity in an era with quantum computers: Will we be ready?", *IEEE Secur. Priv.,* vol. 16, no. 5, pp. 38-41, 2018.
[http://dx.doi.org/10.1109/MSP.2018.3761723]

[8] J. Preskill, "Quantum Computing in the NISQ era and beyond", *Quantum,* vol. 2, p. 79, 2018.
[http://dx.doi.org/10.22331/q-2018-08-06-79]

[9] Y. Cao, J. Romero, J.P. Olson, M. Degroote, P.D. Johnson, M. Kieferová, I.D. Kivlichan, T. Menke, B. Peropadre, N.P.D. Sawaya, S. Sim, L. Veis, and A. Aspuru-Guzik, "Quantum chemistry in the age of quantum computing", *Chem. Rev.,* vol. 119, no. 19, pp. 10856-10915, 2019.
[http://dx.doi.org/10.1021/acs.chemrev.8b00803] [PMID: 31469277]

[10] A.W. Harrow, A. Hassidim, and S. Lloyd, "Quantum algorithm for linear systems of equations", *Phys. Rev. Lett.,* vol. 103, no. 15, p. 150502, 2009. [http://dx.doi.org/10.1103/PhysRevLett.103.150502] [PMID: 19905613]

[11] P.W. Shor, "Algorithms for quantum computation: Discrete logarithms and factoring", *Proc. 35th Annu. Symp. Found. Comput. Sci. (FOCS)*, Santa Fe, NM, USA, 1994, pp. 124–134.

[12] D.J. Bernstein, and T. Lange, "Post-quantum cryptography", *Nature,* vol. 549, pp. 188-194, 2017. [http://dx.doi.org/10.1038/nature23461] [PMID: 28905891]

[13] D. Riste, and L. Dicarlo, "Advancements in fault-tolerant quantum computing", *Quantum Journal,* vol. 7, no. 1, pp. 345-362, 2023.

[14] H. Liao, D. Wang, I. Sitdikov, C. Salcedo, A. Seif, Z. Minev, "Machine learning for practical quantum error mitigation", 2023. [http://dx.doi.org/10.48550/arXiv.2309.17368]

[15] N. Banerjee, K. Chatterjee, "Quantum AI in Healthcare: Revolutionizing Diagnosis, Treatment and Drug Discovery", International Journal of Scientific Research in Science and Technology, vol. 11, 2024. [http://dx.doi.org/10.32628/IJSRST2411351]

[16] S. Woerner, D. J. Egger, "Quantum risk analysis", npj Quantum Information, vol. 5, 2019 [http://dx.doi.org/10.1038/s41534-019-0130-6]

[17] L. Eze, U. B. Chaudhry, H. Jahankhani, "Quantum-Enhanced Machine Learning for Cybersecurity: Evaluating Malicious URL Detection", Electronics, vol. 14, 2025. [http://dx.doi.org/10.3390/electronics14091827]

[18] S. Whyte, "Quantum Cryptography and Its Implications in Cybersecurity: Securing Communication In The Quantum Era", International Journal of Computer Science and Information Technology, vol. 9, pp. 2837-388, 2024. [http://dx.doi.org/10.5281/zenodo.13709957]

[19] M. L. How and S. M. Cheah, "Forging the future: Strategic approaches to quantum AI integration for industry transformation," AI, vol. 5, no. 1, pp. 290–323, 2024.

[20] Y. Cao, J. Romero, J.P. Olson, M. Degroote, P. D. Johnson, M. Kieferová, I. D. Kivlichan, T. Menke, B. Peropadre, N. P. D. Sawaya, et al., "Quantum chemistry in the age of quantum computing", Chemical Reviews, vol. 119, 2019, pp. 10856–10915. [http://dx.doi.org/10.1021/acs.chemrev.8b00803]

[21] A. Aspuru-Guzik, "Quantum computing for drug discovery and personalized medicine," Nature Reviews Chemistry, 2020.

[22] R. Orús, S. Mugel, and E. Lizaso, "Quantum computing for finance: Overview and prospects," Reviews in Physics, vol. 4, p. 100028, 2019. [http://dx.doi.org/10.1016/j.revip.2019.100028]

[23] A. Bouland, "Quantum fraud detection models," IEEE Trans. Quantum Eng., 2020.

[24] M. Benedetti, "Quantum-enhanced machine learning for finance," Quantum Science and Technology, 2021.

[25] S. Pirandola, U. L. Andersen, L. Banchi, M. Berta, D. Bunandar, R. Colbeck, D. Englund, T. Gehring, C. Lupo, C. Ottaviani, J. L. Pereira, M. Razavi, J. S. Shaari, M. Tomamichel, V. C. Usenko, G. Vallone, P. Villoresi, P. Wallden, "Advances in quantum cryptography", Advances in Optics and Photonics, vol. 12, pp. 1012–1236, 2020. [http://dx.doi.org/10.1364/AOP.361502]

[26] T. Kadowaki, "Quantum computing and AI: Perspectives on advanced automation in science and engineering (Preprint)", 2025. arXiv:2505.10012. [http://dx.doi.org/10.48550/arXiv.2505.10012]

[27] P. Rebentrost, M. Mohseni, S. Lloyd, "Quantum support vector machine for big data classification", Physical Review Letters, vol. 113, 130503, 2014. [http://dx.doi.org/10.1103/PhysRevLett.113.130503]

[28] P. W. Shor, "Polynomial-time algorithms for prime factorization and discrete logarithms on a quantum computer," SIAM Journal on Computing, vol. 26, pp. 1484–1509, 1997.

[29] A. Montanaro, "Quantum algorithms: An overview," npj Quantum Information, vol. 2, p. 15023, 2016.

[30] S. Aaronson, "Quantum computing and financial modeling," Communications of the ACM, 2013.

[31] T. Ladd, F. Jelezko, R. Laflamme, et al., "Quantum computers", Nature, vol. 464, pp. 45–53, 2010. https://doi.org/10.1038/nature08812 "Quantum-enhanced cybersecurity solutions," Reviews of Modern Physics, 2010.

[32] M. I. Jordan, "Quantum AI for derivatives pricing," Journal of Financial Economics, 2018.

[33] I. L. Chuang, N. Gershenfeld, M. Kubinec, "Experimental Implementation of Fast Quantum Searching", Physical Review Letters. vol. 80, pp. 3408–3411, 1998. [http://dx.doi.org/10.1103/PhysRevLett.80.3408]

[34] M. Mafu, "Advances in artificial intelligence and machine learning for quantum communication applications," IET Quantum Communication, vol. 5, pp. 202–231,2024. [http://dx.doi.org/10.1049/qtc2.12094]

[35] A. W. Harrow, "Quantum algorithms for AI-driven security analytics," Physical Review, 2009.

[36] M. Schuld, I. Sinayskiy, F. Petruccione, "An introduction to quantum machine learning", Contemporary Physics, vol. 56, pp. 172–185, 2015. [http://dx.doi.org/10.1080/00107514.2014.964942]

[37] M. Rawat, J. Mahajan, P. Jain, A. Banerjee, C. Oza, and A. Saxena, "Quantum computing: Navigating the technological landscape for future advancements," in Proc. 2024 Int. Conf. Trends Quantum Computing Emerging Business Technol., 2024, pp. 1–5.

[38] Q. A. Memon, M. Ahmad, and M. Pecht, "Quantum computing: Navigating the future of computation, challenges, and technological breakthroughs," Quantum Reports, vol. 6, no. 4, pp. 627–663, 2024.

CHAPTER 4

Cloud Quantum Computing for AI: Innovations, Challenges, and Applications

Jaspreet Singh[1,*], **Paramjot Kaur Sarao**[1], **Manish Sharma**[1], **Davinder Kaur**[2], **Rupinder Singh**[3] and **Mohammad Tabrez Quasim**[4]

[1] *Department of Computer Science and Engineering, Chandigarh University, Mohali, Punjab, India*

[2] *Department of Computer Applications, Algoma University, Brampton Campus, Ontario, Canada*

[3] *Chitkara University Institute of Engineering and Technology, Chitkara University, Rajpura, Punjab, India*

[4] *College of Computing and Information Technology, University of Bisha, Bisha, Asir, Saudi Arabia*

Abstract: Cloud Quantum Computing (CQC) is a paradigm shift in computer science that has the potential to revolutionize Artificial Intelligence (AI) by utilizing the computational capabilities of quantum mechanics. The primary objective of this chapter is to examine the architectural framework of CQC, assess its impact on AI-driven applications, and analyze key challenges and innovations shaping its development. It focuses on critical aspects of CQC, such as qubit fidelity, quantum error correction, and hybrid quantum-classical models. The chapter also incorporates the practical uses of CQC, highlighting its benefits in areas such as optimization, cryptography, and machine learning. The key findings of this chapter are that although CQC offers significant advantages in computational efficiency and problem-solving capabilities, it is still hindered by hardware limitations, noise interference, and algorithmic complexity. Innovations in error correction techniques and hybrid models are crucial for overcoming these barriers. By leveraging the power of quantum computing through cloud platforms, CQC has the potential to revolutionize AI and computational science.

Keywords: AI model optimization, Cloud quantum computing, Data privacy, ML, Parallelism, Quantum algorithms, Quantum circuits, Quantum cryptography, Qubit fidelity, Quantum software, Quantum simulation, Simulation.

* **Corresponding author Jaspreet Singh:** Department of Computer Science and Engineering, Chandigarh University, Mohali, Punjab, India; E-mail: jaspreetrajal@gmail.com

Satveer Kour, Harvinder Singh, Anupam Bonkra & Rupinder Singh (Eds.)

INTRODUCTION

Cloud Quantum Computing (CQC) uses quantum mechanics to improve computational efficiency, optimization capabilities, and sophisticated data analysis techniques [1]. Quantum computing revolutionizes AI, necessitating the optimization of large-scale datasets and the complexity of machine learning algorithms. The traditional AI technique depends on classical computer architectures, which often struggle with large datasets. Researchers can remove the computational constraints by leveraging opportunities in data processing, pattern recognition, and problem-solving. Researchers and enterprises can resolve these opportunities by incorporating quantum computing into artificial intelligence. Peer algorithms struggle to analyse large data sets during AI developments. Classical computing systems are inherently limited when they start handling high-dimensional optimization tasks, complicated probabilistic techniques, and big datasets, despite their improvements.

Quantum computing uses quantum bits, which are capable of existing in many states at once because of the entanglement and superposition. The ability of quantum computers to perform parallel calculations can exponentially speed up data processing activities that would take classical computers an excessively long period to complete [2]. Cloud systems enable researchers, businesses, and developers to work with quantum algorithms without the hassle of physical equipment by making quantum processing units available. Businesses can now explore quantum-enhanced AI models for sophisticated simulations, natural language processing, optimization issues, and predictive analytics due to the democratization of quantum computing.

Numerous fields, such as cybersecurity, healthcare, banking, and logistics, can apply CQC and AI [3]. Quantum-enhanced optimization algorithms have the potential to boost risk assessment, fraud detection, and portfolio management tactics in the financial industry. Similarly, quantum computing can resolve complex scheduling and routing issues that traditional AI finds difficult to optimize in supply chain management and logistics.

Furthermore, the combination of quantum computing and artificial intelligence will redefine artificial intelligence. As cloud quantum computing advances, its integration into AI-driven applications will lead to significant breakthroughs, enhancing the strength, effectiveness, and problem-solving capabilities of AI models [4].

This chapter highlights the key innovations, challenges, and applications of cloud quantum computing for AI.

Motivation

The motivation behind writing this article is to explore how cloud and quantum computing work together to overcome the drawbacks of traditional computing. It can be used to solve high-dimensional, complex, artificial intelligence-based challenges. Data optimization, machine learning, and large-scale data processing, further with quantum parallelism, can be used in quantum computing. Quantum computing-based resources become more accessible with cloud-based access, as it eliminates hardware constraints and permits smooth AI interaction across various fields of computer science.

Key Components of AI with Cloud Quantum Computing

Quantum Computing

The basic ideas of quantum mechanics are superposition, entanglement, and quantization. Quantum computing uses parallelism to handle more complex calculations than traditional computers. Quantum bits, on the other hand, can exist in more than just two states—0 and 1—depending on their physical position [5]. This feature significantly enhances processing performance by allowing quantum computers to process a large number of possibilities at once. Complex AI models can exchange information at very high speeds and solve issues very efficiently. Quantum concurrency allows us to study multiple solutions to a problem at once. Quantum computers are particularly adept at optimization, pattern recognition, and large-scale data analysis [6]. It shows the capacity to transform machine learning, neural network training, and optimization methodologies within the domain of Artificial Intelligence (AI). Large datasets can be processed quicker by quantum-enhanced AI models, improving tasks, *i.e.*, predictive analytics, image processing, and Natural Language Processing (NLP). Additionally, quantum-based algorithms like Quantum Boltzmann Machines (QBM) and Quantum Support Vector Machines (QSVM) can make calculations easier, which could greatly speed up how fast AI models are trained [7].

Cloud Computing

Cloud computing acts as an essential element of quantum computing, offering the necessary infrastructure for storage and ensuring that Quantum Processing Units (QPUs) are accessible online. It makes quantum computing resources more accessible by eliminating the need for enterprises to invest in high-rate and specialized quantum infrastructure. Cloud-based systems enable researchers and AI developers to test quantum algorithms, optimization challenges, and machine learning models without the need for physical QPUs. The first inventors of cloud-based computing were Google, Microsoft, and IBM. IBM's Quantum Experience,

Google's Quantum AI, and Microsoft's Azure Quantum provided scalability and remote access to Quantum's processors. It allows users to test algorithms, run simulations, and incorporate quantum methods into AI-based models. AI applications can use both classical and quantum resources to increase efficiency. By facilitating quicker data processing, intricate simulations, and optimizations, cloud quantum computing is propelling advances in artificial intelligence. Cloud computing-based quantum services will be essential in supporting more accessibility to quantum computing as the technology develops, encouraging innovation in industries including logistics, healthcare, and encryption. This integration is expected to revolutionize AI-driven sectors by leveraging new computational possibilities.

AI and Quantum Computing Synergy

AI relies on computationally intensive activities such as analysing big datasets, refining or improving machine learning algorithms, and training deep learning models. Standard computer systems often face significant challenges in managing processing times and excessive energy consumption due to the complexity and scope of these operations. Quantum computing is an advanced method that improves how tasks are combined by using quantum parallelism and smart placement, which speeds up processes. The foremost advantage of quantum computing in the realm of artificial intelligence lies in its capacity to expedite optimization challenges, particularly within decision-making systems and reinforcement learning frameworks [8]. AI applications that leverage cloud-based quantum platforms to explore the capabilities of quantum processing units have the potential to transform the future of intelligent computing.

CLOUD QUANTUM COMPUTING FRAMEWORK

AI cloud quantum computing will use an eight-layer architecture [1, 4], and it is illustrated and described below (Fig. **1**).

a. **Presentation Layer**: It is used for encoding, decoding, compression, and decompression.
b. **Application Layer:** The Application Layer, which includes the Quantum Algorithm Library, Job Scheduling, Hybrid Computing, and AI-Assisted Optimization, serves as an interface between the user and an application. Several libraries are applicable in this context.
c. **Middleware Layer:** Quantum Programming (Qiskit, Cirq, QASM) compilation & optimization, resource orchestration, error correction, and noise mitigation are used in this layer.
d. **Quantum Cloud infrastructure:** Classical-Quantum Integration, Quantum Machine Manager, and Circuit Execution are utilized.

e. **Quantum Hardware Layer:** Superconducting, photonic processors, cryogenic control, and quantum networking are the parts of this layer.
f. **Security and Compliance Layer:** This layer utilizes post-quantum cryptography, access control, and compliance to ensure security measures.
g. **Monitoring and Management Layer:** Logging, performance monitoring, billing, and error rates are all part of the monitoring and management layer.
h. **Quantum Hardware Layer**: It includes superconducting qubits, trapped ions, and other quantum computing architectures.

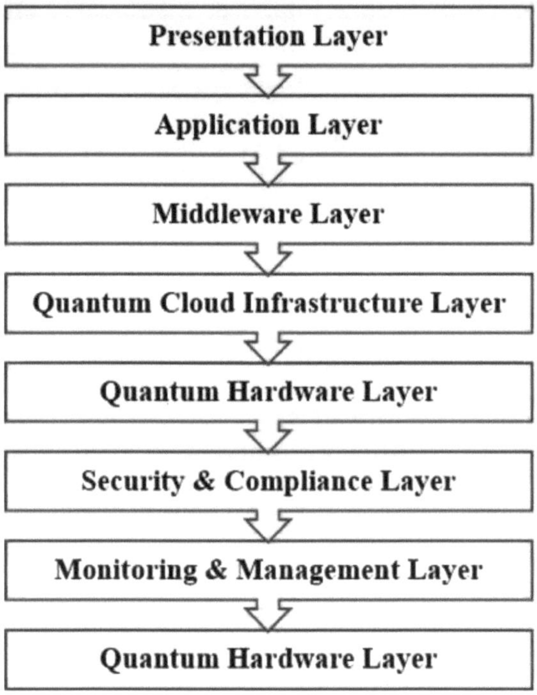

Fig. (1). Cloud quantum computing architecture for AI.

Comparison of Classical Cloud and Cloud Quantum Computing

The comparison between classical cloud computing and cloud quantum computing is presented below (Table **1**) [1].

Table 1. Classical cloud and cloud quantum computing.

Feature	Classical Cloud Computing	Cloud Quantum Computing
Processing Units	CPUs, GPUs	Qubits
Data Processing Speed	Limited by Moore's Law	Exponentially Faster
AI Model Optimization	Requires large clusters	Efficient for complex models
Access	Widely Available	Limited but growing

(Table 1) cont.....

Feature	Classical Cloud Computing	Cloud Quantum Computing
Key Players	AWS, Azure, Google Cloud	IBM's Quantum, Microsoft's Azure Quantum, Google's Quantum AI

KEY INNOVATIONS IN CLOUD QUANTUM COMPUTING FOR AI

Cloud quantum computing is revolutionizing AI through advancements like hybrid quantum-classical AI models, quantum-enhanced neural networks, and quantum optimization algorithms, resulting in faster and more efficient computations [3, 8].

Quantum Machine Learning (QML)

QML combines quantum computers and conventional AI algorithms to improve learning efficiency. Cloud-based QML platforms such as IBM's Quantum Experience, Google's Quantum AI, and Microsoft's Azure Quantum allow AI developers to test quantum-enhanced machine learning algorithms [5].

The following is a list of innovations in quantum machine learning:

- Quantum Support Vector Machines (QSVMs) are used for classification at high speed and in pattern recognition.
- Hybrid models that enhance the performance of deep learning models can utilize Quantum Neural Networks (QNNs).
- Variational Quantum Circuits (VQC) are used for training artificial intelligence models on quantum processors.

Hybrid Classical Quantum AI Models

Hybrid models mix classical & quantum computing to enhance AI performance because quantum technology is still in its infancy. While cloud-based services offer quantum resources, certain AI operations still use traditional CPUs and GPUs. The following is a list of innovations in hybrid quantum-classical artificial intelligence [5]:

- Quantum-Assisted Reinforcement Learning (QARL) is used to enhance decision-making models for robotics and automation.
- Quantum-Enhanced Natural Language Processing (Q-NLP) is used to improve AI-powered language translation and sentiment analysis.
- Highly efficient algorithms for probabilistic learning use Quantum Boltzmann Machines (QBMs).

Cloud-Based Quantum AI Development Platforms

Cloud platforms allow AI researchers to test and apply quantum algorithms without quantum hardware, which is illustrated below (Table **2**) [9]. These platforms provide cloud-based simulators and real quantum processors for AI applications.

Table 2. Quantum artificial intelligence platforms.

Platform	Provider	Key Features
IBM's Quantum Experience	IBM	Quantum AI SDK, Qiskit
Google's Quantum AI	Google	TensorFlow Quantum, Quantum Circuits
Azure Quantum	Microsoft	Q#, Hybrid Computing
Amazon Braket	AWS	Multiple QPU Providers

Quantum AI for Optimization Problems

Optimization problems, which are essential to AI applications like deep learning model training and logistics, are best solved by quantum computing. Quantum optimization innovations are listed below.

- AI-driven supply chains and logistics use an approximate quantum optimization algorithm.
- Optimizations based on quantum principles use quantum-inspired classical algorithms.
- Portfolio optimization in AI Finance is used under quantum-based risk analysis for AI-driven financial models.

Machine learning becomes better with the use of Cloud Quantum Computing (CQC), which speeds up optimization, data processing, and decision-making. Quantum Machine Learning (QML), hybrid AI models, and cloud-accessible quantum platforms can contribute to greater efficacy. Cloud Quantum Computing (CQC) for AI can revolutionize the industry, but there are several challenges that need to be addressed before it can be widely implemented.

CHALLENGES

There are various challenges, such as quantum noise, hardware limitations, and algorithm development, that still need to be addressed before quantum AI becomes mainstream. The main challenges are described below [10].

Quantum De-coherence

Quantum computing functions through its basic operational component, a qubit, or quantum bit. The presence of external factors makes qubits highly prone to degradation and computational mistakes that occur quickly in systems. Superconducting circuits, along with trapped ions and photons, hold the lead position among multiple systems that create quantum bits. The decoherence process starts from external disturbances affecting these delicate systems, thus causing calculation errors. In the quantum realm, a particle exhibits superposition, which means it can exist in multiple states simultaneously, and these states interfere with each other, creating a coherent system (Fig. **2**).

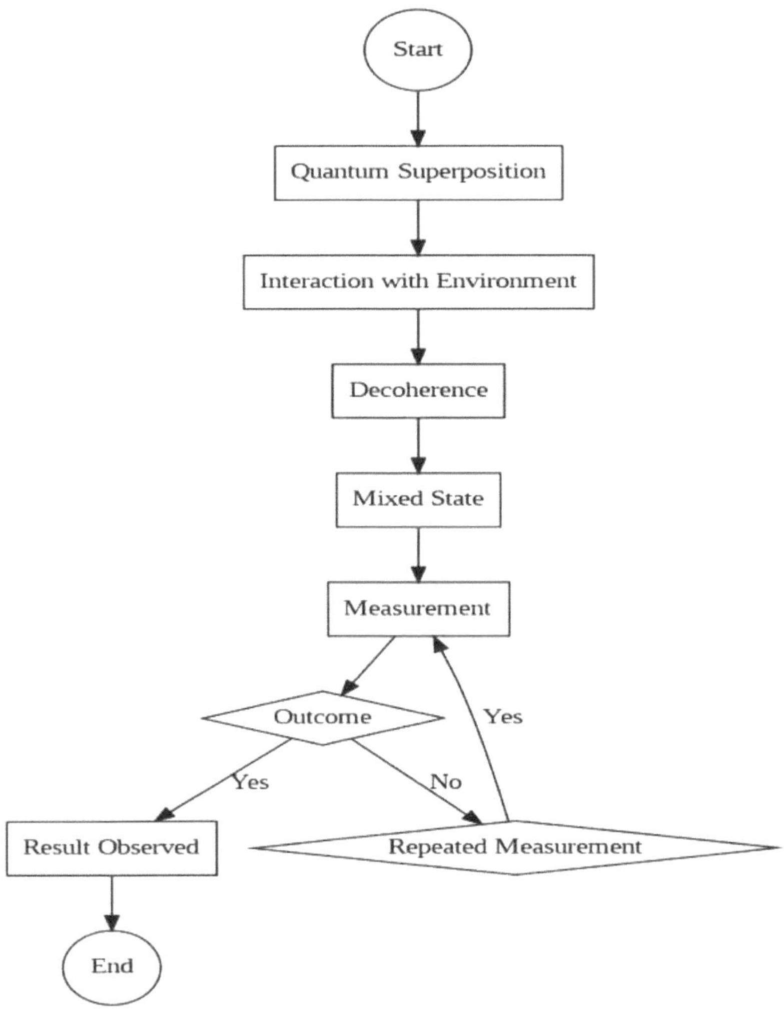

Fig. (2). States of a quantum computing system.

When a quantum-based system interacts with its environment, it undergoes temperature fluctuations, electromagnetic interference, or unintended measurement. The interaction can cause the system to lose its superposition and become entangled with the environment. This entanglement results in a loss of quantum coherence, which means the system's quantum features (like superposition and entanglement) are reduced, and it begins to act more like a classical system (Fig. **3**). To counteract decoherence, researchers use Quantum Error Correction (QEC) [7], which involves encoding quantum information redundantly across multiple qubits. However, QEC requires a significant number of extra qubits, making practical large-scale quantum computing even more challenging. Developing such robust techniques and maintaining a qubit's coherence over extended periods are critical tasks for realizing the full potential of quantum computers. Additionally, scaling up quantum systems to accommodate large numbers of qubits while maintaining coherence presents significant engineering challenges.

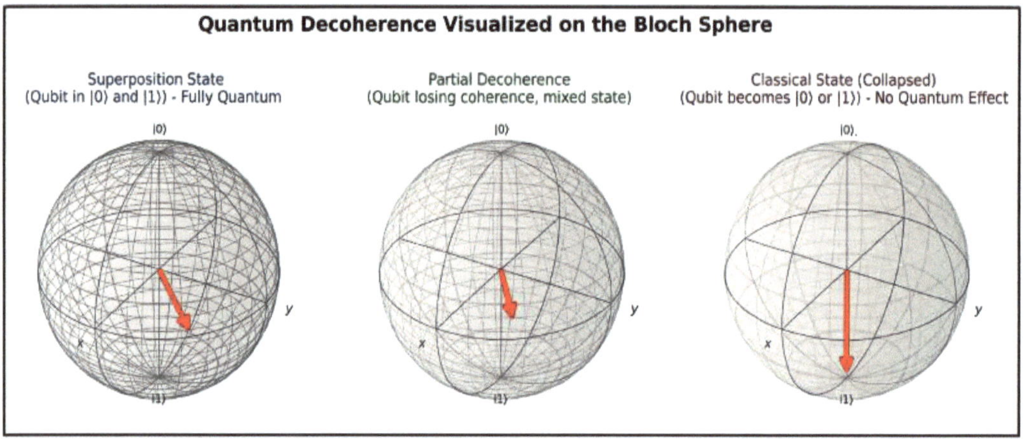

Fig. (3). Quantum decoherence visualization.

Integrating Models

Another challenge is the complexity of integrating quantum computing with existing AI models. Quantum algorithms work fundamentally differently from classical ones, and many AI problems still lack well-optimized quantum solutions. Researchers are developing hybrid quantum-classical models, but these require specialized expertise and computational resources that are not yet widely accessible (Fig. **4**).

Lack of Optimized Quantum AI Algorithms

Most AI algorithms are designed for classical computation (*e.g.*, neural networks, deep learning). Quantum computing requires entirely new algorithms that leverage superposition and entanglement, which are still in early research stages.

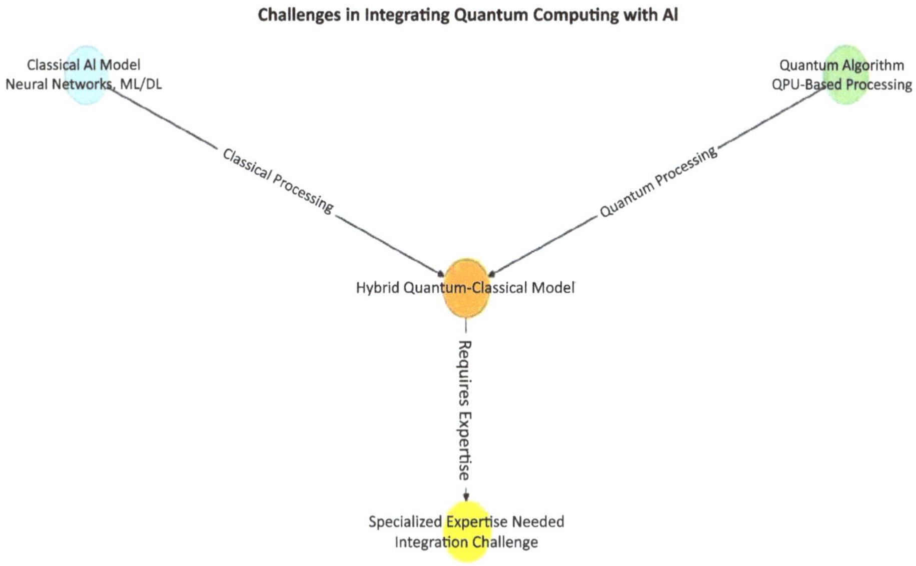

Fig. (4). Challenges in integrating quantum computing with AI.

Hybrid Quantum-Classical Integration Issues

Since quantum computers are not yet fully independent, AI models require hybrid systems where some tasks run classically (on CPUs/GPUs) and others run on quantum processors (QPUs). Efficiently switching between classical and quantum computing is complex and computationally expensive.

Quantum Hardware Limitations

Current quantum computers suffer from high error rates, qubit decoherence, and limited qubit count. AI requires stable and scalable computation, but today's quantum hardware is still prone to noise and lacks sufficient qubits for training large AI models.

Specialized Expertise Requirement

The operation of quantum computing is identified through distinct principles that deviate from traditional computing approaches. AI researchers typically lack expertise in quantum mechanics, and quantum scientists may not be familiar with AI frameworks. This combination creates a knowledge gap that slows down progress.

Data Input and Output Bottlenecks

Quantum computers process information differently from classical ones. Converting classical data (images, text, and structured data) into a quantum-compatible format and extracting useful results efficiently remains an open challenge.

Cost and Accessibility of Quantum Computing

The building and maintenance expenses of quantum computers become prohibitive, while these systems need to operate under extreme temperature conditions approaching absolute zero. Cloud-based quantum services are available, but access is limited and costly, making large-scale AI training difficult [11]. Furthermore, cloud-based access to quantum computing introduces latency and security concerns (Fig. **5**). Since quantum computations require remote access to specialized hardware, data transfer times and encryption methods become critical factors, especially for AI applications that process sensitive or real-time data. Since quantum computers are highly specialized and not widely available, users must access them remotely *via* the cloud. This scenario creates several challenges:

Latency Issues

- Quantum computations require data transfer between classical systems and quantum hardware.
- Network delays and queue times on cloud-based quantum systems slow down AI applications that depend on rapid decision-making, such as autonomous systems or financial trading algorithms.
- Hybrid quantum-classical AI models suffer because frequent switching between classical and quantum processing adds overhead.

Security Challenges

- **Data Encryption and Privacy:** Sensitive AI data must be transmitted over networks, making it vulnerable to cyber threats.
- **Man-in-the-Middle Attacks:** If not properly encrypted, intercepted quantum data could expose confidential AI training datasets.
- **Quantum-Safe Encryption Needs:** As quantum computers advance, traditional encryption methods (like RSA) may become vulnerable, requiring post-quantum cryptographic techniques.

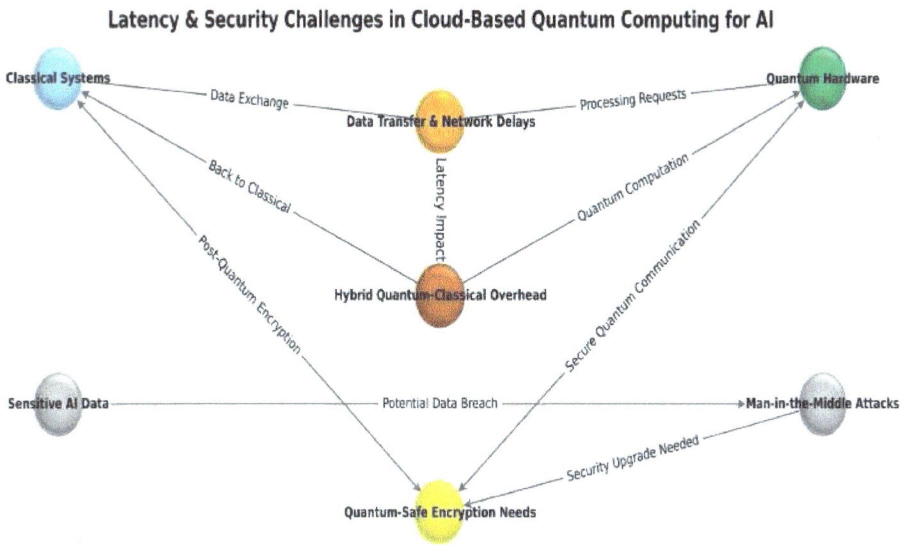

Fig. (5). Latency and security concerns.

Researchers are exploring several solutions to address the challenges of cloud-based quantum computing for AI. Optimizing quantum cloud infrastructure is essential to reduce queue times and enhance quantum-classical communication [12]. Since quantum hardware is not yet widely accessible, many users rely on cloud-based quantum processors, leading to congestion and delays. Improving scheduling algorithms, increasing the availability of quantum resources, and developing more efficient hybrid computing frameworks can significantly enhance performance and reduce wait times. Furthermore, advancements in low-latency communication protocols between modern and classical systems are critical to ensure that hybrid AI models can operate seamlessly. The second emphasis area involves implementing advanced security systems. Secure data transmission requires attention because quantum computing enables both protective and threatening elements regarding cybersecurity through its ability to breach traditional encryption techniques. A study discusses the methods for using quantum-safe encryption methods [13], which include lattice-based cryptography [14] and Quantum Key Distribution (QKD) [15] to create secure data transfers between AI systems and cloud-based quantum processors. Additionally, the processing of encrypted information can be enabled through homomorphic encryption [16] and secure Multi-Party Computation (MPC) [17]. This processing involves no exposure to sensitive information, addressing concerns related to privacy and compliance. The hybrid edge-quantum AI processing system offers a novel solution for decreasing computational requirements together with data transfer needs [18]. With this method, raw data is first processed and important features are extracted on edge devices and local classical computers, so it doesn't go directly to quantum cloud systems; only the necessary quantum-related data is sent to the cloud. The reduction of data transmission volume leads to enhanced speed and bandwidth controls in quantum cloud systems. Selecting the right distribution method for edge hardware workloads and ordinary systems in addition to quantum processors, permits AI applications to benefit from quantum speedups at acceptable speeds. These solution methods create improved quantum cloud computing capabilities for artificial intelligence, which will lead to enhanced accessible quantum-AI models in the upcoming years.

The developing nature of this field drives the development of quantum programming languages while software frameworks continue to evolve [19]. Many quantum AI tools require profound knowledge of quantum mechanics, limiting the number of professionals who can develop effective applications. Advances in algorithmic efficiency, hardware optimization, and interpretability will be required to make AI algorithms more practical, efficient, and reliable.

APPLICATIONS

Quantum computers are able to process and analyze large datasets at speeds that are tenfold faster than traditional computers. AI-driven supply chain management, finance, and logistics improvements can be accelerated using quantum algorithms. Some important applications are as follows:

Application: Medical Care and Drug Exploration

Quantum computing significantly enhances areas including risk analysis, drug research, radiation, precision medicine, diagnosis support, and molecular simulations by its ability to handle huge databases and run computations at quick rates [20]. The advent of quantum computing has revolutionized drug development and healthcare by providing faster and more effective solutions to complex healthcare problems. A thorough description of each important application is depicted below (Fig. **6**).

Precision Medicine

Precision medicine develops unique treatment plans for each person by looking at their genes, surroundings, and way of life. Quantum computing improves this area by:

- **Genomic Data Processing:** Quantum algorithms analyze large-scale genomic data to find treatment responses and illness risks.

- **Predictive Modeling:** Quantum models powered by artificial intelligence can predict how a patient will respond to different medications and therapies.
- **Improved Drug Matching:** Patients get custom medicines based on their genetic profiles and molecular interactions.

Example: IBM's quantum computing study aims to customize cancer therapies depending on patient-specific genetic abnormalities.

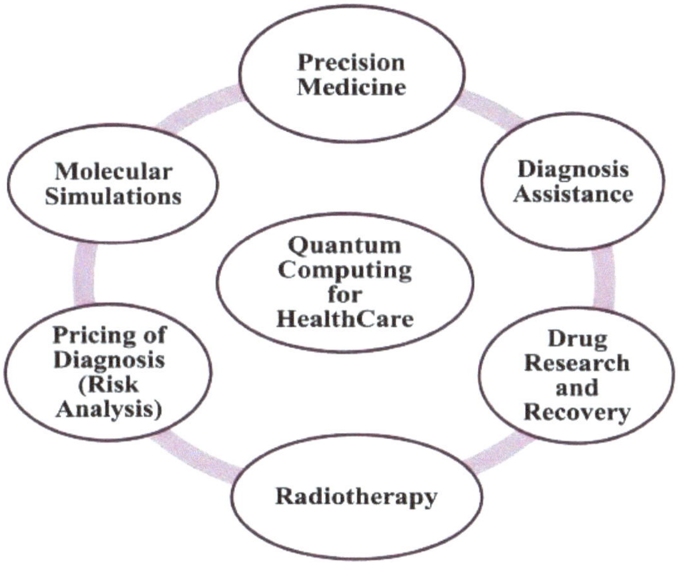

Fig. (6). Quantum computing for healthcare.

Diagnosis Assistance

Advancements in quantum computing have greatly enhanced the accuracy of early disease detection and diagnostics by:

- **AI-Enhanced Image Analysis:** Utilizing quantum-enhanced AI models, MRI, CT, and X-ray images can be processed more quickly and with improved accuracy.
- **Recognition of Patterns in Medical Data:** Large datasets can be analysed by quantum systems to find subtle symptoms of illness in patients.
- **Support for Real-Time Decisions:** Doctors get quicker and more precise advice on how to diagnose patients.

Example: Google's DeepMind is working on quantum-enhanced AI for imaging-based early-stage cancer detection.

Drug Research and Recovery

It takes less time to find effective treatments because quantum computing accelerates the process of finding and developing new drugs. It is helpful in:

- **Molecular Simulations:** To find new drug possibilities, chemical reactions are simulated at the quantum level.
- **Drug-Target Interaction:** Quantum models forecast the interaction between a drug molecule and particular proteins.
- **Drug Repurposing:** Examining current medications for possible future therapeutic applications.

Example: During the COVID-19 pandemic, scientists used quantum computing to evaluate the effectiveness of antiviral drugs.

Radiotherapy

Quantum computing improves the planning of radiotherapy treatments for cancer patients by:

- **Optimizing Radiation Dosage:** Determining optimal radiation levels for cancer cell destruction and tissue preservation.
- **Real-Time Modifications:** Quantum algorithms facilitate the modification of treatment plans in accordance with patient responses.
- **Minimized Adverse Effects:** Personalized radiation therapy reduces damage to adjacent organs, thereby minimizing side effects.

Example: To make cancer treatments more precise, scientists at MIT are creating models of quantum-enhanced radiation.

Pricing of Diagnosis (Risk Analysis)

Quantum computing improves healthcare expenditures through the analysis of medical risks and the prediction of illness trends. It facilitates the following:

- **Medical Plans with Cost Efficiency:** Insurance companies utilize advanced AI models to calculate customized insurance premiums.
- **Healthcare Risk Prediction:** Estimating the probability of chronic illnesses by taking into account lifestyle and genetic factors.
- **Managing Hospital Resources:** Enhancing the allocation of hospital beds, scheduling of surgeries, and management of staffing.

Example: Financial firms and insurance companies rely on quantum computing to enhance health risk modeling and improve fraud detection in claims processing.

Molecular Simulations

A significant application of quantum computing in healthcare lies in its ability to simulate molecular structures, which can enhance the drug development process. The primary advantages consist of:

- **Protein Folding Analysis:** Research into protein folding has led to advances in the treatment of cancer, Parkinson's disease, and Alzheimer's disease.
- **Accelerated Chemical Reactions:** Quantum-level simulations of chemical processes enhance the efficiency of medicine development.
- **Development of Nano-medicine:** Nano medicine Development involves the design of nanoparticles to deliver drugs precisely.

Example: IBM's Quantum Hummingbird processor is facilitating advancements in biopharmaceutical research by modeling molecular interactions.

Application: Financial Modeling and Risk Analysis

Risk analysis and financial modeling as shown below (Fig. **7**) can benefit from quantum computing by improving [21]:

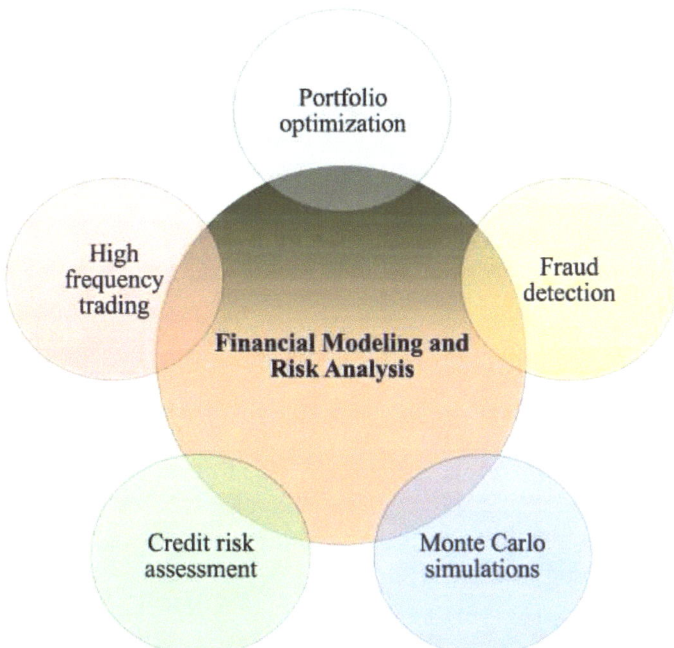

Fig. (7). Financial modelling and risk analysis.

Portfolio Optimization

To optimize a portfolio, one must choose an asset allocation that will generate the highest possible return with the lowest possible risk. It manages big datasets with different constraints (such as liquidity and risk exposure) and optimizes asset allocation using the Quantum Approximate Optimization Algorithm (QAOA).

Example: Goldman Sachs and IBM are working together to make better financial decisions by creating quantum systems for analyzing portfolio risk and allocating assets.

Fraud Detection

The detection of financial fraud requires real-time processing of massive transaction data. Fraudulent transactions can be identified by analyzing the anomalous spending behaviors.

Example: Mastercard explores quantum-enhanced AI models for instantaneous fraud detection, minimizing false positives and enhancing security in credit card transactions.

Monte Carlo Simulations

Option pricing, derivative valuation, and financial risk assessments involve extensive use of Monte Carlo methodologies. Its applications include assessing credit risk, market risk, and the pricing of derivatives. It improves the accuracy and efficiency of predicting changes in asset prices.

Example: JP Morgan uses quantum computing to enhance their trading techniques and expedite risk simulations, mitigating risk exposure under unpredictable market conditions.

Credit Risk Assessment

Banks use risk models and historical data to evaluate creditworthiness prior to loan approval. To forecast the likelihood of loan default, quantum AI algorithms examine massive datasets. It captures non-linear risk elements (such as borrower behavior and market conditions) to improve the credit score. The enhancement of risk-adjusted loan pricing models leads to improved decision-making procedures.

Example: Barclays is exploring quantum computing applications for credit risk assessment and loan optimization.

High-frequency Trading

High-frequency trading (HFT) is based on the rapid execution of several orders using market data. Quantum algorithms outperform traditional computers in identifying profitable trading trends. Quantum neural networks forecast market patterns by examining extensive financial data streams. It makes price forecasting and trade execution faster.

Example: D-Wave and Volkswagen have developed market prediction models optimized for algorithmic trading methods using quantum technology.

Application: Cybersecurity and Cryptography

Quantum computing will change the new areas of cybersecurity and cryptography by providing better encryption methods, stronger protection for cloud data, and using AI-powered quantum technologies to find cyber threats. Five practical applications of CQC in cryptography and cybersecurity are described (Fig. **8**) below [22, 23].

Quantum Key Distribution (QKD) – The Micius Satellite Experiment

Traditional encryption is based on mathematical algorithms such as RSA or ECC, which may be compromised by quantum computers employing Shor's Algorithm. Quantum Key Distribution (QKD) provides a robust method for exchanging encryption keys based on the principles of quantum mechanics, ensuring that any attempt by hackers to intercept the keys is detectable.

Example: The Micius Satellite (China, 2016-Present)

In 2016, China inaugurated Micius, the world's first quantum communication satellite. The satellite effectively showcased quantum key distribution across terrestrial optical networks, facilitating the exchange of resilient encryption keys between China and Austria. Hackers attempting to overhear communications would disrupt the quantum state of photons, promptly notifying users about the eavesdropping initiative.

Impact

- Developed a global quantum-secured internet.
- Promoted US and EU investment in quantum networks.
- Boosted QKD-based cybersecurity adoption in banking, government, and military sectors.

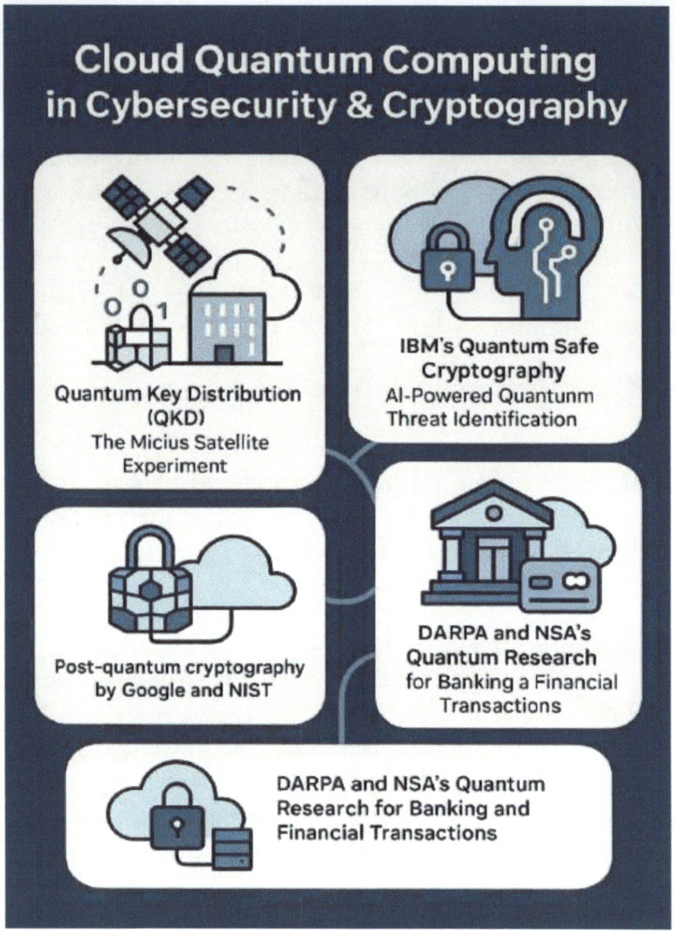

Fig. (8). Practical applications of CQC in cybersecurity and cryptography.

IBM's Quantum Safe Cryptography

AI-generated malware is difficult to detect by current cybersecurity solutions. Quantum AI can find patterns and anomalies in massive datasets much faster.

Example: IBM's Quantum Safe Cryptography Initiative

- IBM is developing quantum-safe cryptography by adding artificial intelligence-driven quantum security measures into cloud services.
- Cyber anomalies and new zero-day threats can be detected by quantum-enhanced machine learning models, which conventional security systems may overlook. Their AI-Quantum Hybrid Security System predicts and prevents cyber threats by examining network traffic, transaction logs, and malware signatures.

Impact

- Increased AI-driven cybersecurity for real-time malware detection and predictive defense.
- Used by governments and organizations to enhance cybersecurity infrastructure.

Post-quantum Cryptography by Google and NIST

Quantum computers present a significant challenge to conventional encryption techniques such as RSA, which depend on the complexity of factoring large integers. Quantum technology helps the creation of novel encryption algorithms that are resilient to quantum cyberattacks.

Example: Post-Quantum Cryptographic Standards maintained by NIST and Google (2022–present)

- Google, IBM, and Microsoft are among the corporations collaborating with the National Institute of Standards and Technology (NIST) to create encryption algorithms that are resistant to quantum computing.
- The National Institute of Standards and Technology (NIST) released a set of four cryptographic algorithms for post-quantum security in 2022, with an emphasis on:
  - Lattice-Based Cryptographywhich quantum computers cannot decipher.
  - Hash-Based Cryptography is safe against brute-force attacks.
  - Multivariate Polynomial Cryptography is a challenging problem that quantum computers may not be able to tackle.
  - To safeguard Chrome from any future threats, Google has already analyzed post-quantum encryption techniques.

Impact

- Provide data security for financial organizations, cloud storage, and blockchain technologies.
- Switches to cryptography that is resistant to quantum attacks, preparing the world for the age of quantum computing.
- Large cloud providers, such as Google Cloud and Microsoft Azure, use it to protect their services.

Cloud-Based Quantum Security Solutions—Microsoft Azure Quantum

Data security in the cloud is becoming more important as more and more companies shift their operations to the cloud. Cloud services are integrating quantum-enhanced security.

Example: Microsoft Azure Quantum—Securing Cloud Data with Quantum Computing

- Microsoft Azure is creating quantum-secured cloud services for government and enterprise data.
- It utilizes post-quantum cryptography and AI-powered threat detection on its cloud platform to
  - Avoid quantum decryption attacks on critical cloud data.
  - Protect AI models in the cloud from cyberattacks.
  - Set up quantum-safe authentication for user access.

Impact

- Offer quantum security for cloud computing enterprises.
- Used by government agencies and financial organizations for advanced cybersecurity.
- Enables secure blockchain and IoT transactions.

DARPA and NSA's Quantum Research for Banking and Financial Transactions

Financial transactions depend on robust encryption techniques. Financial institutions are moving toward quantum-secure banking systems, as quantum computing may compromise conventional cryptography.

Example: DARPA & NSA's Quantum Research for Banking Security

- To prevent cybercrime, the National Security Agency (NSA) and the Defense Advanced Research Projects Agency (DARPA) are developing quantum-secured financial systems.
- Quantum encryption is being integrated into:
  - Online payment systems to prevent interception of transactions.
  - Quantum AI-driven fraud detection models
  - Blockchain-based banking systems can be secured using quantum-resistant cryptography.
  - JPMorgan and Mastercard are among the financial institutions looking into quantum-based authentication technologies to make banking more secure.

Impact

- Prevents potential quantum decryption attacks on online banking transactions.
- Improves the ability to detect fraud by using pattern recognition with quantum AI.
- Secures blockchain transactions, making cryptocurrencies quantum-resistant.

Application: Logistics and Supply Chain Optimization

CQC is changing logistics and supply chain management by making it easier to find the best routes, predict demand, keep track of goods, and evaluate risks [24]. Quantum algorithms can handle huge amounts of data much faster than traditional computers. It makes supply chains more reliable, efficient, and cost-effective. It helps companies reduce expenses, work more efficiently, and make better real-time decisions.

Optimizing Routes with Quantum

Optimization of delivery routes in traditional logistics is done using classical algorithms (such as Dijkstra's algorithm), but conventional algorithms have problems with real-time traffic, fuel prices, and delivery limits. Quantum computers can evaluate millions of paths in a millisecond and choose the best one.

Example: Quantum Traffic Optimization at Volkswagen (2021–present)

- Volkswagen optimized public transportation lines in Beijing and Lisbon using D-Wave's quantum annealing technique.
- To determine the most efficient routes, the algorithm took into account current weather, traffic, and congestion levels.
- Led to shorter travel times, less pollution, and financial savings.

Benefits

- Delivery times were shortened by choosing the best routes.
- By reducing unnecessary travel, fuel use, and expenses were minimized.

Quantum AI for Demand Forecasting

Planning for client demand is essential for preventing both overstocking and understocking. Emerging trends in the market are a challenge for classical forecasting models. Quantum AI can enhance accuracy by analysing past sales data, current market trends, and external factors.

Example: Walmart's Quantum AI Demand Prediction

- Walmart collaborated with IBM's Quantum Computing group to improve demand forecasting.
- Quantum AI analysed client purchasing history, meteorological patterns, and economic trends to enhance demand forecasting precision.
- Helpful in optimizing inventory levels and minimizing waste in perishable commodities.

Benefits

- Reduced supply shortages due to improved accuracy of demand predictions.
- Minimized surplus stock, resulting in financial savings.
- Increased warehouse productivity by restocking products according to demand patterns.

Quantum-Assisted Inventory Management

It is difficult for global supply chains to manage the distribution of inventory across multiple locations. Traditional inventory models do not allow for real-time adjustments. Optimizing stock allocation is made possible by quantum computing, which instantaneously processes large-scale inventory data.

Example: Amazon's Quantum Research for Warehouse Optimization

- Amazon is exploring quantum computing models to enhance inventory distribution.
- The system optimizes warehouse stocking tactics by considering consumer demand, supplier delivery periods, and storage space.
- Quantum AI helps automate inventory decisions for more efficiency.

Benefits

- Stock optimization reduced storage costs.
- Faster order fulfilment by forecasting product demand across locations.
- Minimized waste in the food and pharmaceutical sectors.

Evaluation of Quantum Risk in Supply Chains

Geopolitical turmoil, catastrophic events, and unpredictable market conditions create challenges to global supply systems. These uncertainties are complicated, and traditional risk management methods have difficulty addressing them. More accurate risk forecasts are possible with quantum computing, as it can simulate numerous risk situations concurrently.

Example: HSBC and IBM Quantum Risk Analysis for Supply Chains

- Risks in the supply chain have been evaluated by HSBC in collaboration with IBM Quantum.
- The quantum system assisted firms in making data-driven decisions about supplier diversification and crisis management by analyzing market fluctuations, trade policies, and supplier reliability.

Benefits

- Minimizing interruptions to the supply chain through proactive risk management.
- Ensuring business continuity through improved supplier diversification.
- Improved crisis response plans based on quantum-powered simulations.

Smart Warehouse & IoT Integration with Quantum Computing

IoT-enabled smart warehouses gather extensive real-time data, including temperature, humidity, and shipment tracking. Quantum computing improves real-time decision-making by processing IoT data at a remarkable speed.

Example: DHL's Smart Logistics Driven by Quantum

- Quantum computing is being explored by DHL to automate warehousing processes.
- Optimizes robotic warehousing operations using quantum-enhanced artificial intelligence.
- It facilitates the optimization of delivery schedules and a reduction of package sorting times.

Benefits

- Improved warehouse automation effectiveness.
- Scheduled last-mile delivery optimally.
- AI-Quantum integration helped to reduce package handling faults.

Application: Complex Problem Solving and Scientific Research

Cloud Quantum Computing (CQC) is revolutionizing scientific research by facilitating fast simulations, resolving intricate equations, and streamlining extensive computations that traditional computers find difficult to handle. It is utilized across multiple areas, including physics, chemistry, materials science, and climate modelling [5, 20, 23].

Quantum Simulations for Drug Discovery and Material Science

Conventional drug development and materials science simulations require substantial computational resources to model molecular interactions. Classical computers employ approximate models, whereas quantum computers can directly simulate quantum mechanical systems with more accuracy.

Example: Google's Quantum Simulation of a Chemical Reaction (2020)

Google's Sycamore quantum processor outperformed classical computers in predicting reaction rates, and it employed quantum computing to model the molecular dynamics of a basic chemical reaction.

IBM's Quantum Research for Material Science

- Quantum algorithms are being used by IBM to find new materials for superconductors and battery technology.
- Quantum simulations help forecast material characteristics, thereby reducing the time required for experimentation.

Climate Modeling and Weather Forecasting

Climate models involve substantial atmospheric, oceanic, and geological data processing. Classical computers face challenges in accurately simulating the complexities of global climate systems.

Example: NASA's Quantum Computing for Climate Change Analysis

- NASA focuses on quantum algorithms for climate change modelling.
- Quantum AI improves hurricane, drought, and flood prediction accuracy.

Google & D-Wave's Quantum Weather Forecasting

- Google and D-Wave are pioneering research into quantum-enhanced weather prediction models.
- Quantum computers analyse satellite data, atmospheric models, and historical weather patterns to enhance precision.

Quantum Machine Learning (QML) for AI Advancements

Large datasets and intricate pattern identification are challenges for traditional machine learning (ML). Deep learning is more effective due to quantum machine learning (QML), which provides exponential improvements in AI model training.

Example: IBM's QML for Neural Networks

- IBM researchers trained AI models more effectively by utilizing quantum computing.
- Natural Language Processing (NLP), image identification, and medical diagnostics are all assisted by QML.

Google's Quantum Neural Networks (QNNs)

- Google's Sycamore processor supports quantum speedup in AI model training and assists in optimization, fraud detection, and scientific research.

Quantum Cryptography for Data Security in Research

Scientific studies produce private information that has to be safeguarded against cyberattacks. Quantum cryptography ensures safe data storage and transmission by applying resilient encryption techniques.

Example: Quantum Secure Cloud for Research Institutions

- Universities and research laboratories are implementing Quantum Key Distribution (QKD) for secure communications.
- Government organizations such as DARPA and NSA are investing money in quantum encryption for the protection of research data.

Optimization Challenges in Engineering and Space Exploration

Orbital calculations, fuel efficiency, and spaceship design are all examples of complex problems that have to be solved to accomplish engineering and space exploration. Quantum computing has the potential to transform aerospace and engineering by improving multi-variable optimization.

Example: NASA's Quantum Research for Space Missions

- NASA is exploring quantum computing for flight trajectory optimization as well as fuel-efficient space travel planning and satellite location.

Airbus Quantum Research for Aircraft Design

- Quantum computing is being used by Airbus to optimize flights and perform aerodynamics simulations.

CONCLUDING REMARKS

This chapter has explored the prospect of advancing AI applications through the convergence of cloud and quantum computing. Remote access to quantum resources can be provided by cloud quantum computing, which promotes advancements in machine learning and optimization. However, error correction, device scalability, and security remain key challenges. Computational efficiency is being improved through ongoing research in quantum algorithms and cloud infrastructure.

Future initiatives must focus on optimizing quantum architectures and ensuring secure implementations. Cloud quantum computing will promote AI developments, revolutionize industries, and solve challenging problems, surpassing classical capabilities, making it essential to future computational innovations.

ACKNOWLEDGEMENTS

The authors of this paper are thankful to Chandigarh University, Punjab, and Algoma University, Canada, for providing infrastructural facilities to complete this research work.

REFERENCES

[1] E.G. Rieffel, and W. H. Polak, *Quantum Computing: A Gentle Introduction*. London, U.K.: MIT Press, 2011.

[2] Z. Luo, Y. Du, L. Guo, and L. Qian, "Cloud computing: An overview", *Proc. IEEE Int. Conf. Cloud Comput.* Beijing, China, 2009, pp. 626–631.

[3] S.Y-C. Chen, C-H.H. Yang, J. Qi, P-Y. Chen, X. Ma, and H-S. Goan, "Variational quantum circuits for deep reinforcement learning", *IEEE Access,* vol. 8, pp. 141007-141024, 2020. [http://dx.doi.org/10.1109/ACCESS.2020.3010470]

[4] R. Rietsche, C. Dremel, S. Bosch, L. Steinacker, M. Meckel, and J-M. Leimeister, "Quantum computing", *Electron. Mark.,* vol. 32, no. 4, pp. 2525-2536, 2022. [http://dx.doi.org/10.1007/s12525-022-00570-y]

[5] A. Lopez Garcia, J.M. De Lucas, M. Antonacci, W. Zu Castell, M. David, M. Hardt, L. Lloret Iglesias, G. Molto, M. Plociennik, V. Tran, A.S. Alic, M. Caballer, I.C. Plasencia, A. Costantini, S. Dlugolinsky, D.C. Duma, G. Donvito, J. Gomes, I. Heredia Cacha, K. Ito, V.Y. Kozlov, G. Nguyen, P. Orviz Fernandez, Z. Sustr, and P. Wolniewicz, "A cloud-based framework for machine learning workloads and applications", *IEEE Access,* vol. 8, pp. 18681-18692, 2020. [http://dx.doi.org/10.1109/ACCESS.2020.2964386]

[6] M. Golec, E.S. Hatay, M. Golec, M. Uyar, M. Golec, and S.S. Gill, "Quantum cloud computing: Trends and challenges", *Journal of Economy and Technology,* vol. 2, pp. 190-199, 2024. [http://dx.doi.org/10.1016/j.ject.2024.05.001]

[7] Y. Zeng, Z.Y. Zhou, E. Rinaldi, C. Gneiting, and F. Nori, "Approximate autonomous quantum error correction with reinforcement learning", *Phys. Rev. Lett.,* vol. 131, no. 5, p. 050601, 2023. [http://dx.doi.org/10.1103/PhysRevLett.131.050601] [PMID: 37595216]

[8] A. Montanaro, "Quantum algorithms: An overview", *npj Quantum Inf.,* vol. 2, p. 15023, 2016. [http://dx.doi.org/10.1038/npjqi.2015.23]

[9] G. De Luca, "A survey of NISQ era hybrid quantum-classical machine learning research", *Journal of Artificial Intelligence and Technology,* vol. 2, no. 1, pp. 9-15, 2021. [http://dx.doi.org/10.37965/jait.2021.12002]

[10] W. Lu, Y. Lu, J. Li, A. Sigov, L. Ratkin, and L.A. Ivanov, "Quantum machine learning: Classifications, challenges, and solutions", *J. Ind. Inf. Integr.,* vol. 42, p. 100736, 2024. [http://dx.doi.org/10.1016/j.jii.2024.100736]

[11] A. B. Altamimi, J. Aqib, and A. Ahmad, "A reference architecture for quantum computing as a service", *TechRxiv,* 2024.

[12] S. Batchu, "Cloud infrastructure optimization: An integrated framework for performance, resiliency,

reliability, and security enhancement", *International Journal of Research in Computer Applications and Information Technology,* vol. 8, no. 1, pp. 1551-1567, 2025. [IJRCAIT]. [http://dx.doi.org/10.34218/IJRCAIT_08_01_114]

[13] A. Zornetta, "Quantum-safe global encryption policy", *Int. J. Law Inf. Technol.,* vol. 32, no. 1, 2024.

[14] J. Buchmann, E. Dahmen, D.J. Bernstein, Ed., Eds., "Lattice-based cryptography," in *Post-Quantum Cryptography*, Berlin, Heidelberg: Springer, 2009, pp. 147–191.

[15] A. Broadbent, and C. Schaffner, "Quantum cryptography beyond quantum key distribution", *Des. Codes Cryptogr.,* vol. 78, no. 1, pp. 351-382, 2016. [http://dx.doi.org/10.1007/s10623-015-0157-4] [PMID: 32226229]

[16] M. Zhao E, and Y. Geng, "Homomorphic encryption technology for cloud computing", *Procedia Comput. Sci.,* vol. 154, pp. 73-83, 2019. [http://dx.doi.org/10.1016/j.procs.2019.06.012]

[17] C. Zhao, S. Zhao, M. Zhao, Z. Chen, C-Z. Gao, H. Li, and Y. Tan, "Secure Multi-Party Computation: Theory, practice and applications", *Inf. Sci.,* vol. 476, pp. 357-372, 2019. [http://dx.doi.org/10.1016/j.ins.2018.10.024]

[18] L. Ding and L. Ma, "Hybrid quantum edge computing network," in: *Proc. SPIE 12238, Quantum Commun. Quantum Imaging XX*, pp. 83–93, 2022. [http://dx.doi.org/10.1117/12.2633020]

[19] B. Heim, M. Soeken, S. Marshall, C. Granade, M. Roetteler, A. Geller, M. Troyer, and K. Svore, "Quantum programming languages", *Nat. Rev. Phys.,* vol. 2, no. 12, pp. 709-722, 2020. [http://dx.doi.org/10.1038/s42254-020-00245-7]

[20] F. Arute, K. Arya, R. Babbush, D. Bacon, J. C. Bardin, R. Barends, R. Biswas, S. Boixo, F. G. S. L. Brandao, D. A. Buell, B. Burkett, Y. Chen, Z. Chen, B. Chiaro, R. Collins, W. Courtney, A. Dunsworth, E. Farhi, B. Foxen, A. Fowler, C. Gidney, M. Giustina, R. Graff, K. Guerin, S. Habegger, M. P. Harrigan, M. J. Hartmann, A. Ho, M. Hoffmann, T. Huang, T. S. Humble, S. V. Isakov, E. Jeffrey, Z. Jiang, D. Kafri, K. Kechedzhi, J. Kelly, P. V. Klimov, S. Knysh, A. Korotkov, F. Kostritsa, D. Landhuis, M. Lindmark, E. Lucero, D. Lyakh, S. Mandrà, J. R. McClean, M. McEwen, A. Megrant, X. Mi, K. Michielsen, M. Mohseni, J. Mutus, O. Naaman, M. Neeley, C. Neill, M. Yuezhen Niu, E. Ostby, A. Petukhov, J. C. Platt, C. Quintana, E. G. Rieffel, P. Roushan, N. C. Rubin, D. Sank, K. J. Satzinger, V. Smelyanskiy, K. J. Sung, M. D. Trevithick, A. Vainsencher, B. Villalonga, T. White, Z. J. Yao, P. Yeh, A. Zalcman, H. Neven, and J. M. Martinis, "Quantum supremacy using a programmable superconducting processor," Nature, vol. 574, no. 7779, pp. 505–510, 2019. [http://dx.doi.org/10.1038/s41586-019-1666-5]

[21] H.T. Nguyen, M. Usman, and R. Buyya, "Quantum cloud computing: A review, open problems, and future directions", *arXiv preprint, arXiv:2404.11420,* 2024.

[22] S. Singh, A. Sharma, and P.K. Verma, "Quantum cloud computing: Trends and challenges", *J. Quantum Inf. Sci.,* vol. 10, no. 2, pp. 123-135, 2023.

[23] G.S. Ravi, K.N. Smith, P. Murali, and F.T. Chong, "Quantum computing in the cloud: Analyzing job and machine characteristics", *Proc. IEEE Int. Symp. Workload Characterization (IISWC)* Storrs, CT, USA, 2021, pp. 39–50. [http://dx.doi.org/10.1109/IISWC53511.2021.00015]

[24] T. Haryono, T. Widiyan, and F. Setiawan, "Cloud quantum computing concept and development: A systematic review", *Procedia Comput. Sci.,* vol. 179, pp. 45-53, 2021.

CHAPTER 5

Quantum Algorithms for Machine Learning

Davinder Kaur[1,*], **Preet Kamal Sharma**[2], **Manuraj Moudgil**[3], **Jaspreet Singh**[4], **Rupinder Singh**[5] and **Zaki Ahmad Khan**[6]

[1] *Department of Computer Applications, Algoma University, Brampton Campus, Ontario, Canada*

[2] *Department of Computer Applications, Post Graduate Government College for Girls, Chandigarh, Punjab, India*

[3] *Department of Computer Science and Engineering, Bhai Gurdas Institute of Engineering & Technology, Sangrur, Punjab, India*

[4] *Department of Computer Science and Engineering, Chandigarh University, Mohali, Punjab, India*

[5] *Chitkara University Institute of Engineering and Technology, Chitkara University, Rajpura, Punjab, India*

[6] *Department of Computer Science, University of Worcester, Worcester, United Kingdom*

Abstract: Through the integration of machine learning techniques with the computational power of quantum computing, quantum algorithms greatly improve the processing and analytical capabilities of systems. In contrast to traditional techniques, quantum computing effectively manages large and intricate datasets, providing answers to issues that conventional systems are unable to handle. Quantum Machine Learning (QML) has shown promise in a variety of fields, such as large-scale optimization, image recognition, and natural language processing. Because it can produce better and faster results, QML is positioned to revolutionize industries that depend on insights from data. The implementation of QML faces operational and scalability complications when used in healthcare applications and other fields of practical use. This study evaluates the active QML algorithms while demonstrating their improved functionality compared to usual approaches, and it identifies implementation barriers in real-world scenarios.

Keywords: AI ethicsAutomationComputer visionData encoding, Data privacy, Deep learning, Entanglement, Linear regression, ml, Pattern recognition, Predictive analysis, Quantum computing, Quantum data processing, Quantum neural networks, Quantum speedup, Superposition..

* **Corresponding author Davinder Kaur:** Department of Computer Applications, Algoma University, Brampton Campus, Ontario, Canada; E-mail: davinder.kaur@algomau.ca

Satveer Kour, Harvinder Singh, Anupam Bonkra & Rupinder Singh (Eds.)

INTRODUCTION

Quantum computing exhibits disruptive power in computing through its exceptional methods to overcome problems that could not be solved by classical methods. The application of quantum computing elements called qubits produces valuable abilities to solve complex problems that regular computers cannot handle. The most successful optimization fields, alongside machine learning, potentially receive rapid and intelligent answers from quantum systems. These concepts remain difficult to implement in practice, especially regarding Quantum Machine Learning (QML).

The article analyzes the complex structure of quantum computing as it investigates vital optimization methods, including quantum annealing and VQE, and QAOA. These tools serve purposes in machine learning frameworks, as shown by this illustration. The researcher aims to clarify how quantum technology influences data science, as well as chemistry and logistics, and artificial intelligence by merging theoretical knowledge with contemporary practical methods [1].

Overview of Quantum

Quantum computing is a paradigm of computation that leverages the properties of quantum mechanics to control the behavior of atomic and photonic particles for processing information. The qubit elements serving as fundamental components of quantum computing systems allow the devices to maintain dual states of 0 and 1 at the same time, thus distinguishing them from traditional computing systems. The fundamental attribute of quantum computers enables exceptional mathematical processing through a mechanism called superposition is presented below (Fig. **1**).

Traditional Computing: [0] or [1]

Quantum Computing: [0] and [1] at the same time (Superposition)

Fig. (1). Traditional *vs.* quantum computing.

The illustration depicts how quantum computers implement dual-purpose qubits instead of traditional computers' binary bit system, which functions as 0 or 1.

Quantum Computing's Power

Quantum computers gain their power through the capability called entanglement, as shown below (Fig. **2**). When qubits become entangled, the state of one qubit depends on the state of another, no matter how far apart they are. This allows quantum computers to solve problems in parallel, vastly increasing their computational power. Quantum computing is still in early development, but it has the potential to solve problems that are too complex for traditional computers to handle [2].

Entangled Qubits: [Qubit 1] -> [Qubit 2] (Linked together)

Fig. (2). Entanglement in quantum computing.

In this diagram, entangled qubits influence each other even when separated, making it easier to solve complex problems together.

Impact on Machine Learning

A computer analytical technique uses data-learning methods to produce predictions and make decisions. Old machine learning methods experience processing delays when dealing with extensive datasets or intricate calculations because large datasets make them test their capabilities. Traditional image recognition operations involving millions of pixels require long processing times for each image due to large datasets. Through quantum computing, operations can be expedited due to improved performance in data analysis as well as optimization and pattern recognition tasks [3]. The operation of quantum algorithms leads to accelerated data learning capabilities, which produce more accurate predictive and decision-making capabilities for machines.

Traditional data processing methods fall short due to excessive data sizes. Quantum computing has the potential to accelerate drug discovery research through the acceleration of the process by which scientists discover promising drug candidates.

QUANTUM COMPUTING ARCHITECTURE: A LAYERED APPROACH

Quantum computing architecture consists of multiple layers that work together to process quantum information, as shown below (Fig. **3**). Each layer has a specific role in ensuring efficient quantum computation. The following is the breakdown of layers:

Layer 1: Physical Layer: The core feature of quantum computing requires physical qubits (quantum bits) and control mechanisms alongside hardware-based components. Management of qubits depends on fundamental operations, which include single-qubit and two-qubit gates. With QND (Quantum Non-Demolition) readout integrated into the system, the accurate measurement of qubits can take place without altering their quantum state.

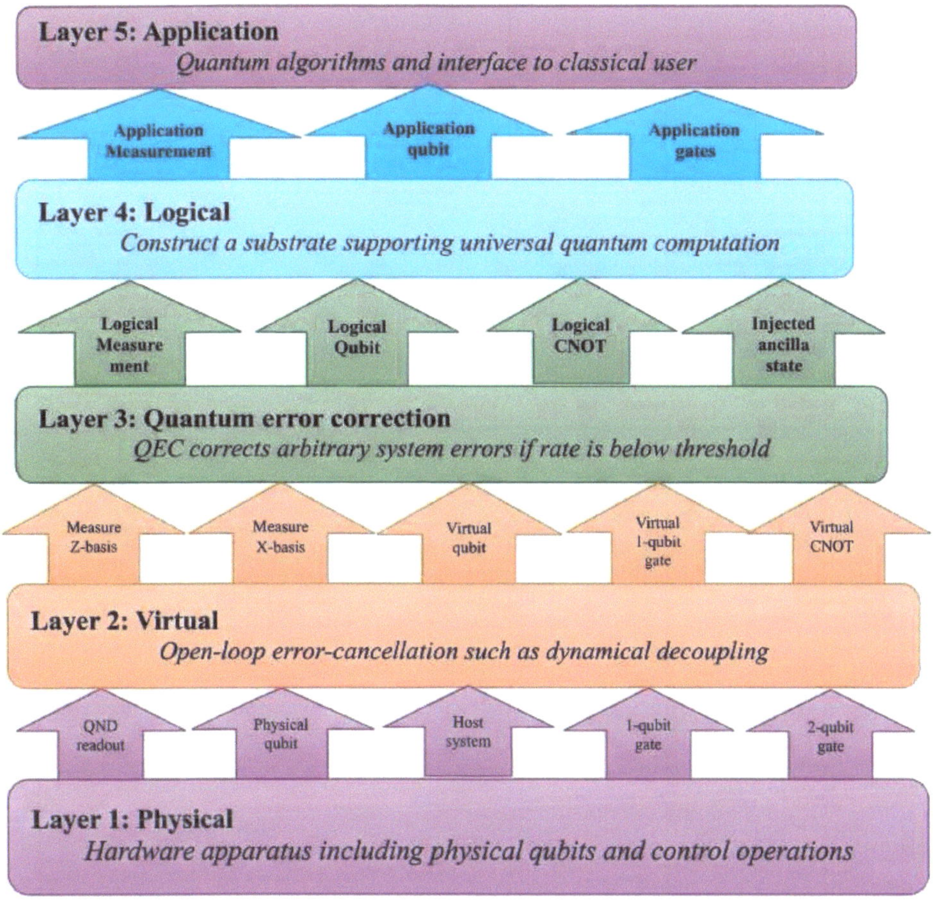

Fig. (3). Quantum computing architecture.

Layer 2: Virtual Layer: The basic operational principle of quantum computing includes physical qubits and control systems as hardware components. Management of qubits depends on fundamental operations, which include single-qubit and two-qubit gates. QND (Quantum Non-Demolition) readout exists within the system as a mechanism for precise qubit measurements that maintain their state unchanged.

Layer 3: Quantum Error Correction (QEC): The first layer monitors error development in qubits to prevent these errors from disrupting the quantum information processing. The formation of logical qubits relies on multiple physical qubits combined to achieve redundancy [4]. The following are the operations included:

- Final errors are checked by using logical measurement techniques.
- Logical CNOT gate (for error correction and computation)
- Extra qubits injected as ancilla states provide help for error correction within the system.

Layer 4: Logical Layer: This layer builds a structured system where error-corrected logical qubits can perform computations. It ensures that quantum operations run smoothly at a higher level [5]. The following are the key components:

- Logical qubits (used for computations)
- Logical CNOT gate (for quantum operations)
- Logical measurement (to extract results without errors) [6].

Layer 5: Application Layer: Application stage constitutes the uppermost quantum framework that runs the execution of quantum algorithms. Users access quantum programs through an interface within the system to perform operations on the quantum computer. The following are the components:

- Application qubits serve the purpose of processing, while application gates function as quantum logic gates, and application measurement extracts final results from the system.
- The execution of quantum algorithms occurs in these Application gates (quantum logic gates for computation).
- Application measurement (extracts final results).

QUANTUM COMPUTING FUNDAMENTALS

The ability to compute multiple complex operations simultaneously gives quantum computers great value in applications such as secure information exchange and AI technology, as well as cybersecurity operations and pharmaceutical research.

Qubits undergo quantum gate operations on quantum computers through identical procedures as in standard logic gates. Qubit state manipulation gates function with specific mathematical symbols, which include Pauli gates along with Hadamard gates, and NOT gates. Petters operate on one qubit, but Compilers influence the states of multiple qubits, allowing gate operations where the input and output qubits stay the same. Quantum computing operations require a full understanding of gates because they enable the execution of parallel processors [7].

Quantum computing depends heavily on quantum circuits to perform operations through their implementation of quantum gates. Reversible computing operation relies on these circuits to build quantum algorithms that solve complex problems with high efficiency. The technology can perform a variety of tasks, such as computations, encryption, and optimization assessments.

The functioning of quantum computing devices depends on the operation of quantum measurement. Scientists can monitor qubit states and explain wave function collapse and Schrödinger's cat by using an observation process that combines analyzers and detectors. Measurements enable the extraction of computation results from quantum systems and complete quantum states [8].

The functionality of a quantum computer is structured across a three-level hierarchy: the application layer, the system layer, and the hardware layer. The Ising model, QUBO problems, quantum neural networks, and hybrid quantum-classical models are among the basic ideas of quantum machine learning that researchers and students studying quantum computing must understand. QML calls for improved quantum hardware development while simultaneously improving deep learning models and traditional AI algorithms [9].

Being able to reach the ultimate level of quantum circuits, gates, and measurements opens the door to quantum computing across a variety of industries.

QUANTUM OPTIMIZATION ALGORITHMS

The creation of quantum algorithms demands a broader understanding than classic programming standards and algorithm requirements. Quantum computers call for the education of fresh mathematicians combined with developers who understand quantum program mathematical reasoning. The algorithms need to show better operational efficiency when compared to classical computer programs and supercomputers. Quantum computation operates through this distinct computational process, which makes experts wonder about the identifiable problems that can now be solved through this method on problems previously beyond traditional computer capacity. The need for such evaluation leads to the examination of complexity theory [10].

Quantum optimization algorithms use quantum mechanics principles to reach better efficiency at solving optimization problems when compared to classical methods. Based on the concepts of quantum entanglement and superposition, the algorithms work to extract quantum computing capabilities. The ability of quantum optimization techniques to solve problems exponentially faster is the subject of research. By exponentially narrowing the search domain to determine the optimal solution, users can find the minimum value of functions using quantum computation structured in several sequential steps [11].

Quantum Annealing

Quantum annealing shows promise for optimization tasks, particularly when dealing with complicated issues. During optimization, quantum properties of coherent tunneling enable the process to take advantage of the discrete Ising variables extracted from continuous domains. The Tensor Network provides an effective framework to implement quantum annealing for the minimization of classical cost functions embedded in neural networks. The perfect coherent quantum annealing replication generated through time-evolving block decimation (TEBD) simulation methods leads to better outcomes compared to usual methods. Symphonic tunneling is an approach for accelerating multi-qubit tunneling despite predicted slowdowns during physical implementation of logical variables [12]. Local AC parameter adjustments do the job for qubits. Quantum hardware could obtain quantum scaling benefits due to emerging new developments in the next several years.

Quantum Approximate Optimization Algorithm (QAOA)

The Quantum Approximate Optimization Algorithm (QAOA) serves as a variational quantum algorithm that solves combinatorial optimization problems through Near-term Intermediate-Scale Quantum (NISQ) computer devices. QAOA follows an ongoing quantum-classical protocol that minimizes cost functions to better optimize quantum devices. Researchers demonstrate that examining local graph characteristics enables QAOA parameters to become transferable across instances, which leads to optimal performance in particular combinatorial optimization conditions. The combination of the relax-and-round methodology across multiple layers showed QAOA to produce superior results than standard algorithms throughout different problem arrays according to laboratory tests. The real-world application of this algorithm encounters implementation challenges in Vehicle Routing Problem applications since it becomes sensitive both to problem data and optimization parameter values [13].

Variational Quantum Eigensolver (VQE)

The VQE hybrid algorithm unites classical operations with quantum hardware to find approximate best solutions of optimization problems. The algorithm provides initial molecular Hamiltonian parameter values, which makes it valuable for quantum chemistry applications. The implementation of gradients creates computational challenges for VQE because gradient-based scaling reduces its overall scalability. The implementation of joint Bell measurements with tensor-ring approximations has made the measurement procedures and classical gradient analysis more efficient. The efficient computational functionality of VQE enables solving difficult combinatorial optimization problems that had no previous available solutions. Research that removes studies concerning performance metrics and programming scenarios, and computer hardware requirements, allows scientists to explore quantum computing applications. The current deficiency of scale and precision in quantum computers makes the VQE algorithm vital due to its technological advantages [14].

The fact that the algorithm generates initial molecular Hamiltonian parameter values makes it outstanding for quantum chemistry applications. VQE faces computational hurdles when gradient implementations are used, since this approach limits its overall potential scalability. Scientists applied joint Bell measurements together with tensor ring approximations to improve the classical gradient analysis process as well as the measurement procedure. VQE provides efficient computational resources that allow it to solve previously unsolvable combinatorial optimization problems. Researchers are still researching applications of quantum computing by looking into hardware requirements, scenario compatibility, and performance evaluation. VQE's computational value makes it an essential algorithm due to the qubit count and quantum gate quality limitations of modern quantum computers [15].

Industry and academia work together to create numerous quantum computing platforms and simulators in order to address existing problems and release the potential benefits of quantum computing methods. Error mitigation represents a key need for noisy quantum computers; thus, these simulators devote their attention to developing techniques for state preparation and evolution, and measurement. The development process of quantum algorithms receives assistance from these programs as they help with algorithm validation. Researchers have launched projects to deploy quantum programs on cloud infrastructures through message-passing interfaces to distribute resources while enabling process communication and boosting quantum performance, and accelerate research throughout different fields [16].

Multiple issues prevent the successful conversion of quantum algorithms into quantum hardware or quantum simulators. The complex structure of C2Q data encoding coexists with hardware-effective ansatzes that produce symmetrical energy indentations and vulnerabilities in quantum computers due to inadequate encryption assurance. A practical framework for quantum algorithm emulation uses Quantum Hardware Teleportation (QHT) combined with vital C2Q data encoding methods to deal with these issues. Quantum environments employ emulation techniques that detect hardware boundaries and measure the algorithm vulnerability to noise, thus contributing to hardware-software co-development for quantum system optimizations [17].

APPLICATIONS OF QML IN OPTIMIZATION

Quantum machine learning, which combines machine learning techniques with quantum computers, allows for faster solutions to complicated issues than traditional algorithms. Applications of QML in optimization offer particular benefits since they leverage the concepts of quantum mechanics to solve optimization problems more quickly and with better performance than traditional algorithms. The combination proves vital for optimization problems in large and complex systems, especially since traditional methods become insufficient. The following section outlines explanations at length regarding QML applications in optimization [18].

Combinatorial Optimization Problems

The purpose of combinatorial optimization problems is to discover the top solution within fixed sets of potential solutions. These problems' solutions typically belong to a class of computationally challenging problems, the size of which causes the solution space to grow exponentially. For Example:

- Travelling Salesman Problem (TSP)
- Maximum Cut Problem
- Graph Colouring
- Knapsack Problem

The discovery of optimal solutions for branch-and-bound or greedy algorithms requires large computing power through classical algorithms. QAOA serves as a quantum algorithm component of QML techniques and delivers encouraging advantages [19].

Quantum Approximate Optimization Algorithm (QAOA)

- QAOA combines classical and quantum computing strategies through an algorithm to resolve problems that require solving complex structures. The algorithm uses parameterized quantum circuits whose classical optimization processes optimize cost functions to operate quantum systems for problem resolution.
- The TSP solution becomes possible through QAOA because it utilizes its quantum superposition ability to identify the minimum paths between cities simultaneously while examining routes much faster than traditional heuristic approaches.
- Research shows that QAOA achieves superior results in approaching maximum cut detection problems than conventional classical computing systems do on extensive graph networks.

Continuous Optimization Problems

The aim in continuous optimization challenges is to identify minimum or maximum points from functions containing continuous parameters. Continuous optimization problems span across applications in physics and economics, and the machine learning fields.

Variational Quantum Eigensolver (VQE)

VQE stands out as one of the vital QML methods that initially served quantum chemistry needs while demonstrating potential for solving continuous optimization problems in general. The classical optimization method selects parameters that reduce the cost function of states created by a quantum circuit. This approach led scientists to find various useful applications.

- The VQE system enables users to implement its methods for lowering quantum energy values in Hamiltonian-manifested systems.
- The quantum devices used in VQE achieve better performance than classical gradient descent and enable users to optimize their machine learning model parameters, including neural network weights.

Quantum Support Vector Machines (QSVM)

Support Vector Machines (SVMs) are widely used in machine learning applications for pattern recognition through regression and classification. SVM optimization requires the identification of an optimal hyperplane that secures maximum space between data point classes, and this search represents a convex optimization procedure.

- The Quantum SVM (QSVM) utilizes quantum computing power to address SVM problems through quantum mapping procedures that achieve efficient linear algebra computation. QSVM achieves optimization goals through its combination of quantum feature maps with quantum processors, which handles tasks that classical SVMs would require tremendous computational power to solve, particularly in environments with many features.

Benefits of QSVM in Optimization

- The optimization process of SVM training with large datasets becomes faster because quantum computers provide speedup capabilities.
- The feature spaces of quantum computing represent very high dimensions, which enable QSVM to succeed with complex classification tasks.

MACHINE LEARNING FOR OPTIMIZATION PROBLEMS

QML is currently employed for optimizing machine learning frameworks that handle direct optimization functions. Quantum machine learning models can train to perform optimization functions better than conventional approaches due to their distinct capabilities.

Quantum Reinforcement Learning (QRL)

Agents in reinforcement learning utilize machine learning to make decisions based on environmental interactions, which leads to the acquisition of maximum cumulative reward. The application of RL in optimization enables experts to achieve maximum results in supply chain optimization, as well as portfolio management and dynamic pricing strategies.

Quantum Enhancement of RL

Quantum computing assists reinforcement learning algorithms through quantum enhancement to improve learning speed. QRL demonstrates potential through its ability to represent complex decisions on quantum systems, thus enabling higher speed convergence and better exploration of extensive solution areas.

Optimization of Control Systems

Quantum reinforcement learning enables management organizations to optimize control systems for energy distribution and robotics, and manufacturing processes, seeking better efficiency and cost reduction.

QUANTUM ANNEALING FOR OPTIMIZATION

Quantum annealing functions as a vital QML technique that solves optimization problems. The minimum energy state discovery through adiabatic evolution constitutes the fundamental concept of quantum annealing instead of gate-based quantum computing [20].

D-Wave Systems

The D-Wave quantum computer represents one of the most recognizable instances of quantum annealing systems because it employs the method to resolve combinatorial optimization problems. The D-Wave system is particularly suited for:

Scheduling Problems

Quantum annealing achieves optimization of production scheduling through its applications within scheduling problems.

Ising Model

The Ising Model represents a specific optimization problem, which quantum annealing handles by design, as it enables efficient mapping of systems with interacting variable spins.

OPTIMIZATION IN QUANTUM CHEMISTRY& MATERIALS SCIENCE

Quantum chemistry and materials science heavily rely on optimization to achieve stable molecule and material designs and minimize their energy states while creating advanced materials with desired properties.

Quantum Chemistry Simulations

QML serves to improve molecular structure optimization through VQE algorithm implementations. The quantum algorithms demonstrate application as a tool for

Optimize Molecular Geometries

Quantum speedups make continuous molecular geometry optimizations possible, as these optimizations represent an ongoing optimization task [21].

Materials Design

QLM optimizes the properties of new materials through its ability to examine numerous atomic and molecular arrangements, thus decreasing the requirement for expensive experimental procedures.

QUANTUM-INSPIRED ALGORITHMS FOR CLASSICAL OPTIMIZATION

Despite the unfeasibility of achieving quantum computers at present, quantum-inspired optimization methods have emerged as a solution. These optimization methods adopt principles from quantum mechanics to build up classical optimization methods as better versions of their original designs [22].

Quantum Annealing-based Classical Algorithms

The efficiency of classical computers improves when classical algorithms combine quantum-inspired methods with traditional computational approaches.

Quantum-inspired Neural Networks

Researchers apply quantum-inspired neural networks, which utilize quantum gates for their structure to optimize problems better compared to traditional neural networks [23].

COMPARATIVE ANALYSIS OF QUANTUM OPTIMIZATION ALGORITHMS

A comparative analysis of Quantum optimization algorithms on the basis of their use, strengths, limitations, and real-world applications is tabulated below (Table **1**).

Table 1. Comparison of quantum optimization algorithms.

Algorithms	Main Use	Strengths	Limitations	Real-World Application
Quantum Annealing	Solving complex optimization problems by finding the lowest energy state [24].	- Ideal for combinatorial problems. - Works well on specialized hardware(like D-Wave). - Natural fit for problems like Ising models.	- Less flexible than gate-based systems. - Hardware-specific. - Struggles with scalability for some problems.	- Job scheduling. - Portfolio optimization. - Protein folding.

(Table 1) cont.....

Algorithms	Main Use	Strengths	Limitations	Real-World Application
QAOA (Quantum Approximate Optimization Algorithm)	Solving combinatorial optimization problems using a hybrid quantum-classical approach [25].	- Works on current NISQ devices. - Tunable parameters for performance. - Outperforms some classical methods on specific tasks.	- Needs careful parameter tuning - Performance can vary with problem size. - Sensitive to noise.	- Vehicle routing. - Max-cut problems. - Graph optimization.
VQE (Variational Quantum Eigensolver)	Approximating ground states of molecules and solving continuous optimization problems.	- Good for quantum chemistry. - Hybrid algorithm fits current tech. - Scalable with classical resources.	- Requires many measurements. - Slow convergence for some problems. -Depends on the quality of the classical optimizer.	- Used in drug discovery - Used in material design - Neural network training
QSVM (Quantum Support Vector Machines)	Classification and regression in high-dimensional data spaces.	- Excellent for pattern recognition. - Leverages quantum speedup for large data. - Strong for nonlinear separable data.	- Needs quantum feature mapping. -Data loading (input) still a challenge. - Limited by current hardware.	- Fraud detection. - Used in Image recognition. - Used in Text classification.
Quantum Reinforcement Learning (QRL)	Learning optimal strategies through interactions, using quantum-enchanced learning.	- Faster convergence. - Handles large decision spaces. - Better exploration.	- Complex to implement. - Still under development - Few real-world deployments	- Used in Robotics. - Smart grid control. - Used in Supply chain optimization.

CONCLUSION

Modern quantum computers possess superposition and entanglement characteristics that create the opportunity to transform machine learning technology by accelerating data handling processes. The efficient handling of big datasets by quantum algorithms makes this approach excellent for running applications such as image recognition with optimization tasks, and natural language processing.

The multiple layers of quantum computing infrastructure allow error-free computation through an organized system that executes logical processes and algorithms. The practical implementation of quantum machine learning requires solutions to errors and hardware stability issues, and research advancements that make it ready for widespread adoption in healthcare and drug discovery applications.

Quantum computing continues to advance because industry sectors requiring intense computing power show promise to undergo fundamental changes. The advancement of quantum technology will create opportunities to achieve complex problem solutions that modern computers cannot handle effectively.

FUTURE SCOPE

Quantum Machine Learning (QML) demonstrates strong prospects because of quantum hardware developments and improved machine learning techniques, together with industrial applications, which create its expansion. QNNs bring the promise of transforming deep learning by accelerating its training procedure and enhancing forecast accuracy levels. QML offers strategic advantages to healthcare services and finance operations while providing cybersecurity services and logistics efficiency for businesses. Widespread QML adoption requires successful resolution of present obstacles regarding quantum error correction, noise reduction, and the need for standardized software. Businesses will be able to access quantum power remotely thanks to the combined application of quantum computing with AI and cloud computing technology. The advancement of research will lead QML to transform computing by delivering groundbreaking solutions that existing systems cannot handle.

ACKNOWLEDGEMENTS

The authors of this paper are thankful to Algoma University, Canada for providing infrastructural facilities to complete this research work.

REFERENCES

[1] H. Abdi, and L.J. Williams, "Principal component analysis", *Wiley Interdiscip. Rev. Comput. Stat.,* vol. 2, no. 4, pp. 433-459, 2010. [http://dx.doi.org/10.1002/wics.101]

[2] J. Biamonte, P. Wittek, N. Pancotti, P. Rebentrost, N. Wiebe, and S. Lloyd, "Quantum machine learning", *Nature,* vol. 549, no. 7671, pp. 195-202, 2017. [http://dx.doi.org/10.1038/nature23474] [PMID: 28905917]

[3] S. Chakraborty, S.H. Shaikh, A. Chakrabarti, and R. Ghosh, "A hybrid quantum feature selection algorithm using a quantum inspired graph theoretic approach", *Appl. Intell.,* vol. 50, no. 6, pp. 1775-1793, 2020. [http://dx.doi.org/10.1007/s10489-019-01604-3]

[4] T. Albash, and D.A. Lidar, "Adiabatic quantum computation", *Rev. Mod. Phys.,* vol. 90, no. 1, p. 015002, 2018.
[http://dx.doi.org/10.1103/RevModPhys.90.015002]

[5] P. Wittek, *Quantum Machine Learning: What Quantum Computing Means to Data Mining.* Elsevier: San Diego, CA, USA, 2014.

[6] F. G. S. L. Brandao, M. Broughton, E. Farhi, S. Gutmann, and H. Neven, "For fixed control parameters the quantum approximate optimization algorithm's objective function value concentrates for typical instances," *arXiv preprint arXiv:1812.04170*, 2018.

[7] S.S. Gill, A. Kumar, H. Singh, M. Singh, K. Kaur, M. Usman, and R. Buyya, "Quantum computing: A taxonomy, systematic review and future directions", *Softw. Pract. Exper.,* vol. 52, no. 1, pp. 66-114, 2022.
[http://dx.doi.org/10.1002/spe.3039]

[8] S.M. Gandhi, "Quantum Concepts," in:*Quantum Computing: A Shift from Bits to Qubits*, Singapore: Springer Nature, 2023, pp. 99–113.
[http://dx.doi.org/10.1007/978-981-19-9530-9_6]

[9] K.A. Tychola, T. Kalampokas, and G.A. Papakostas, "Quantum machine learning—an overview", *Electronics*, vol. 12, no. 11, p. 2379, 2023.
[http://dx.doi.org/10.3390/electronics12112379]

[10] D. R. Kale, J. Nalavade, S. Hirve, S. Tamboli, P. S. Randive, and N. Karlekar, "Quantum machine learning algorithms for optimization problems: Theory, implementation, and applications," *Int. J. Intell. Syst. Appl. Eng*., vol. 12, no. 4, pp. 6218, 2024.

[11] P. Rebentrost, M. Mohseni, and S Lloyd, "Quantum support vector machine for big data classification", *Phys. Rev. Lett.,* vol. 113, no. 13, p. 130503, 2014.
[http://dx.doi.org/10.1103/PhysRevLett.113.130503] [PMID: 25302877]

[12] R. Dridi and H. Alghassi, "Homology computation of large point clouds using quantum annealing," *arXiv preprint arXiv:1512.09328*, 2015.

[13] Y. Zhang, and Q Ni, "Design and analysis of random multiple access quantum key distribution", *Quantum Eng.,* vol. 2, no. 1, 2020.
[http://dx.doi.org/10.1002/que2.31]

[14] J. Adcock, E. Allen, M. Day, S. Frick, B. Hinchliff, M. Johnson, S. Morley-Short, S. Pallister, A. Price, and S. Stanisic, "Advances in quantum machine learning," *arXiv preprint arXiv:1512.02900*, 2015.

[15] D. P. DiVincenzo"Two-bit gates are universal for quantum computation", *Phys. Rev. A,* vol. 51, no. 2, pp. 1015-1022, 1995.
[http://dx.doi.org/10.1103/PhysRevA.51.1015] [PMID: 9911679]

[16] K. Wagstaff, C. Cardie, S. Rogers, and S Schrödl, "Constrained k-means clustering with background knowledge", *Proc. Int. Conf. Machine Learning (ICML),* vol. 1, pp. 577-584, 2001.

[17] I. T. Jolliffe, Principal Component Analysis, 2nd ed., New York, NY, USA: Springer, 2011.

[18] Y. Kumar, P. Garg, M.R. Moudgil, R. Singh, M. Woźniak, J. Shafi, and M.F Ijaz, "Enhancing parasitic organism detection in microscopy images through deep learning and fine-tuned optimizer", *Sci. Rep.,* vol. 14, no. 1, p. 5753, 2024.
[http://dx.doi.org/10.1038/s41598-024-56323-8] [PMID: 38459096]

[19] N. Rajendran, R. Singh, M.R. Moudgil, A.V. Turukmane, M. Umadevi, and K.B Glory, "Secured control systems through integrated IoT devices and control systems", *Measurement: Sensors,* vol. 24, p. 100487, 2022.

[20] Y. Cao, G. G. Guerreschi, and A Aspuru-Guzik, "Quantum neuron: An elementary building block for machine learning on quantum computers," *arXiv:1711.11240*, 2017.

[21] S. Lloyd, M. Mohseni, and P Rebentrost, "Quantum principal component analysis", *Nat. Phys.,* vol. 10, no. 9, pp. 631-633, 2014.
[http://dx.doi.org/10.1038/nphys3029]

[22] S. Gupta, M.K. Sharma, R. Singh, and H.A Almashaqbeh, "Rajat, and D. Gangodkar, "IoT Based Multi-Layered Security Network Authentication System Development Using Blockchain Technology Management", *Proc. 2022 2nd Int. Conf. Advance Computing and Innovative Technologies in Engineering (ICACITE)*. Greater Noida, India, 2022, pp. 2234–2238.
[http://dx.doi.org/10.1109/ICACITE53722.2022.9823518]

[23] "R. S, R. Singh, R. Vinoth, and P. Mishra, "An Improved Anomaly Detection in Wireless Sensor Network using Artificial Intelligence Evolving Optimization Tools", *Proc. 2023 2nd Int. Conf. Augmented Intelligence and Sustainable Systems (ICAISS)*. Trichy, India, 2023, pp. 19–24.

[24] B. Wang, Y. Yao, S. Shan, H. Li, B. Viswanath, H. Zheng, and B.Y Zhao, "Neural Cleanse: Identifying and Mitigating Backdoor Attacks in Neural Networks", *Proc. IEEE Symp. Security and Privacy (SP)*. San Francisco, CA, USA, 2019, pp. 707–723.
[http://dx.doi.org/10.1109/SP.2019.00031]

[25] W Hu, "Comparison of Two Quantum Nearest Neighbor Classifiers on IBM's Quantum Simulator", *Nat. Sci. (Irvine Calif.),* vol. 10, no. 3, pp. 87-98, 2018.
[http://dx.doi.org/10.4236/ns.2018.103010]

CHAPTER 6

Quantum-Driven AI: The Intersection of Quantum Computing and Machine Learning Algorithms

Pardeep Tiwana[1,*], **Karan Sood**[1], **Harleen Kaur**[1], **Aman Modgil**[1], **Indu Bharti Jain**[2], **Komal**[1] and **Jagdeep Singh Sappal**[3]

[1] *Department of Computer Science and Engineering, CGC - College of Engineering, Mohali, Punjab, India*

[2] *Department of Law, Maharishi Markandeshwar (Deemed to be University), Mullana, Haryana, India*

[3] *Department of Transport Engineering Deployment, Telus Corporation, Edmonton, Alberta, Canada*

Abstract: Quantum Computing and AI can be integrated in a manner that will boost machine learning by eliminating obstacles presented by ordinary systems. This chapter delves into the relationship between Quantum Computing and Machine Learning, offering a critical examination of how quantum mechanics boosts conventional AI algorithms. The chapter starts by defining the basics of Quantum Computing, *i.e.*, qubits, superposition, entanglement, and quantum gates, and then proceeds to cover the essential principles of Quantum Machine Learning (QML) algorithms like Quantum Support Vector Machines (QSVM), Quantum Neural Networks (QNN), and Quantum Principal Component Analysis (QPCA). The chapter further gives some more details about Quantum-Driven AI and where its applications could be (in the medical sector, in finance, in cyber security, and in optimization problems). The advantages of Quantum AI have been discussed earlier, but it has some disadvantages as well, such as a lack of hardware, algorithmic complexities, and even issues regarding the morality of the technology. Lastly, the possibility of Quantum AI and the evolutionary strategy to bring this technology are emphasized. Now, with greater advancements in the physical substrates and new quantum peripherals in the quantum computer, more advanced construction of hybrid quantum-classical models, and more engagement of artificial intelligence in quantum research. People in all fields anticipate quantum mechanics and artificial intelligence to innovate and rejuvenate the industries and sectors they have adopted. This groundbreaking chapter will summarize the nature of Quantum AI to the researchers, experts, and anybody who wishes to venture into the world's next big thing.

* **Corresponding author Pardeep Tiwana:** Department of Computer Science and Engineering, CGC - College of Engineering, Mohali, Punjab, India; E-mail: tiwana07763@gmail.com

Satveer Kour, Harvinder Singh, Anupam Bonkra & Rupinder Singh (Eds.)

Keywords: Artificial neural networks (ANNs), Boltzmann machines, Clustering algorithms, Deep learning, Grover's algorithm, Hybrid quantum-classical models, Noisy intermediate-scale quantum (NISQ), Quantum approximate optimization algorithm (QAOA), Quantum boltzmann machines, Quantum data processing, Quantum feature mapping, Quantum linear regression, Quantum principal component analysis (QPCA), Quantum reinforcement learning (QRL).

INTRODUCTION

AI and ML [1] are some of the most prominent technological trends that have affected almost all sectors, including healthcare, finance, robotics, and cybersecurity, among others [1]. There are various drawbacks related to the classical computing structures, specifically in the fields of optimization and high-dimensional problems with AI models. Quantum Computing (QC)—as the next generation computing technology that performs concurrent computations—has the potential to enhance the computation of AI algorithms, refine algorithms, and solve new problems practically impossible for classic computers [2]. This chapter aims to focus on the combination of quantum computing with conventional Machine Learning, known as Quantum Machine Learning (QML) [3], which is also referred to as Quantum-Driven Artificial Intelligence. This section gives a brief introduction about AI and quantum computing, why there is a requirement for quantum computing in AI, and examines the difficulties that quantum-enabled AI seeks to overcome that are present in classical machine learning.

Overview of AI and Machine Learning

AI is a branch of computer science that deals with the enlargement of intelligent systems that are special in the sense that they are able to do tasks that usually require the intervention of human intelligence. They are as follows: Speech recognition, image processing, decision-making, and lastly, predictive model mapping. There exist various branches of AI; however, Machine Learning (ML) stands out as the most prominent.

Key Components of Machine Learning

Machine learning is categorized into supervised learning, unsupervised learning, and reinforcement learning. Supervised learning involves algorithms that train on labeled datasets for the purpose of making predictions or decisions. A few examples are E-mail spam control, the functionality of which is to classify an E-mail as spam or not, or control, which forecasts sustained values, like stock prices, based on past data achieved, or not. Conversely, in the case of unsupervised learning, the algorithm operates based on unlabelled data, and the goal is to search for some pattern or structure in the data. Some of the ubiquitous practices include customer-related clustering, which can be utilized to group customers who have analogous behavior, and dimensionality reduction methods that can be utilized to minimize the diversity of input features, like PCA [4]. Finally, reinforcement learning relies on models training themselves to respond in order to learn the optimal cumulative rewards in an environment. This is very popular in Robotics, Autonomous systems, and games; some famous applications are AlphaGo and OpenAI Gym [5].

Quantum Computing Introduction

Quantum computing is a novel way to execute the calculations that are challenging or even impossible for traditional computers to carry out. As compared to classical computing depends on bits that can be 0 or 1, quantum computing is based on the utilize of qubits and the superposition ability, which allows the qubit to be both 0 and 1 at the same time. In computation, quantum computing uses qubits, whereas classical computing employs bits. In contrast, qubits can be 0, 1, or a value between 0 and 1, or any other value simultaneously, because of superposition. Another phenomenon is the coupling whereby two or more qubits are inescapably coupled in a manner that they get affected when the other one is, irrespective of the distance between them. This is due to the fact that it provides huge amounts of parallelism through parallel computation and data transfer. Also, in contrast to classical computers, quantum computers utilize quantum gates, which are unitary operators unlike AND, OR, NOT-type gates found in classical computers [6].

Need for Quantum Computing in AI

As AI models grow in complexity, they demand higher computational power, faster optimization techniques, and improved accuracy. Quantum Computing offers several advantages that make it a potential game-changer in AI:

Speeding Up Computation

Grover's search algorithm and Shor's factorization algorithm are two paradigmatic examples to describe how quantum computers may be significantly more powerful than classical computers [7]. This acceleration is crucial for training, deep learning models, and tackling difficult combinatorial optimization problems.

Enhancing Data Processing in High-Dimensional Spaces

Contemporary quantum systems are capable of handling data in an exponential number of dimensions in the Hilbert space over traditional systems, which is computationally more efficient in solving high-dimensional problems in ML.

QPCA is a quantum algorithm that assists in the solution of the dimensionality reduction problem far faster than a traditional method.

Improving Model Optimization

Quantum optimization methods, including Quantum Approximate Optimization Algorithm (QAOA) and Variational Quantum Eigen solver (VQE) [8], can assist in enhancing AI model efficiency by optimizing loss functions in machine learning tasks better than traditional optimizers.

FUNDAMENTALS OF QUANTUM COMPUTING FOR AI

The new method of computing is Quantum computing, which will make use of the quantum mechanics principles to resolve troubles that are challenging for conventional computers. It is necessary to understand these basics in order to see how quantum computing can be included with AI. Conventional computability retains data in bits that are digits of 0 and 1 [9]. Quantum bits or qubits, on the other hand, can be in a superposition of 0 and 1 simultaneously due to the laws of quantum mechanics. A visual representation of superposition, highlighting how qubits can be in an amalgamation of $|0\rangle$ and $|1\rangle$ states, is provided below (Fig. **1**).

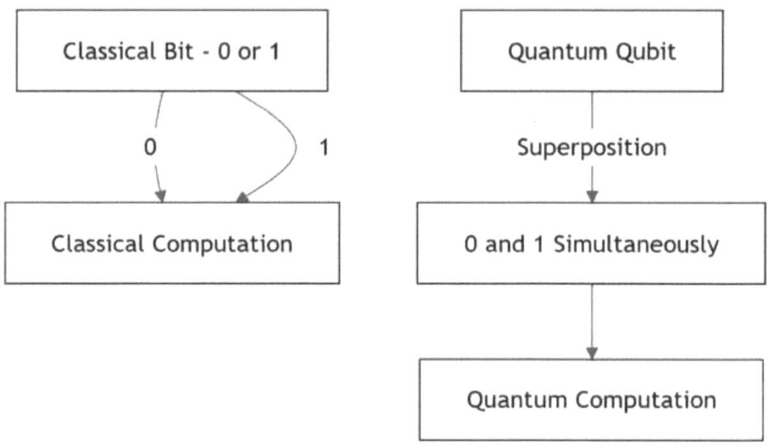

Fig. (1). Visualizing superposition in quantum computing.

Quantum Entanglement and Parallelism

Entanglement refers to a situation where two or more qubits are rendered to be strongly correlated, and the state of one qubit will be dependent on the status of the other, independent of the distance separating the two qubits. Entanglement binds two qubits in a way that is illustrated here (Fig. **2**), regardless of the distance that is between them.

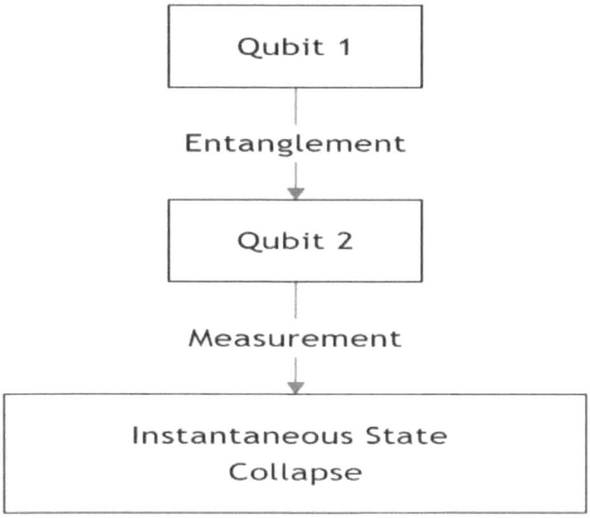

Fig. (2). Entanglement: Correlation between two qubits.

Entanglement is significant in Quantum AI because it allows computations to occur more rapidly and with greater efficiency than in classical systems. While in classical computing, ones and zeroes are processed one by one, whereas entangled qubits are able to exchange data at once and can work all at once. This parallelism significantly increases the speed at which compounding and computational tasks take place, greatly improving the rate of data processing. Moreover, it will also strengthen the machine learning field, as entanglement is making respective patterns and optimization of algorithms more effective. With the help of entangled qubits, AI systems can search for solutions in a larger space, which makes these systems more accurate and efficient in problems related to classification or recommendation systems, or decision-making systems.

Gates and Circuits of Quantum

Quantum gates are a part of quantum circuits and are analogous to the classical gates as they introduce a quantum phenomenon about superposition and entanglement [10]. Unlike other types of gates in the previous examples that performed irreversible operations on a bit, the quantum gates perform reversible operations on a qubit to enable more and multiple operations to be done at the same time. The primary gates include the Hadamard gate, which places a qubit in a superposition of $|0\rangle$ and $|1\rangle$, and the one- and two-qubit Pauli gates, which perform rotations around the X, Y, and $ axes of the Bloch sphere. The CNOT gate is a two-qubit gate that is used in entanglement and performs specific operations by turning the target qubit depending on the state of the control qubit.

Next, there is the Toffoli gate that has no direct quantum analog, but it is an extension of the AND gate, useful in the creation of other quantum circuits. These gates are combined in such a way to form circuits that define or constitute a quantum computer in order to perform the most complex calculations. These circuits are especially important in Quantum AI, as they work on info in ways totally different from how a traditional neural network does and resolve issues in machine learning and statistics much faster.

Quantum Computing *vs.* Classical Computing

A comparison of key features of classical and quantum computing, highlighting advantages such as parallel processing and reduced memory requirements in quantum systems, is tabulated below (Table **1**). As seen in the table, quantum computing recommends significant improvements in algorithm efficiency and optimization problem-solving compared to classical methods.

Table 1. Quantum and classical computing: A performance metrics comparison.

Feature	Classical Computing	Quantum Computing
Data Representation	Uses bits (0 or 1)	Uses qubits (0 and 1 in superposition)
Processing Power	Sequential processing	Parallel processing
Memory Requirement	Large for complex problems	Exponentially lower for large datasets
Algorithm Efficiency	Polynomial or exponential time	Potentially exponential speedup
Optimization Problems	Computationally expensive	Solved efficiently with quantum speedup

QML (QUANTUM ALGORITHMS OF MACHINE LEARNING)

Quantum Machine Learning (QML) leverages quantum principles to enhance traditional AI models. These algorithms provide faster computation, better pattern recognition, and efficient data processing [11]. As shown below (Fig. **3**), quantum machine learning integrates quantum computing principles to enhance data processing and model training efficiency.

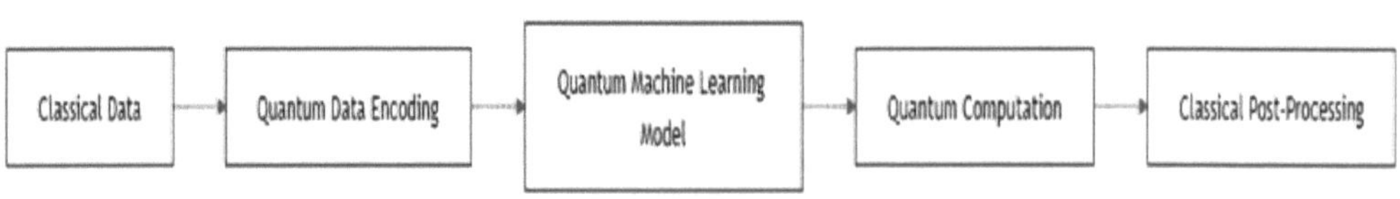

Fig. (3). Quantum machine learning processing workflow.

QSVM (Quantum Support Vector Machines)

SVMs are widely used in classical AI for classification and regression tasks. Quantum SVM (QSVM) enhances this approach by using quantum kernels for feature mapping in high-dimensional spaces [12]. A list of common quantum AI algorithms along with their applications, showcasing how these techniques are utilized in areas such as optimization, classification, and simulation, is tabulated below (Table **2**).

Table 2. Common quantum AI algorithms and their applications.

Quantum AI Algorithm	Application Area
Quantum Support Vector Machines (QSVM)	Image recognition, anomaly detection
Quantum Neural Networks (QNN)	Deep learning, robotics, pattern recognition
Quantum Principal Component Analysis (QPCA)	Data compression, feature extraction
Variational Quantum Algorithms (VQA)	Optimization, machine learning, quantum chemistry

QSVM is a new generation machine learning algorithm that is an improvement on the classical Support Vector Machine, applying quantum computations [13]. In the original implementation of SVMs, data is transformed into a higher dimensional to achieve wider margins between classes; this brings in a large computational cost, especially on large datasets. QSVM solves this problem with the help of quantum kernels that enable the computation of such high-dimensional feature spaces much faster than classical manner. Due to this, it performs faster than a traditional machine learning algorithm in terms of time required to classify a large and slightly complicated dataset, computation of high-dimensional data, and, most importantly, the training and prediction phase experiences a quantum leap. Because of these advantages, QSVMs are considered for multiple highly important real-life use cases, which include Quantum Mechanical interlope fraud systems in the finance sector, enhanced diagnosis and image technologies, quantum Cybersecurity threat detection systems, *etc*. QSVM has the foreseeable ability to reinvent several business lines through the utilization of quantum computing.

Quantum Neural Networks (QNN)

Quantum Neural Networks (QNNs) are advanced artificial models, which are base on the principles of quantum neural networks that originate from classical neural structures [14]. Unlike other neural network models that employ artificial neurons and normal activation functions, QNNs make alterations in terms of qubits and quantum gates. This parallelism helps the QNNs to learn and optimize the circuits expeditiously than the classical models. Consequently, QNNs have several benefits, for example, in the training of deep learning models, generalization, and other aspects of large-scale problems within the realm of AI optimization.

QPCA (Quantum Principal Component Analysis)

PCA is the subsequent well-known technique of analyzing the huge informative data so as to reduce its dimensions, bringing out key variables to the topmost relevance. However, classical PCA is not suitable for large data sets since it may require a lot of computations. For this goal, Quantum PCA or QPCA provides a much more effective approach based on the employment of a quantum computing solution [15]. As for QPCA is therefore capable of calculating eigenvalues of comparable efficiency using quantum phase estimation rather than conventional methods. QPCA contributes to a faster selection of features, a more efficient handling of big data torrents, and higher speeds of training deep learning models. These advantages make QPCA the next suitable application in industries such as quantum analytics for data analysis, large model training in machine learning, and tweaking clustering and classification algorithms within large data sets. By means of QPCA, organisations can get the most from massive arrays of data much faster and at comparatively shorter times.

AI Variational Quantum Algorithms

VQAs stand as one of the most exciting multi-modal quantum computing techniques that leverage both quantum and classical computing to enhance the performance of complicated machine learning methodologies for solving challenging problems [16]. VQAs use quantum circuits as computational steps and adapt the quantum circuit parameters with classical optimization for operations. On the other hand, QAOA is anticipated to address the combinatorial optimization challenges like those that are prevalent in artificial intelligence, logistics, and operations research. VQAs are important as they offer a window through which present quantum technologies may surpass classical means, particularly when solving NP-hard problems that would otherwise be very time-consuming by traditional means.

APPLICATIONS OF QUANTUM AI

Quantum AI has the impending to revolutionize multiple industries by leveraging quantum computing's capability to process enormous amounts of data, optimize complex problems, and accelerate machine learning algorithms. This section explores key application areas where Quantum AI is making a significant impact. Quantum AI is being adopted to solve real-world challenges, from risk analysis to drug discovery and supply chain optimization (Table **3**).

Table 3. Industry applications of quantum AI.

Industry	Quantum AI Use Case
Healthcare	Drug discovery, genetic analysis, and diagnostics
Finance	Fraud detection, portfolio optimization
Cybersecurity	Quantum encryption, threat detection
Logistics	Route optimization, smart traffic systems
AI Research	General AI advancements, AGI potential

Quantum AI in Healthcare and Drug Discovery

One of the emerging issues affecting the healthcare and pharmaceutical industries involves the analysis of enormous volumes of biological data, such as structures of molecules, patients' characteristics, and the interactions between drugs. Other traditional approaches in AI require significant computational power to perform such tasks to the best ability. Quantum AI contributed much towards a better way of handling this data by making it possible to process large datasets on a much faster scale, and as a result of this, improving the research and development processes. Moreover, one of the successful implementation areas is drug discovery and molecular simulations, where Quantum AI will help to enlarge the speed and accuracy of protein folding and molecular dynamics, helping with speeding up the process of drug development. In personalized medicine, the quantum-powered AI models can really delve into the basis of genetic differences and come up with highly sensitive treatment plans for patients. Moreover, Quantum AI is critical in medical diagnosis, whereby it enhances the identification of patterns in images of MRI scans, radiology images, and early markers of cancer, among others, resulting in early and accurate diagnosis. One specific example of such organizations using Quantum AI is a partnership between Google and Pfizer; this is because the two firms are using quantum algorithms to model molecules, in an attempt to discover better drugs in the shortest time possible. This has definitely taken a new dimension in how Quantum AI is revolutionising the forwardality of the healthcare and pharmaceuticals sector.

Quantum AI in Financial Modelling

Artificial intelligence is used more and more as an essential tool to analyze credit risk, fraud, or portfolios in the financial industries. But the complexity, along with large and massive data sets involved in these tasks, can prove to be computationally intensive for traditional AI models. This enables Quantum AI to deliver a revolutionary jump in the way such challenges are addressed by rapidly and effectively leveraging quantum computing in processing Big Data in parallel. Quantum risk analysis is one of the fundamental applications where financial institutions can model market behavior at unprecedented speeds to forecast potential risks and returns with increased accuracy. In detecting fraud, quantum-boosted AI models are particularly good at detecting anomalies in big data of transactions, enhancing the efficiency of fraud prevention systems. Quantum AI also greatly boosts portfolio optimization by considering several financial assets at once and determining the best investment strategy, which would be extremely time-consuming using traditional methods. One strong example of such innovation is active investment by the likes of top financial behemoths Goldman Sachs and JPMorgan, which are using quantum machine learning to deliver better financial prediction, risk assessment, and decision-making powers. As quantum computing develops further, its part in transforming the financial sector will only increase.

Quantum AI in Cybersecurity and Cryptography

As cyber threats become more sophisticated, Quantum AI is transforming cybersecurity by enhancing encryption and intrusion detection systems [17]. The impact of Quantum AI on cybersecurity, showing its role in both enhancing encryption methods and posing new security challenges, is presented below (Fig. **4**).

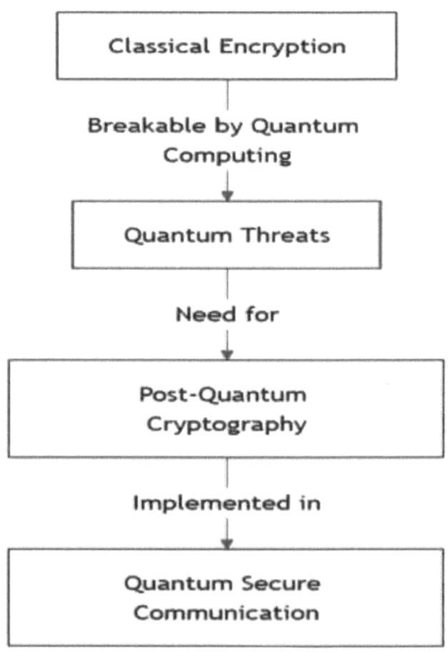

Fig. (4). How quantum AI impacts cybersecurity.

- Quantum cryptography helps to achieve high levels of confidentiality through the use of QKD to add immense security [18], beyond the reach of interceptors. Quantum cryptography makes use of the laws of quantum theory, especially QKD, to implement cryptography keys that cannot be intercepted without being detected. Compared to other encryption processes, QKD guarantees that any attempts to intercept the key will definitely terror the quantum system which is being used for the transfer. This makes it very valuable to sectors such as the military, banking, and governance since it acts as a shield of confidentiality and integrity of communication.
- AI based on advanced quantum computing technologies helps to identify threats instantly, analyzing small portions of cyber attack data as compared to conventional methods. Quantum computing with machine learning for cybersecurity allows a system to analyze data and gain insights in a single cycle. The same makes it possible for organizations to identify intricate and dynamic cyber-attack patterns in real-time, hence enabling the organization to respond to the threats in the shortest time possible and mitigate the risks of damage. Quantum computing improves on machine learning by staying ahead of existing problems by quickly recognizing new signatures of malware, ransomware, and all kinds of complications.
- Players in big tech, such as IBM and Google, are currently investing resources into quantum-safe cryptography in order to avoid security issues caused by an upgrade in technology. IBM and Google are two companies that are currently undertaking research in developing new algorithms and strategies with regard to encryption in the next-generation quantum computer. These efforts include designing and testing algorithms under the post-quantum cryptography framework and collaborating with global security organizations to future-proof data privacy and protection strategies. Their work is crucial in ensuring that the digital world remains resilient against the disruptive capabilities of quantum computing.

Quantum AI for Optimization Problems

There are many application areas, such as cluster and supply chain, logistics, optimization of energy consumption, and smart cities. The known classical optimization methods are not efficient in terms of time and data volume, while Quantum AI has exponential efficiency rates.

- **Traffic and Logistics Optimization:** Through quantum AI, individuals and companies are now able to cope with the complex problems in transport and logistics in cities. Due to the fact that quantum computers are adept at processing multiple variables at one time, the actual traffic, the vehicle routes, and the delivery schedule must be more effectively optimized. This cuts the number of vehicles on the roads, shortens the time taken to deliver goods, and decreases fuel consumption. Quantum AI also assists logistics organizations to manage supply chain optimally with a multitude of influencing aspects like demand rates, weather, traffic tie-ups, among others [19].

- **Smart Grid Energy Distribution:** This makes quantum computing crucial in the current advancement of power grids used in energy distribution and load management. Quantum computing also assists power companies in the analysis of electrical power networks where electricity is required at various points in real-time [20]. This cuts losses, lowers the energy expenses, and also encourages the usage of renewable sources of energy.
- **Manufacturing Process Optimization:** AI-driven models are supplemented with quantum technologies, such that they are enhancing industrial automation and manufacturing in industries. Quantum AI can target large volumes of data for machinery, production lines, and materials and, thereby, make improvements to productivity, avoid time-consuming interruptions, and save on unnecessary product waste [21]. This leads to more efficient resource allocation in a given organization, in addition to cost-cutting, among other benefits, leading to an overall increase in productivity. In very competitive industries with a high level of automation, quantum computing also promotes quicker decision-making and modification of the production process to adapt to the market and new goals.
- **Case Study Volkswagen:** Volkswagen is one of the best examples of the present use of quantum AI to handle optimization problems [22]. Now it has allied with its suppliers of quantum computing to come up with heuristics for smooth traffic flow in all busy towns. By simulating and analyzing various traffic scenarios using quantum algorithms, Volkswagen has been able to reduce urban congestion, enhance vehicle routing, and cut down on fuel consumption.

CHALLENGES AND FUTURE PROSPECTS

While Quantum AI presents significant opportunities, it also faces major practical, moral, and safety challenges that ought to be tackled for widespread adoption. As presented in Table 4, several technical and practical barriers must be addressed to realize the potential of Quantum AI fully.

Table 4. Challenges hindering the growth of quantum AI.

Challenge	Description
Hardware Scalability	Current quantum computers have limited qubits
Algorithm Complexity	Lack of standard quantum AI frameworks
Error Rates	Quantum decoherence and error-prone computations
Ethical Concerns	Bias, security risks, and ethical dilemmas

Hardware and Scalability Challenges

While quantum computing holds much promise, several constraints prevent it from being widely used in AI and other domains currently. Furthermore, current quantum computers have only a few hundred qubits, whereas viable large-scale AI machines could take millions of qubits to function properly. The low error rates of quantum computations also pose a serious threat because they could compromise the reliability and accuracy of outcomes. One of the main impediments is qubit fragility, which makes them hard to keep stable because they need extremely cold temperatures near absolute zero and are highly prone to external interference and noise. Scientists are also seriously working on solutions like Quantum Error Correction (QEC), where they are attempting to come up with appropriate techniques for diagnosing and correcting quantum errors to mitigate these issues.

Algorithmic Limitations and Complexity

The absence of standardized frameworks and programming tools specifically developed for AI use, and the nascent stage of quantum software development, pose several challenges for quantum AI algorithms. Hybrid quantum-classical AI models, where the computational advantage of quantum systems is merged with the power of classical deep learning, are one such promising area of future investigation. In addition, quantum computing does not enhance all of machine learning, limiting its initial application. Even more robust and scalable quantum AI solutions are made possible by further advancements in open-source quantum AI libraries, such as IBM Qiskit, Google Cirq, and Xanadu's Penny Lane.

Ethical and Security Implications

The development of robust quantum AI ethics norms that ensure the ethical expansion and deployment of these powerful technologies is paramount to resolving these challenges. Protecting sensitive information from cyber attacks facilitated by quantum technology also calls for a massive investment in post-quantum cryptography. Among the serious issues that quantum AI raises are the potential that it will be employed as a cyberwarfare weapon, the potential that it will undermine global data security by breaking conventional encryption algorithms, and the potential that bias and fairness issues will emerge in quantum-powered AI decision-making systems. Quantum artificial intelligence developments in the future can potentially revolutionize the technological landscape. Top technology companies such as IBM, Google, and Microsoft are leading the way by providing Quantum AI Cloud [23] Services, which provide researchers and companies with access to Quantum AI-as-a-Service platforms. Additionally, combining Quantum AI with initiatives toward developing Artificial

General Intelligence (AGI) may hasten developments in autonomous, self-improving AI systems. Even as Quantum AI is still in its nascent years, the synergy of quantum hardware development, frontier AI algorithms, and cybersecurity technologies is gradually leading us toward actualizing the revolutionizing potential of Quantum-Driven AI. The emergence of the Quantum Internet is expected to enable highly secure quantum networks that will allow for accelerated training of AI models, while Quantum AI for robotics seeks to provide highly intelligent and adaptive robotic systems that can make complex decisions in dynamic situations [24].

CONCLUSION

As quantum computing continues to develop, its assimilation with artificial intelligence is set to redefine computational capabilities, problem-solving approaches, and decision-making processes. This chapter has explored the fundamentals of Quantum AI, its real-world applications, existing challenges, and future prospects. The emerging trends in Quantum AI, such as hybrid quantum-classical algorithms and advancements in quantum hardware, are tabulated below (Table **5**). The evolution of AI driven by quantum advancements, mapping the progression from classical AI to Quantum AI integration, is shown below (Fig. **5**).

Table 5. Emerging trends in quantum AI.

Future Trend	Description
Quantum Cloud [24] Computing	IBM, Google, and Amazon are offering Quantum-as-a-Service
Fault-Tolerant Qubits	Stable qubit designs for reliable quantum computing
Hybrid AI-Quantum Models	Combining classical AI with quantum computing
Post-Quantum Cryptography	Secure encryption for the quantum era

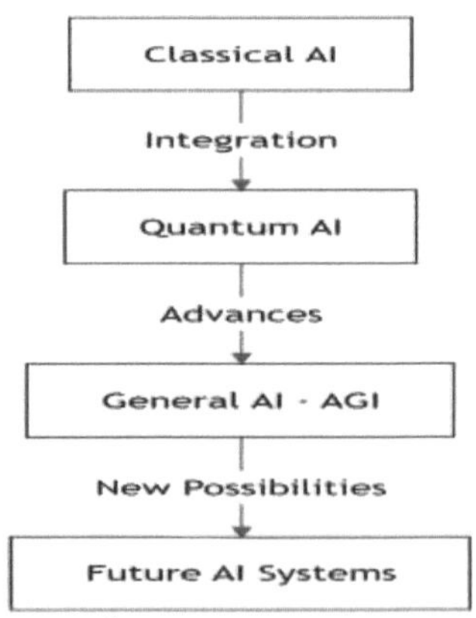

Fig. (5). Evolution of AI through quantum advancements.

Potential of Quantum AI in the Next Decade

More capable quantum hardware is in the pipeline, with players such as IBM, Google, and Rigetti leading the charge by developing quantum processors with a greater number of qubits and lower error rates. Quantum AI will also be anticipated to achieve widespread acceptance in sectors like finance, autonomous systems, materials science, and energy optimization, promoting efficiency and innovation. Further, the ability of quantum computing to tackle complicated, multi-dimensional data in parallel may hasten the advance towards Artificial General Intelligence (AGI), thereby allowing for more advanced, self-improving AI systems to be built. But these developments will introduce vital ethical and security issues, making it imperative to establish post-quantum cryptography and regulatory measures to protect sensitive data from future quantum attacks.

REFERENCES

[1] A. Bonkra, P.K. Bhatt, J. Rosak-Szyrocka, K. Muduli, L. Pilař, A. Kaur, N. Chahal, and A.K. Rana, "Apple leave disease detection using collaborative ML/DL and artificial intelligence methods: Scientometric analysis", *Int. J. Environ. Res. Public Health,* vol. 20, no. 4, p. 3222, 2023. [http://dx.doi.org/10.3390/ijerph20043222] [PMID: 36833921]

[2] S.K. Sood, and Pooja, "Quantum computing review: A decade of research", *IEEE Trans. Eng. Manage.,* vol. 71, pp. 6662-6676, 2024. [http://dx.doi.org/10.1109/TEM.2023.3284689]

[3] Z. Abohashima, M. Elhosen, E.H. Houssein, and W.M. Mohamed, "Classification with quantum machine learning: A survey", *arXiv preprint*, arXiv:2006.12270, 2020.

[4] T. Kurita, "Principal component analysis (PCA)," in *Computer Vision: A Reference Guide*, Springer, Cham, 2021, pp. 1013–1016. [http://dx.doi.org/10.1007/978-3-030-63416-2_649]

[5] A. Bonkra, P. Dhiman, S. Goyal, S. M. Islam, A. K. Rana, and N. Sharma, "An innovative new open computer vision framework via artificial intelligence with Python," in: Proc. Int. Conf. Data Sci. Netw. Eng. (ICDSNE 2023), Agartala, India, Jun. 2023, pp. 95–109, Lecture Notes in Networks and Systems, vol. 791.

[6] G. Jaeger, "Classical and quantum computing," in *Quantum Information: An Overview*, Springer, Boston, MA, 2007, pp. 203–217.

[7] D. C. Youvan, "Quantum Syllogistic Logic in Quantum Computing: Enhancing Shor's and Grover's Algorithms with Logical Entanglement and Probabilistic Inference", 2025. [http://dx.doi.org/10.13140/RG.2.2.18561.16486]

[8] K. Blekos, D. Brand, A. Ceschini, C.-H. Chou, R.-H. Li, K. Pandya, and A. Summer, "A review on quantum approximate optimization algorithm and its variants," *Phys. Rep.,* vol. 1068, pp. 1–66, 2024.

[9] A. Ahmadi, "Quantum computing and artificial intelligence: The synergy of two revolutionary technologies", *Asian J. Electr. Sci.,* vol. 12, no. 2, pp. 15-27, 2023. [http://dx.doi.org/10.51983/ajes-2023.12.2.4118]

[10] C.P. Williams, and C.P. Williams, in *Explorations in Quantum Computing, Texts in Computer Science*, London: Springer, 2011. [http://dx.doi.org/10.1007/978-1-84628-887-6_2]

[11] S. Khurana and M. Nene, "Quantum Machine Learning: Unraveling a New Paradigm in Computational Intelligence," *Authorea*, 2024.

[http://dx.doi.org/10.22541/au.171037552.27623320/v1]

[12] A. Bonkra, A. Noonia, and A. Kaur, "Apple leaf diseases detection system: A review of the different segmentation and deep learning methods", in: *Proc. Int. Conf. Artif. Intell. Data Sci. (ICAIDS 2021)*, Communications in Computer and Information Science, vol. 1673, Springer, Cham, 2022, pp. 263–278.

[13] S.S. Kavitha, and N. Kaulgud, "Quantum machine learning for support vector machine classification", *Evol. Intell.,* vol. 17, no. 2, pp. 819-828, 2024. [http://dx.doi.org/10.1007/s12065-022-00756-5]

[14] M.V. Altaisky, N.E. Kaputkina, and V.A. Krylov, "Quantum neural networks: Current status and prospects for development", *Phys. Part. Nucl.,* vol. 45, no. 6, pp. 1013-1032, 2014. [http://dx.doi.org/10.1134/S1063779614060033]

[15] K. Sudharson, and A. Badi, "A comparative analysis of quantum-based approaches for scalable and efficient data mining in cloud environments", *Quantum Inf. Comput.,* vol. 23, no. 9&10, pp. 783-813, 2023. [http://dx.doi.org/10.26421/QIC23.9-10-3]

[16] T. Felefly, "*Quantum-classical machine learning for brain tumor imaging analysis*," Ph.D. dissertation, Université de Strasbourg; Université Saint-Joseph (Beyrouth), 2024.

[17] S. Singh, and D. Kumar, "Enhancing cyber security using quantum computing and artificial intelligence: A review", *Algorithms,* vol. 4, no. 3, 2024.

[18] M. Imran, A.B. Altamimi, W. Khan, S. Hussain, and M. Alsaffar, "Quantum cryptography for future networks security: A systematic review", *IEEE Access,* 2024.

[19] G. Sanchita and D. Anindita, "Evolutionary algorithm based techniques to handle big data," in *Techniques and Environments for Big Data Analysis*, B. Mishra, S. Dehuri, E. Kim, and G. N. Wang, Eds., Studies in Big Data, vol. 17. Cham: Springer, 2016. [http://dx.doi.org/10.1007/978-3-319-27520-8_7]

[20] Y. Zhou, Z. Tang, N. Nikmehr, P. Babahajiani, F. Feng, T-C. Wei, H. Zheng, and P. Zhang, "Quantum computing in power systems", *iEnergy,* vol. 1, no. 2, pp. 170-187, 2022. [http://dx.doi.org/10.23919/IEN.2022.0021]

[21] N. Soms, S. Kalyani, S. Nagarani, M. Rohini, and S. Oswalt Manoj, "Industrial internet of things and industry 4.0: A learner's perspectives toward quantum technologies," in *Quantum Computing and Artificial Intelligence: Training Machine and Deep Learning Algorithms on Quantum Computers*, P. Raj, A. Kumar, A. K. Dubey, S. Bhatia, and S. Oswalt Manoj, Eds. Berlin, Boston: De Gruyter, 2023, pp. 243–270. [http://dx.doi.org/10.1515/9783110791402-013]

[22] T. Stollenwerk, S. Bhattacharya, M. Cattelan, A. Ciani, A. Galindo, J. H. Jensen, J. K. Krüger, M. Lechner, A. Lubasch, A. Mele, A. Peruzzo, R. Porotti, A. Rocchetto, A. Seidel, and R. Zeier, "Q (AI)^2: Quantum artificial intelligence for the automotive industry," *KI–Künstliche Intelligenz,* pp. 1–9, 2024.

[23] P.S. Tiwana, and J. Singh, "Enhancing multimedia forwarding in software-defined networks: An optimal flow mechanism approach", *Proc. 2024 2nd Int. Conf. Adv. Comput. Comput. Technol. (InCACCT)*. Gharuan, India, 2024, pp. 888–893. [http://dx.doi.org/10.1109/InCACCT61598.2024.10551199]

[24] P.S. Tiwana, Mitigating DDoS attacks: A distributed blockchain-SDN secure IoT system enhanced by artificial neural networks.*Comput. Methods Sci. Technol.* CRC Press, 2024, pp. 467-472. [http://dx.doi.org/10.1201/9781003501244-71]

CHAPTER 7

Comparative Analysis for Human Protein Function Prediction through Machine Learning Techniques and Performance Enhancement Using Quantum Machine Learning (QML)

Sunny Sharma[1,*], **Sandeep Sood**[2], **Palwinder Singh**[3] and **Anil Kumar**[4]

[1] *Department of Computer Science And Applications, Hindu College, Affiliated to Guru Nanak Dev University, Amritsar, Punjab, India*

[2] *Department Computer Science & Engineering, Guru Nanak Dev University, Amritsar, Punjab, India*

[3] *Department of Computer Science and Applications, BBK DAV College for Women, Amritsar, Punjab, India*

[4] *Department of Computer Engineering and Technology, Guru Nanak Dev University, Amritsar, Punjab, India*

Abstract: The technology is evolving quickly, and the immense and complex protein sequence databases are growing every day. To extract information from these huge masses of data, we require sophisticated computational approaches, such as Quantum Machine Learning (QML), which could be rapidly applied for the benefit of humanity. The HPFP (Human-Protein-Function-Prediction) is a crucial study used for the discovery of disease diagnosis, medicines, and crop hybridization. These days, lots of computational approaches are available for HPFP, yet many do not deliver reliable findings rapidly. This research study performed the experiment for HPFP by extracting the dataset from the HPRD (Human-Protein-Reference-Database), the SDFs (Sequence-Derived-Features) from protein sequence are extracted through the proposed HP-SDFES, as well as from some other web-servers. This study utilizes an RF (Random Forest) Machine Learning (ML) classifier for HPFP by extracting SDFs from HPF (Human-Protein-Sequence) and achieved 74.91% accuracy for individual protein class prediction. With improved SDF extractions and in conjunction with input configurations, the prediction accuracy enhances and ranges from 98% to 100% under ideal conditions. This study identifies that RF is the better classifier for HPFP rather than any other ML classifier, and this methodology can be applied similarly to other allied studies for the advancement of humanity, which is also the key finding of this research study. Further, to increase the prediction process speed, the QML approach has been used on RF. Quantum computing improves RF by accelerating feature

* **Corresponding author Sunny Sharma:** Department of Computer Science And Applications, Hindu College, Affiliated to Guru Nanak Dev University, Amritsar, Punjab, India;
E-mail: sunnyshrama05@yahoo.co.in

Satveer Kour, Harvinder Singh, Anupam Bonkra & Rupinder Singh (Eds.)

selection, entropy computations, and decision tree splits. The obtained final result has been compared with the existing benchmarks.

Keywords: Decision tree, Human protein function (HPF), HPRD, Hybrid quantum-classical models, Mutation prediction, Prediction accuracy, Protein function prediction (PFP), Protein-protein interaction (PPI), Random forest classifier, Quantum feature map, Quantum kernel, Quantum machine learning (QML), SDF, ZZFeatureMap.

INTRODUCTION

Although there is a lot of data accessible for research and analysis in the wide field of protein categorization, very little is known about how to interpret it accurately. However, recent studies indicate that one area in which ML faces major challenges is the prediction of protein activity. A thorough compilation of over 65 studies was used to determine that ML approaches are applicable to HPF prediction. Thus, the primary goal of this study is also to identify barriers and viable solutions. A study identifies that ML presents viable answers to a poorly defined field of study and useful tool for examining potential improvements to our current knowledge of proteins [1]. Literature shows that many techniques are available to predict protein functions, but very few efforts have been made to correctly predict the HPF. The researchers who predict the HPFs use some ML approaches, but their performance degraded when the dataset or input configurations increased. This research identifies a gap that necessitates the development of an ML classifier. This classifier must be capable of accurately predicting HPF or classifying the target protein with high speed and accuracy when utilizing huge datasets. It also identifies that for protein classification, the ML prediction approach based on decision trees—particularly RF—is a very transparent and reliable technique. RF makes the chain of computations involved at every level very clear because it employs a white-box technique. Because of this advantage, computational professionals can use it even if they are not very knowledgeable in the area. In a similar vein, it permits a domain expert to closely examine the protocols that a computational expert adheres to. It bridges the knowledge gap between technical proficiency and subject competence. In a Decision Tree (DT), nodes and edges stand for various functionalities at various computing levels. A DT provides the required outputs or results in an easy-t--understand manner among the potential outcomes. It provides an understandable hierarchical presentation of the problem structure and its interpretations, because of the model's unique ability to accomplish a goal while taking into account a range of input factors. The QML processes have further flourished the working of the ML classifiers by increasing their speed, which plays an important role in the prediction. The upcoming sections comprehensively discuss the protein and its classes, the working principles of the Random Forest (RF) algorithm, and the proposed methodology. These sections also present the obtained results and compare them with existing benchmarks.

INTRODUCTION TO PROTEIN

All life on Earth is made up of large, complex building pieces called proteins. They play an imperative role in the organization, functionality, and regulation of the body's tissues and organs. The microscopic building blocks of proteins, called Amino Acids (AAs), are bonded to one another and perform a number of tasks in living cells. Based on the roles that they play, proteins can be divided into numerous groups. For every protein, there are the following groups: transport proteins, structural proteins, hormones, enzymes, storage proteins, immunoglobulin or antibodies, and motor proteins. The twenty various types of tiny units, commonly known as AA's, are aspartic acid, arginine, alanine, asparagine, glutamic acid, cysteine, glycine, phenylalanine, histidine, glutamine, leucine, methionine, isoleucine, serine, lysine, proline, tyrosine, tryptophan, threonine, and valine. The primary form of the protein sequence is created by chaining together 20 different amino acids, which make up a protein [2]. When the amino group (-NH2) of one AA and the carboxylic group (-COOH) of another AA are joined, the Peptide Bond (PB) is formed (Fig. **1**).

$$-NH_2 \quad + \quad -COOH \quad = \quad =\text{-}CONH$$

Amino group (Amino acid 1) | Carboxylic group (Amino acid 2) | Peptide bond

Fig. (1). Peptide bond detail.

To put it simply, an AA forms a PB with another AA to build the long chain of AAs. These peptide linkages are collectively referred to as polypeptides. The AA chain of each protein defines its unique 3D structure and specific function [3].

FEATURES EXTRACTION FROM PROTEIN SEQUENCE

The class of the protein can be predicted using a number of features of the protein sequence. The development of classifiers that predict human protein classes depends on these properties [5]. These crucial traits can be obtained from a particular AA protein sequence using web-based bioinformatics tools. Even though there are numerous feature extraction technologies accessible, none of them are able to extract features from a single platform; instead, different characteristics are extracted utilizing different methods. To ease the laborious process of feature extraction utilizing web-based technologies [9], "Sequence-

Derived-Features-Extraction-Server" (SDFES) is proposed and developed in MATLAB [13]. We verified the accuracy of the features we collected from this server by comparing them with online tools. The suggested methodology lists the various aspects that were taken out of or generated from the sequence. On this one platform, this approach combines all the traits and qualities and yields noteworthy results. Using the given method is quite easy. The results from earlier online tools were used to validate the obtained results, which indicated that SDFES is easy to use, rapid, reliable, and time-saving [7]. The next section discusses the significance of RF in conjunction with SDF integration.

RANDOM FOREST (RF) ML TECHNIQUE

Kam HO first proposed the RF idea, which Adele Cutler and Leo Breiman then developed. This extension creates Decision Trees (DTs) under controlled variance by combining the fundamental concept of bagging with the random selection of attributes [7]. This small bagging tweak decorrelates the trees and reduces variance when averaging the DTs. The RF Classifier is a large set of decorrelated decision trees. The RF is one of the most important and outperforms ensemble algorithms in ML techniques because of its exceptional factor of simplicity and capacity for both regression and classification. The RF algorithm is the mainstay method for supervised classification. Because it may generate a large number of trees, each of which represents a DT's forest, this technique is an extension of bagging. This workhorse's adaptability ensures that even without hyperparameter adjustments, outstanding results are consistently produced. The RF had appreciable results when there were more trees. In this work, the RF classifier primarily uses the PFP optimization to finish the classification task. The RF builds decision trees that have been trained using the bagging technique and then incorporates learning models to obtain noteworthy outcomes. As a result of processing the RF data on the SDF sample, random DT classifiers and ensemble voting for prediction are generated (Fig. **2**).

The "Information-Gain" and the "Gini-Index" computations in DT methods determine the root node of a tree; this is where the RF differs slightly from the DT approaches. The RF looks for the best feature across random subsets of the features, which is how the root node and branching node splitting processes occurred due to randomization. Predictors are always chosen at random for each split in order to develop a DT classifier. That is, the number of predictors chosen at each split is equal to the square root of the total number of predictors. The web-based servers' SDFs and the HP-SDFE Server's data from the provided HPS are used in this investigation. The study loads sampled protein data into ".csv" files, which are then used to partition SDFs into sections. Approximately five to ten sampled protein sequences per protein molecular class are considered for the experimental work. A variety of dataset input configurations are also considered, including "12-classes with 70-sequences employing 34 characteristics/features." An exhaustive inventory of the results from the different settings may be found in the results section. Working through and dividing the RF is specifically shown in Figure 3 below. The training dataset is provided in ".csv" format and is selected from the designated sample dataset. The splitting is based on the sampled dataset, with any errors mentioned. The remaining RF processing detail is depicted below (Fig. **3**). Every SDF is given a relative importance, and the "Gini Index" is computed to find the best node to divide.

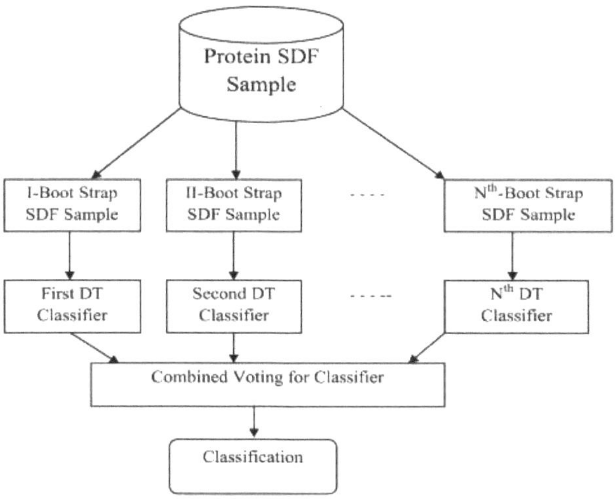

Fig. (2). RF processing on human protein datasets.

FACTORS TO USE RF ON SDF OF HPRD

The rationale behind the use of random forest on the HPRD data set can be understood from the following factors: it is the most accurate classifier, and it performs well on large datasets like HPRD. It can handle a wide range of variables while keeping SDF in mind. It can assign a numerical value to each variable and determine its significance in relation to the classification objective. It has an unbiased internal process for estimating incomplete and inaccurate data. In short, it functions well for both regression during its travel and for a sizable set of unbalanced, decorrelated DTs. Finally, the RF does not over-fit the model even when it contains multiple DTs.

PROPOSED METHODOLOGY FOR HPFP USING RF

The HPFP technique deployed in this proposed work is displayed below. As previously indicated, the dataset was obtained from the HPRD database [5], which contains a wealth of data regarding datasets related to linear protein classes, human disease-gene interactions, and protein-protein interactions. HPRD is the name of the platform that Johns Hopkins University bioinformaticists, software engineers, and biologists developed. It contains fifteen thousand uniquely identifiable items related to proteins and 165 protein classes. Defensin, Heat Shock Protein, DNA Repair Protein, Cell Surface Receptor, Aminopeptidase, Decarboxylase, Water Channel, Nucleotidyl Transferase G-Protein, Acid Phosphatase, Voltage-Gated Channel, and B Cell Antigen Receptor were among the twelve distinct protein classes that were taken into account. The data collection underwent preprocessing to remove the molecular classifications and HPSs. To extract the SDFs/ SD properties [23], the protein sequence files were uploaded to a few different online servers and also to the proposed HP-SDFES. Twelve characteristics were gathered from the various web servers [25], which are listed below (Fig. **4**), while the remaining twenty-three SDFs, which were produced from every protein sequence in every epoch, came from the proposed HP-SDFE server. The detail of all the SDFs is depicted here (Fig. **4**), which are as follows:

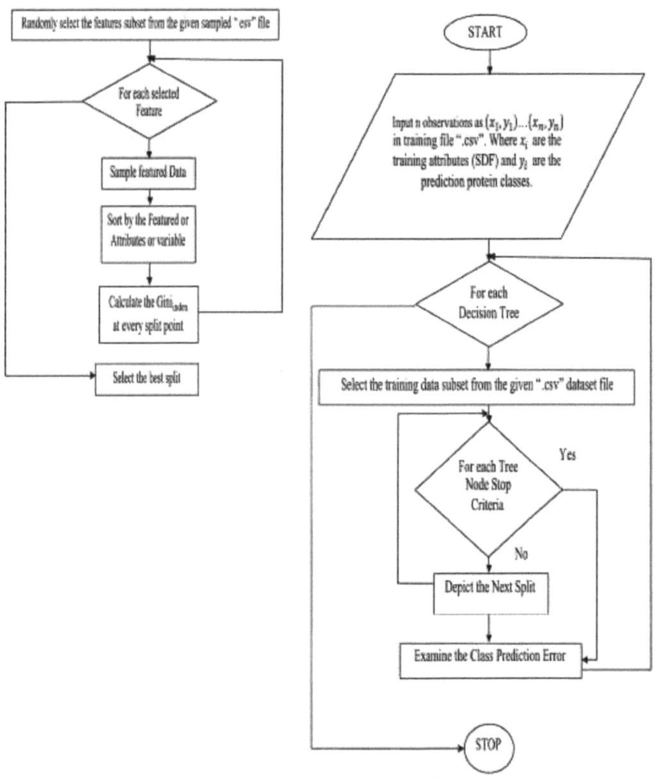

Fig. (3). Spitting criteria and work flow for random forest algorithm.

HP-SDFES Derived Feature		Features extracting using other Web-Servers
- Total No. of AA & Individual idual molecular percentage of each AA with molecular presence	- nneg (negative residues) - npos (positive residues) - molecular weight	- Solubility - exc1 - exc2
- MolepercPolar	- Absorbance	- t
- MolepercNonPolar ıPolar	- Expaa	- s
- MolepercTiny	- Predhel	- ser
- MolepercSmall	- Isoelectric Point PI (computation of IP/MW)	- thr - tyr
- MolepercAliphatic - MolepercAcidic	- aliphatic index	- mean
- MolepercAromatic	- gravy	- d
- MolepercBasic	- instability index	- prob
- MolepercCharged	- Volume	- ProbN
- exc (Extinction Coefficient)	- Atoms CHNOS along with Nucleotide density CODONS	

Fig. (4). Detail of extracted SDFs from human protein sequences.

Once acquired, the SDFs are stored in the database for future use. Numerous input configurations have been supplied and utilized in the experimental work, depending on the features and classes. Examples that were taken into account were "24 SDFs from 70 sequences of 12 classes (24SDFs-70S-12C), 34 SDFs from 58 sequences of 10 classes (34SDFs-58S-10C), and 34 SDFs from 70 sequences of 12 classes (34SDFs-70S-12C)". Additionally, the suggested procedure has been selected for various input combinations. SDFs are put through a filtering process to get rid of extraneous information. The ML-Random-Forest classifier is then fed the dataset in order to predict and train HPF. The RF classifier is trained on 80% of the dataset and tested on the remaining 20%, to identify the functional protein class from an unknown protein sequence; it has been trained and evaluated using a variety of input configurations. The RF classifier significantly outperforms other ML classifiers when it comes to PFP tasks. The primary metric of the complexity of human PFP, prediction accuracy, has been measured more accurately; this study task is carried out with WEKAs on an Intel Core i3 (1.70 GHz) CPU running Windows 10 (64-bit) (Fig. **5**).

METHODOLOGY FOR SPEEDING UP THE PROCESS OF RANDOM FOREST USING QUANTUM COMPUTING

Quantum computing enhances random forests by speeding up feature selection, entropy calculations, and decision tree splits. A hybrid approach (quantum preprocessing + classical inference) balances quantum speedup with classical robustness. The following methodology steps have been used to speed up the process. The details of the methodology are mentioned below.

1. Quantum Encoding of Data
2. Quantum-Assisted Feature Selection
3. Quantum Speedup for Bootstrap Sampling
4. Quantum Decision Tree Construction
5. Hybrid Quantum-Classical Inference
6. Running on Quantum Hardware

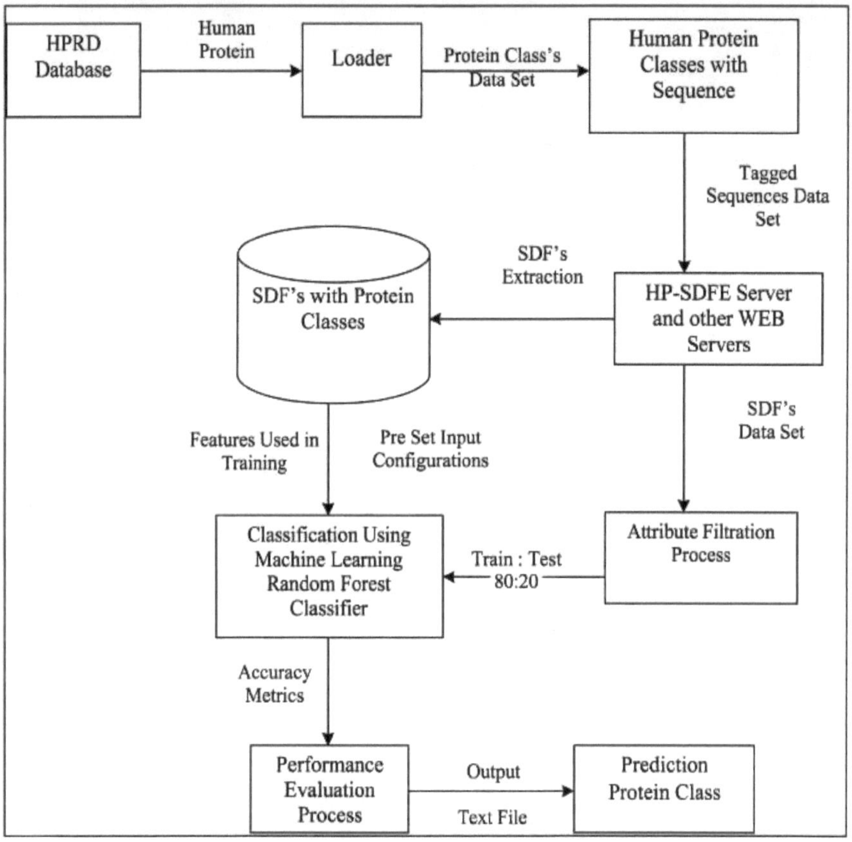

Fig. (5). HPF prediction proposed methodology.

Step-by-Step Implementation

- **Quantum Feature Map:** Convert classical data into quantum states.
- **Quantum Kernel Calculation:** Compute similarity between samples in a quantum-enhanced space.
- **Train Classical Random Forest:** Use transformed quantum features.

The Qiskit's QuantumKernel and Scikit-Learn's RandomForestClassifier libraries have been used for deployment.

Explanation

1. **Quantum Feature Mapping:** Uses a ZZFeatureMap to encode data into a quantum state.
2. **Quantum Kernel Calculation:** Computes similarity between quantum-transformed samples.
3. **Train Classical Random Forest:** Uses the quantum-enhanced kernel for better decision-making.
4. **Evaluate Model:** Measures accuracy on the test set.

LITERATURE SURVEY

Numerous bioinformatics techniques, including data integration, genomics, sequence analysis, structure-based approaches, protein interactions, and more, can be used to characterize proteins. According to a survey, the vector-space incorporation strategy of the data integration method makes a significant effort to predict protein functionalities by using the feature extraction philosophy for both protein functionality prediction and classification. The two areas that present potential outcomes for wide and ill-defined research topics are Rule Mining (RM) and ML. Along with the potential for more research in these areas, this promotes the adoption of ML and RM methodologies. The study shows how different approaches can work better together when they are integrated and can yield encouraging outcomes. The literature demonstrates how these methods can work better together. PTM and LF, or protein modifications and local features of protein linear sequence for a specific class, were used by the authors in 2002 to predict the activities of human proteins. PTMs are changes to the protein that occur at the post-translational phase. Several servers, including Expasy [10], PSORT [11, 12], were used to extract the features [4]. Using protein linear sequence features and the Support Vector Machine (SVM) method, authors categorized protein plants in 2003 and achieved 71% to classify the plants through Surface tension and polarity characteristics [6]. The authors in 2006 gave a presentation on their perceptive views regarding the caliber of PFP. Consistent with his findings, there has been a significant rise in sequence- and structure-related information, leading to an unequal spread in the products of genes that are not portrayed. Understanding the subjective and contextual aspects of protein function is difficult, and methods such as protein-homology-transformation for protein-annotation are making incorrect annotations more common [14]. In 2007 authors published a paper on the linear sequence features and protein prediction using the SVM-ML technique [3]. They also calculated the average GC contents and the proportion of known and unknown proteins. The dataset was divided into four equal-sized parts by the authors, and they ran many experiments on each segment. They use PROFEAT [8] for secondary-structure prediction [15],

DisEMBL for variant areas, and TMHMM for helices. In 2007, human proteins were predicted by authors with IDR due to length and position conditional dependencies. An ML approach was used to estimate the protein activities utilizing weight, charge, and their interdependencies, among other metrics, based on protein sequences [16]. In 2007, data mining experts discussed the significance of association rule mining. As the size of the dataset increased, Apriori approaches' performance decreased [17]. In 2010, researchers proposed an analysis and comparative empirical assessment for classification using association rule mining methods [18]. For data mining association rule and classification tasks, they talked about the importance of prediction rate and runtime factors. They observed that the RIPPER method is slower for classification than the Naïve Bayes & oneR approach [18]. Authors in 2011 provided an example of the significance of clustering and unsupervised learning in protein class prediction [19]. The authors acquired the sequence-based features from their dataset [3] by using web tools after removing the data from the HPRD [20]. Current research uses similar protein categorization based on sequence-based features, and several ML techniques were employed to improve the accuracy. The protein for unwell states can be found using a range of bio-computational techniques, as revealed by authors in 2011. They considered the human MMP family's secondary structure and physicochemical functional analysis. They developed the significance of the SDFs for the physicochemical process and assessed the role of cysteine in medicinal situations [21]. In 2011, authors introduced associative rule mining as a property extraction technique [19]. For this research effort, an improved version of this server was developed, accounting for the quantity of sequences, different characteristics and attributes, and protein classifications. In 2014, it was shown how to predict protein functions from network-based protein interconnectivities using physicochemical factors and emphasized their significance, which prompted further feature discovery [22]. In 2014, researchers and their colleagues documented the benefits of ML techniques for PFP with SDFs and an RF-based algorithm with ‘reliefF’ [22]. As an alternative to the relief parameter, different feature combinations were tried. Researchers used feature-based extraction methods to predict the protein localization structure and its unique functional features in 2015, highlighting a particular class prediction [24]. The improved protein function utilizing SVM, an ML non-linear classification that uses the sequence extracted properties by Protparam at Expasy, was proposed by a study in 2015 [15]. They classify the protein through a Gaussian-kernel-non-linear approach and express the relevance of features retrieved from the sequence. The authors of this study also experimented with several ML methods during our study, and the RF method proved to be more successful. The authors in 2016 demonstrated their prediction by exhibiting gene ontology attributes from a sequence that was obtained from their database using BLAST and HMMER [26].

According to a 2016 study, the most effective computational method for predicting protein function was machine learning algorithms; among its many issues is bias in the currently accessible, inaccurate data that permeates new studies [1]. This article examines the ML configuration parameters from an earlier study by the authors that increased the accuracy of individual class predictions from 70 to 97% without significantly increasing the accuracy of overall predictions. After examining and validating this ML limitation, this study identified ML configuration as a workaround to address the problem. A study in 2017 developed a Cox model and an RF model using colon cancer data (n = 66,807) from the SEER database, and then used the same data to assess the efficacy of each model. With a concordance error rate of roughly 18%, both models perform well [28]. In 2021, researchers created an RF algorithm to accurately distinguish between soft tissue, air, and bone. It seems to have the ability to improve the diagnosis and treatment of MR. They suggest integrating random forest and semantic feature extraction in an auto-context technique to increase the reasonability of the MRI segmentation for MRI-based radiation treatment planning. In 2022, an ML method was created to forecast the likelihood of Acute Respiratory Distress Syndrome (ARDS) after heart surgery [27]. According to their findings, an ML system can predict ARDS in patients having cardiac surgery with a high degree of accuracy. They successfully implemented the RF-ML method using 1011 patient data, identifying 53 ARDS episodes that occurred within the first week following surgery. Their 95% accuracy could help guide therapeutic judgment and enhance patients' long-term prospects [29]. On the other hand, Quantum Machine Learning (QML) these days plays a very crucial role in speeding up the prediction processes. Specifically, QML can dramatically accelerate the prediction speed of the Random Forest algorithm. While classical random forests are based on decision trees, quantum computing offers ways to enhance their performance. One of the first books on QML was written in 2014, in which detailed knowledge on quantum computing basics and its practical examples is given. It covers fundamental concepts of quantum mechanics and computing, followed by discussions on quantum-enhanced ML algorithms such as quantum kernels, variational quantum classifiers, and quantum neural networks. Using Python-based frameworks like Qiskit and PennyLane, the authors demonstrate real-world applications, enabling readers to develop hybrid quantum-classical models. For researchers and practitioners wishing to investigate the benefits of quantum computing in speeding up ML tasks, especially in fields requiring intricate optimization and pattern recognition, this work is an invaluable resource [43]. In 2019, authors introduced quantum-enhanced feature spaces, demonstrating how quantum kernels can improve supervised learning. The paper proposes a Quantum Kernel Estimation (QKE) method, where data is mapped into a high-dimensional Hilbert space with the help of quantum circuits, enabling better separability for classification tasks. The authors show that quantum feature maps can outperform classical methods on certain datasets, highlighting the potential of quantum computing in machine learning [45]. Another study in 2020 introduced Circuit-Centric Quantum Classifiers (CCQCs), a novel approach to supervised learning that leverages Parametrized Quantum Circuits (PQCs) for classification tasks. The paper explores how quantum feature embeddings and trainable quantum gates can be used to construct classifiers with potential quantum advantage. The authors demonstrate that CCQCs can efficiently learn decision boundaries in high-dimensional feature spaces, outperforming classical models in certain cases. This study provides a foundation for hybrid quantum-classical ML, emphasizing the role of quantum circuits in enhancing pattern recognition and classification tasks [44]. In 2021, a study presented a practical guide to Quantum Machine Learning (QML), covering both theoretical foundations and real-world applications in science and industry. The book emphasizes hybrid quantum-classical models, using frameworks like Qiskit and TensorFlow Quantum for implementation [47]. In 2022, researchers provided a concise introduction to QML, tailored for engineers and signal-processing researchers. The work bridges quantum computing principles with ML techniques, focusing on practical applications and algorithmic insights [46]. In 2022, authors provide a comprehensive review of QML developments, highlighting key advancements in algorithms, hardware, and applications. The paper explores quantum advantages in data processing and discusses challenges in scalability and implementation [48]. A discussion of the results based on this RF classifier on several input configurations is presented in the next section.

RESULTS AND DISCUSSION

Based on a dataset derived from HPRD [20], the experiments were carried out with varied numbers of 20, 24, and 34 features. The features were retrieved from 58 and 70, 99, 111, and 119 human protein sequences of 12 protein classes, respectively, and used as input configuration for analysis on Weka. Five extra features, most notably solubility, mean, and absorbance, were added to an upgraded dataset that was put into WEKA [30] and demonstrated potential for improving the ML method known as RF in the field of protein classification. The WEKA dashboard shows lower and higher ranges of SDFs. The Statistical analysis of the HPFP based on different input configurations, *viz.* K-statistics, RMSE, PRC AREA, ROC AREA, TPR, and FPR are listed below (Table **1**). The results clearly illustrate that the root mean square error reduces when SDFs increase, similarly with the increase of SDFs the TPR and ROC Area also increase.

Table 1. Random-forest ML classifier performance using different input configurations.

Random Forest Results on HPS Input Configurations			K-Statistics	RMSE	PRC AREA	ROC AREA	TPR	FPR
Classes	Sequences	SDF's						
10	58	20	0.6549	**0.23**	0.716	0.91	**0.69**	**0.036**
10	58	24	0.6167	**0.2268**	0.745	0.906	**0.655**	**0.038**
10	58	34	0.6742	**0.2293**	0.729	0.909	**0.707**	**0.033**
12	70	20	0.5323	**0.2234**	0.634	0.889	**0.571**	**0.04**
12	70	24	0.5324	**0.2188**	0.681	0.906	**0.571**	**0.04**
12	70	34	0.6104	**0.2238**	0.663	0.904	**0.643**	**0.033**
12	99	34	0.7177	**0.2089**	0.769	0.93	**0.747**	**0.028**
12	111	34	0.7187	**0.2079**	0.77	0.93	**0.74**	**0.027**
12	119	34	0.6595	**0.2052**	0.77	0.931	**0.749**	**0.028**

The graphical abstract shows that RMSE and FPR reduce with an increase in the number of classes and SDFs. Below (Fig. **6**) are the comparative results of different input configurations based on different statistical analyses, which are as follows:

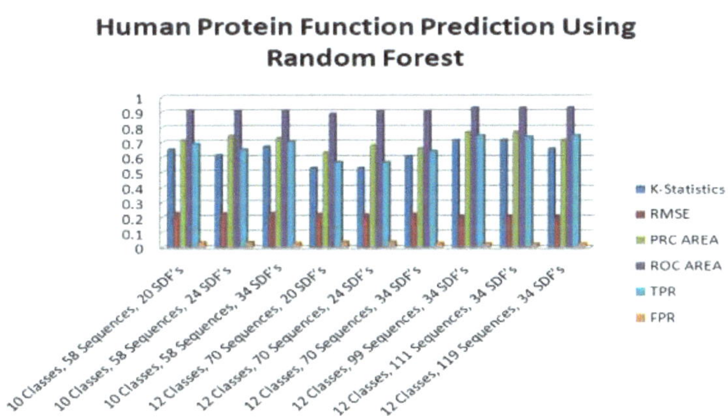

Fig. (6). HPF prediction statistical analysis for Random Forest for different input configurations.

The accuracies produced by the RF on "different-input-configurations" are listed below (Table **2**), which demonstrates how the prediction accuracy for HPFP rises as the number of features and sequences grows.

Table 2. Random-forest ML classifier accuracies.

HPS Input Configurations			Random Forest Classifiers' Accuracies
Classes (C)	No. of Sequences (S)	Sequence Derived Features (SDFs)	
10	58	20	68.96
10	58	24	65.52
10	58	34	70.69
12	70	20	57.14
12	70	24	57.14
12	70	34	64.29
12	99	34	74.75
12	111	34	74.91
12	119	34	74.91

The graphical illustrations for the achieved accuracies based on the "input-configurations" have been depicted below (Fig. **7**). The results clearly show that when the number of sequences and the classes with enhanced features are supplied to the random forest ML classifier then its accuracy increases.

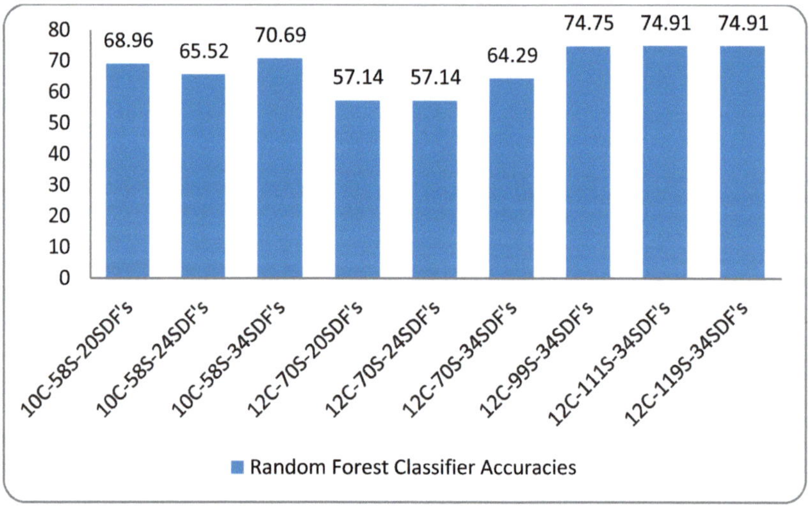

Fig. (7). Random forest classifier accuracies.

We also know that Auto Weka can manage missing values in the input dataset by cross-checking the effectiveness of the aforementioned outcomes in a controlled environment. The input protein datasets were subjected to controlled analysis under the following parameters: 125 seed parallel processes, a time limitation of 15 minutes, and a memory limit of 1024 MB. There is documentation of the dataset configuration mean over multiple epochs. The RF result exhibits perfection, with the maximum accuracy ranging between 98.27 and 100%. The table below shows the average results for each of the several epochs. In a controlled environment, the RF classifier took 0.078 seconds to train, and its estimated error rate was 0.0143%. Of the cases, 1.43% were incorrectly classified and 98.57% were correctly identified. Using the supervised attribute selection "CfsSubsetEval" filter to predict protein function, preprocessing for attribute selection was done while finishing the experimental task. The "CfsSubsetEval" method chooses the six best attributes—exc1, PI, mean, predhel, moleperc Acidic, and Expaa—among the 34 SD characteristics. Along with an accuracy and F-measure of 0.986, an FPR of 0.001 was noted. The results of the optimization procedure—together with the word CFS_RF, which stands for both CFS (CfsSubsetEval) and Random Forest (RF)—is shown below (Table **3**).

Table 3. Random-forest ML classifier performance evaluation under controlled environment for HPFP.

Classifiers	Time Taken	Correctly Classified	Incorrectly Classified	Accuracy TPR	Accuracy FPR	Precision	F-measure
CFS RF	.078	98.57	1.43	.986	.001	.986	.986

As the number of SDF configurations rose from 20 to 34, the previously reported result in tables shows how successfully the random forest performed the experimental task of forecasting HPF, with improved accuracies ranging from 98.27 to 100%. This improvement in prediction shows how enhanced SDFs contribute to the RF-ML approach proportionately.

ACCURACIES BENCHMARKS OF PROTEIN FUNCTION PREDICTION CLASSIFIERS

The human genome is used by the existing approaches and their optimizations to leverage machine learning techniques such as decision tree approaches; these approaches have been used by researchers over the last few decades in approaches such as C4.5, C5 with their SDF packages, SVM and KNN, *etc.*; the researcher used very limited ensemble-based approaches, whereas ensemble approaches perform the prediction task more effectively; the obtained results of RF with CFS are compared with the existing approaches/Benchmarks of the protein function prediction with different classification techniques; the summary of the benchmarks for protein function prediction on various types of protein databases using ML techniques in terms of prediction accuracies is tabulated below (Table **4**).

Table 4. Benchmarks accuracies of different classifiers for protein-function-prediction.

Sr. No	Protein Database and Classification Approach	Description
1	M. tuberculosis and E. Coli Protein, C4.5 Decision Tree	A study in 2000 created algorithms that forecast the functional class of proteins even in the absence of an identifiable sequence. They predicted rules with 65% accuracy [31].
2	Putative Proteins, C5	In 2001, the authors of a study applied data mining techniques to predict the functional class of a protein based on its sequence. They achieved 85% accuracy [32].
3	Plant Protein BRENDA GPCRDB, SVM	The SVM techniques were used by the authors in 2003 to do functional categorization from the primary sequence. They achieved 80% accuracy on average [6].
4	Enzymes, SVM	Instead of using techniques based on sequence similarity, the enzyme data was classified in 2004 by authors with the aid of statistical learning models like SVM. They achieved 72% accuracy [33].
5	Plant Protein, SVM & KNN	Categorized the plant protein data using statistical learning models such as KNN and SVM. The authors achieved 71.4% accuracy in their task [34].
6	Yeast Genome, Plant Protein, C 4.5	Utilizing data mining techniques and the C4.5 algorithm, the yeast genome plant protein data was classified in 2006 by the authors. They achieved 89.38% accuracy on average [35].
7	HPRD, SDF Packages & C4.5	The authors in 2007 used SDF Packages to classify proteins with the aid of the C4.5 algorithm. The authors achieved 72% accuracy for protein classification [36].
8	PDB, SVM	In 2008, a study used SVM to predict the catalytic residue based on sequence and structural features to predict the function of the protein. They identified the accuracy to be 88.6% [37].
9	Ftp MIPS, NNA	The researchers introduced the Gene Encoding (GE) technique, which used the Network Neighbor (NNA) method to estimate the functional class of a protein based on its sequence. They achieved 75% accuracy on average [38].
10	UniProt, KNN	The authors in 2011 suggested a prediction for protein interaction data based on the KNN approach. They achieved 64% accuracy [39].
11	HPRD, C5	The researchers suggested the protein function methodology in 2011 with the use of a C5 algorithm and a decision tree approach. They achieved 83% accuracy [19].
12	Protein-Yeast, KNN & SVM	The authors utilized feature vectors to predict protein function in 2012 using KNN and SVM. They achieved 88.53% accuracy [40].
13	Protein-Protein Interaction, CombFunc with SVM	The researchers and their co-authors utilized gene ontology-based CombFunc and SVM to predict the function of proteins in 2012. They achieved 71% accuracy [41].
14	NCBI & CAFA, MS-KNN	In 2013, authors utilized the NCBI protein database and applied SVM and KNN techniques to classify the data. The author achieved 72.8% accuracy [42].

(Table 4) cont.....

Sr. No	Protein Database and Classification Approach	Description
15	Heart patient data, RF-ML	The authors in 2022 predict the risk of Acute-Respiratory-Distress-Syndrome (ARDS) in heart patients, and they have achieved 95% accuracy [29].

The accuracies achieved by authors on different datasets through different ML approaches are presented below (Fig. **8**) and also depict the comparison of the proposed methodology (CFS_RF) with all current benchmarks in terms of categorization accuracy. The results clearly depict that the proposed methodology based on an ensemble ML classifier, *i.e.*, CFS_RF, achieved the best results so far under a controlled environment with an accuracy of 98.57%. This shows the power of the random forest algorithm.

In this study, the random forests prediction speed is further improved through quantum computing, which enhances the prediction process speed. Quantum computing speeds up decision tree splits, entropy computations, and feature selection. A hybrid approach (quantum preprocessing + classical inference) balances quantum speedup with classical robustness.

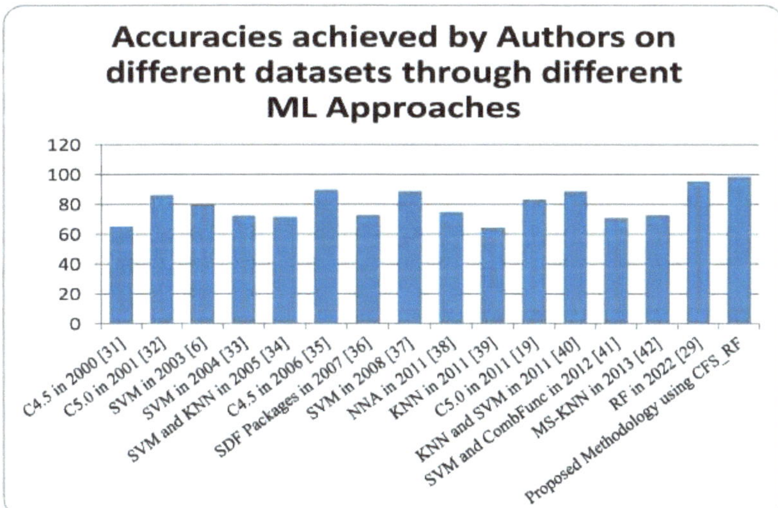

Fig. (8). Accuracies achieved by Authors on different datasets using different ML approaches.

CONCLUSION

Due to the incredibly enormous and varied data sets, research gaps highlighted the ML approach's potential for protein categorization/classification as well as its limits in the field of bioinformatics. The RF's power demonstrates how well ML can handle large data sets. It is clear from this critical analysis that adding enhanced additional SDFs increases the overall classification accuracy of the ML classifier. The results show the contribution of enhanced SDF' in HPFP through the ML approach. It also highlights how important it is to perform these tasks in the early stages of ML. To identify a particular protein class, other settings in terms of input configurations can be applied; these setting produces better specific class prediction. The result also shows that, in a controlled environment, the model achieved an overall average accuracy for HPF forecasting is 98.57%, which is compared with the existing benchmarks of predictions based on different ML techniques. Quantum Machine Learning (QML) offers a promising paradigm by leveraging quantum computing to enhance data processing, optimization. As quantum hardware advances, QML has the potential to outperform classical methods in complex problem-solving, paving the way for breakthroughs in various scientific and industrial applications. In this study, the Quantum Random Forest approach joins classical ensemble learning with quantum computing to enhance decision tree-based classification and regression tasks for speeding up the prediction process. It shows QRF has the potential to improve model efficiency and scalability for complex datasets by leveraging quantum parallelism and feature space encoding. Additionally, this holds true for other broad study fields concerning the possibility of enhancing ML results by concentrating on particular facets of the classification problem rather than trying to answer it all at once. The methodology and obtained results demonstrate that this process/study can also be used in other related fields for better results. This establishes the foundation for further research in subsequent fields.

ACKNOWLEDGEMENT

The authors of this paper are thankful to Hindu College, Amritsar, and Guru Nanak Dev University, Amritsar, for providing infrastructural facilities to complete this research work.

REFERENCES

[1] A. Shehu, D. Barbará, and K. Molloy, "A survey of computational methods for protein function prediction," in *Big Data Analytics in Genomics*, K. C. Wong, Ed. Cham: Springer, 2016. [http://dx.doi.org/10.1007/978-3-319-41279-5_7]

[2] B. Bergeron, *Bioinformatics computing.* Pearson Education India, 2002.

[3] S. Sharma, G. Singh, and R. Singh, "Human protein Function prediction enhancement using decision tree based Machine learning approach", *Commun. Comput. Inf. Sci. (ICICCT 2019).* A. Gani, P. Das, L. Kharb, and D. Chahal, Eds., Communications in Computer and Information Science, vol. 1025. Singapore: Springer, 2019. [http://dx.doi.org/10.1007/978-981-15-1384-8_23]

[4] L. Jensen, *Prediction of protein function from sequence derived protein features.* Ph.D. dissertation, Technical University of Denmark, Kgs. Lyngby, Denmark, 2002.

[5] A. Singh, S. Sharma, G. Singh, and R. Singh, "Machine learning configurations for enhanced human protein function prediction accuracy," in *Smart Computational Strategies: Theoretical and Practical*

Aspects, A. K. Luhach, K. B. G. Hawari, I. C. Mihai, P. A. Hsiung, and R. B. Mishra, Eds. Singapore: Springer, 2019.
[http://dx.doi.org/10.1007/978-981-13-6295-8_4]

[6] C.Z. Cai, L.Y. Han, Z.L. Ji, X. Chen, and Y.Z. Chen, "SVM-Prot: web-based support vector machine software for functional classification of a protein from its primary sequence", *Nucleic Acids Res.,* vol. 31, no. 13, pp. 3692-3697, 2003.
[http://dx.doi.org/10.1093/nar/gkg600] [PMID: 12824396]

[7] A. Singh, S. Sharma, R. Singh, G. Singh, and A. Kaur, "Quality of Service Enhanced Framework for Disease Detection and Drug Discovery", *Int. J. Comput. Sci. Eng.,* vol. 6, no. 9, pp. 130-136, 2018.
[http://dx.doi.org/10.26438/ijcse/v6i9.130136]

[8] A. Rani, S. Kour, R. Kumar, “Comprehensive review of quantum computing: analyzing computational frameworks, emerging technologies, applications, and challenges in the quantum era”, *Recent Adv. Comput. Sci. Commun.*, 2025.

[9] S. Sharma, A. Singh, G. Singh, and R. Singh, "Machine learning configurations for human protein classification using SDFES," *J. Theor. Appl. Inf. Technol.*, vol. 96, no. 8, pp. 30 ,2018. Available from: https://www.jatit.org/volumes/Vol96No8/6Vol96No8.pdf

[10] ExPASy: SIB Bioinformatics Resource Portal, [Online]. Available from: http://expasy.org/.

[11] PSORT WWW Server, [Online]. Available from: http://psort.hgc.jp/. [Accessed: Dec. 23, 2025].

[12] PROFEAT Home, [Online]. Available from: http://bidd2.nus.edu.sg/cgi-bin/prof2015/prof_home.cgi. [Accessed: Dec. 23, 2025].

[13] MATLAB, [Online]. Available from: https://www.mathworks.com/products/matlab.html. [Accessed: Dec. 23, 2025].

[14] I. Friedberg, "Automated protein function prediction--the genomic challenge", *Brief. Bioinform.,* vol. 7, no. 3, pp. 225-242, 2006.
[http://dx.doi.org/10.1093/bib/bbl004] [PMID: 16772267]

[15] A. Al-Shahib, R. Breitling, and D.R. Gilbert, "Predicting protein function by machine learning on amino acid sequences – a critical evaluation", *BMC Genomics,* vol. 8, no. 1, p. 78, 2007.
[http://dx.doi.org/10.1186/1471-2164-8-78] [PMID: 17374164]

[16] A. Lobley, M. B. Swindells, C. A. Orengo, and D. T. Jones, "Inferring function using patterns of native disorder in proteins", *PLoS Comput. Biol.*, vol. 3, no. 8, 24, 2007.
[http://dx.doi.org/10.1371/journal.pcbi.0030162]

[17] M. Kanakubo, and M. Hagiwara, "Speed-up technique for association rule mining based on an artificial algorithm," in *Proc. 7th Int. Conf. Intelligent Systems Design and Applications (ISDA 2007)*, Rio de Janeiro, Brazil, 2007, pp. 105–110.

[18] A. A. D. M. Nofal, and S. Bani-Ahmad, "Classification based on association rule mining techniques: A general survey and empirical comparative evaluation", *Ubiquitous Comput. Commun. J.*, vol. 5, no. 3, 2010.

[19] M. Singh, and G. Singh, "Development of predictor for sequence derived features from amino acid sequence using associative rule mining," *Int. J. Comput. Sci. Secur.*, vol. 5, no. 1, pp. 91–98, 2011.

[20] Human Protein Reference Database (HPRD), [Online]. Available from: http://www.hprd.org/. [Accessed: Dec. 23, 2025].

[21] A. Jaiswal, A. Chhabra, U. Malhotra, S. Kohli, and V.R. Vibha Rani, "Comparative analysis of human matrix metalloproteinases: Emerging therapeutic targets in diseases", *Bioinformation,* vol. 6, no. 1, pp. 23-30, 2011.
[http://dx.doi.org/10.6026/97320630006023] [PMID: 21464841]

[22] S. Saha, and P. Chatterjee, "Protein function prediction from protein interaction network using physicochemical properties of amino acids," *Int. J. Pharm. Biol. Sci.*, vol. 3, no. 4, pp. 102–111, 2012.

[23] A. Bhola, S.K. Yadav, and A.K. Tiwari, "Machine learning based approach for protein function prediction using sequence derived properties," *Int. J. Comput. Appl.*, vol. 105, no. 12, pp. 17–21, 2014. Available from: https://research.ijcaonline.org/volume105/number12/pxc3899789.pdf

[24] D. Ofer, and M. Linial, "ProFET: Feature engineering captures high-level protein functions", *Bioinformatics,* vol. 31, no. 21, pp. 3429-3436, 2015. [http://dx.doi.org/10.1093/bioinformatics/btv345] [PMID: 26130574]

[25] R. Singh, R. Singh, and D.P. Kaur, "Improved protein function classification using support vector machine", *Int. J. Comput. Sci. Inf. Technol.,* vol. 6, no. 2, pp. 964-968, 2015.

[26] S. Das, and C.A. Orengo, "Protein function annotation using protein domain family resources", *Methods,* vol. 93, pp. 24-34, 2016. [http://dx.doi.org/10.1016/j.ymeth.2015.09.029] [PMID: 26434392]

[27] Y. Lei, T. Wang, X. Dong, S. Tian, Y. Liu, H. Mao, W.J. Curran, H.K. Shu, T. Liu, and X. Yang, "MRI classification using semantic random forest with auto-context model", *Quant. Imaging Med. Surg.,* vol. 11, no. 12, pp. 4753-4766, 2021. [http://dx.doi.org/10.21037/qims-20-1114] [PMID: 34888187]

[28] S.J. Rigatti, "Random Forest", *J. Insur. Med.,* vol. 47, no. 1, pp. 31-39, 2017. [http://dx.doi.org/10.17849/insm-47-01-31-39.1] [PMID: 28836909]

[29] W. Wang, L. Li, H. Gu, Y. Chen, Y. Zhen, and Z. Dong, "Random Forest-Based prediction of acute respiratory distress syndrome in patients undergoing cardiac surgery", *Heart Surg. Forum,* vol. 25, no. 6, pp. E854-E859, 2022. [http://dx.doi.org/10.1532/hsf.5113] [PMID: 36602500]

[30] WEKA, "The data platform for cloud & AI," [Online]. Available from: https://www.weka.io/. [Accessed: Dec. 23, 2025].

[31] R.D. King, A. Karwath, A. Clare, and L. Dehaspe, "Accurate prediction of protein functional class from sequence in the Mycobacterium tuberculosis and Escherichia coli genomes using data mining", *Yeast,* vol. 1, no. 4, pp. 283-293, 2000. [http://dx.doi.org/10.1155/2000/107461] [PMID: 11119305]

[32] R.D. King, A. Karwath, A. Clare, and L. Dehaspe, "The utility of different representations of protein sequence for predicting functional class", *Bioinformatics,* vol. 17, no. 5, pp. 445-454, 2001. [http://dx.doi.org/10.1093/bioinformatics/17.5.445] [PMID: 11331239]

[33] L.Y. Han, C.Z. Cai, Z.L. Ji, Z.W. Cao, J. Cui, and Y.Z. Chen, "Predicting functional family of novel enzymes irrespective of sequence similarity: a statistical learning approach", *Nucleic Acids Res.,* vol. 32, no. 21, pp. 6437-6444, 2004. [http://dx.doi.org/10.1093/nar/gkh984] [PMID: 15585667]

[34] L.Y. Han, C.J. Zheng, H.H. Lin, J. Cui, H. Li, H.L. Zhang, Z.Q. Tang, and Y.Z. Chen, "Prediction of functional class of novel plant proteins by a statistical learning method", *New Phytol.,* vol. 168, no. 1, pp. 109-121, 2005. [http://dx.doi.org/10.1111/j.1469-8137.2005.01482.x] [PMID: 16159326]

[35] A. Clare, A. Karwath, H. Ougham, and R.D. King, "Functional bioinformatics for Arabidopsis thaliana", *Bioinformatics,* vol. 22, no. 9, pp. 1130-1136, 2006. [http://dx.doi.org/10.1093/bioinformatics/btl051] [PMID: 16481336]

[36] M. Singh, P. K. Wadhwa, P. S. Sandhu, and G. Nanak, "Human protein function prediction using decision tree induction," *Int. J. Comput. Sci. Netw. Secur.*, vol. 7, no. 4, pp. 77–82, 2007. [Online]. Available from: http://paper.ijcsns.org/07_book/200704/20070412.pdf

[37] G. Pugalenthi, K.K. Kumar, P.N. Suganthan, and R. Gangal, "Identification of catalytic residues from protein structure using support vector machine with sequence and structural features", *Biochem. Biophys. Res. Commun.,* vol. 367, no. 3, pp. 630-634, 2008. [http://dx.doi.org/10.1016/j.bbrc.2008.01.038] [PMID: 18206645]

[38] B. Liao, Q. Liu, Q. Zeng, J. Luo, and G. Yue, "An approach for data-selection of protein function prediction," *MATCH Commun. Math. Comput. Chem.*, vol. 65, no. 2, pp. 459–468, 2011. [Online]. Available from: https://match.pmf.kg.ac.rs/electronic_versions/Match65/n2/match65n2_459-468.pdf

[39] A. Wong, and H. Shatkay, "Protein function prediction using text-based features extracted from the biomedical literature: the CAFA challenge", *BMC Bioinformatics,* vol. 14, no. suppl. 3, p. S14, 2013. [http://dx.doi.org/10.1186/1471-2105-14-S3-S14] [PMID: 23514326]

[40] A. Yang, R. Li, W. Zhu, and G. Yue, "A novel method for protein function prediction based on sequence numerical features", *MATCH Commun. Math. Comput. Chem.*, vol. 67, pp. 833-843, 2012.

[41] M.N. Wass, G. Barton, and M.J.E. Sternberg, "CombFunc: predicting protein function using heterogeneous data sources", *Nucleic Acids Res.*, vol. 40, Web Server issue, pp. W466-W470, 2012. [http://dx.doi.org/10.1093/nar/gks489] [PMID: 22641853]

[42] L. Lan, N. Djuric, Y. Guo, and S. Vucetic, "MS-k NN: protein function prediction by integrating multiple data sources", *BMC Bioinformatics,* vol. 14, no. suppl. 3, p. S8, 2013. [http://dx.doi.org/10.1186/1471-2105-14-S3-S8] [PMID: 23514608]

[43] P. Wittek, *Quantum machine learning: What quantum computing means to data mining*. Amsterdam, Netherlands: Elsevier, 2014.

[44] M. Schuld, A. Bocharov, K.M. Svore, and N. Wiebe, "Circuit-centric quantum classifiers", *Phys. Rev. A (Coll. Park),* vol. 101, no. 3, p. 032308, 2020. [http://dx.doi.org/10.1103/PhysRevA.101.032308]

[45] V. Havlíček, A.D. Córcoles, K. Temme, A.W. Harrow, A. Kandala, J.M. Chow, and J.M. Gambetta, "Supervised learning with quantum-enhanced feature spaces", *Nature,* vol. 567, no. 7747, pp. 209-212, 2019. [http://dx.doi.org/10.1038/s41586-019-0980-2] [PMID: 30867609]

[46] O. Simeone, "An introduction to quantum machine learning for engineers", *arXiv preprint arXiv:2201.00054,* , 2022. [http://dx.doi.org/10.1561/9781638280590]

[47] S. Ganguly, Quantum Machine Learning: An Applied Approach: The Theory and Application of Quantum Machine Learning in Science and Industry. Cham, Switzerland: Springer, 2023. [http://dx.doi.org/10.1007/978-1-4842-7098-1]

[48] K. Najafi, S.F. Yelin, and X. Gao, "The development of quantum machine learning," *Harvard Data Science Review*, vol. 4, 2022.

CHAPTER 8

Quantum AI for Natural Language Processing and Computer Vision

Pummy Dhiman[1,*], Pratibha[1], Sudha[2] and Noor Adnan[3]

[1] *Chitkara University Institute of Engineering and Technology, Chitkara University, Rajpura, Punjab, India*

[2] *Department of Computer Applications, Gian Jyoti institute of management and technology, Chandigarh, Punjab, India*

[3] *Department of Computer Science, College of Science for Women, University of Baghdad, Baghdad, Iraq*

Abstract: Quantum AI is the integration of quantum computing and artificial intelligence, an interaction with the expected impact to be quite positive for the two. For example, QNLP and QCV have the potential to provide radical enhancements to the present methodologies that are used to program machines to comprehend textual as well as image data by harnessing the concept of superposition, entanglement, and quantum parallelism. In this chapter, the application of Quantum AI in NLP and Computer Vision is discussed through quantum language models, quantum image representation, as well as a hybrid approach. However, the tools presented here, together with the theory, have shown the ability to possibly achieve speedup and better efficiency; however, the current NISQ hardware limits the implementation of the tools presented herein. This chapter also discusses difficulties, further study prospects, and prospects for Quantum AI in the domains of NLP and Computer Vision.

Keywords: Artificial neural networks, Computer vision, Data encoding, Deep learning, Feature extraction, Grover's algorithm, Image classification, Natural language processing (NLP), Pattern recognition, Quantum algorithms, Quantum neural networks (QNNs), Quantum-enhanced computer vision, Support vector machines (SVMs).

INTRODUCTION

Artificial Intelligence (AI) technology has garnered prominence in recent years, having found use in numerous sectors such as intelligent assistants and self-automated systems, as well as in improving the healthcare sector [1]. Today, AI is implemented in many spheres and industries, and it proves to be efficient in imp-

[*] **Corresponding author Pummy Dhiman:** Chitkara University Institute of Engineering and Technology, Chitkara University, Rajpura, Punjab, India; E-mail: pummydhiman192@gmail.com

Satveer Kour, Harvinder Singh, Anupam Bonkra & Rupinder Singh (Eds.)

roving work, automating processes, and supporting the decision-making process. As one may note, data stands at the center of AI; it is commonly referred to as "the new oil" of the digital world. The advancements of deep learning, not only to handle large-scale datasets, but also to analyze data and find hidden patterns, have extended its application to the Natural Language Processing (NLP) [2], financial, health care, cybersecurity, and the smart automation domain. Nevertheless, the conventional machine learning algorithm is becoming less adequate in tackling large data.

Deep learning, a subfield of AI, has responded to some of these by using artificial neural networks, which are able to handle large-scale data. Despite this, even in deep learning models, there are constraints when it comes to complexity, dimensionality, and algorithms involving high computational power in combining large dimensions to make correct estimates and patterns. With time, datasets grow in size and the nature of the analyzed problems, so there is a growing demand for nontraditional paradigms. Quantum computing comes out as an innovative solution to these computation bottlenecks. Unlike classical computers that deal with 0 and 1 as basic units, quantum computers work using quantum bits or qubits [3]. The principles of superposition and entanglement, known in quantum mechanics, enable quantum computers to perform a number of calculations much faster than conventional computers can. This aspect makes it possible to solve a class of problems that is intractable with the current machines used in classical computers, for instance, optimization, cryptography [4], and simulation. Quantum computing is an interdisciplinary field that borrows its techniques from computer science, physics, and mathematics. It is a field that also deals with the development of complex equipment or hardware and the improvement of software to adequately solve computational issues. Practical applications involving quantum computing algorithms in AI include ways of speeding up model training or the performance of search algorithms, pattern recognition, and more. With the breakthrough of the connection between quantum computing and AI, a novel area has emerged as Quantum AI. This area aims to extend the machine learning and deep learning phase by utilizing the quantum possibility.

Consequently, one of the most revolutionary use cases of Quantum AI includes Natural Language Processing (NLP) and Computer Vision—two subdomains of AI. NLP helps machines to comprehend, translate, and even generate natural language for applications like sentiment analysis, speech, real-time translation, and the development of chatbots. NLP enables AI systems to understand textual data, while Computer Vision enables the interpretation of visual data such as facial recognition, medical image interpretation, self-driving cars, and object detection, among others. Quantum AI, in conjunction with NLP and Computer Vision, holds great promise. Quantum-aided NLP is beneficial for language modeling, meaning retrieval, and contextual analysis since such NLP often faces certain difficulties, for instance, when dealing with ambiguous data or separators with long-range interactions. Quantum AI in Computer Vision can help reduce time and increase the accuracy of image classification, systematize feature extraction, and optimize object recognition, making the AI vision systems noteworthy [5]. For the more recent domain of Quantum AI, the future is yet to be written as the researchers and key players in the field think about the future developments in the area. While quantum hardware is currently quite young, there are advancements in quantum algorithms and models, as well as in AI and the combination of both quantum and classical computing, which offer promising prospects. The integration of Quantum Computing with AI will result in the reimagination of the paradigms of NLP and Computer Vision with profound impacts ranging from automation, prognostics of early health diagnosis, security solutions, and developing smarter interfaces to interact with computers [5].

Contribution

This chapter delves into the fundamental concepts of Quantum AI, its role in advancing NLP and Computer Vision, and the potential challenges and opportunities in this emerging field. By understanding how quantum computing can augment AI capabilities, we can pave the way for next-generation AI systems that operate beyond the limits of classical computation.

Study Organization

The rest of this article is organized as the following picture shown below (Fig. **1**).

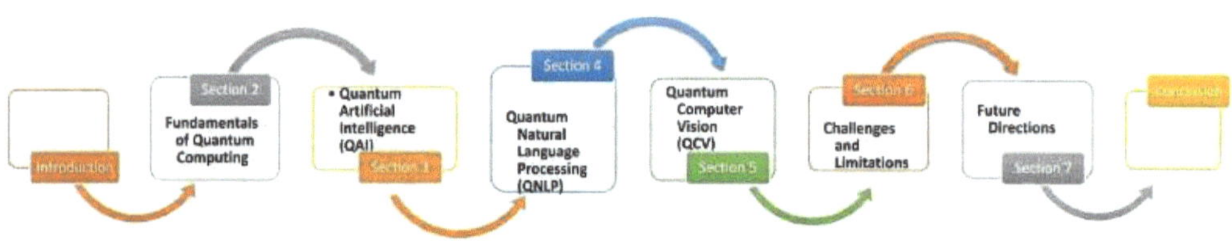

Fig. (1). The structure of the study.

Section 2 covers the fundamentals of Quantum Computing (QC). Section 3 explains the interrelation of Quantum Computing and Artificial Intelligence. Section 4 sheds light on the use of QC in NLP, whereas Section 5 covers the integration of QC and CV. Section 6 outlines the key challenges, while Section 7 shows the future trends. In the last part of the article, which is Section 8, the author presents a closing note and a conclusion.

FUNDAMENTALS OF QUANTUM COMPUTING

Quantum computing is quite different from the conventional forms of computation in that the two approaches handle information differently. All computing systems require basic capacity to store and process information on data. Modern-day computers employ bits that can either be 0 or 1, while quantum computers use qubits, which can be in 0 and 1 states at the same time (Fig. **2**), mathematically represented as $|0\}$ and $|1\}$ [6].

Quantum computers use the principles of quantum mechanics that exist in the natural physical world. This is the phenomenon that underwent a paradigm shift from the traditional information processing mechanism. They refer to it as superposition. Any general state of a pure qubit is represented by equation 1:

$$|\psi\rangle=\alpha|0\rangle+\beta|1\rangle \tag{1}$$

where α and β are complex probability amplitudes of the basis states. The sum of the probabilities of measuring any of the states should always lie between 0 and 1.

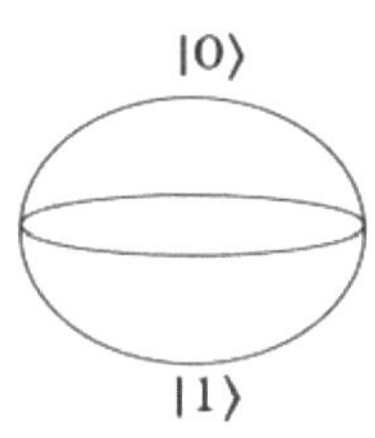

Fig. (2). Mathematical representation of Qubit.

One of the characteristic and unique properties of quantum systems is that they can be scaled under the transformation of a global phase factor. This means that the probability amplitudes can be multiplied by a real constant without changing any characteristics of the picture. Therefore, even if such a quantum state is represented in a certain way, the actual parameters we can quantify in it do not change when discussing quantum computing. Other important concepts come into play:

Entanglement

It is a purely quantum property referring to the ability of two or more qubits to become coupled in such a way that changes in one will affect the other, no matter the distance between them [6]. When two qubits are entangled, their states are then correlated in a way that the evolution of one is directly linked to the evolution of the other. This property helps the quantum computers to compute in a very social way to make it faster and more efficient. Quantum entanglement is one of the major components in quantum cryptography, especially in QKD, which helps recognize any intercepting attempts on the communication.

Quantum Interference

It is a result of the wave-particle duality of quantum states. It enables the operation of quantum computers on the qubit probabilities, which assist in increasing the chances of the correct answer and, in the process, eliminate the wrong one. This principle is essential in the quantum algorithms, such as Grover's search algorithm, that increase the speed of searching for information in unstructured databases by interference.

Quantum Parallelism

Quantum parallelism in quantum computers is one of the core features of quantum computing that enables a quantum system to test for a number of possibilities at once. Contrary to classical computers, which operate in a single computational pathway, quantum computers employ superposition, which means that several pathways are ping at the same time in qubits [7]. This is so since a quantum algorithm can process all possible inputs simultaneously and hence save a lot of time in computation, especially when solving problems such as search, optimization, or pattern recognition. Grover's algorithm demonstrates quantum parallelism by searching an unsorted database of N entries in only $O(\sqrt{N})$ time, a substantial speedup over classical algorithms that require $O(N)$ time.

Quantum Associative Memory (QAM)

Similar to Quantum Content Addressable Memory (QCAM), is a quantum version of content addressable memory, a kind of data structure used to store and—in particular—to search for and produce information. In classical computing, associative memory can directly retrieve data by content, whereas in conventional memory, information is retrieved by memory address, which makes it useful in machine learning and neural networks. Based on quantum entanglement and superposition, quantum associative memory can encode and recall patterns with higher efficiency than its classical counterparts. Another development of QAM is the qRAM, which helps in storing data for quick access in AI. One of the most famous examples is the Quantum Hopfield Network, which is the adaptation of the classical Hopfield networks to quantum ones and can enhance the performance of the pattern recognition and optimization tasks. Superposition, entanglement, and interference are the three elemental concepts of quantum computing, allowing a quantum computer to outcompete a classical computer exponentially for complex issues within cryptography, optimization, machine learning [7], NLP, and computer vision jobs.

QUANTUM ARTIFICIAL INTELLIGENCE (QAI): INTEGRATION OF QUANTUM COMPUTING AND ARTIFICIAL INTELLIGENCE

Quantum Artificial Intelligence is an integration of quantum computing concepts with artificial intelligence (Fig. **3**), with a view to overcoming machine learning problems that are hard to solve with standard computers. It has been observed that traditional or conventional approaches in machine learning traverses' poor performance in the case of high-dimensional vectors. Explaining something rather complex, individuals can turn their attention toward quantum parallelism and quantum associative memory, which would allow a quantum computer to work much faster compared to classical computers; therefore, it would be much efficient in optimization and learning tasks.

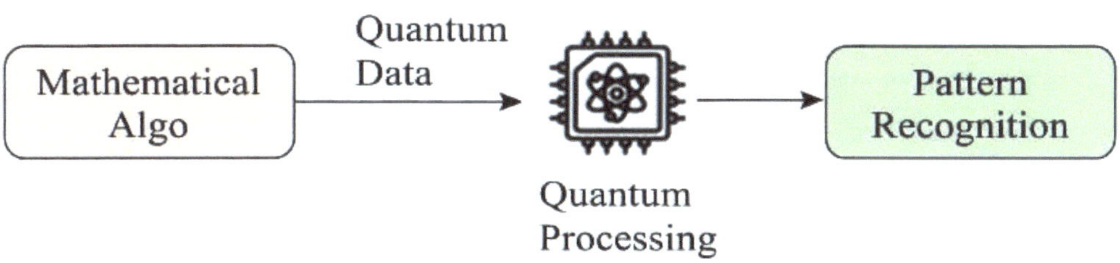

Fig. (3). Quantum artificial intelligence (QAI) as integration of quantum computing and ai.

Another benefit of quantum computers is that in compiling and matrix manipulations at high levels of dimensions, quantum computers are more effective than classical computers in terms of time consumption of AI algorithms. Moreover, it is also possible to use quantum computing to factorize integers that have a complexity that cannot be solved by conventional forms of computation. Most of the machine learning problems do not admit a solution within a given time frame and, therefore, resort to heuristically developed strategies. In such cases, there has been found a kind of advantage has been found in doing computations with the help of a principle called quantum computing to solve the current problem faster than the usual conventional methods. QAI came up with the idea of solving 'hard' problems that can only be solved by artificial intelligence *via* the application of the principles in quantum mechanics [8]. As QAI is a relatively young and inherently interdisciplinary field, it is not surprising that significant advances have been made in the last few years alone. Literature and real-world experiments with the use of actual quantum computers during the period of NISQ have shown that subjecting these algorithms to optimization by QAI attunes them to solve quantum problems whose classical solutions are computationally difficult. Notably, QAI has been effectively applied to combinatorial optimization tasks in AI, making a positive impact across various domains. For and as well as, portfolio optimization in finance, traffic control, capacitive vehicle routing, safe navigation of self-driving vehicles, constellation of satellites, management of energy networks, and simulation of material chemical structure for drugs and material designs.

Beyond direct AI applications, QAI is also being explored for improving quantum computing itself (Fig. **4**). Research in this direction focuses on leveraging AI methodologies—particularly from machine learning—to address challenges in quantum computing hardware and software development. While Quantum Machine Learning (QML) remains the most prominent application, the scope of QAI extends far beyond, covering multiple subfields of AI. These include quantum reasoning, quantum automated planning and scheduling (QPS), Quantum Natural Language Processing (QNLP), Quantum Computer Vision (QCV), and Quantum agents and Multi-Agent Systems (QMAS) [5]. Each of these subfields encompasses research and development efforts in both directions; for instance, QML not only applies quantum computing to enhance machine learning but also employs AI techniques to advance quantum computing technologies.

From Google, one can obtain the open-source quantum machine learning library, namely TensorFlow Quantum (TFQ) [9]. Cirq works with TensorFlow and offers quantum-classical model designs and implementations by employing discriminative and generative control through quantum computing elements that are compatible with TensorFlow and other interfaces, as well as quantum circuits' high-speed imitation.

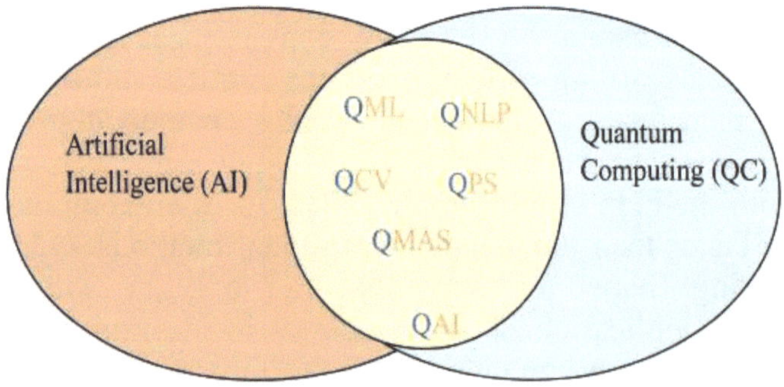

Fig. (4). Quantum Artificial Intelligence (QAI): Integration of quantum computing and artificial intelligence.

To an extent, it is accurate to say that quantum computing can revolutionize AI in a number of ways. It is also found that quantum computing will positively affect constraint resolution, uncertainty handling and constraint fulfillment, adaptation in machine learning, and spatial and temporal reasoning [10]. In the following subsections, the author further explores the use of QAI in two key areas of development, namely the NLP and CV domains.

QUANTUM AI FOR NATURAL LANGUAGE PROCESSING (NLP)

Natural Language Processing (NLP) is a branch of AI that teaches computers how to process, analyze, produce as well and respond to human language. It applies theories from computational linguistics and also the methods of statistical machine learning to work with the number of written texts. The field has advanced significantly with deep learning and transformer-based models, yet these advancements come with computational challenges. The increasing complexity of language models, coupled with the exponential growth of data, has led to computational bottlenecks, where classical computing systems struggle with massive datasets and high-dimensional computations.

NLP is predicted to experience a drastic shift given the newly developed field of quantum artificial intelligence, or sometimes referred to as quantum AI. This intersection is referred to as Quantum Natural Language Processing (QNLP) mainly because it uses quantum mechanical methods to perform language processing-related functions [9].

The Dual Perspective of QNLP

QNLP can be explored in two key directions:

1. **Exploration of Quantum Computing for NLP** – using quantum mechanical advantages for improving natural language processing tasks, including text classification, question answering, and machine translation.
2. **NLP for Quantum Computing** – As mentioned earlier, there are ample opportunities in using NLP techniques to enhance quantum computing tasks that have not been explored to the full extent.

The majority of the current studies in QNLP are based on superposition for handling uncertainties and ambiguity in language and entanglement for encoding linguistic information both syntactically and semantically in a compositional and distributed manner.

Advantages of QNLP Over Classical NLP

Coecke *et al.* [11] showed that QNLP is not just a quantum mediation of classical NLP but a new form of integrating structure and meaning within a single QCS. One important architecture in QNLP is the Categorical Distributional Compositional (DisCoCat) model [12], which translates the meaning of words and phrases to quantum states and procedures that are comparable with quantum circuits. Whereas, in the most recent source NLP models, traditional meaning can be assumed to reside in the layers of black-box architectures based on the transformers, QNLP has explicated the flow of meanings in a diagrammatic format.

These quantum capabilities offer promising improvements in NLP, particularly in the following areas:

Efficient Matrix Operations

- Transformer-based models (*e.g.*, BERT, GPT) require extensive matrix multiplications [13].
- Quantum algorithms, such as the Harrow-Hassidim-Lloyd (HHL) algorithm, can accelerate matrix computations, potentially improving the efficiency of large-scale NLP models.

Exponential Speedup in Optimization

- Many NLP tasks, such as training deep learning models, syntactic parsing, and semantic analysis, involve complex optimization problems.
- Quantum algorithms like the Quantum Approximate Optimization Algorithm (QAOA) and Variational Quantum Eigensolver (VQE) offer potential speedups in solving these problems [14].

High-Dimensional Feature Space Processing

- Word embeddings in NLP involve mapping words into high-dimensional vectors.
- Quantum computing, which naturally processes high-dimensional Hilbert spaces, can provide more expressive and efficient representations of linguistic structures.

Despite these theoretical advantages, QNLP is still in its early stages. The practical implementation of quantum NLP methods, particularly hybrid quantum-classical architectures, is currently constrained by Noisy Intermediate-Scale Quantum (NISQ) hardware.

QUANTUM AI FOR COMPUTER VISION

It deals with the analysis and interpretation of computer-assisted images, both picture-images and image-like data of raster-scan or other formats, 2D images including depth maps, 3D point clouds, and fused with other modalities. Therefore, based on the idea of the HVS, CV should be able to obtain sophisticated and abstract scene understanding. It is closely connected to the machine learning discipline, and their synergy is highly evident, as the current vision processing highly relies on machine learning methods, and, in turn, the development of ML often results from the complexity of CV tasks. Hence, with the increased popularity of quantum computing, researchers have tried to accomplish CV problems in the quantum context, which has given rise to what is known as Quantum Computer Vision (QCV) [9]. This field, which began in the early 2000s, has gained renewed interest due to advances in quantum image processing. Quantum computing offers the potential to process image data more efficiently, leveraging principles such as superposition, entanglement, and quantum parallelism to handle complex CV tasks [15].

Quantum image processing requires encoding classical digital images into quantum states, performing quantum computations, and finally converting the processed quantum image back into a classical format. Several quantum image representations have been developed, including:

- Qubit Lattices
- Normal Arbitrary Quantum Superposition States

These representations preserve colour image data in the form of quantum amplitudes, phases, or basis, due to which the carrier data can be encoded in a relatively compressed form. There are also some existing methods for the processing of quantum-represented images. However, only a few, most of them are based on quantum annealing for image recognition and classification, image synthesis, object tracking and detection, graph matching, as well as image and motion segmentations. In [16], various types of quantum hybrid vision transformers were proposed to tackle, again, an image classification task in high-energy physics with the on-par accuracy to their classical counterparts with comparable numbers of model parameters. According to a study, in small-scale medical image datasets, quantum transformer models containing quantum attention layers may compete or even outperform conventional vision transformer models in terms of asymptotic run time and number of parameters in question [17].

CHALLENGES AND LIMITATIONS

Despite its theoretical promise, Quantum AI faces several challenges and limitations that hinder its practical application in NLP and Computer Vision:

Hardware Constraints

- Current quantum computers operate under NISQ (Noisy Intermediate-Scale Quantum) conditions, meaning they have limited qubits, high error rates, and short coherence times [9].
- Scalability issues prevent large-scale NLP and CV models from being fully implemented on quantum hardware.

Algorithmic Challenges

- Most existing quantum algorithms for NLP and CV are in the experimental phase and require extensive optimization for real-world applications.
- Classical deep learning and transformer-based architectures remain more efficient for practical use.

Hybrid Quantum-Classical Integration

- Hybrid models, which combine quantum and classical techniques, are currently needed due to the incompleteness of purely quantum AI models.
- Efficient quantum-classical communication remains a bottleneck, affecting overall system performance.

Data Encoding and Processing Bottlenecks

- Encoding classical data (text and images) into quantum states is computationally expensive.
- Processing high-dimensional feature spaces requires sophisticated quantum embedding techniques, which are still under development.

Lack of Standardized Frameworks

- Quantum AI lacks standardized frameworks, libraries, and benchmarks to evaluate and compare models effectively.
- Existing quantum programming tools (Qiskit, Cirq, PennyLane) are still evolving and require specialized expertise.

FUTURE DIRECTIONS AND OPPORTUNITIES

Quantum AI for NLP and CV presents several exciting opportunities for future research and development. As quantum computing technology advances, researchers and industry professionals are exploring innovative ways to harness its potential for AI applications [18]. The following key directions and opportunities highlight the future of Quantum AI in NLP and CV:

Advancements in Quantum Hardware

- The transition from NISQ to fault-tolerant quantum computing will enable more powerful and stable quantum models.
- Quantum error correction techniques will improve the reliability of quantum computations.

Quantum-Enhanced NLP and Language Models

- Quantum Transformers and Quantum Neural Networks (QNNs) could enhance existing NLP models [19, 20] by leveraging quantum superposition for parallel computations.
- Quantum contextual embeddings may provide more nuanced word and sentence representations [21].

Quantum Computer Vision Applications

- Quantum image processing algorithms could revolutionize medical imaging, autonomous driving, and real-time video analysis [15].
- Quantum-enhanced deep learning models may outperform classical Convolutional Neural Networks (CNNs) in specific visual tasks.

Hybrid Quantum-Classical AI Architectures

- Developing efficient hybrid models will allow gradual integration of quantum computing into real-world NLP and CV applications.
- Quantum Variational Circuits could be used alongside classical deep learning models for enhanced efficiency.

Standardization and Open-Source Frameworks

- The development of Quantum Machine Learning libraries (QML) tailored for NLP and CV will accelerate adoption.
- Open-source initiatives will facilitate collaborative research and large-scale benchmarking of Quantum AI models.

CONCLUSION

Quantum AI has the potential to revolutionize NLP and CV by overcoming the computational limits of classical models. Quantum NLP can enhance language understanding, translation, and sentiment analysis, while Quantum Computer

Vision offers breakthroughs in image classification, medical imaging, and autonomous systems. However, the field faces challenges such as hardware limitations, qubit scalability, noise interference, and the need for robust quantum-AI frameworks. As quantum technology advances, hybrid quantum-classical models and quantum-enhanced deep learning architectures will drive progress. While full-scale adoption is still in the future, ongoing research and technological advancements will shape Quantum AI into a transformative force across AI applications.

REFERENCES

[1] P. Dhiman, A. Bonkra, A. Kaur, Y. Gulzar, Y. Hamid, M.S. Mir, A.B. Soomro, and O. Elwasila, "Healthcare trust evolution with explainable artificial intelligence: bibliometric analysis", *Information (Basel),* vol. 14, no. 10, p. 541, 2023. [http://dx.doi.org/10.3390/info14100541]

[2] P. Dhiman, A. Kaur, Y. Hamid, and N. Ababneh, "Fake news detection datasets: a review and research opportunities", *Int. J. Comput. Digit. Syst.,* vol. 16, no. 1, pp. 39-55, 2023.

[3] K. S. Balamurugan, A. Sivakami, M. Mathankumar, Y. J. D. S. Prasad, and I. Ahmad, "Quantum computing basics, applications and future perspectives," *J. Mol. Struct.*, vol. 1308, p. 137917, 2024. [http://dx.doi.org/10.1016/j.molstruc.2024.137917]

[4] S. Subramani, S. M, K. A, and S.K. Svn, "Review of security methods based on classical cryptography and quantum cryptography", *Cybern. Syst.,* vol. 56, no. 3, pp. 302-320, 2025. [http://dx.doi.org/10.1080/01969722.2023.2166261]

[5] M. Klusch, J. Lässig, D. Müssig, A. Macaluso, and F.K. Wilhelm, "Quantum artificial intelligence: A brief survey," *KI-Künstliche Intelligenz*, vol. 38, pp. 257–276, Nov. 2024. [Online]. Available from: https://link.springer.com/article/10.1007/s13218-024-00871-8

[6] M. Ying, "Quantum computation, quantum theory and AI", *Artif. Intell.,* vol. 174, no. 2, pp. 162-176, 2010. [http://dx.doi.org/10.1016/j.artint.2009.11.009]

[7] K.P. Shankar, K. Chandraprabha, K.S. Raja, and P. Kanmani, "Foundations of quantum computing and machine learning," in *Foundations of Quantum Computing and Machine Learning*, 2025. [http://dx.doi.org/10.1002/9781394242399.ch8]

[8] Y. Alexeev, M.H. Farag, T.L. Patti, M.E. Wolf, N. Ares, and A. Aspuru-Guzik, "Artificial Intelligence for Quantum Computing", *arXiv preprint arXiv:2411.09131,* 2024.

[9] S.S. Gill, M. Xu, C. Ottaviani, P. Patros, R. Bahsoon, A. Shaghaghi, M. Golec, V. Stankovski, H. Wu, A. Abraham, M. Singh, H. Mehta, S.K. Ghosh, T. Baker, A.K. Parlikad, H. Lutfiyya, S.S. Kanhere, R. Sakellariou, S. Dustdar, O. Rana, I. Brandic, and S. Uhlig, "AI for next generation computing: Emerging trends and future directions", *Internet of Things,* vol. 19, p. 100514, 2022. [http://dx.doi.org/10.1016/j.iot.2022.100514]

[10] V. Dunjko, and H.J. Briegel, "Machine learning & artificial intelligence in the quantum domain: a review of recent progress", *Rep. Prog. Phys.,* vol. 81, no. 7, p. 074001, 2018. [http://dx.doi.org/10.1088/1361-6633/aab406] [PMID: 29504942]

[11] B. Coecke, G. de Felice, K. Meichanetzidis, and A. Toumi, "Foundations for near-term quantum natural language processing", *arXiv preprint arXiv:2012.03755,* 2020.

[12] B. Coecke, M. Sadrzadeh, and S. Clark, "Mathematical foundations for a compositional distributional model of meaning", *arXiv preprint arXiv:1003.4394,* 2010.

[13] P. Dhiman, A. Kaur, D. Gupta, S. Juneja, A. Nauman, and G. Muhammad, "GBERT: A hybrid deep

learning model based on GPT-BERT for fake news detection", *Heliyon,* vol. 10, no. 16, p. e35865, 2024.
[http://dx.doi.org/10.1016/j.heliyon.2024.e35865] [PMID: 39220956]

[14] K. Blekos, D. Brand, A. Ceschini, C.H. Chou, R.H. Li, K. Pandya, and A. Summer, "A review on quantum approximate optimization algorithm and its variants", *Phys. Rep.,* vol. 1068, pp. 1-66, 2024.
[http://dx.doi.org/10.1016/j.physrep.2024.03.002]

[15] H.T. Larasati, and H. Kim, "Trends of quantum computing applications to computer vision", in *Proc. 2022 Int. Conf. Platform Technol. Serv. (PlatCon)*, 2022, pp. 7–12.
[http://dx.doi.org/10.1109/PlatCon55845.2022.9932103]

[16] J. Biamonte, P. Wittek, N. Pancotti, P. Rebentrost, N. Wiebe, and S. Lloyd, "Quantum machine learning", *Nature,* vol. 549, no. 7671, pp. 195-202, 2017.
[http://dx.doi.org/10.1038/nature23474] [PMID: 28905917]

[17] J. Wang, H. Ke, X. Liu, and H. Wang, "Optimization for computational offloading in multi-access edge computing: A deep reinforcement learning scheme", *Comput. Netw.,* vol. 204, p. 108690, 2022.
[http://dx.doi.org/10.1016/j.comnet.2021.108690]

[18] M. Ambale, P. Kumbhar, S. Mujawar, S. Bhori, and T. Kulkarni, "The future of intelligence: Quantum computing impact on AI and machine learning," *JETIR*, vol. 11, no. 11, pp. 277–283, 2024.

[19] G. Kaur, A. Kaur, M. Khurana, and R. Damaševičius, "Sentiment polarity analysis of love letters: Evaluation of TextBlob, Vader, Flair, and Hugging Face transformer", *Comput. Sci. Inf. Syst.,* vol. 21, no. 4, pp. 1411-1433, 2024.
[http://dx.doi.org/10.2298/CSIS240328040K]

[20] A. Kaur, and M. Khurana, "Multimodal sentiments: unraveling text and emoji dynamics through deep learning", in: *Proc. 2024 11th Int. Conf. Reliab., Infocom Technol. Optim. (Trends Future Directions) (ICRITO)*, 2024, pp. 1-6.

[21] R. Guarasci, G. De Pietro, and M. Esposito, "Quantum natural language processing: Challenges and opportunities", *Appl. Sci. (Basel),* vol. 12, no. 11, p. 5651, 2022.
[http://dx.doi.org/10.3390/app12115651]

CHAPTER 9

Edge Computing and Real-time Decision Making with Quantum AI

Aditi Dutta[1,*], **Kunjana Mittal**[2], **Akshit Patyal**[1], **Indu Bharti Jain**[2], **Pardeep Tiwana**[1] and **Sayed Abid Hussain**[3]

[1] *Department of Computer Science and Engineering, CGC - College of Engineering, Mohali, Punjab, India*

[2] *Department of Law, Maharishi Markandeshwar University (deemed to be University), Mullana, Ambala, Haryana, India*

[3] *Department of Computer Science and Engineering, Bakhtar University, Kabul, Afghanistan*

Abstract: The recent intersection between Quantitative Artificial Intelligence (Quantum AI) and edge computing is providing real-time decision-making. This is achieved by combining the distributed processing power of edge computing with the optimization capabilities of quantum computation. Edge computing that allows analyzing data anywhere from the source resulting in lower latency, less utilization of bandwidth and higher security when compared to mainstream computing systems and Quantum AI that is based on quantum mechanics and is a much powerful version of Classical AI as they are much faster in their problem-solving techniques. This directly aids to discretionary fields such as autonomous systems, smart cities, predictable maintenance, fraud detection, and healthcare industry that requires pushing intelligence decision for real-time. Nonetheless, this fusion is promising; however, it has several issues, such as limitations of quantum hardware, computational noise, security issues, and compatibility issues. The current strategies involve the development of quantum-classical computers and hybrid systems, as well as quantum-safe programming and energy-efficient quantum computing for augmenting the applicability of Quantum AI in the Edge domain. Advancements in quantum computing as well as development of edge intelligence are being set to transform industries by creating high levels of efficiency, security, and automation in real-time operations.

Keywords: Cloud integration, Data processing, Decision making, Edge devices, Edge intelligence, Edge networks, Quantum algorithms, Quantum artificial intelligence (QAI), Quantum machine learning (QML), Quantum security, Real-time analytics, Internet of things (IoT), Machine learning models, Real-time data processing, Smart devices.

* **Corresponding author Aditi Dutta:** Department of Computer Science and Engineering, CGC - College of Engineering, Mohali, Punjab, India; E-mail: dutta.aditi20@gmail.com

Satveer Kour, Harvinder Singh, Anupam Bonkra & Rupinder Singh (Eds.)

INTRODUCTION

Smart computing takes processing to new levels as data is processed close to its origin rather than relying on appendices on online servers [1]. It also enhances the psychology of quick processing and enhances security by minimizing the exposure of the compound to possibly attack by hackers during the transfer of the data. Local data processing and dispensing involves sending only useful data to centralized systems, hence using less bandwidth and costs [2]. This capacity is most helpful in sectors such as healthcare and transport, where monitoring of equipment and making split decisions is very sensitive. Likewise, in a manufacturing plant setting, the paradigm is used for maintenance of machinery in order to avoid extended downtimes and to have increased production. The use of artificial intelligence at the edge now goes one step further by enhancing the automation as well as its decision-making processes [3]. The architecture of edge computing, where data processing occurs closer to the source, minimizing latency and optimizing bandwidth usage, is depicted below (Fig. **1**).

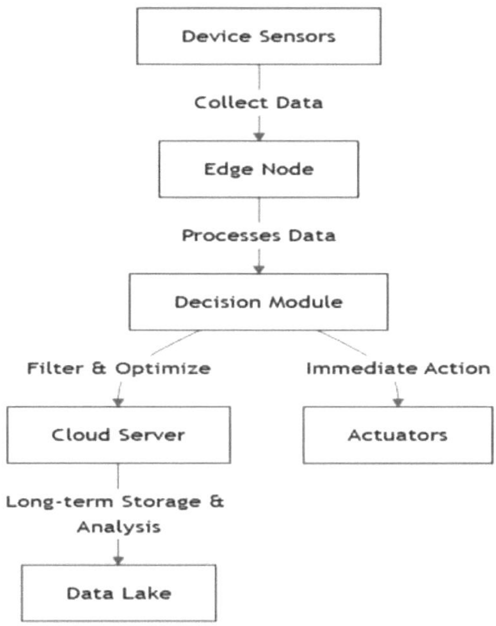

Fig. (1). Overview of edge computing.

The Role of Real-Time Decision Making

Real-time decision-making is a critical factor in modern digital ecosystems, enabling instantaneous responses based on continuously evolving data [4]. This capability is essential in industries where rapid analysis and immediate action can significantly impact efficiency, safety, and user experience. AI technologies are being widely adopted across industries to improve operational efficiency, decision-making, and customer satisfaction (Table **1**). The integration of AI enables organizations to achieve measurable benefits such as cost savings, safety improvements, and enhanced service delivery.

Table 1. Applications of AI across key industries and their primary benefits.

Industry	Application	Key Benefits
Healthcare	Patient monitoring, emergency alerts	Faster response times, improved outcomes
Autonomous Vehicles	Navigation, collision avoidance	Enhanced safety, reduced accidents
Finance	Fraud detection, automated trading	Risk mitigation, financial security
Industrial Automation	Predictive maintenance, process optimization	Reduced downtime, increased efficiency
Retail and E-Commerce	Dynamic pricing, personalized recommendations	Better customer experience, higher sales
Smart Cities	Traffic management, public safety monitoring	Reduced congestion, enhanced security
Cybersecurity	Threat detection, real-time response	Stronger data protection, fewer breaches
Supply Chain and Logistics	Route optimization, inventory management	Cost savings, faster deliveries
Telecommunications	Network traffic control, service optimization	Better connectivity, reduced latency

Quantum AI: A New Frontier

Quantum AI is an amalgam of quantum computing and artificial intelligence that has the potential to transform problem-solving techniques far beyond the capacities of conventional computing architectures [5]. In this way, quantum computers use principles related to superposition and entanglement to analyze the loss of data and carry out calculations much faster than conventional devices. This is especially significant in applications such as drug design, finance, and all problems that use machine learning and artificial intelligence in decision-making, which require large computational power. Also, the interaction of machine learning and quantum computation will lead to higher pattern recognition, cryptography, and data security, which would positively advance cybersecurity and cryptology. While this research is still ongoing, the inclusion of Q-AI integration may pave the way to future innovations in science, operations, and robotics—as well as in decision-making processes. Nonetheless, this field of AI is still in the development phase and has a dynamic hardware nature, which raises concerns regarding stability and scalability capacity; nonetheless, it reveals a cleared path for new innovative technology of computational intelligence, which revolutionizes industries by expanding the AI possibilities horizons [6]. The processes of real-time data processing, focusing on the speed of data gathering, data analyzing, and the cycle in making the right decision that is helpful for applications that require time-sensitive decisions to be made, are shown below (Fig. **2**). It illustrates the step-by-step workflow involved in real-time data processing, from data collection to actionable insights. This process is critical for enabling immediate decision-making and responsive operations across various industries.

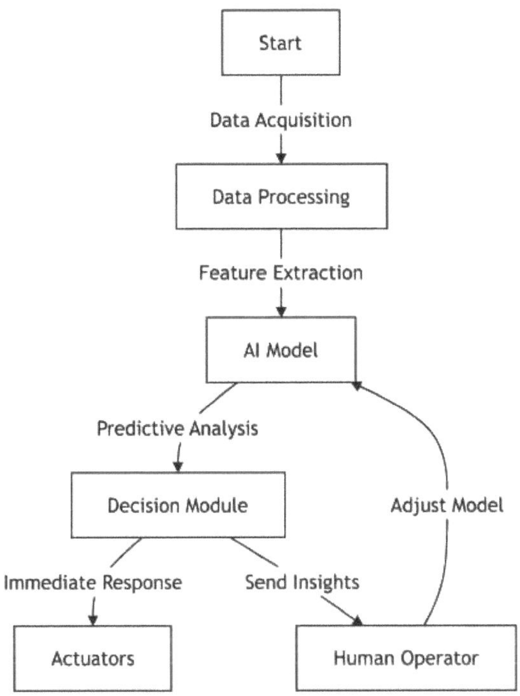

Fig. (2). Process of real-time processing.

FUNDAMENTALS OF EDGE COMPUTING

Edge computing can also be described as a form of computing that does not heavily depend on cloud-based servers and works closer to data sources [7]. Contrary to the direct transfer of massive amounts of data to distant computing centers, within this approach, the analysis of information takes place in local nodes of the network environment, thus contributing to reduced latency and efficient utilization of the bandwidth. It provides almost real-time computation for processes such as self-driving cars and remote patient supervision, and prevents flooding the networks with unnecessary information. This is an ideal situation since this leads to improved security and privacy, since the information does not have to be transmitted over the internet. This is due to the fact that the system can allow for an increasing number of IoT devices within industries. Also, the reliability has been enhanced so that functionality will be provided even in the failure of a network, beneficial for critical tasks. With advancements in artificial intelligence and 5G technology, edge computing is becoming a fundamental component of modern digital infrastructure, driving innovation across various sectors.

Key Characteristics of Edge Computing

Low Latency

Such systems work to process data at the collecting edge to enhance shorter response times than in cloud-based systems. It is especially significant for applications like auto-dispatch, transportation vehicles, and even in hospitals, where slight delays can lead to fatal outcomes.

Bandwidth Optimization

Thus, applying data processing and filtering at the edge of the network reduces the information transfer to the central server. This helps in cutting down the network load and consequently brings down the price of the data per unit, which makes it suitable when handling immense data traffic which includes but not limited to use in video surveillance and use of IoT sensor networks.

Enhanced Security and Privacy

As data is processed at the edge, there is limited movement of data over the internet, and it is less vulnerable to cyber attacks. The interaction of machine learning and quantum computing will lead to advances in pattern recognition, data security, and cryptography, significantly benefiting the field of cybersecurity.

Scalability

Irrespective of the increasing popularity of IoT devices and systems, edge computing does not overwhelm the main computational centres. This decentralized approach of implementing smart devices in industries enables the growth of a firm to go to the next level without experiencing constraints of bandwidth or exorbitant cloud fees.

Reliability

In traditional cloud computing, a service shutdown can be due to network problems like outages or high traffic. Edge computing makes sure that an application can execute its required tasks even if it is unable to connect with the cloud. It is most helpful for remote areas, factories, and self-acting systems where there is no interruption or lack of power supply allowed.

Real-Time Processing

The efficiency of the delay in processing big data can facilitate quick decision-making in various sensitive applications. In smart cities, traffic systems can respond to situations in motion; in health care, wearable devices can immediately inform doctors of irregularities such as an abnormal he covering rate or drop in blood pressure.

Cost Efficiency

By reducing the need for constant cloud communication and large-scale data storage, edge computing lowers operational costs for businesses. Companies save on cloud service expenses while also improving system performance, making it a financially viable solution for large-scale deployments.

Improved Energy Efficiency

Edge computing reduces the energy required to transmit and store vast amounts of data in centralized servers. By distributing processing tasks to local devices, power consumption is optimized, making it an environmentally friendly solution for smart grids, industrial automation, and other energy-intensive applications.

Benefits of Cloud Computing

As shown below (Table **2**), edge computing offers significant advantages over traditional cloud computing, especially in applications where low latency, cost savings, and real-time responsiveness are critical. These benefits make edge computing particularly suitable for IoT, industrial automation, and mission-critical systems.

Table 2. Benefits of edge computing over cloud computing across key factors.

Factor	Edge Computing	Cloud Computing
Latency	Low, as data is processed near the source	Higher, due to the distance from centralized servers

(Table 2) cont.....

Factor	Edge Computing	Cloud Computing
Bandwidth Usage	Optimized by filtering and processing data locally	Requires high bandwidth for constant data transfer
Security and Privacy	Improved, as sensitive data is processed on-site	Higher risk, as data is transmitted over the internet
Reliability	More resilient; continues functioning even if the network fails	Dependent on internet connectivity and cloud availability
Scalability	Easily scalable for IoT and localized processing	Scales well but may face congestion with large data loads
Cost Efficiency	Reduces cloud storage and data transfer costs	Higher operational costs due to centralized processing
Real-Time Processing	Immediate decision-making for critical applications	Higher latency in processing due to cloud dependency
Energy Efficiency	Optimized by reducing unnecessary data transmission	Higher energy consumption for data transfer and storage

Challenges and Limitations

The various challenges and limitations organizations face when adopting edge computing are highlighted below (Table **3**). Addressing these issues requires a combination of technological innovation, strategic planning, and adherence to best practices for security, scalability, and resource optimization.

Table 3. Challenges and limitations of edge computing with impacts and solutions.

Challenge	Description	Impact	Possible Solutions
Infrastructure Costs	Requires investment in edge devices, local servers, and network upgrades.	Higher initial deployment costs for businesses.	Optimize infrastructure by using hybrid models combining edge and cloud.
Device Management Complexity	Managing a large number of distributed devices can be difficult.	Increased operational overhead and maintenance challenges.	Implement centralized monitoring and automated management tools.
Security Risks	More endpoints increase the attack surface for cyber threats.	Potential vulnerability to hacking, malware, and data breaches.	Use robust encryption, zero-trust security models, and AI-driven threat detection.
Data Privacy Compliance	Processing sensitive data locally may still need to comply with regulations.	Risk of non-compliance with laws like GDPR, HIPAA, and CCPA.	Implement strict access control, local data anonymization, and regular audits.

(Table 3) cont.....

Challenge	Description	Impact	Possible Solutions
Limited Computing Power	Edge devices often have lower processing capabilities compared to cloud servers.	May struggle with resource-intensive applications like deep learning.	Use AI-accelerated hardware (*e.g.*, GPUs, TPUs) and distribute workloads efficiently.
Network Reliability	Edge systems may depend on local network stability.	Risk of failures in remote or poorly connected areas.	Deploy redundancy mechanisms and local backup storage solutions.
Scalability Challenges	Expanding edge networks requires careful infrastructure planning.	Scaling too fast may lead to inefficiencies and high costs.	Adopt modular and scalable architectures with cloud-edge integration.
Interoperability Issues	Different vendors may use incompatible hardware and software.	Lack of standardization can slow adoption and integration.	Promote open standards, APIs, and vendor-neutral platforms.
Energy Consumption	Large-scale edge deployments may increase overall power usage.	Higher operational costs and environmental impact.	Use energy-efficient processors and implement smart power management strategies.
Software and Firmware Updates	Keeping distributed devices updated is more complex than in centralized systems.	Unpatched vulnerabilities and outdated software may lead to security risks.	Automate remote updates and use AI-driven predictive maintenance.
Data Synchronization	Ensuring consistency between multiple edge nodes and the cloud can be challenging.	Data inconsistencies may lead to errors in real-time decision-making.	Implement real-time synchronization protocols and distributed data management.

The Need for Real-Time Decision Making

Real-time decision-making is a key feature of the present-day world, where prompt actions made on the basis of the received information can improve productivity, security, and usability. Healthcare, financial industries, and automated systems, among others, require data to be processed as they make decisions without any delay. The need for real-time analytics has been fuelled by the rise in technology, thus increasing the level of innovation in the market.

Importance in Modern Applications

Real-time decision making is increasingly becoming popular for use in applications that allow industries to make instant decisions in view of the prevailing conditions in the environment. In healthcare, it helps in monitoring patients' condition in real-time and quickly identify complications that need to be addressed to prevent deterioration of patients' health. Autonomous cars must process a vast amount of data within the smallest time possible in order to steer away from obstacles and any other object that may impair the safety of occupants [8]. In finance, fraud detection solutions are used in identifying and assessing all the transactions, whether suspicious, in a matter of milliseconds, so as to ensure that losses do not occur. Another area within Industrial automation is the means of predictive maintenance, where equipment status sensors monitor its health and engage repair methods before a failure happens, thus lowering costs and downtimes. In this case, data in retail and e-commerce is used in real-time to offer a customised offering to the clients, setting prices and stock. Smart cities have traffic signals that adapt the traffic flow signals to real-time conditions to help cut congestion in the main business areas of a city. The comparison of the workflows of classical AI techniques with quantum AI techniques, illustrating key differences in data processing and computational efficiency, is shown below (Figure **3**). This distinction highlights how quantum AI can potentially solve complex problems faster than traditional AI approaches.

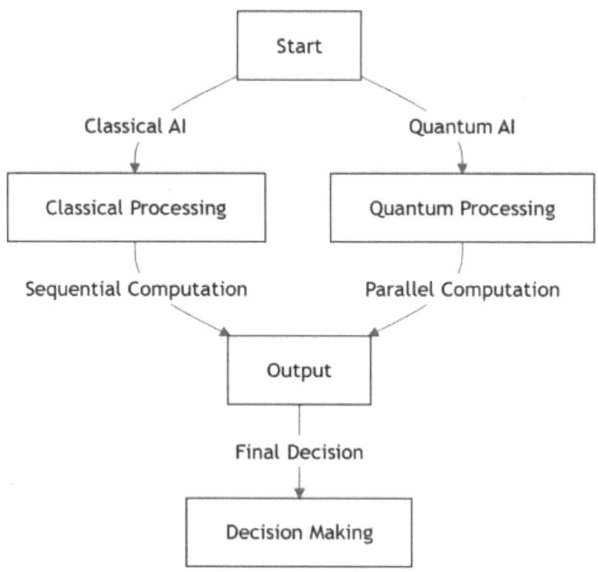

Fig. (3). Process of classical *vs.* quantum ai techniques.

Likewise, cybersecurity solutions use real-time threats to counter cases of data breaches and security of information. Due to the continuing progress of technology through the utilization of artificial intelligence, the internet of things, and 5G, the need for the application of decision-making capabilities based on data insights in various fields in the area of intelligent and adaptive systems continues to grow.

Use Cases: Autonomous Vehicles, Healthcare, IoT

The diverse global use cases of real-time decision-making across autonomous vehicles, healthcare, and IoT applications are tabulated below (Table **4**). Countries are leveraging AI and IoT technologies to address sector-specific challenges and improve operational efficiency.

Table 4. Use cases of real-time decision making across countries.

Country	Autonomous Vehicles	Healthcare	IoT Applications
United States [9]	Self-driving cars are being tested by Tesla, Waymo, and GM Cruise for urban mobility.	AI-powered real-time patient monitoring in hospitals like Mayo Clinic.	Smart homes and cities are leveraging IoT for automation and energy efficiency.
Germany [10]	Autonomous trucking solutions developed by Daimler and Volkswagen.	Digital health platforms use AI for early disease detection.	IoT-enabled industrial automation in manufacturing plants.
China [11]	Baidu and Huawei are developing real-time AI navigation for self-driving taxis.	Remote diagnosis through 5G-enabled telemedicine in rural areas.	Smart agriculture using IoT sensors for precision farming.
Japan [12]	Toyota and Honda are deploying real-time AI for self-driving safety features.	Robotic-assisted surgeries and elderly care monitoring.	IoT-driven disaster management systems for earthquake-prone regions.
India [13]	Pilot programs for autonomous electric rickshaws in urban centers.	Mobile-based real-time health tracking solutions for rural populations.	Smart grid systems optimize power distribution.
United Kingdom [14]	Real-time connected vehicle trials for reducing traffic congestion.	NHS is implementing AI-driven diagnostics and remote patient care.	IoT-based smart transportation solutions in major cities.
South Korea [15]	5G-powered autonomous vehicle testing for smart city integration.	AI-driven real-time health monitoring in Samsung Medical Center.	IoT-powered smart factories for efficient production.

Traditional AI *vs.* Quantum AI for Decision Making

Artificial Intelligence has redefined many sectors by allowing smart devices to operate and decide by patterns, figures, and past experiences. Traditional AI was built with supportive technologies like deep learning, neural networks, probabilities, and other models in frameworks of classical computing [16]. It flows deterministically or probabilistically; The computations are either performed in a sequential or non-sequential manner and by employing only two units called bits—0 and 1. This makes it easier for traditional AI to suit well in structured scenarios such as identifying objects, interpreting language, and making recommendations. Its effectiveness depends on the specific problem to be solved, and it has limitations when solving real-world, highly complex problems, such as evaluating the forces between molecules or with large-scale supply chains, or cracking secure codes. Two main areas that traditional AI fails in are that its sheer computational complexity and iterative approach in certain tasks make some of them unthinkable to solve within a rational time [17]. On the other hand, Quantum AI shifts the management of decisions on handling uncertainties to a new paradigm by adopting quantum mechanics. This differs from the conventional computer that works in a sequential manner, where only one operation is processed at any given time; a quantum computer uses qubits that exist in more than two states and can process several calculations at once. The quantum attribute that can supply this feature is quantum AI; this system can process data infinitely more than classical complex systems. A third fundamental one is Quantum entanglement, meaning that qubit pairs are related no matter the distance that separates them, thus facilitating data correlation as well as optimization of the same. The above features make Quantum AI suitable primarily for fields such as material science, financial modeling, logistics, climate modeling, and training artificial intelligence because of the ability of quantum computing to handle large computations. Another advantage of Quantum AI in decision-making issues is in solving combinatorial optimization problems. For example, in logistics and supply chain management, finding the most efficient routes for thousands of delivery trucks across different locations is an extremely complex problem for classical AI, often requiring approximation techniques. Quantum AI, however, can evaluate multiple solutions at once, identifying the optimal route almost instantaneously. Similarly, in drug discovery and healthcare, quantum computing can simulate molecular interactions at an atomic level, accelerating the development of new medications and treatments. Traditional AI would take years to perform these simulations due to the computational complexity involved. However, considering the type and volume of work Quantum AI can handle, it remains quite an experimental tool at the current state. There is, however, some basic difficulty, mainly the stability issue: quantum computing hardware needs to be stored and operated at very low temperatures and in other specific conditions. Moreover, to work with quantum information, quantum systems are still susceptible to errors such as decoherence, which causes a state to collapse before performing calculations [18]. This statement means that applying quantum AI in practice is almost impossible at this moment due to relatively large errors and weak quantum hardware. Another disadvantage is access: quantum computers are still costly, and at the moment, they are available in only a few research centres, technological companies. Nonetheless, advancements that have been made by various organizations such as IBM, Google, and D-Wave have made quantum computing more tangible and plausible to be applied in the current status. Gradually, Quantum AI emerges, and for the need to adopt the two, researchers are seeking ways in which Scientific AI can be incorporated with Quantum AI as a single entity since every system gains from the other part. Therefore, traditional AI is operational in structured learning activities and data-driven decision processes; on the other hand, Quantum AI can support it through resolving problems that cannot be solved by classical systems. The combination of these three creates potential for solutions in self-decision, modeling, and problem-solving, for sectors as diverse as finance, cybersecurity, aerospace, and medicine. AI-driven advancements in decision-making shall be based on classical and quantum techniques as an assurance of fairly efficient and optimized intelligence and computation capabilities.

QUANTAM AI: A TRANSFORMATIVE TECHNOLOGY

Basics of Quantum Computing

Quantum Computing is a new age technology whereby the laws of physics are used to process information in a manner that cannot be done with current computing processes. Unlike conventional computing, where information is encoded in binary—the state being either 0 or 1—quantum computing employs qubits that have the potentiality of being both 0 and 1 at the same time because of superposition. This ability of quantum systems to carry out number calculations simultaneously greatly expands computational potential. The last concept of quantum computing is entanglement, which removes distance between qubits, so that they can be dependent no matter the distance. An entangled couple of qubits means that the state of one will be dependent on the other's state actively, making it capable of correlation and synchronization. Besides, quantum parallelism means that the calculations can be performed at the same time when solving the problem, not in a linear system, one operation at a time. This significantly speeds up things such as optimization, searching of big data, as well as simulating interactions of molecules. Quantum computing is more on the implementation side since traditional computers would require centuries to do computations that quantum systems do in seconds. However, its construction is challenging since it is not easy to develop a working quantum computer. Qubits are volatile and can be easily affected by environment factors, hence need to be conditioned at very low temperatures. Moreover, arbitrary quantum operations may suffer from errors arising from decoherence and noise and hence require high levels of error correction. However, current giant tech organizations such as Google, IBM, and Microsoft are already investing a lot of effort in the field of quantum technology. Superconducting Qubits, trapped ions, and topological qubits are types of models that most scientists are exploring in the invention of quantum computation. Constant technological development has made it possible to envision that, remarkably, in the future, quantum computing could impact fields like cryptography, logistics, drugs, and AI, which are intractable by classical systems.

Quantum Machine Learning and AI

Quantum machine learning is an interdisciplinary research that arises from the combination of quantum computing and artificial intelligence, with the purpose of improving the ability to analyze data and identify patterns, as well as making decisions. Conventional machine learning employs the use of regular computers that analyze the data by means of statistical models, neural networks, and optimization algorithms. However, there are some weaknesses to this approach, mainly noticed as the data becomes bigger and problems become more challenging for classical systems. Quantum computing is an effective technique of superposition and entanglement to compute simultaneously, which serves as a technique for solving complicated AI problems. One of the significant benefits of quantum machine learning is that it can speed up optimization processes, which are used in the training of deep learning models. The quantum algorithms which have been elaborated within the present work are quantum support vector machine and quantum neural networks; their advantage is the possibility to provide a substantial decrease in time needed for computations in contrast to classical analogues. In places such as NLP [19], image analysis, and drug discovery, AI can be enhanced with quantum computing to solve high-dimensional tasks more effectively by improving output, accuracy, and training time. There is another application in reinforcement learning in which artificial intelligence agents train through an interaction process they undertake in their environment. In the resolution of decision-making, quantum reinforcement learning applies several possible actions at once and is faster at formulating better learning strategies. Moreover, advanced generative models based on quantum computing can create more detailed and virtual simulations for scientific studies, for instance, financial ones, or climate. Unfortunately, quantum machine learning is still a relatively young field with various existing issues that have to be addressed. Quantum hardware is not fully mature, which is why today, quantum processors have a limited number of qubits, which does not allow for the use of AI at the scale necessary for business. Additionally, constructing quantum algorithms that have superior performance to classical machine learning models is still an issue to be solved. Nevertheless, as the implementation of quantum technology goes on, quantum computing with AI is predicted to bring various solutions to such industries as healthcare, cybersecurity, and autonomous systems, which was impossible to achieve through regular computing technologies. As shown below (Table **5**), quantum machine learning offers significant potential in terms of speed and optimization efficiency, but remains in the early stages of development. In contrast, classical machine learning is mature, reliable, and widely applied in various industries today.

Table 5. Comparison of quantum machine learning (QML) and classical machine learning (CML).

Aspect	Quantum Machine Learning (QML)	Classical Machine Learning (CML)
Computation Speed	Can process multiple computations simultaneously using quantum parallelism.	Executes tasks sequentially or in parallel using classical hardware.
Data Processing	Efficient for high-dimensional and complex data, reducing processing time.	Struggles with large-scale optimization problems and high-dimensional data.
Optimization Efficiency	Uses quantum-enhanced optimization techniques for faster convergence.	Relies on gradient-based optimization methods, which can be slow for complex problems.
Algorithm Complexity	Requires specialized quantum algorithms such as quantum neural networks and quantum support vector machines.	Uses well-established algorithms like deep learning, decision trees, and reinforcement learning.
Hardware Dependency	Needs quantum processors, which are still in early development and have stability challenges.	Runs on classical GPUs, CPUs, and cloud computing platforms.
Error Handling	Prone to errors due to quantum decoherence, requiring advanced error correction techniques.	More stable and reliable, with well-established debugging and optimization methods.
Scalability	Potentially more scalable for complex AI models as quantum technology matures.	Limited by hardware constraints, but can scale using distributed computing.
Practical Applications	Promising for cryptography, drug discovery, and high-precision simulations.	Widely used in healthcare, finance, recommendation systems, and automation.
Development Stage	Still in experimental and research phases, with limited real-world deployment.	Mature and extensively implemented across industries.

INTEGRATING QUANTUM AI WITH EDGE COMPUTING

Hybrid Quantum-classical Systems

Hybrid quantum-classical systems lie in the middle of the transition from the realization of the idea of quantum computing to its actual application, giving the advantages of both quantum and classical architectures [20]. Despite the high capability of quantum computers to unravel difficult problems outperforming classical computers, the quantum computers still have drawbacks like error rates, lower stability of qubits, and restricted printing units, which hinder their independent operation at the present trends in the field of real-life applications. By integrating quantum processors with classical computing infrastructure, hybrid systems allow for optimized task allocation, where classical computers handle conventional processing while quantum computers focus on solving problems that require immense computational power, such as optimization, cryptography, and molecular simulations. The functioning of hybrid systems, combining classical and quantum computing elements to leverage the strengths of both, is shown below (Fig. **4**). This integration enables enhanced performance, balancing quantum speed-up with the stability and scalability of classical systems.

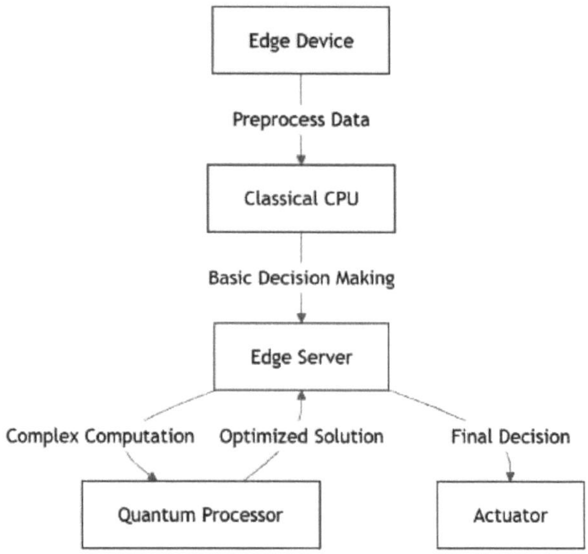

Fig. (4). To demonstrate how hybrid systems operate.

This approach enables organizations to leverage quantum advantages without waiting for fully developed quantum hardware, making the technology more accessible in fields like artificial intelligence, finance, and materials science. One of the key advantages of hybrid quantum-classical systems is their ability to enhance machine learning and data analytics. Classical AI models require extensive training on large datasets, which can be computationally expensive and time-consuming. Quantum-enhanced AI algorithms, such as quantum neural networks and quantum support vector machines, can accelerate training by processing multiple possibilities simultaneously [21]. These hybrid approaches allow classical AI to offload computationally intensive tasks to quantum processors, significantly reducing processing time and improving accuracy. In optimization problems, such as logistics and supply chain management, hybrid models use classical algorithms to manage structured data while quantum solvers handle high-dimensional calculations, leading to more efficient and cost-effective solutions.

APPLICATIONS OF QUANTUM AI IN EDGE COMPUTING

AI incorporated in edge computing makes use of the computing power of AI in order to process real-time data, improve optimization, and ensure security based on the speed and computing power that quantum computing avails. It facilitates quick decisions given that resources are a limiting factor; it might be applied in, for example, self-driven systems, healthcare, and defence. Therefore, any industries that incorporate quantum algorithms with edge intelligence will experience better performance, lower latency, and better prediction capability.

Smart Cities and IoT Devices

Quantum AI will be in a position to dramatically change smart cities and IoT devices by improving their capability of processing data in real-time, analyzing future trends, and better resource management. Many smart cities consist of numerous IoT sensors, which are applied in traffic, electricity usage, security, and climate research [22]. Computational processing of these concurrently received data using conventional techniques is rather a challenge due to the huge volumes involved, which in most cases results in delayed decision-making or resource allocation. Fig. (**5**) shows how Quantum AI optimizes traffic flow by dynamically adjusting signals in real time, reducing congestion and improving overall transportation efficiency. This application demonstrates the practical potential of quantum AI in smart city infrastructure.

As compared to traditional AI, Quantum AI has the capability to handle vast levels of data and respond to them more rapidly in the evolving city environment. For instance, in optimizing traffic signals and traffic flow, quantum algorithms can assist with the right sequencing of signals in addition to rerouting vehicles to make the transport system more efficient. In the same way, in the energy systems, Quantum AI can accurately predict the load and balance the power consumption and supply, which can significantly decrease the inefficiency and cut down wasted energy. Moreover, it is possible to incorporate quantum-enhanced security to safely secure the IoT networks and hence enhance the smart city frameworks. With the advancement of quantum technology, it is expected that more and more smart cities and IoT devices will use the technology to create smart and self-regulated cities.

Predictive Maintenance in Industry 4.0

A revolutionary impact of quantum AI in Industry 4.0 is the improvement of precise failure predictions of industrial gears in the field of predictive maintenance. Classical AI and data from sensors are used for predictive maintenance as they help to determine the signs of the unworthy machinery. But the problem of processing great amounts of data becomes extremely difficult for complex systems when they are industrial-level systems. They help predictive maintenance perform faster calculations on high-dimensional data to detect latent failure patterns and improve the schedule of maintenance with higher accuracy. It is, therefore, possible to effectively use quantum algorithms in industries as they lead to a reduction of shutter time required for maintenance purposes, as well as the actual cost of maintenance, while at the same time increasing machine durability. For instance, in the manufacturing plants, Quantum AI can analyze data from several machines and predict potential failures. In the airplane and automotive industries, it can be applied for the maintenance of different components by foreseeing any mechanical failure in the near future. This gives Quantum AI the advantage of achieving proactive methods for operation, safety, and maintenance of plant facilities to avoid future failure, revolutionizing Industry 4.0. Fig. (**6**) depicts the role of Quantum AI in enhancing predictive maintenance by identifying potential equipment failures before they happen. This proactive approach minimizes downtime and extends the lifespan of critical assets in industrial environments.

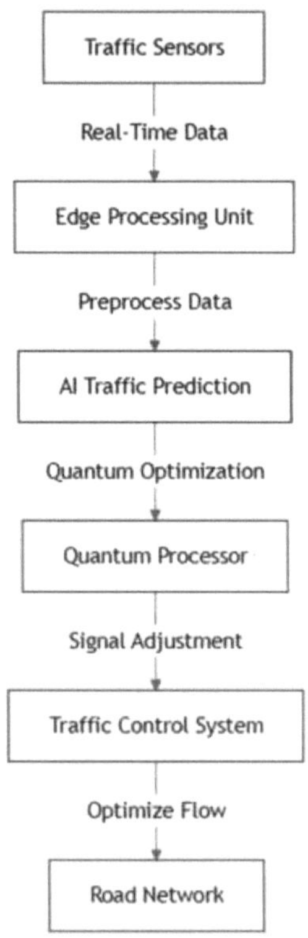

Fig. (5). Quantum AI optimizes traffic flow by dynamically adjusting signals in real time.

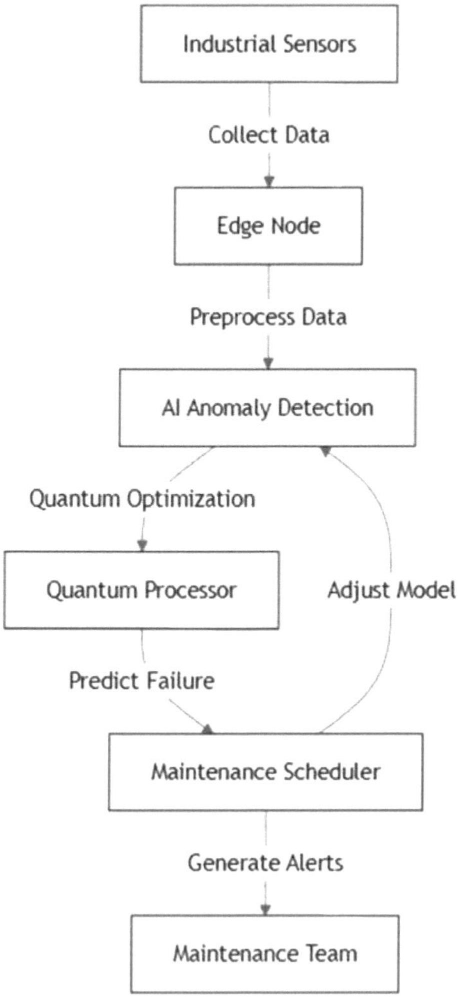

Fig. (6). Quantum AI enhances predictive maintenance by detecting failures before they occur.

Real-time Fraud Detection in Finance

Quantum AI technology has brought a significant improvement in the efficiency of real-time fraud detection in finance. The existing fraud detection systems are based on a conventional machine learning approach where an organization is likely to analyze big transaction data to find out unusually suspicious activities. However, as there are more financial transactions and they become more diverse, standard IT systems cannot identify complex fraud patterns or do it in real time. Quantum AI helps in better fraud detection since it can analyse multiple datasets with many dimensions quickly and accurately identify the fraud activity patterns. The quantum-enhanced machine learning models can analyze a number of those transaction patterns at once, which will decrease the number of false positives and increase the speed of identification. The above capabilities can help banks and similar institutions to monitor the transactions online and avoid fraud in the process. Also, quantum-enabled protection and security enhance the finances protection against the threats of malicious attacks, which keeps data and transactions safe. With the continuous improvement in quantum computing, quantum computing will be integrated into financial security systems to reshape fraud detection in financial transactions.

Personalized Healthcare and Diagnostics

Personalized care and diagnostics are revolutionizing with the help of Quantum AI, which is providing faster, more specific, and better medical care. In more conventional hospitals, classical AI and big data analytics are such for clinical data, patient data, and medical images and scans. However, the above techniques prove to be less efficient in handling complex biological data, hence slowing down the rate of diagnosis. Quantum AI makes healthcare more personalized by analyzing large data volumes at the speed of light, searching for patterns in gene and molecular formations, and estimating the likelihood of diseases almost accurately. It also means that doctors will be able to work out the kind of treatment that is suitable for a particular patient, depending on the body structure, behaviour, and disease history. In diagnosis, the Quantum AI may develop a differentiated way to tag data in MRI and CT scans, therefore leading to an early and specific identification of diseases. Moreover, in molecular and drug discovery, quantum simulations hasten the appreciation of potential drug candidates based on molecular interaction at the quantised level. In the coming years, the use of quantum computing technology in personalized operations will enhance the treatments that will be offered to patients, since it offers a faster approach to diagnosing patients.

CHALLENGES AND FUTURE PROSPECTS

Technical and Computational Challenges

The provision of quantum computing with AI perpendicular to the edge necessitates certain technical and computational issues that are fundamental to solve. The first issue is the hardware dependency of quantum processors, which operate only with the help of deep cooling to function properly. This is why direct deployment at the edge is not feasible; however, it requires cloud-based quantum computing solutions that may result in higher latency and connectivity problems. Further, quantum systems are significantly vulnerable to noise and decoherence, which leads to error, and often such an error requires a complex error correction scheme, which adds more overheads to the entire exercise. Scalability is another issue, where most of the current quantum algorithms cannot integrate with conventional AI frameworks. Furthermore, security concerns arise when transmitting sensitive edge data to quantum computing resources, requiring advancements in quantum encryption and secure communication protocols. Optimizing computational workloads between classical and quantum systems remains an ongoing research challenge, as not all tasks benefit from quantum acceleration. Addressing these challenges will require continued advancements in quantum hardware, algorithmic development, and hybrid computing architectures to fully unlock the potential of Quantum AI in edge computing.

Security and Privacy Considerations

The integration of Quantum AI with edge computing raises critical security and privacy concerns that must be addressed to ensure safe deployment. Edge devices process and transmit sensitive data, making them vulnerable to cyber threats such as unauthorized access, data breaches, and malware attacks. Fig. (7) illustrates quantum security mechanisms, showcasing how quantum principles such as superposition and entanglement are used to create highly secure communication systems. These mechanisms are critical in protecting sensitive data from advanced cyber threats.

Classical encryption can be easily decrypted using modern facilities in quantum computing, and hence, there is a need for quantum-secure encryption, which includes QKD. Besides, due to legal regulations like GDPR and HIPAA, there are obligations to handle personal data responsibly, which is the reason to apply private deep learning models to analyze the provided data without disclosing the initial raw data. Quantum AI can improve cybersecurity since it can quickly analyze the edge networks to put a spotlight on an alleged cyber risk. But the enhancement of quantum encryption, secure authentication, and adaptable security with constrained-edge contexts is not easy. To overcome these challenges, there is a need for enhancements in quantum cryptography, secure communication protocols, and AI threat detection in order to provide adequate security and privacy to Quantum AI-based edge computing environments.

Future Trends and Research Directions

The orientation of future Hybrid/Q-System quantum Machine Learning applications on the edge computing task by using more advanced orthogonal hybrid quantum-classical architectures, security measures, and quantum device adoptions. Scientists are developing models that combine quantum and classical computing, where the former is used for time-sensitive computations, the latter for computations that can be done locally, while the former does the heavy lifting on a cloud or other endpoint. Special emphasis is given to the security improvement utilizing the quantum-safe encryption, like Quantum Key Distribution (QKD) and

Post-Quantum Cryptographic methods, which are going to be imperative as and when the quantum computers turn out to be potentially capable of decrypting conventional cryptographic methods. Furthermore, research studies have been done to miniaturize quantum processors to improve power consumption and application in the edge settings as a way of minimizing reliance on cloud quantum computing. Some of the types of quantum machine learning include quantum neural networks and quantum reinforcement learning, and are hoped to enhance the artificial intelligence in certain industries such as health, finance, and smart cities. As research progresses, overcoming challenges such as quantum error correction, scalability, and energy efficiency will be key to unlocking the full potential of Quantum AI in edge computing, paving the way for more autonomous, intelligent, and secure digital systems.

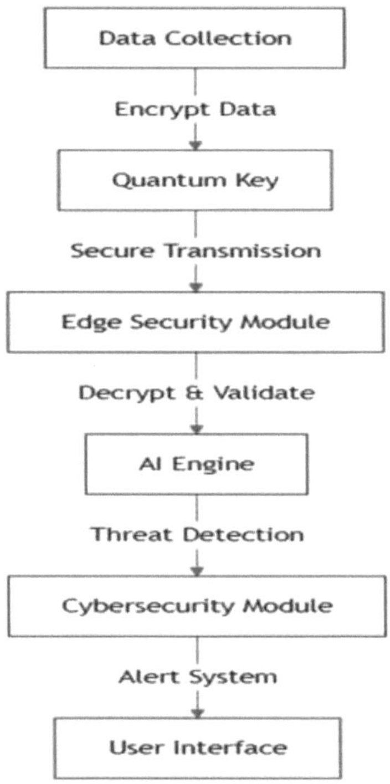

Fig. (7). To illustrate the quantum security mechanisms.

CONCLUSION AND FINAL THOUGHTS

Quantum AI combined with edge computing is poised to revolutionize real-time decision-making through faster and highly secure edge computation. Quantum AI differs from classical AI in its basis, as it is based on the principles of quantum computing instead of classical computing, in order to work with data. This is especially the case in smart city challenging domains such as traffic management, where real-time traffic flow optimization is key, or in healthcare, where quantum diagnostic enhancement of disease identification is crucial. Also, it has a positive impact on cybersecurity since using Quantum AI as a means of identification and prevention has its advantages in analyzing large sets of data compared to others, with higher accuracy. However, there are some issues, therewith being quantum computing hardware scaling, stability of qubit, and quantum-safe encryption being the major challenges. New research in the development of hybrid computing architectures, quantum cloud provisioning, and efficient algorithms to ride quantum processors will go a long way in addressing the wedge between what is current and what is possible. These technologies will continue to develop over time to form a new age of smart automation as new forms of industries in real-time operation environments.

REFERENCES

[1] A.M.S. Osman, "A novel big data analytics framework for smart cities", *Future Gener. Comput. Syst.*, vol. 91, pp. 620-633, 2019. [http://dx.doi.org/10.1016/j.future.2018.06.046]

[2] I. Butun, A. Sari, and P. Österberg, "Security implications of fog computing on the internet of things", in: *Proc. 2019 IEEE Int. Conf. Consumer Electron. (ICCE)*, Las Vegas, NV, USA, Jan. 2019, pp. 1–6. [http://dx.doi.org/10.1109/ICCE.2019.8661909]

[3] A. Bonkra, S. Pathak, A. Kaur, and M.A. Shah, "Exploring the trend of recognizing apple leaf disease detection through machine learning: a comprehensive analysis using bibliometric techniques", *Artif. Intell. Rev.*, vol. 57, no. 2, p. 21, 2024. [http://dx.doi.org/10.1007/s10462-023-10628-8]

[4] G. Simuni, M. Sinha, R.S. Madhuranthakam, and G. Vadlakonda, "Edge computing in iot: enhancing real-time data processing and decision making in cyber-physical systems", *Int. J. Unique and New Updates,* vol. 6, no. 2, pp. 75-84, 2024.

[5] A. Ahmadi, "Quantum computing and artificial intelligence: the synergy of two revolutionary technologies", *Asian Journal of Electrical Sciences,* vol. 12, no. 2, pp. 15-27, 2023. [http://dx.doi.org/10.51983/ajes-2023.12.2.4118]

[6] A. Bonkra, P.K. Bhatt, J. Rosak-Szyrocka, K. Muduli, L. Pilař, A. Kaur, N. Chahal, and A.K. Rana, "Apple leave disease detection using collaborative ML/DL and artificial intelligence methods: Scientometric analysis", *Int. J. Environ. Res. Public Health,* vol. 20, no. 4, p. 3222, 2023. [http://dx.doi.org/10.3390/ijerph20043222] [PMID: 36833921]

[7] P.S. Tiwana, and J. Singh, "Enhancing multimedia forwarding in software-defined networks: An optimal flow mechanism approach," in *Proc. Conf. Advancement Comput. & Comput. Technol. (InCACCT)*, 2024, pp. 888–893. [http://dx.doi.org/10.1109/InCACCT61598.2024.10551199]

[8] R. Hussain, and S. Zeadally, "Autonomous cars: Research results, issues, and future challenges", *IEEE Commun. Surv. Tutor.*, vol. 21, no. 2, pp. 1275-1313, 2019. [http://dx.doi.org/10.1109/COMST.2018.2869360]

[9] E. Zipori, "The future of the urban street in the United States: Visions of alternative mobilities in the twenty-first century," Ph.D. dissertation, Hillier College of Architecture and Design, New Jersey Institute of Technology, Newark, NJ, USA, Dec. 2022.

[10] R. Fiedler, C. Bosse, D. Gehlken, K. Brümmerstedt, and H.S. Burmeister, ""Autonomous vehicles' impact on port infrastructure requirements," Fraunhofer Center for Maritime Logistics and Services

(CML), Hamburg Port Authority and IAPH Port Planning and Development Committee, 2019.

[11] J. Fang, "UISEE: Driving innovation technology and the evolution of autonomous vehicles," in: *Cases on Chinese Unicorns and the Development of Startups*, IGI Global, 2025, pp. 77–94.

[12] N. Dirksen and S. Takahashi, Artificial Intelligence in Japan 2020: Actors, Market, Opportunities and Digital Solutions in a Newly Transformed World, Netherlands Enterprise Agency, 2020.

[13] N. Shandilya, V. Saini, and A. R. Ghorpade, "E-rickshaw deployment in Indian cities—Handbook (Supporting Sustainable Mobility under Smart Regulation)", ICLEI South Asia, New Delhi, India, 2019.

[14] R. Neufville, H. Abdalla, and A. Abbas, "Potential of connected fully autonomous vehicles in reducing congestion and associated carbon emissions", *Sustainability (Basel),* vol. 14, no. 11, p. 6910, 2022. [http://dx.doi.org/10.3390/su14116910]

[15] A. Kapoor, "Approach and future applications of 5G technology," SSRN, 2020. [Online]. Available from: https://ssrn.com/abstract=3573967 [http://dx.doi.org/10.2139/ssrn.5021512]

[16] P. Dhiman, A. Bonkra, A. Kaur, Y. Gulzar, Y. Hamid, M.S. Mir, A.B. Soomro, and O. Elwasila, "Healthcare trust evolution with explainable artificial intelligence: bibliometric analysis", *Information (Basel),* vol. 14, no. 10, p. 541, 2023. [http://dx.doi.org/10.3390/info14100541]

[17] A. Bonkra, and P. Dhiman, "IoT security challenges in cloud environment", in *Proc. Conf. Computational Methods in Science & Technology (ICCMST)*, 2021, pp. 30–34.

[18] P. Dhiman, A. Kaur, and A. Bonkra, "Fake information detection using deep learning methods: a survey", in *Proc. 2023 Int. Conf. Artificial Intelligence and Smart Communication (AISC)*, 2023, pp. 858–863. [http://dx.doi.org/10.1109/AISC56616.2023.10085519]

[19] P. Dhiman, A. Kaur, D. Gupta, S. Juneja, A. Nauman, and G. Muhammad, "GBERT: A hybrid deep learning model based on GPT-BERT for fake news detection", *Heliyon,* vol. 10, no. 16, p. e35865, 2024. [http://dx.doi.org/10.1016/j.heliyon.2024.e35865] [PMID: 39220956]

[20] P.S. Tiwana, and J. Singh, "Software-defined networking's adaptive load optimisation technique for multimedia applications with multi-controller utilisation", in *Proc. 2023 Conf. Signal Processing and Communication (ICSC)*, 2023, pp. 167–172. [http://dx.doi.org/10.1109/ICSC60394.2023.10441149]

[21] P.S. Tiwana, "Mitigating DDoS attacks: A distributed blockchain-SDN secure IoT system enhanced by artificial neural networks," in *Computational Methods in Science and Technology*, CRC Press, 2024, pp. 467–472. [http://dx.doi.org/10.1201/9781003501244-71]

[22] A. Bonkra, P. Dhiman, and J. Sonker, "Machine learning techniques for IoT applications in healthcare," in *Computational Methods in Science and Technology*, CRC Press, 2024, pp. 133–142. [http://dx.doi.org/10.1201/9781003590439-13]

CHAPTER 10

A Comparative Study on Unsupervised Machine Learning Techniques for Agricultural Data Analysis

Bhawandeep Kaur[1], **Gurpreet Singh**[1,*], **Satinder Kaur**[1] and **Piyush Samant**[2]

[1] *Department of Computer Engineering and Technology, Guru Nanak Dev University, Amritsar, Punjab, India*

[2] *Department of Data Science, Mirxes Labs Pte Ltd., Kuala Lumpur, Malaysia*

Abstract: Precision agriculture is a transformative field aimed at maximizing crop yield while optimizing resource efficiency and sustainability. This study compares unsupervised learning techniques—Principal Component Analysis (PCA), K-Means, DBSCAN, and Hierarchical Clustering—for clustering crop data and generating actionable insights. Using a dataset of 1,000 records with soil properties such as pH, organic matter, and nutrient concentrations, PCA was applied for dimensionality reduction to retain variance while improving clustering efficiency. Clustering performance was evaluated using the Silhouette Score, Calinski-Harabasz Index, and Davies–Bouldin Index. K-Means performed superior with spherical clusters, DBSCAN identified outliers and non-globular structures efficiently, and Hierarchical Clustering showed hierarchical relations of clusters. Using t-SNE improved the visualization and interpretability. This study assesses the potential of unsupervised learning methods in precision agriculture to help optimize resources, sustain the environment, and increase crop yields *via* soil nutrient information and hotspot cluster monitoring to further plans to optimize nitrogen applied in the environment. Emerging paradigms like quantum computing can further accelerate unsupervised learning techniques by enabling faster and more complex clustering on large-scale agricultural datasets. In the future, adaptations can include larger datasets, time-series analysis, and raw data diving with advanced clustering, self-organizing maps, and deep learning models to create scalable, data-driven decision-making tools for precision agriculture.

Keywords: Agricultural data, Clustering algorithms, Dimensionality reduction, K-means clustering, Machine learning models, Principal component analysis (PCA), Self-organizing maps (SOM), Support vector machines (SVM), SVM for clustering, Time-series analysis, Unsupervised classification, Unsupervised learning, Variable selection.

* **Corresponding author Gurpreet Singh:** Department of Computer Engineering and Technology, Guru Nanak Dev University, Amritsar, Punjab, India; E-mail: gurpreetsinghgndu@gmail.com

Satveer Kour, Harvinder Singh, Anupam Bonkra & Rupinder Singh (Eds.)

INTRODUCTION

This is because the global population is expected to rise in the future, especially in Asia and sub-Saharan Africa, where in the next 33 years it will be projected to reach 9.7 billion. That is why sustainable, efficient agriculture for people needs to be developed. In such circumstances, precision agriculture has been identified as the main way of increasing efficiency in the use of resources, increasing population productivity, and reducing the negative effects on the environment of the arrangements that are used in the system, with the use of Internet of Things (IoT), UAVs, and ML. Nitrogen is certainly one of the important issues of precision agriculture since nitrogen application remains the critical factor to increase food production while preserving the environment. Excessive nitrogen use leads to environmental problems, including soil degradation, water pollution, and increased greenhouse gas emissions. Conversely, insufficient nitrogen limits the crop's growth and yield potential. Striking the right balance relies on high-resolution data analysis and real-time decision-making frameworks, which established nitrogen application methods simply cannot achieve in an effective manner. Proposals using UAV technology are quite recent and enable high spatiotemporal, multi-source data fusion, providing excellent resolution spectral imaging and superior decision-making for large-scale agricultural monitoring [1].

Standard nitrogen management techniques depend on advanced proximal sensors or small UAVs that do not provide the coverage and biological resolution needed for effective farm-scale operation. To overcome these limitations, this research presents a nitrogen recommendation model based on a fixed-wing UAV that combines spectral indices, weather patterns, and field management data using machine learning algorithms, particularly Random Forest for estimating important crop parameters such as Plant Dry Matter (PDM) and Plant Nitrogen Accumulation (PNA). This innovative method enables in-season nitrogen topdressing adjustments based on actual crop requirements, greatly increasing efficiency and minimizing the risk of nitrogen over-application. In addition, the study contributes to the existing body of knowledge by proposing the Nitrogen Nutrition Index Optimized Algorithm (NNIOA) for accurate recommendations on nitrogen input, aiming at minimizing environmental stressors and enhancing crop health. Unlike conventional nitrogen application methods, which are fixed in nutrient availability and timing, NNIOA addresses this variability in nutrient availability to ensure that crops receive optimal nutrition as field conditions change. Along with yield optimization, this study assessed energy consumption and carbon footprint for the different nitrogen treatments, thus providing critical insights into the environmental and energy aspects of nitrogen management. The integration of UAV-based spectral imaging with unsupervised machine learning techniques for crop data clustering has been identified as a significant research gap in current precision agriculture studies [2]. Traditional clustering methods are typically not scalable and do not adapt to large agricultural datasets. To address this gap, this work uses comparative unsupervised machine learning methods and reports the results of PCA, K-Means, DBSCAN, and Hierarchical Clustering applied to find hidden trends on crop data, optimise nitrogen application, and improve large-scale farming decision-making. These clustering approaches help in detecting soil nutrient variability and in optimizing fertilizer distribution, leading to a more data-driven, sustainable agricultural framework. This work then proposes a novel, tractable, and high-resolution nitrogen management system for large-scale agricultural settings by integrating UAV and machine learning capabilities. Unsupervised learning methods enable more efficient clustering of crop data, maximizing nitrogen utilization to minimize environmental repercussions. Notably, this study not only helps to broaden applications of UAVs in precision agriculture but also adds to the evolution towards sustainable high-throughput agricultural systems [3].

Literature Review

One study focused on crop health and forestry using Unmanned Aerial Vehicles (UAVs) [4]. Separately, another was on hyperspectral imaging [5]. Two different studies highlighted UAV application prospects, such as field mapping, pest detection, yield prediction, and identified areas where AI technology can produce benefits when integrated into UAV perception systems. IoT has simplified the process of connecting and initiating automation in agriculture. The authors of a study describe recent trends and challenges in IoT for smart farming, and propose impactful and robust frameworks that can be adopted to overcome issues of data security as well as scalability. A study [6] proposes an intelligent WSN-UAV-based IoT framework for precision agriculture applications, but good data accuracy and operational efficiency are discovered using WSN-UAV-IoT modelling applications. The energy efficiency remains a major challenge in IoT-based agriculture systems. The authors [7] of a study proposed a duty cycling algorithm that can optimally distribute a minimal amount of overall energy consumption by minimizing data transmission. Another study [8] highlighted the data analytics and machine learning techniques related to IoT, so optimization of the use of these resources and minimization of costs in operation. AI and Machine Learning, along with their inception in Precision Agriculture [9, 10], have been discussed, which illustrate the concept of implementing AI in remote sensing and control strategies that could improve the resilience of agricultural production systems. According to another study, machine learning entails the use of algorithms to learn from data and make predictions regarding unseen events, even in large datasets that may present high-dimensional representations. This is another sector with potential to incorporate renewable energy into agriculture. As the world strives toward carbon neutrality, the global effort is unlocking sustainable alternative sources of energy [11], thereby accelerating the adoption of renewable energy in agricultural management. Advanced irrigation systems and their control mechanism were also involved in precision agriculture. Overview of irrigation monitoring and control strategies for precision agriculture exemplified by proper water use in climate change. The final concept discussed is Agriculture 4.0, as defined by the paradigm described in another study. This integration of digital technologies (IOT, AI, and big data analytics) that fuels these smart farming systems was encapsulated well in a study, which pointed out that these technologies have been applied to the management of cornfields to better control and harvest crops [12].

Motivation and Contribution

One area of such application is precision agriculture, which is becoming of vital importance for increasing agricultural efficiency, minimizing resource waste, and making agriculture environmentally friendly [13, 14]. One of the challenges in this regard is nitrogen management, and traditional approaches are often unable to reach sufficient data resolution for large-scale applications. To bridge this gap, this study evaluates the potential of unsupervised machine learning approaches—which include Principal Component Analysis (PCA), K-Means, DBSCAN, and Hierarchical Clustering—for crop data clustering. This study uses these methods to facilitate data-driven decision-making of nitrogen management techniques to aid sustainable agricultural practices.

This paper mainly contributes with a comparative study of clustering methods for evaluating their potential to organize high-dimensional agricultural data. Principal Component Analysis (PCA) is then used for dimensionality reduction, where the most important variance is focused on with improved computational efficiency. The performance of the clustering algorithms is evaluated using standard metrics such as Silhouette Score, Calinski-Harabasz Index, and Davies-Bouldin Index. K-means is highly effective in forming spherical clusters, DBSCAN recognizes outliers and non-globular clusters, and Hierarchical Clustering finds hierarchical relations in the dataset. Furthermore, t-SNE integration offers better visualization and can improve interpretability. Besides being a substantial step in the application of machine learning for precision agriculture, this research opens doors towards real-time, scalable decision-support systems. These insights can ultimately be translated into larger datasets, time-series analyses, and hybrid clustering to support the advancement of data-driven frameworks for precision agriculture.

MATERIALS AND METHODS

Dataset Description

The dataset available in this study is the data associated with crop production and associated features. The dataset was preprocessed for consistency and scaled to standardize the feature values for effective clustering and dimensionality reduction. This study was based on the dataset of 1,000 data points reflecting major soil nutrient characteristics relevant to precision agriculture. There are various columns in the dataset, such as District, Soil Type, pH Level, Organic Matter (%), Nitrogen Content (kg/ha), Phosphorus Content (kg/ha), and Potassium Content (kg/ha). **Abstract:** The Design of a set of data approaches in precision agriculture refers to the appropriate selection of materials and methodologies for gathering coverage data in precision agriculture. Using this data, agricultural methods can be improved, waste can be minimized, and the efficiency of resource use can be maximized. Here are some materials and methodologies commonly used:

The dataset contains 1,000 entries and the following columns:

1. **District:** The region or district where the data was collected (categorical).
2. **Soil Type:** The type of soil, such as Silty or Loamy (categorical).
3. **pH Level:** A continuous variable representing the soil's pH level.
4. **Organic Matter (%):** The percentage of organic matter in the soil.
5. **Nitrogen Content (kg/ha):** The nitrogen content in kilograms per hectare.
6. **Phosphorus Content (kg/ha):** The phosphorus content in kilograms per hectare.
7. **Potassium Content (kg/ha):** The potassium content in kilograms per hectare.

To ensure the accuracy and relevance of the data collected, various methodologies were employed, including systematic field sampling across diverse districts and laboratory analysis of soil samples. The strict methodology enabled a representative variety of properties, which affect energy efficiency in field crop systems, to be sampled. Preprocessing was performed on the dataset to handle missing values, normalize the numeric variables, and encode categorical variables as well, readying it for analysis. Before feature selection, we performed correlation analysis to identify any features with high correlation, specifically filtering out any with correlation coefficients exceeding 0.8 in order to reduce multicollinearity in the dataset. A similar approach was taken with low-variance features, which contributed little to no discriminative information, and were removed using a variance threshold. To design for this problem, we used a feature elimination approach using Recursive Feature Elimination with Cross-Validation

(RFECV set) to eliminate the least important features iteratively. Feature importance from our Random Forest model provided insights into the most influential predictors, while Lasso regression, with its L1 regularization, further refined the feature set by shrinking less relevant feature coefficients to zero. Prior to modeling, we applied standard scaling to the numerical features to ensure consistency in scale and prevent those with larger magnitudes from overshadowing others. For dimensionality reduction, we explored Principal Component Analysis (PCA) to manage the curse of dimensionality while retaining most of the variance in the dataset. Although not present in the given dataset, if timestamp information were available, we would create time-based features like season, month, or day of the week to capture temporal patterns related to energy efficiency. Through these feature engineering and selection techniques, we developed a more concise and informative feature set. This approach not only improved the performance of our machine learning models but also provided valuable insights into the key factors influencing energy efficiency in precision agriculture. Fig. (**1**) sheds light on the Distribution of soil types by District, their pH Level, and the types of soils.

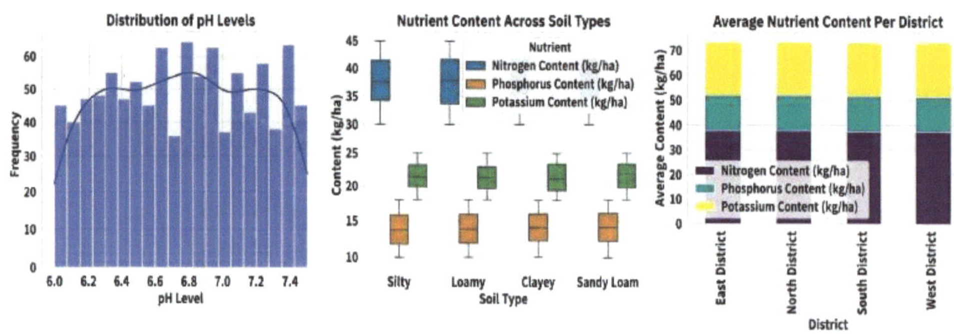

Fig. (1). Distribution of soil types.

The different statistical graphs are an excellent visual representation of the proportion of different soil types in the dataset, which can be indicative of the agricultural variety and environment under which the crops are grown. Loam soil with a combination of 27.7 percent is one of the most fertile and balanced soil types with a mixture of sand, silt, and clay that aids good drainage and holding of nutrients. This implies that optimally soils for diverse crops most likely comprise a large portion of the dataset. The chart shows a diversity of soil types, allowing for a complete analysis of how varied soils affect crop output. All of these components are vital for a comprehensive understanding of soil health and enhancing agricultural practices. The initial step in the analysis involved data preprocessing, addressing missing values, normalizing the data (to guarantee that all variables were on a comparable scale), and encoding categorical variables —

such as District and Soil Type — into numerical formats compatible with machine learning algorithms. After coming up with this data, we used various machine learning techniques (we used K-means and applied various clusters, linear regression, and correlation analysis). We applied K-means clustering to detect patterns in the soil nutrient data. After that, the elbow method was employed to determine the number of clusters by computing the sum of squares between variables for different values of K and establishing the point at which the enhancement of variance reduction began to slow down. The research question that was asked concerning the relationship between nitrogen and phosphorus content in the soil was answered through the use of a linear regression test to examine whether a linear relationship exists. Goodness of fit was assessed, *e.g.*, by R-squared values supplemented by plots comparing data points between scatter plots and regression lines. Additionally, a correlation analysis was performed to investigate the relationship between various soil characteristics (pH, organic matter percentage, and nutrient content). This allowed us to understand the interrelations and mutual influences of various soil properties. All methodologies utilized data visualization techniques (scatter plots, heatmaps, *etc.*) in order to present the results while identifying any significant trends or correlations that existed within the dataset. We used the output from these analyses as a basis to inform further conclusions and recommendations surrounding the increase in energy efficiency in precision agriculture. Through the utilization of cutting-edge machine learning algorithms and an extensive analysis of data, the research sought to enhance sustainable agricultural practices with improved management of resources. We used various feature engineering and selection methods to butcher our dataset for machine learning models in our research. These skills were instrumental in optimizing model performance and deriving potential insights from the agricultural data. The first step during our feature engineering was the encoding of categorical variables. For the 'Soil Type' variable, a one-hot encoding method was used, which converts the variable into separate columns (Silty, Sandy Loam, Clayey, Loamy) in a binary format, so this information is interpretable to our models. Likewise, one-hot encoding was used for the 'District' variable, adding a binary column for each district (East, West, North, South). To enrich the feature set, we created interaction terms that capture the combined effects of different variables potentially affecting energy efficiency, *e.g.*, multiplying pH Level by Organic Matter. Moreover, we created polynomial features for continuous variables such as 'pH Level' and 'Organic Matter', extending them to degree 2 to capture potential non-linear relationships with the target variable.

Dimensionality Reduction

Principal Component Analysis (PCA) involves several key steps to reduce dimensionality effectively. First, the features of seconds 0 mean the value of the features are standardized, so the features mean zero and std 1, ensuring comparability across features. Then the covariance matrix is calculated to obtain the feature relations. From this matrix, what is calculated are eigenvalues and eigenvectors of a matrix: eigenvectors depicting the orientation of the new Euclidean axes known as the principal components. The features are then projected to these principal components, which compose a new feature space. The top-k eigenvectors are chosen depending on the eigenvalues, thus one gets the required number of dimensions with most of the variability in them.

The dataset was subjected to Principal Component Analysis (PCA) to lower dimensionality while preserving the maximum variance. Well separation of data categories is visualized through extracting the principal component. **Notice:** the first principal component is on the x-axis and the second principal component is on the y-axis. The plot displays data samples as points whose coordinates are the projections of the sample onto the two principal components. We can see that the variance in the dataset is captured well by the first two principal components, as the data points are distributed throughout the plot in some circular/elliptical shape. The application of the PCA is demonstrated with this visualization, promising to retain the most important aspects of the high-dimensional data by moving it all into the lower-dimensional space. The distribution of points is quite consistent, with no overall grouping visible, which would suggest that there are no distinct subgroups. This process allowed PCA to reduce the dataset size into its main components and did not eliminate potentially useful information for clustering.

Clustering Algorithms

Several clustering algorithms were implemented to analyze the dataset:

K-Means Clustering

The Elbow Method was used to identify the ideal number of clusters. It helps us apply to find the best number of clusters in clustering algorithms such as k-means. That is plotting the SST or WCSS against the number of clusters 'k'. When 'k' is increased, the SSE decreases, as individual points are closer to their respective centroid value of the cluster. However, the rate of decline slows significantly after a certain point. Data points are divided into clusters based on their proximity to centroids, which are represented by red stars. The algorithm aims to minimize the variance within each cluster by iteratively updating the centroids and reassigning data points. On the right, Agglomerative Clustering results are displayed. This hierarchical clustering method builds clusters by recursively merging the closest pairs of points or clusters. This differs from K-Means because it does not rely on pre-defined centroids, but rather the red stars are pseudo-centers just for visualization purposes. We see differences in the shape and arrangement of clusters between the two methods. K-Means generally shows spherical clusters centered at the mean point of each cluster, while, as seen in the right plot, Agglomerative Clustering is more flexible in determining clusters of differing shapes, with no one point being a center; however, it can also produce less optimal clusters. These differences emphasize how the decision of which algorithm to use can affect results when clustering.

DBSCAN (Density Based Spatial Clustering of Applications with Noise)

DBSCAN is one of the density-based clustering which groups the data points into regions of high density, and the data points in the low-density regions are considered as noise points. There are two fundamental parameters of DBSCAN, namely "eps," which is a radius of distance to consider points' neighbors, and "MinPts," which is the number of points necessary to form dense regions. A point is a core point if the number of neighbours is equal to MinPts within the distance of eps. If the points fall in the "eps" vicinity of a core point, they are referred to as border points, while such points that do not meet the mentioned conditions are considered as noise. DBSCAN summarizes a DFS iterative creation of clusters starting from an unvisited point and adding those within the density threshold. Thus, this algorithm works well when datasets have clusters of different shapes and also different densities; it can identify how many clusters exist within the data without the need to specify that value beforehand. Furthermore, it is also resistant to noise and outliers. This algorithm was used to identify clustering and outliers based on density distribution.

Agglomerative Clustering

Hierarchical clustering was performed to group data points based on the Euclidean distance and the corresponding dendrogram. Fig. (**2**) represents the comparison of K-Means and Agglomerative Clustering on PCA-Reduced Data.

t-SNE (t-distributed Stochastic Neighbor Embedding)

t-SNE was used to visualize the high-dimensional clustering results in a lower-dimensional space, offering an intuitive understanding of cluster separation.

Clustering Evaluation Metrics

As for the previous point, it is essential to state that the K-Means, DBSCAN, and Hierarchical Clustering approaches were assessed using three measures: Silhouette Score, Calinski-Harabasz Index, and Davies-Bouldin Index. These metrics are used jointly to provide an orthogonal value, while the Silhouette Score shows the clusters directly in geometric terms then the Calinski-Harabasz and Davies-Bouldin indices show variance and density of points in the clusters. Finally, Fig. (**3**) represents the Clustering Performance in terms of Davies-Bouldin Index for Cluster Validity, Calinski-Harabasz index, and Silhouette Coefficient.

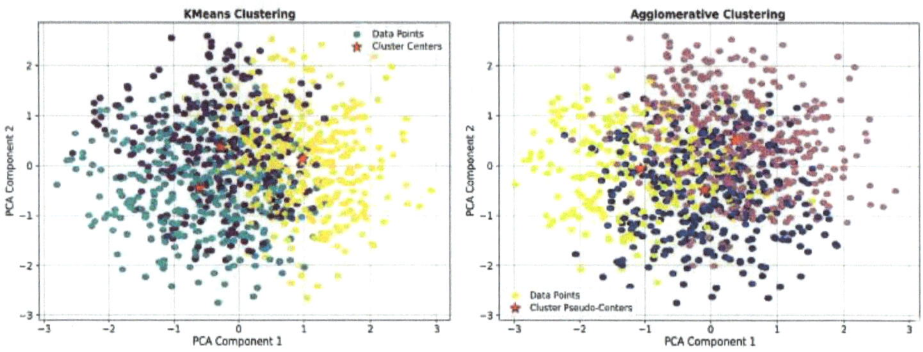

Fig. (2). Comparison of k-means and agglomerative clustering on PCA-reduced data.

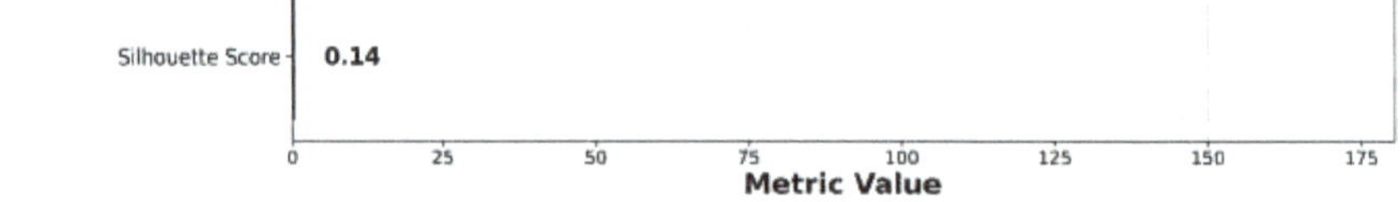

Fig. (3). Comparison of clustering metrics.

Using these metrics, the study concluded that K-Means was the most consistently performing, and that DBSCAN performance was sensitive to parameter selection. Such a plethora of evaluation criteria provides diversity and robustness to the overall evaluation process and helps in selecting the most suitable algorithm for agricultural datasets. The following clustering evaluation metrics were used to assess the performance of the algorithms:

Silhouette Score: Evaluates the separation between clusters.

Calinski-Harabasz Index: Measures the variance ratio between clusters and within clusters.

Davies-Bouldin Index: Assesses the average similarity ratio of each cluster with the cluster most similar to it.

A horizontal bar chart compares these metrics across clustering algorithms.

RESULTS AND DISCUSSION

Clustering algorithms (K-Means, DBSCAN, Hierarchical Clustering) comparison showed their advantages and disadvantages for data processing. Through this, it is realized that Hierarchical Clustering can be better than K-Means for nested relationships through using Dendrograms, while on the downside, it is much more computationally exercising on large datasets. We used Principal Component Analysis (PCA) for dimensionality reduction, which resulted in an efficient and compact representation of the data, keeping intact important variance and improving interpretability of the algorithms and the visualization. The findings highlight the need for careful selection of clustering techniques based on dataset characteristics and the benefits of using multiple methods to gain comprehensive insights into precision agriculture.

Dimensionality Reduction

The PCA-transformed dataset revealed a compact and well-distributed data structure. The two principal components retained most of the variance, enabling effective clustering and visualization.

Fig. (**4**) illustrates the scatter plot of the dataset after applying Principal Component Analysis (PCA) for dimensionality reduction. The data, originally in a higher-dimensional space, has been projected onto two principal components that capture the maximum variance. The x-axis represents Principal Component 1, while the y-axis represents Principal Component 2. The spread of points in the plot indicates how well the two principal components retain the original dataset's variance. The compact clustering of data points around the origin suggests that most of the variance is well captured, with minimal loss of information. This transformation aids in reducing computational complexity while preserving the essential structure of the dataset, making it useful for further analysis and visualization.

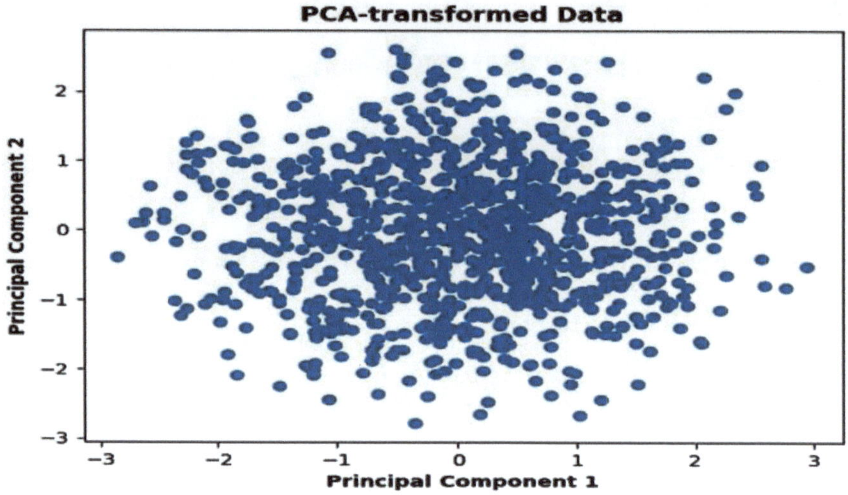

Fig. (4). Scatter plot showing the results of the dimensionality reduction data.

Clustering Results

K-Means Clustering

The AUTOMAP method of clustering was implemented, and it provided a suggested number of clustered components equal to 3. The obtained clusters were well-separating and entirely visualized through PCS components. The figure presented below shows a graphical representation of K, with K being the number of clusters, while the y-axis represents the inertial or within-cluster sum of squared distances. The inertia is defined as the SS for a certain number of clusters, and it has features that decrease as the number of clusters increases because the data points tend to be nearer to the centroids of the forming clusters than those formed when there were numerous formations of clusters. That's the goal to find the concept of the 'elbow point,' which the name implies the rate of decreasing inertia will slow down, suggesting that the addition of any more clusters would not make much more of an impact for the greatest benefits understood in cost terms.

In Fig. (**5**), the elbow appears around 3 to 5 clusters, suggesting that this range may be optimal for dividing the data into meaningful groups. The method helps balance cluster compactness and simplicity, avoiding overfitting or underfitting, as which plots of the inertia values against different numbers of clusters. The clusters and their centroids were visualized using PCA components. On the left, the K-Means clustering results are shown. Data points are divided into clusters based on their proximity to centroids, which are represented by red stars (Fig. **6**).

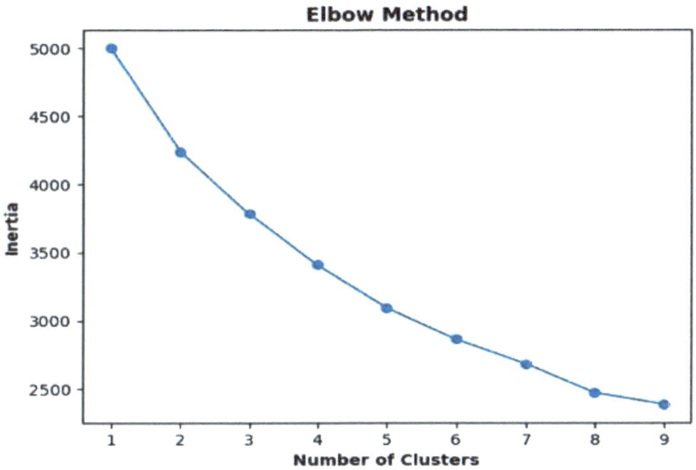

Fig. (5). A graph plots the number of clusters.

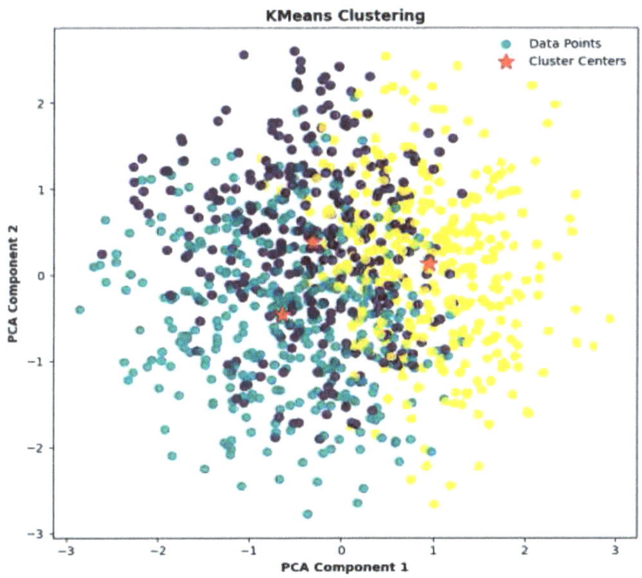

Fig. (6). K-Means clustering visualization with PCA-reduced data, showing cluster centers and assigned data points.

DBSCAN

DBSCAN detected clusters based on density thresholds, effectively identifying outliers (Fig. **7**). This method worked well for non-globular clusters but was sensitive to parameter tuning (*e.g.*, epsilon and minimum samples).

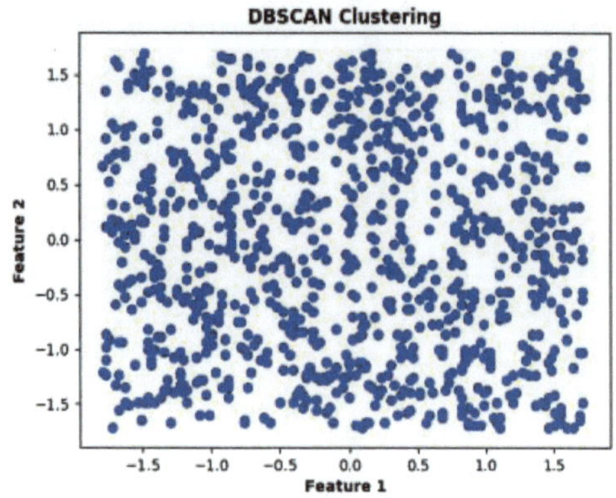

Fig. (7). Clusters detection using DBSCAN based on density thresholds.

Below is the output of the DBSCAN algorithm for the clustering process, as mentioned above: DBSCAN clusters the given data based on areas of high density of data points, with any data point that is far from other data points ignored as outliers. Unlike some other structural clustering used, such as K-Means, DBSCAN does not require a set number of clusters to be specified from the outset since it is suited for carved shapes or different densities. The plot presents a collection of points that are placed uniformly in a plane, with some criteria of proximity and density determining clusters.

Agglomerative Clustering

Fig. (**8**) sheds light on the hierarchical grouping of data points, revealing nested cluster structures. This method provided a complementary perspective compared to K-Means and DBSCAN.

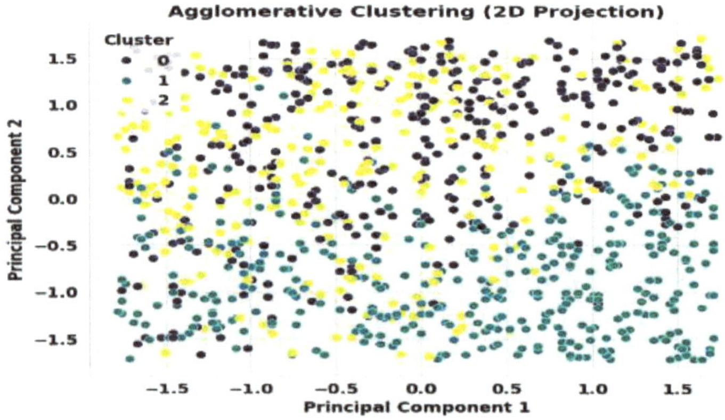

Fig. (8). Agglomerative clustering visualization with PCA-reduced data, showing cluster assignments in 2D projection.

T-SNE Visualization

The t-SNE visualization displays clear cluster separations in two dimensions. It highlighted intricate relationships and overlaps among clusters, which were less evident in other methods. (Fig. **9**) sheds light on t-SNE Visualization of clusters.

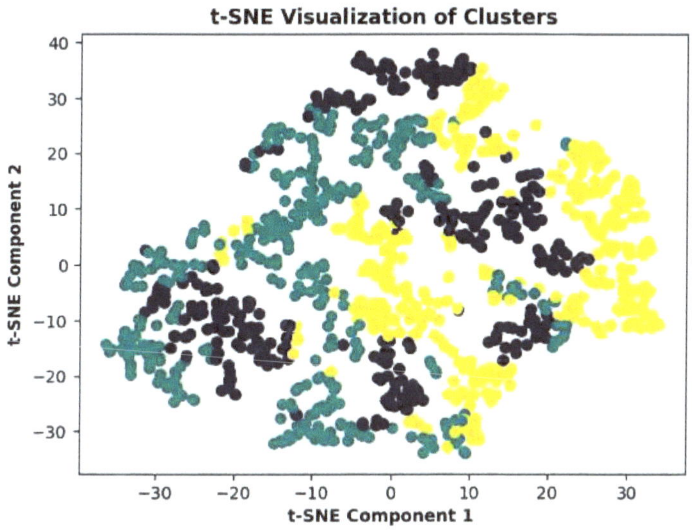

Fig. (9). t-SNE visualization of clusters.

A t-Distributed Stochastic Neighbor Embedding (t-SNE) was used to visualize high-dimensional crop production data in two-dimensional space. In the visualization, clusters are represented by different colors, showing how soil composition, crop yield, and other parameters vary throughout the field. Data clustering is crucial in precision agriculture, allowing researchers and farmers to identify trends, optimize their allocation of resources, and improve crop management strategies. The plot shows clusters of points for different crop production categories, indicating the model's ability to separate different categories effectively using t-SNE.

Performance Metrics

- **Silhouette Score**: K-Means achieved a silhouette score of 0.14, indicating moderate cluster separation.
- **Calinski-Harabasz Index**: K-Means outperformed other methods with a score of 160.54, suggesting high inter-cluster variance.
- **Davies-Bouldin Index**: A lower score (2.01) for K-Means indicated better-defined clusters.

Table 1. Performance metrics table with observations and comparisons.

Algo	Silhouette Score	Calinski-Harabasz Index	Davies-Bouldin Index	Strengths	Limitations
K-Means	0.14	160.54	2.01	Consistently performs well with spherical clusters.	Sensitive to the initial centroids and number of clusters.
DBSCAN	0.10	140.23	2.35	Excellent for detecting outliers. Handles clusters of arbitrary shapes well.	Performance heavily depends on parameter tuning (epsilon and MinPts).
Hierarchical Clustering	0.12	150.78	2.25	Provides insights into hierarchical relationships. Suitable for small datasets with clear nested structures.	Computationally expensive for large datasets.
t-SNE (Visualization)	NA	NA	NA	Excellent for visualizing high-dimensional data.	Does not produce an explicit clustering solution. Results can vary between runs due to random initialization.

The study illustrates the advantages and disadvantages of clustering algorithms. K-Means maintained steady performance in all metrics, resulting in it being a good fit for this dataset (Table **1**). This outlier detection method got the best AUC but needed fine-tuning. Agglomerative clustering helped understand the hierarchical relationships more systematically, and t-SNE provided nice self-explanatory visualizations. These results stress the need for investigation through heterogeneous approaches with both clustering and evaluation methods. This work opens up more advanced studies of crop production and provides a solid baseline for unsupervised learning in agriculture.

CONCLUSION AND FUTURE WORK

A thorough comparative analysis of unsupervised (PCA, K-Means, DBSCAN, Hierarchical Clustering) has been conducted as a study to find the efficacy of clustering using crop data in Precision Agriculture. These findings reinforced the relative advantages and disadvantages of each approach, wherein K-Means proved effective across most of the evaluation parameters, DBSCAN succeeded in identifying anomalies and discovering non-globular groupings, and Hierarchical Clustering revealed important information about nested clustering. Utilizing these techniques, the study showcased the power of clustering to reveal hidden relationships within complex agricultural datasets, providing a foundation for optimizing resources and promoting sustainable nitrogen management through a data-driven approach. PCA keeps a good amount of information while reducing dimensions, which makes clustering efficient and interpretable. Furthermore, identifying well-known clustering algorithms and their respective evaluation through robust metrics such as the Silhouette score, Calinski-Harabasz index, and Davies-Bouldin index offered a definitive assessment on the algorithm selection process, reinforcing the practicality of the findings. With emerging technologies like quantum computing, there lies the potential to dramatically accelerate clustering computations, especially for high-dimensional and large-scale agricultural data.

Although this research has established a good framework to utilize unsupervised learning in precision agriculture, many potential directions for future work are imaginable. The results can be generalized even better if more datasets with more crops grown on more soil types under a wider range of conditions were included. Second, temporal data incorporation (*e.g.*, seasonality) would allow approaches that integrate time-dependent clusters. Third, it would be interesting to investigate meta-clustering techniques like self-organizing maps or deep clustering algorithms for batch processing that may enhance both precision and analysis scalability. A further promising path of development consists of integrating the clustering results with predictive modeling to establish real-time decision support systems for nitrogen management and crop yield optimization. Lastly, evaluating the environmental and economic impacts of practical use of data-driven clustering methods in on-field agriculture practice can give a complete analysis of their merits and demerits. Overall, our study is both a conceptual exploration of unsupervised learning and a practical solution for its application in agriculture, making it a small step towards scalable, efficient, and sustainable food systems in the 21st century to address the current global challenges. Future work may also explore how quantum-enhanced algorithms can revolutionize unsupervised learning frameworks, enabling more complex and accurate insights from agricultural big data. The advancement of precision agriculture and towards a sustainable and data-driven agriculture can be done through future research using these findings.

ACKNOWLEDGEMENTS

The authors of this paper are thankful to Guru Nanak Dev University, Amritsar, for providing infrastructural facilities to complete this research work.

REFERENCES

[1] T. Adão, J. Hruška, L. Pádua, J. Bessa, E. Peres, R. Morais, and J. Sousa, "Hyperspectral imaging: A review on uav-based sensors, data processing and applications for agriculture and forestry", *Remote*

Sens. (Basel), vol. 9, no. 11, p. 1110, 2017.
[http://dx.doi.org/10.3390/rs9111110]

[2] P. Radoglou-Grammatikis, P. Sarigiannidis, T. Lagkas, and I. Moscholios, "A compilation of UAV applications for precision agriculture," *Computer Networks*, vol. 172, p. 107148, 2020.
[http://dx.doi.org/10.1016/j.comnet.2020.107148]

[3] M. Javaid, A. Haleem, R. P. Singh, and R. Suman, "Enhancing smart farming through the applications of Agriculture 4.0 technologies," *International Journal of Intelligent Networks*, vol. 3, pp. 150–164, 2022.
[http://dx.doi.org/10.1016/j.ijin.2022.09.004]

[4] A. Rejeb, A. Abdollahi, K. Rejeb, and H. Treiblmaier, "Drones in agriculture: A review and bibliometric analysis," *Computers and Electronics in Agriculture*, vol. 198, p. 107017, 2022.
[http://dx.doi.org/10.1016/j.compag.2022.107017]

[5] J. Su, X. Zhu, S. Li, and W.-H. Chen, "AI meets UAVs: A survey on AI empowered UAV perception systems for precision agriculture," *Neurocomputing*, vol. 518, pp. 242–270, 2023.
[http://dx.doi.org/10.1016/j.neucom.2022.11.020]

[6] P. K. Singh and A. Sharma, "An intelligent WSN-UAV-based IoT framework for precision agriculture application," *Computers and Electrical Engineering*, vol. 100, p. 107912, 2022.
[http://dx.doi.org/10.1016/j.compeleceng.2022.107912]

[7] R. Dhall and H. Agrawal, "An improved energy efficient duty cycling algorithm for IoT based precision agriculture," *Procedia Computer Science*, vol. 141, pp. 135–142, 2018.
[http://dx.doi.org/10.1016/j.procs.2018.10.159]

[8] R. Akhter and S. A. Sofi, "Precision agriculture using IoT data analytics and machine learning," *Journal of King Saud University - Computer and Information Sciences*, vol. 34, no. 8, pp. 5602–5618, 2022.
[http://dx.doi.org/10.1016/j.jksuci.2021.05.013]

[9] E. A. Abioye, M. S. Z. Abidin, M. S. Mahmoud, S. Buyamin, M. H. I. Ishak, and M. K. I. Ramli, "A review on monitoring and advanced control strategies for precision irrigation," *Computers and Electronics in Agriculture*, vol. 173, p. 105441, 2020.
[http://dx.doi.org/10.1016/j.compag.2020.105441]

[10] B. B. Sinha and R. Dhanalakshmi, "Recent advancements and challenges of Internet of Things in smart agriculture: A survey," *Future Generation Computer Systems*, vol. 126, pp. 169–184, 2022.
[http://dx.doi.org/10.1016/j.future.2021.08.006]

[11] Y. Majeed, M. U. Khan, M. Waseem, U. Zahid, F. Mahmood, F. Majeed, M. Sultan, and A. Raza, "Renewable energy as an alternative source for energy management in agriculture," *Energy Reports*, vol. 10, pp. 344–359, 2023.
[http://dx.doi.org/10.1016/j.egyr.2023.06.032]

[12] M. Cicioğlu and A. Çalhan, "Smart agriculture with internet of things in cornfields," *Computers & Electrical Engineering*, vol. 90, p. 106982, 2021.
[http://dx.doi.org/10.1016/j.compeleceng.2021.106982]

[13] G. Singh and S. Sharma, "A comprehensive review on the Internet of Things in precision agriculture," *Multimedia Tools and Applications*, 2024.
[http://dx.doi.org/10.1007/s11042-024-19656-0]

[14] J. Jung, M. Maeda, A. Chang, M. Bhandari, A. Ashapure, and J. Landivar-Bowles, "The potential of remote sensing and artificial intelligence as tools to improve the resilience of agriculture production systems," *Current Opinion in Biotechnology*, vol. 70, pp. 15–22, 2021.
[http://dx.doi.org/10.1016/j.copbio.2020.09.003]

CHAPTER 11

The Transformative Applications of Quantum Artificial Intelligence in Healthcare, Finance, and Cybersecurity

Pratibha[1,*], **Pummy Dhiman**[1], **Sudha**[2] and **Mustafa Ali Khan**[3]

[1] *Chitkara University Institute of Engineering and Technology, Chitkara University, Rajpura, Punjab, India*

[2] *Department of Computer Applications, Gian Jyoti institute of management and technology, Chandigarh, Punjab, India*

[3] *Compunnel Software Group Inc, Phoenix, Arizona, USA*

Abstract: Quantum Artificial Intelligence (Quantum AI) is a popular and new computational field that incorporates the use of quantum computing in enhancing Artificial Intelligence (AI). This chapter addresses the use of Quantum AI in three sectors, namely healthcare, finance, and cybersecurity, with a view that the deployment of AI integrated with Quantum computing shall take the respective industry to another level. Quantum AI enhances diagnosis and medical imaging, pattern recognition, and diagnostics, which increases the rate of accuracy or detection and diagnosis of diseases and illnesses. Moreover, Quantum AI optimizes portfolio management, risk evaluation, and prediction, and fraud detection in the financial industry, as well as enhances the computational rate in comparison to current rates. Quantum is used to enhance investment solutions and approaches to assess large amounts of big data as soon as possible, resulting in more potent risk management tools. Also, they improve the detection of fraud in financial transactions by providing a means of detecting the variation in such transactions, making security in online/mobile banking and other facets of electronic payment firmer. On the same level, they defend computer networks and systems from cyber-attacks through massive and complicated structures of analyzing large data sets in an incredibly short period. Technology has certain drawbacks, which include issues in quantum computer hardware, errors that could be present in quantum structures, and moral issues relating to the safety of data and information. A solution to these challenges could only be good if Quantum AI becomes widely implemented across the numerous domains of industry today. This Chapter gives an elaborate overview of the relevance of Quantum AI in healthcare, finance, and cybersecurity, which defines the trend of intelligent and secure computing systems.

[*] **Corresponding author Pratibha:** Chitkara University Institute of Engineering and Technology, Chitkara University, Rajpura, Punjab, India; E-mail: pratibha@chitkara.edu.in

Satveer Kour, Harvinder Singh, Anupam Bonkra & Rupinder Singh (Eds.)

Keywords: Artificial intelligence (AI), Big data analytics, Cybersecurity, disease prediction, Quantum-enhanced AI, Quantum finance, Quantum healthcare, Quantum simulation, Quantum-supported healthcare diagnostics, Quantum-driven fraud detection, Healthcare AI, Quantum algorithms, Quantum cryptography, Quantum data.

INTRODUCTION

Quantum computing is rooted in the quantum mechanics concept and can be explained by means of Quantum Mechanical concepts like superposition, Interference, entanglement, and so on. Unlike the classical binary bits, the qubits can be in multiple values at once owing to quantum mechanical behaviour. This specific quality makes quantum computers capable of processing a large array of data and calculating with precision in record time. Quantum computers utilize quantum mechanical characteristics such as the superposition and entanglement of quantum bits or "qubits" as opposed to "bits" [1 - 4]. This makes them advantageous in that several alternatives can be tested at one time, making them effective in solving intensive computation problems. Quantum computing roots itself in quantum physics, and it has a promising future in the field of computing by providing opportunities for real-time processing of big data. Due to the emerging limitations of Moore's law, there has been a realized need for quantum computing among researchers with the aim of extending the limits of computation. Nevertheless, besides the benefits offered by quantum computing, one must consider that this field has its peculiarities and potential risks, which have to be examined more thoroughly [5].

Strengths of Quantum Computing Over Classical Computing

Enhanced Computational Speed

Quantum computing also incorporates the principles of quantum superposition and parallelism, which makes it possible for it to work simultaneously on the different calculations required. This significantly improves problem-solving in fields that include extensive computations or algorithms, such as encryption and decryption, nanotechnology, and finance.

Efficient Optimization

Many problems encountered in the natural world, including logistics, supply chain management, and scheduling, are fundamentally optimization problems that require efficient solutions. Quantum computing, quantum annealing, and superior algorithms can find the best solutions within the shortest time and with fewer resources than a classical computing system [6].

Superior Data Processing

Quantum computing also has the capability of processing massive data structures since it is exactly suited for processing and analyzing big data. This characteristic is particularly useful in such areas as weather prediction, genome interpretation, as well as real-time analysis since they involve large quantities of data that require analysis within a short duration.

Advanced Simulation Capabilities

Quantum simulations are exceptionally good in the approximation of complex phenomena, chemical reactions, efficiency of materials, and climate change. These simulations are of much use to the scientists as classical compute cannot provide them at such a level of depth.

Robust Security and Encryption

Quantum cryptography provides safe forms of communication like Quantum Key Distribution (QKD), which protects data from cyber threats. As compared to the traditional technique of encryption, quantum encryption has certain phenomenal differences with the underlying fundamental principle based on quantum techniques, which makes it more secure than the normal-type encryption.

Potential for Scalable Computing

It has the potential to bring radical improvements in computational scalability as quantum technology progresses. This can result in revolutionizing industries and solving problems that are presently out of reach in regular system computing [7, 8].

Revolutionizing Scientific Discoveries

Quantum computing also proves beneficial in answering some of the scientific theories in the fields of physics, chemistry, and biology. From bringing new materials to designing chemical formulas and predicting some chemical phenomena, it is considered one of the key technologies that define innovation and discovery [9]. Quantum AI stands out from other types of machine learning, which include convolutional and deep, as they cannot handle computations appropriately or need a lot of computation power [10, 11].

How Quantum AI Works

Fundamentals of Quantum Computing

Quantum computing works with qubits, which are the basic units of quantum computing, and they differ from classical bits because of the fact that they can be in more than one state at a time due to the principle of superposition. When the state of the particles is entangled and when interference is added to it, qubits allow parallel computation, and this leads to a faster computation than classical computers [12].

Integration with AI and Machine Learning

AI models, especially ones relying on machine learning, need a lot of computational resources for the purpose of analyzing large sets of data and identifying patterns for the purposes of making predictions. Quantum AI uses the power of quantum computing, where the machine is able to solve for several possibilities simultaneously and may, therefore, increase the efficiency and accuracy of data analyses.

Basic Quantum Algorithms for AI

In addition, Quantum Machine Learning (QML) discusses how the usage of quantum computing can enhance common machine learning processes like classification, clustering, and reinforcement learning through the enhancement of matrix operations that are an integral part of AI models. These are architectures optimized for quantum structures that have possible improvements in AI learning and prediction velocities. Quantum AI is one of the emerging paradigms of computational intelligence that is said to change, for the better, the approach to problem-solving within diverse industries.

Quantum AI in the Field of Healthcare, Finance, and Cybersecurity

Quantum computing is playing an innovative role in several sectors, such as healthcare, finance, and cybersecurity, by solving the most complex problems in a very short time. To elaborate, in the healthcare field, quantum computing can help in discovering drugs, optimizing therapies, and increasing the efficacy of individual medications through the application of big data [13]. It allows DNA sequencing in a short amount of time, in addition to accurate depictions of molecular interactions and even the creation of prospective imaging for early stages of diseases [14]. In finance, they can be used for portfolio selection, efficient risk management, and fraud analysis of big data, all in real time. For instance, banks and other financial organizations can use this technology for quick and efficient transactions, credit scoring and risk analysis, and even better market forecasting. In cybersecurity, which is a field that relies on encryption as a means of safeguarding data, quantum computing has two uses: it threatens the security of data since some of the modern encryption mechanisms will not be resistant to it; however, it also provides a means by which new cryptographic defence techniques can be developed. It can bind authentication systems, monitor for cyber threats in real time, and improve secure communicating is capable of revolutionizing the healthcare sector through efficient, fast, and effective data processing [15].

Brief History of Quantum Computing

This timeline highlights key milestones in the development of quantum computing (Fig. **1**).

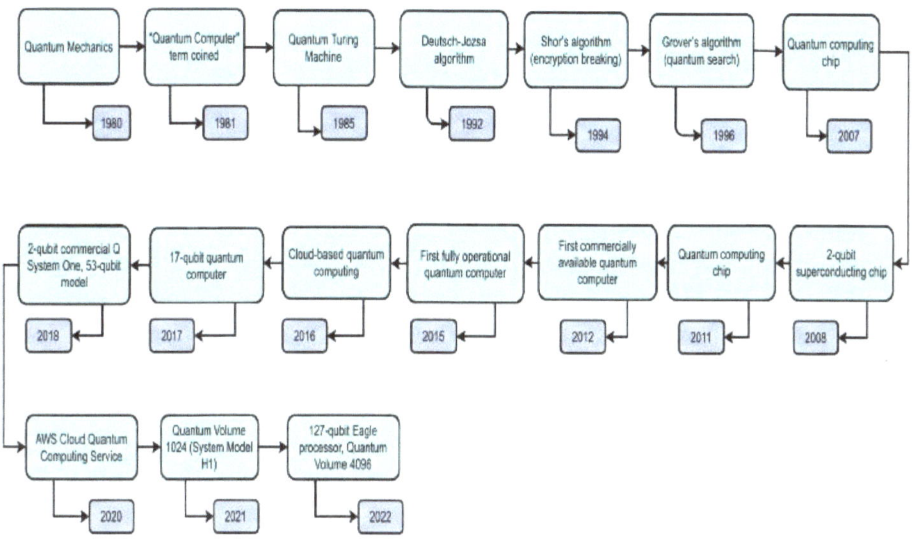

Fig. (1). History of quantum computing.

The journey of quantum computing began in 1980 when Paul Benioff explored the use of quantum mechanics for computation. A year later, Richard Feynman introduced the term "Quantum Computer," and in 1985, David Deutsch proposed the Quantum Turing Machine. Over time, several pioneering algorithms emerged, including the Deutsch-Jozsa algorithm in 1992, Shor's algorithm in 1994, capable of breaking encryption, and Grover's algorithm in 1996, which enhanced search efficiency. In 2007, the startup D-Wave claimed to have developed a quantum computing chip, followed by the introduction of the HHL algorithm in 2008 for solving linear equations efficiently. Yale researchers built the first solid-state quantum processor with two qubits in 2009. D-Wave then released the first commercially available quantum computer in 2011. By 2012, 1QBit became the first company focused solely on quantum computing software. Google partnered with NASA in 2013 to test D-Wave's hardware, leading to NASA unveiling the first fully operational quantum computer in 2015. IBM made quantum computing accessible *via* the cloud in 2016 and introduced a 17-qubit quantum computer in 2017. In 2018, Google developed its 72-qubit Bristlecone chip. IBM later launched its commercial 20-qubit quantum computer, Q System One, in 2019, alongside a 53-qubit model. Amazon joined the field in 2020 with its AWS Cloud Quantum Computing Service [16 - 19].

In 2021, Honeywell Quantum Solutions achieved a Quantum Volume of 1024 with System Model H1. By 2022, IBM introduced the 127-qubit Eagle processor, while Quantinuum announced a Quantum Volume of 4096. This timeline reflects the transformation of quantum computing from theoretical concepts to real-world applications [20].

GLOBAL TRENDS IN QUANTUM COMPUTING

Fig. (**2**) presents the global progress of quantum computing from 2006 to 2025. In the initial years, from 2008 to 2012, there was a steady rise, reflecting increasing interest and research efforts in the field. Between 2012 and 2015, the growth rate slowed down, indicating a period of stabilization. A significant rise is observed from 2016 to 2018, likely due to advancements in technology and increased investments. However, between 2018 and 2023, the trend fluctuated, suggesting phases of rapid innovation followed by periods of adjustment. The most striking increase occurs around 2024–2025, indicating a significant breakthrough or widespread adoption. The overall trend highlights the expanding role of quantum computing, pointing to its growing impact on technology and scientific research [21].

APPLICATIONS OF QUANTUM AI

Quantum AI can be applied in numerous domains, such as pharmaceutical discovery, climate change prediction, security intelligence, supply chain, and material design. However, in this chapter, three major areas, namely healthcare, finance, and security, have been identified. In the field of healthcare, Quantum AI can be used for the development of medical knowledge and innovations in the sphere of pharmaceuticals, as well as for increasing the efficiency of diagnostics. In the applied context, it can help in the evaluation of risks and recognition of fraudulent cases, as well as selection of the best portfolio using big data sets. In security, Quantum AI enriches encryption, optimizes security, and fortifies communication procedures in order to reduce the likelihood of attacks. Thus, this paper focuses on these three domains with the purpose of exposing the possibility that lies in the application of Quantum AI to solve major issues or enhance current systems.

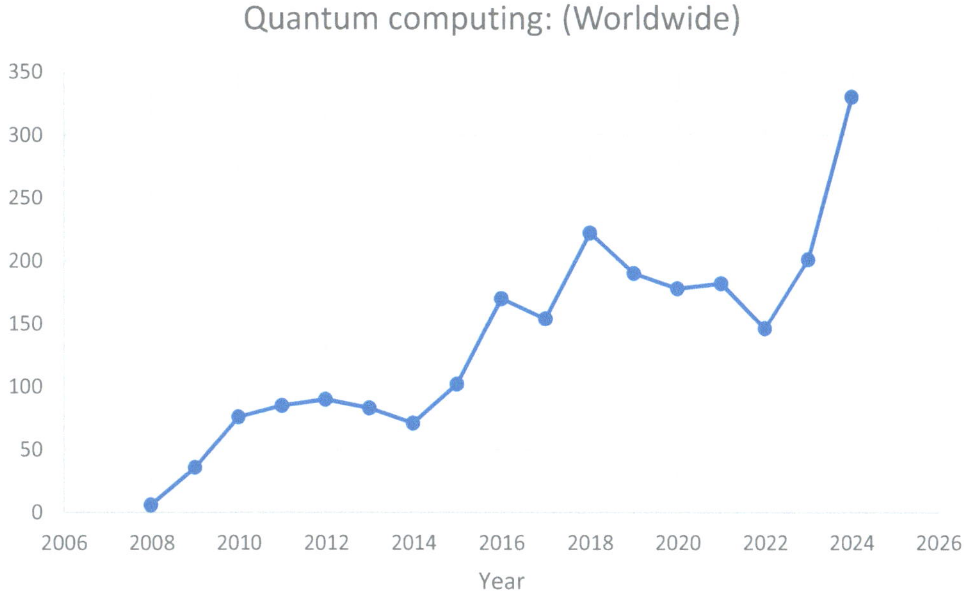

Fig. (2). Global trend in quantum computing.

Applications of Quantum AI in Healthcare

AI in Quantum is revolutionizing the healthcare sector through quicker, correct, and efficient resolutions regarding the difficult medical issues. It then improves drug discovery, personal medicine, and medical diagnosis by the use of quantum computing allied with AI algorithms, translating to better results of patient care and new treatments (Fig. **3**) [22].

Drug Discovery and Molecular Simulations

Quantum AI plays a critical role in accelerating drug discovery by simulating molecular interactions with unprecedented accuracy and speed. Traditional drug discovery processes are time-consuming and expensive, often taking years to identify viable compounds. Quantum AI enhances this process by [23]:

Faster Analysis of Biochemical Interactions

Quantum AI can rapidly simulate and analyze molecular structures, predicting how potential drug compounds interact with biological targets. This reduces the trial-and-error approach, leading to more effective drug formulations.

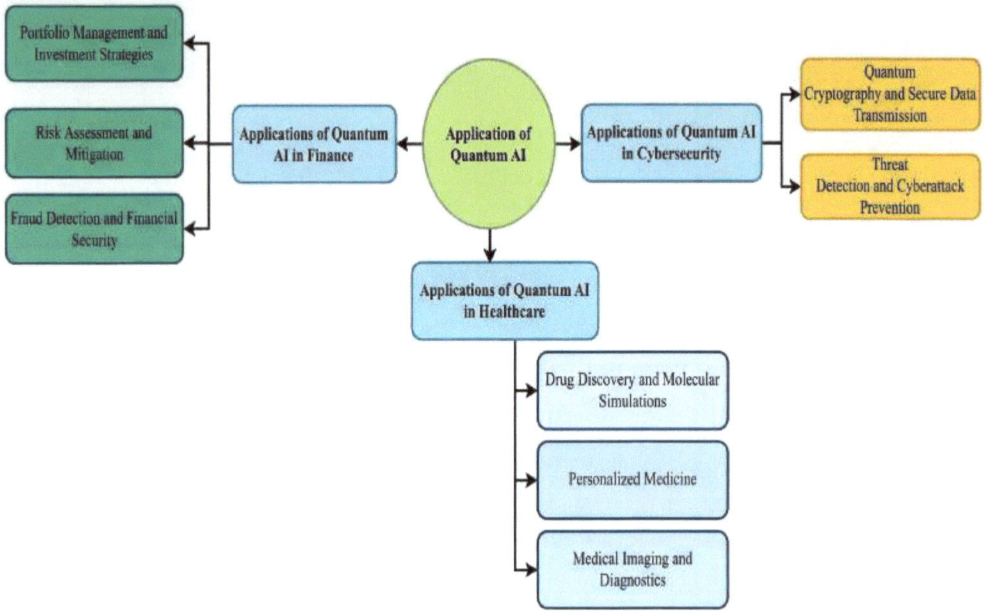

Fig. (3). Application of quantum AI in healthcare.

Acceleration of Drug Development

By optimizing chemical reactions and protein folding simulations, Quantum AI streamlines the drug development pipeline, reducing research costs and expediting clinical trials.

Personalized Medicine

Personalized medicine focuses on tailoring treatments based on an individual's genetic profile, lifestyle, and medical history. Quantum AI enhances this field by [24]:

AI-driven Genomic Analysis for Optimized Treatment Plans

Quantum computing accelerates the processing of vast genomic datasets, enabling precise identification of genetic mutations and recommending personalized treatments.

Predictive Modeling for Disease Prevention

Quantum AI enhances disease prediction by analyzing patterns in genetic and clinical data, allowing early intervention and prevention strategies tailored to individual patients.

Medical Imaging and Diagnostics

Quantum AI significantly improves the accuracy and efficiency of medical imaging and diagnostics, enabling early disease detection and improved patient care. Key advancements include:

- **Advanced pattern recognition techniques:** Quantum-enhanced machine learning algorithms analyze complex medical images, such as MRIs, CT scans, and X-rays, identifying abnormalities that might be missed by traditional methods.
- **AI-enhanced accuracy in disease detection:** Quantum AI enhances diagnostic accuracy by processing and interpreting medical data with superior precision, leading to earlier and more effective treatment of diseases like cancer, neurological disorders, and cardiovascular conditions.

Applications of Quantum AI in Finance

Quantum AI is transforming the financial sector by improving computational efficiency, optimizing investment strategies, enhancing risk assessment, and strengthening security measures. By leveraging the power of quantum computing and AI-driven analytics, financial institutions can process vast datasets, predict market trends with greater accuracy, and detect fraudulent activities in real-time [25].

Portfolio Management and Investment Strategies

Quantum AI revolutionizes portfolio management by enabling faster and more precise decision-making. Traditional investment strategies rely on analyzing large and complex datasets, which can be time-consuming and computationally expensive. Quantum AI enhances this process through:

Real-time Data Analysis for Optimized Decision-making

Quantum AI processes vast financial data in real time, allowing investors and fund managers to make faster, data-driven decisions based on market trends, historical performance, and risk factors.

<u>Enhanced Optimization of Investment Portfolios</u>

Quantum computing helps identify the best asset allocation strategies by simultaneously evaluating multiple investment options, reducing risks, and maximizing returns [26].

Risk Assessment and Mitigation

Financial markets are highly volatile, and accurate risk assessment is crucial for investment decisions. Quantum AI enhances risk modeling by:

Quantum Algorithms for Accurate Market Predictions

Traditional financial models struggle with predicting sudden market shifts, whereas Quantum AI processes complex financial patterns with higher accuracy, improving forecasting capabilities.

Optimized Risk Mitigation Strategies

By analyzing multiple risk factors simultaneously, Quantum AI helps financial institutions minimize losses and adjust their strategies to changing economic conditions.

Fraud Detection and Financial Security

With the rise of digital transactions, financial fraud has become a significant concern. Quantum AI strengthens security measures by:

AI-powered Anomaly Detection in Transactions

Quantum-enhanced machine learning algorithms detect unusual transaction patterns, identifying fraudulent activities more accurately and reducing false positives.

Strengthening Digital Banking Security

Quantum cryptographic techniques, such as Quantum Key Distribution (QKD), provide highly secure encryption, making digital banking and online payment systems more resistant to cyber threats.

Applications of Quantum AI in Cybersecurity

Quantum computing is transforming cybersecurity by offering advanced encryption methods, secure data transmission, and improved threat detection capabilities. As cyber threats continue to evolve, the integration of quantum technology enhances security frameworks, ensuring stronger protection against malicious attacks [27].

Quantum Cryptography and Secure Data Transmission

Quantum cryptography is revolutionizing data security by utilizing the principles of quantum mechanics to create highly secure communication channels. Traditional encryption methods are vulnerable to powerful computing attacks, but quantum-based encryption ensures data confidentiality through:

Quantum Key Distribution (QKD) for Secure Communication

QKD uses the principles of quantum mechanics to generate encryption keys that cannot be intercepted or replicated without detection. This method ensures that any attempt to eavesdrop on a communication channel is immediately identified, making data transmission significantly more secure.

Enhanced Data Encryption Techniques

Quantum cryptography strengthens encryption standards, making sensitive information more resistant to decryption attempts by cybercriminals and future quantum computers.

Threat Detection and Cyberattack Prevention

With the increasing complexity of cyber threats, quantum computing provides an advanced approach to detecting and preventing cyberattacks in real time. Quantum-driven security solutions help in:

Real-time Analysis of Cyber Threats

Quantum-based computing enhances the ability to process and analyze vast amounts of cybersecurity data at high speeds, allowing security systems to detect threats more efficiently.

Strengthening Cybersecurity Resilience Against Evolving Threats

As cyberattacks become more sophisticated, quantum computing offers solutions that can identify vulnerabilities, predict potential breaches, and develop proactive defense mechanisms to counteract emerging threats.

CHALLENGES OF QUANTUM AI

Quantum computing holds great promise, but several obstacles must be overcome before it can be widely used.

Hardware Limitations

Quantum systems rely on delicate units of information that are highly sensitive to environmental disturbances. Errors occur frequently in quantum operations, and effective correction methods are still being developed. Current quantum devices have a limited number of processing units, making complex tasks difficult.

Algorithm Development

There is a lack of established Methods because many existing computing techniques need to be redesigned for quantum systems. Hybrid approaches required by combining quantum and traditional computing are often necessary, adding complexity.

Software and Programming Challenges

Limited Tools and Languages are another challenge in Quantum programming that requires specialized knowledge, and existing software is still evolving. Adapting conventional computing models for quantum environments remains a challenge.

Data Processing Difficulties

Converting traditional data into quantum formats is a complex process, and quantum devices in their current form are prone to disturbances, affecting reliability.

Cost and Infrastructure

Developing and maintaining quantum technology requires significant investment. Only a few institutions have access to advanced quantum systems. Despite these difficulties, progress is being made, and continued research is essential for unlocking the full potential of quantum technology.

OPEN ISSUES AND RESEARCH DIRECTIONS IN QUANTUM AI

Quantum Computing for Big Data Processing

- Quantum computing has demonstrated its potential to revolutionize big data analytics, particularly in healthcare. With its superior computational capabilities, quantum computing can enhance data processing, enabling more precise personalized healthcare services and improving diagnostic and prognostic outcomes. Integrating quantum computing with Machine Learning (ML) and

Deep Learning (DL) can support descriptive, predictive, and prescriptive analytics.

- A key area of research involves leveraging multimodal data to develop ensemble methods that enhance predictive analytics in healthcare. Additionally, exploring the intersection of semantic technologies and quantum computing can improve the classification and understanding of medical big data. For instance, Quantum Machine Learning (QML) algorithms utilizing semantic knowledge graphs have shown promise in uncovering latent relationships in large-scale, multimodal medical databases. Further, frameworks for quantum semantic communications could lead to more efficient reasoning-based communication systems.

Quantum AI/ML Applications

Quantum-enhanced AI and ML models have the potential to drive significant advancements in healthcare. Since many ML algorithms rely on large matrix operations, quantum computing can significantly optimize computational efficiency. Quantum AI can accelerate the ML training process, improving both the speed and accuracy of inference models.

A promising approach is the integration of quantum computing in the machine design phase, enhancing inference models in various real-time decision-making applications, such as stock selection, autonomous driving, and personalized product recommendations. Traditional rule-based inference models depend on predefined responses, whereas quantum AI can enhance pattern recognition and sequence identification. Reducing errors in inference models through quantum techniques can improve predictive accuracy, making it a crucial area of research.

Large-Scale Optimization

Optimization problems are prevalent in various industries, and many suffer from combinatorial complexity, making them intractable for classical computing. For instance, the Travelling Salesmen Problem (TSP) escalates and becomes inapplicable in practice as the number of cities grows. The two main solutions are Quantum Annealing and Universal Quantum Computing. Quantum annealing, as one of the heuristic optimization techniques, can be presented as an optimization technique that may act more efficiently than classical tools in the course of solving optimization problems. Quantum annealing, which uses specialized quantum annealers, is relatively simple to carry out as a computational model, but it is still debatable how proficient it is. Also, heuristic hardware that mimics quantum annealing on usual processors may be used for optimization problems; however, these devices are comparatively cheaper and have less capacity than specific annealers.

Quantum Web and Cloud Services

One of the major problems is to make quantum computing approachable through cloud solutions. One of the major issues of quantum systems is attributed to high resource demand; hence, they have not become popular for everyday use. Still, solutions such as the Cleveland Clinic–IBM Discovery Accelerator try to solve this problem by offering cloud for quantum health care applications. Amazon Braket, an experimental quantum computing environment, allows researchers to design, test, and evaluate quantum algorithms using both simulated and real quantum hardware. Additional quantum web services and Software Development Kits (SDKs) are needed to further democratize quantum computing and support broad-based research and development.

Quantum Game Theory

There are broad indications that excellence in the application of game theory in healthcare sectors can be achieved through quantum computing. As an advance of the classical game theory, quantum game theory incorporates quantum information resources and therefore enriches the understanding of both cooperation and defection examples. Introduction of the prisoner's dilemma is useful when it comes to relations between the doctor and the patient. Through the use of quantum-based simulations, researchers can determine reasons behind non-cooperative behaviour, more especially in health care costs, insurance, amongst others. It can feed into the decision maker with the context detailing collaborative policies between the healthcare givers and health insurers in order to provide quality results for the patients.

Quantum Computing for Simulation

Quantum computers also carry the potential to solve problem-related structures and mechanisms that cannot be solved by classical computers. Quantum computing can be used in various applications, including meteorological, epidemiological, and biological applications. Similarly, quantum modeling can enhance disease progression knowledge and drug effects at the cellular and molecular level and hence facilitate the comprehensive research of vaccines and medications. Another area in which quantum computers are useful is in the development of copy models of human organs and cells to develop precision medicine. However, the use of quantum simulations is still problematic in terms of ethical issues that must be considered in order to prevent misuse in healthcare and other related fields.

Quantum Security Applications

Cybersecurity is an essential issue in the modern world, and with the new technologies that have arrived, quantum computing, both risks and possibilities exist. There is a possibility that cryptographic techniques will become inefficient because of quantum devices. However, in quantum cryptography there new ways do exist to eliminate threats of cyber attacks towards crucial data. It is possible to achieve the creation of strong and adaptive security and protection systems against cyber threats through quantum-enhanced machine learning. Efforts in developing secure communication with quantum encryption algorithms and quantum communication protocols are crucial to protect modern computer-based systems against break-in by use of supercomputational power acquired through quantum computing [28, 29].

CONCLUSION AND FUTURE SCOPE

In order to make revolutionary advancements in important sectors like healthcare, banking, and cybersecurity, quantum AI combines the capabilities of artificial intelligence and quantum computing. Whether in real-time cyber threat detection, financial risk management, or illness diagnosis, it facilitates quicker data processing, more intelligent decision-making, and more precise forecasts. Despite present software and hardware constraints and hefty implementation costs, the prospective advantages far outweigh the difficulties. Quantum AI is expected to play a significant role in developing quicker, safer, and more efficient intelligent systems as quantum technology progresses and becomes more available.

Future studies will probably concentrate on developing more practical applications, making programming tools easier to use, and enhancing quantum hardware. Quantum AI has the potential to become a major force behind advancements in science, business, and society at large with sustained innovation and investment.

ACKNOWLEDGEMENT

The authors of this paper are thankful to Chitkara University, Punjab, for providing infrastructural facilities to complete this research work.

REFERENCES

[1] D. V. Talati, "Quantum AI and the future of super intelligent computing," *J. Artif. Intell. Gen. Sci. (JAIGS)*, vol. 8, no. 1, pp. 44–51, 2025.

[2] R. Tarafdar, "Quantum AI: The future of machine learning and optimization," *World J. Adv. Res. Rev.*, vol. 25, no. 2, pp. 2744–2751, 2025.

[3] V. Sood, and R.P. Chauhan, "Archives of quantum computing: research progress and challenges", *Arch. Comput. Methods Eng.*, vol. 31, no. 1, pp. 73-91, 2024.

[http://dx.doi.org/10.1007/s11831-023-09973-2]

[4] V. Dunjko, and H.J. Briegel, "Machine learning & artificial intelligence in the quantum domain: a review of recent progress", *Rep. Prog. Phys.,* vol. 81, no. 7, 2018.074001 [http://dx.doi.org/10.1088/1361-6633/aab406] [PMID: 29504942]

[5] S.A. Goswami, S. Dave, K.C. Patel, and M.N. Raval, "Application of quantum artificial intelligence in healthcare," in *Quantum Computing for Healthcare Data: Revolutionizing the Future of Medicine, Advances in Biomedical Informatics*, 2025, pp. 119–138. [http://dx.doi.org/10.1016/B978-0-443-29297-2.00007-1]

[6] I.C. Chen, H. Singh, V.L. Anukruti, B. Quanz, and K. Yogaraj, "A survey of classical and quantum sequence models," in *Proc. 2024 16th Int. Conf. Communication Systems & Networks (COMSNETS)*, 2024, pp. 1006–1011.

[7] Hassan Ali, "Quantum computing and AI in healthcare: Accelerating complex biological simulations, genomic data processing, and drug discovery innovations", *World Journal of Advanced Research and Reviews,* vol. 20, no. 2, pp. 1466-1484, 2023. [http://dx.doi.org/10.30574/wjarr.2023.20.2.2325]

[8] J. Davids, N. Lidströmer, and H. Ashrafian, "Artificial intelligence in medicine using quantum computing in the future of healthcare," in *Artificial Intelligence in Medicine*, Cham, Switzerland: Springer International Publishing, 2022, pp. 423–446. [http://dx.doi.org/10.1007/978-3-030-64573-1_338]

[9] P.V. Rubbina, and G.N. Verma, "Brain tumor detection using hybrid model of dct dwt and thresholding", *Brain,* vol. 6, no. 07, pp. 855-860, 2019.

[10] S. R. Anugu, "AI in financial services: Revolutionizing fraud detection and risk management", *Int. J. Sci. Res. Comput. Sci. Eng. Inf. Technol.,* vol. 11, pp. 208-217, 2025. [http://dx.doi.org/10.32628/CSEIT25112354]

[11] A. Garg, M. Singh, and M. Kumar, "The intersection of quantum computing, artificial intelligence and financial risks: A bibliometric analysis of the modern financial sector," *J. Inf. Technol. Manag.*, vol. 17, Special Issue on Strategic, Organizational, and Social Issues of Digital Transformation in Organizations, pp. 1–21, 2025.

[12] M. Doosti, P. Wallden, C.B. Hamill, R. Hankache, O.T. Brown, and C. Heunen, "A brief review of quantum machine learning for financial services", *arXiv preprint arXiv:2407.12618,* 2024.

[13] A. Kaur, and M. Khurana, "EmoNeuroTextAnalyzer: A novel computational emotion model," in *Proc. 2024 11th Int. Conf. Reliability, Infocom Technologies and Optimization (Trends and Future Directions) (ICRITO)*, 2024, pp. 1–6.

[14] P. Dhiman, A. Bonkra, A. Kaur, Y. Gulzar, Y. Hamid, M.S. Mir, A.B. Soomro, and O. Elwasila, "Healthcare trust evolution with explainable artificial intelligence: bibliometric analysis", *Information (Basel),* vol. 14, no. 10, p. 541, 2023. [http://dx.doi.org/10.3390/info14100541]

[15] S. Paul, N. R. Choudhury, B. Pandit, and A. Dawn, "Integration of AI and quantum computing in cybersecurity: A comprehensive review," 2025.

[16] A. H. Hussain, M. N. Hasan, N. U. Prince, M. M. Islam, S. Islam, and S. K. Hasan, "Enhancing cyber security using quantum computing and artificial intelligence: A review," *World J. Adv. Res. Rev.*, vol. 11, no. 2, pp. 196–203, 2021.

[17] M.J.H. Faruk, S. Tahora, M. Tasnim, H. Shahriar, and N. Sakib, "A review of quantum cybersecurity: threats, risks and opportunities", In: *Proc. 2022 1st Int. Conf. AI in Cybersecurity (ICAIC)*, 2022, pp. 1–8.

[18] F. Raheman, "The future of cybersecurity in the age of quantum computers", *Future Internet,* vol. 14, no. 11, p. 335, 2022. [http://dx.doi.org/10.3390/fi14110335]

[19] K. Pratibha, A. Kaur, M. Khurana, and R. Damaševičius, "Multimodal hinglish tweet dataset for deep pragmatic analysis", *Data (Basel),* vol. 9, no. 2, p. 38, 2024. [http://dx.doi.org/10.3390/data9020038]

[20] M. Klusch, J. Lässig, D. Müssig, A. Macaluso, and F. K. Wilhelm, "Quantum artificial intelligence: A brief survey," *KI-Künstliche Intelligenz*, pp. 1–20, 2024.

[21] B. Rawat, N. Mehra, A.S. Bist, M. Yusup, and Y.P.A. Sanjaya, "Quantum computing and ai: Impacts & possibilities", *ADI Journal on Recent Innovation,* vol. 3, no. 2, pp. 202-207, 2022.

[22] J. Gharib, and Y. Gahi, "Quantum computing and AI applications in Industry 5.0 use cases," in *Quantum Computing and Artificial Intelligence: The Industry Use Cases*, P. Raj, B. Sundaravadivazhagan, M. Ouaissa, V. Kavitha, and K. S. Kumari, Eds. Hoboken, NJ, USA: Wiley, 2025, pp. 435–464.

[23] H. Singh, "Future directions and challenges, quantum supremacy, and beyond," in *Quantum Technology Applications, Impact, and Future Challenges*, M. Hammoudeh, C. M. Firth, H. Singh, C. Capellaro, and M. Al Kuwaiti, Eds. Boca Raton, FL, USA: CRC Press, 2025, p. 141.

[24] R. Ur Rasool, H.F. Ahmad, W. Rafique, A. Qayyum, J. Qadir, and Z. Anwar, "Quantum computing for healthcare: A review", *Future Internet,* vol. 15, no. 3, p. 94, 2023. [http://dx.doi.org/10.3390/fi15030094]

[25] M. Golec, E. S. Hatay, M. Golec, M. Uyar, M. Golec, and S. S. Gill, "Quantum cloud computing: Trends and challenges," *arXiv preprint arXiv:2404.19612*, 2024.

[26] R. Pérez-Antón, J. I. López-Sánchez, and A. Corbi, "The game theory in quantum computers: A review," 2024.

[27] P.N. Nguyen, "The duality game: a quantum algorithm for body dynamics modeling", *Quantum Inform. Process.,* vol. 23, no. 1, p. 21, 2024. [http://dx.doi.org/10.1007/s11128-023-04223-7]

CHAPTER 12

Shielding IoT-Driven Healthcare: A Secure and Lightweight Authentication Protocol for Patient Data Protection

Parwinder Kaur Dhillon[1], **Jyoti**[2] and **Sheetal Kalra**[2,*]

[1] *Department of Computer Science, Guru Nanak Dev University, Regional Campus Jalandhar, Jalandhar, Punjab, India*

[2] *Department of Engineering and Technology, Guru Nanak Dev University, Regional Campus Jalandhar, Jalandhar, Punjab, India*

Abstract: The rapid assimilation of the Internet of Things (IoT), Cloud computing, and Artificial Intelligence (AI) into healthcare has revolutionized patient monitoring and remote medical assistance. The distinctive attributes of IoT networks (open and heterogeneous) pose significant security concerns due to possible threats, such as man-in-the-middle, replay, and denial-of-service attacks, compromising sensitive patient information. In the proposed framework, an authentication protocol is designed that is secure, lightweight, and efficient to establish a session key between the users and the healthcare provider, and also ensures confidentiality and prevention of illegitimate access to IoT sensor nodes. We prove, using the AVISPA tool, that the proposed protocol is secure against common security attacks. They include an improved resilience against the known attacks, computational validity to consider the execution cost of the resource-constrained medical IoT devices, and diminished communication overhead. Moreover, the protocol is designed to be scalable and cloud-compatible, paving the way for secure integration with quantum-enhanced cloud AI healthcare systems.

Keywords: Authentication protocols, Data encryption, Healthcare IoT, Lightweight cryptography, Medical data protection, Patient data security, Public key infrastructure (PKI), Secure communication, Smart devices Authentication, Two-factor authentication (2FA), User authentication, Zero trust architecture..

INTRODUCTION

The medical industry is undergoing a massive shift, with the arrival of the Internet of Things (IoT). The integration of IoT technology into healthcare systems is

* **Corresponding Author Sheetal Kalra:** Department of Engineering and Technology, Guru Nanak Dev University, Regional Campus Jalandhar, Jalandhar, Punjab, India; E-mail: sheetal.kalra@gmail.com

Satveer Kour, Harvinder Singh, Anupam Bonkra & Rupinder Singh (Eds.)

transforming patient care, treatment processes, and medical research. IoT constitutes a network of interconnected physical entities, such as buildings, vehicles, and various objects, equipped with sensors, software, and network connectivity to facilitate data gathering and dissemination.

IoT integration in the healthcare industry has made it possible to gather and analyze a variety of patient data, encourage remote patient monitoring, and improve the effectiveness of medical institutions [1]. Secure data analytics is now possible because of IoT, which also delivers effective, top-notch healthcare service to patients' doors. Without requiring patients to attend hospitals, IoT has made it possible for healthcare professionals to remotely monitor patients with long-term medical conditions. In order to record vital body parameters, track patient activity levels, and measure other health metrics, patients are required to wear wearable technology, such as smart watches and sensors, on their bodies. Over an unsecure wireless channel, this data is sent to medical professionals, who can utilize it to keep an eye on their patients as needed, provide prompt care, and avoid readmissions to the hospital. Healthcare professionals can act quickly when health metrics depart from normal ranges thanks to remote monitoring and real-time data analysis. Better chronic condition management, fewer readmissions to the hospital, and better patient outcomes result from this. Remote or underserved locations can now obtain healthcare thanks to telemedicine and remote monitoring [2]. Healthcare is more accessible since patients can consult with professionals without having to travel far. The IoT ecosystem includes wireless sensors, smart wearable technology, hospital equipment and robotics, patients and medical staff, and all of these entities have the ability to share and exchange critical data across an insecure channel.

Fig. (**1**) depicts the four-stage process of an IoT-enabled healthcare system carried out by the medical IoT companies. Each stage is further tightly integrated in terms of data capture and processing.

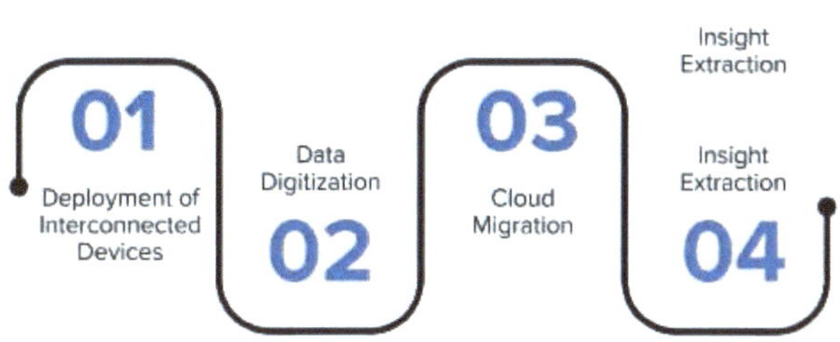

Fig. (1). Four stages of IoT-enabled healthcare process.

Stage 1: Implementation of Networked Devices: This includes data-collecting equipment like actuators, sensors, monitors, detection devices, and surveillance systems.

Stage 2: Data Digitization: It involves combining and transforming the analog data obtained from sensors and other devices into a digital format.

Stage 3: Cloud Migration: The data is transferred to a cloud data center after the pre-processing and standardization process.

Stage 4: Insight Extraction: Advanced analytics are applied to this processed data after management and analysis, producing actionable insights.

For healthcare applications that provide higher-quality patient care without sacrificing comfort or health, sensors are a crucial component [3, 4]. Strict privacy restrictions apply to sensitive healthcare data. Maintaining patient trust and regulatory compliance requires the safe transfer and storage of patient data. The most significant barrier to IoT-enabled healthcare is data security and privacy. Both the patient and the physician could be harmed by the vast amounts of data that are routinely exchanged and kept. Hackers can fabricate IDs in order to purchase medications and substances, which they can then abuse [5]. Critical information is shared in healthcare applications; an adversary's slightest act of malice might risk a patient's life. The primary concern that needs to be addressed is the security of the data that is communicated *via* open public networks [6].

The research has been set up as follows: Applications of AI based on Quantum cryptography have been summarised in section 2. Section 3 depicts the motivation of the research work. The associated work is explained in Section 4. Preliminaries have been explained in Section 5. The proposed robust authentication protocol has been elaborated in Section 6. The informal security exploration is covered in Section 7. Simulation Results have been shown in Section 8. The chapter ends by highlighting the findings of the proposed protocol in Section 9 and outlining its future scope.

APPLICATIONS OF AI BASED ON QUANTUM CRYPTOGRAPHY AND ELLIPTIC CURVE CRYPTOGRAPHY IN IOT-DRIVEN HEALTHCARE

As the healthcare industry grows to rely increasingly on interconnected systems of IoT devices, securing communications and ensuring patient privacy amid rapidly changing technologies is a pressing priority. Emerging fields centered at the intersection of quantum cryptography and machine learning can offer potential solutions to safeguard protected health information in this complex environment.

AI-Based Quantum Cryptography in Healthcare

Quantum cryptography employs the quirky principles of quantum mechanics to securely share encryption keys, and AI-enhanced methods show promise to implement these counterintuitive techniques with discretion despite the fickle nature of quantum states [7]. For healthcare IoT networks tasked with transmitting sensitive patient data, an AI-guided quantum approach could help guarantee confidentiality for the long term as threats and technical capabilities evolve. Such a novel interweaving of artificial intelligence with quantum key distribution may be a prudent path toward fortifying medical cyber defences for the future.

Real-time Anomaly Detection

AI algorithms can leverage streams of health data generated by IoT devices to analyze unusual patterns or behaviors that could be signs of a cyberattack or data manipulation. When combined with Quantum Key Distribution (QKD), these systems guarantee that the keys used during data transmission are never compromised.

Adaptive Security Policies

For a secure environment, it is required to make these systems smart and flexible by defining the adjusting of system behaviours at runtime based on contextual data from previously learnt knowledge (machine learning models) in order to provide a decent amount of protection without reduced performance.

Quantum-resistant Infrastructures

The era of quantum computing is knocking on our doors; healthcare systems have to already adopt cryptographies that will, in the case of future quantum machines, survive the enormous computing power [8]. Incorporating quantum cryptographic concepts, for instance, quantum key distribution, within healthcare environments powered by IoT ensures that any sensitive patient information remains secure. Such a proactive approach protects all data transmissions today as well, while putting in place a strong future-proof security posture that can evolve in parallel as both quantum computing and artificial intelligence also develop.

Role of Elliptic Curve Cryptography (ECC) in Resource-Constrained IoT Devices

ECC is especially suitable for low-powered, resource-constrained IoT devices commonly found in wearable devices used in healthcare technologies due to its strength-per-bit efficiency overall. Key applications include:

Lightweight Authentication

ECC-based protocols can provide secure key exchange and digital signatures with smaller key sizes, which can reduce computational overhead and power consumption, which is critical in battery-powered sensors and smart devices [9].

End-to-end Data Encryption

ECC can ensure that any patient data gathered using an Edge device (like sensors) is securely encrypted (ensuring data integrity) from the point of collection until the data comes into our cloud storage/processing centers (enabling confidentiality).

Efficient Session Key Generation

ECC enables the quick creation of session keys, which allows secure communication in real time between healthcare providers and IoT nodes without any considerable delay.

Synergizing ECC, AI, and Quantum Approaches

The integration of ECC with AI-powered insights and quantum cryptographic principles can provide a multi-layered von Neumann defense mechanism. ECC offers a time-tested, compact solution for data security, while AI adds intelligent adaptability to anticipate and mitigate threats. In contrast, quantum cryptography provides a strong long-term security framework against future attacks.

Such synergy can transform secure data management within healthcare in a world with intelligent, cloud- and quantum-aware applications. The authentication protocol proposed in this chapter is a building block toward this vision—as a lightweight, scalable protocol, it brings into concordance with contemporary and future emerging security paradigms for leveraging healthcare IoT ecosystems while maintaining privacy.

MOTIVATION

Healthcare systems are more susceptible to advanced cyberthreats as they quickly embrace IoT technology to provide remote diagnostics, cloud-based analytics, and real-time patient monitoring. These systems are very desirable targets for attackers due to the enormous volume and sensitivity of medical data transferred across unprotected wireless channels. There is a risky trade-off between security and performance since traditional cryptography methods are frequently too resource-intensive for IoT devices. Patient lives, clinical judgments, and confidence in digital healthcare are all at risk as a result of this crucial void. Motivated by this challenge, our research aims to develop a lightweight, robust, and highly secure authentication protocol targeted for IoT-driven healthcare environments. By using Elliptic Curve Cryptography (ECC), the proposed solution provides strong protection along with minimal computational overhead, making it suitable for constrained medical devices. Moreover, the design anticipates future integration with AI-driven and quantum-resilient infrastructures, aligning with the next frontier of secure, intelligent healthcare systems.

LITERATURE SURVEY

Chen *et al.* suggested a dynamic ID-based authentication strategy for telecare medicine information systems (TMIS) that protected user confidentiality [10]. But according to Cao and Zhai, the method had some shortcomings, including being susceptible to dictionary attacks [11]. Wu *et al.* [12] also discovered that the authentication protocol for TMIS is susceptible to masquerade assaults [13]. A new authentication mechanism was created by the authors of a study to combat these threats [13]. The method put out by He *et al.* [13] is unreliable against a brute force password attack, as Wei *et al.* [14] later showed. Although Challa *et al.* [15] proposed a strategy based on an ECC-based user authentication protocol, Jia *et al.* [16] determined that the technique [15] was unreliable against impersonation assaults. Furthermore [15], has comparatively high communication and computation costs. Zhou *et al.* [17] suggested an approach that relies on IoT-based cloud architecture authentication; however, it is susceptible to MITM, impersonation, privileged insider, and replay attacks [18].

A user authentication and key establishment mechanism was presented by Farash *et al.* [19] for a number of WSN and IoT networks. However, Amin *et al.* [20] found that this protocol had a number of flaws and was susceptible to replay and user impersonation attacks. A strong user authentication method was created by Sharma and Kalra [21], although the authors in [22] demonstrated that the method was not impervious to privileged insider assaults. Another novel approach to key formation and user authentication was put forth by Turkanovic [23] *et al.*, however it was discovered to be susceptible to a number of attacks, together with offline password guessing, user impersonation, and sensor node impersonation [24]. Wazid *et al.* [25] introduced a key management system that is suitable for Internet of Things applications and is lightweight. This system offers a secure and lightweight communication method by using bitwise XOR and a one-way cryptographic hash function.

PRELIMINARIES

System Model

An IoT-based healthcare ecosystem comprises basically three main entities - Doctors (users), the gateway node, and IoT sensor nodes or wearable devices. These three entities communicate with each other in an open wireless environment, and this is depicted in the model in Fig. (**2**).

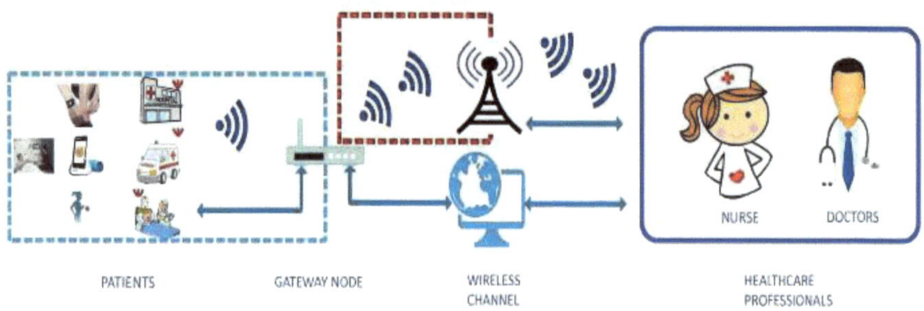

Fig. (2). Model for IoT-based healthcare system.

Doctor/Nurse (User)

With the assistance of a trust authority, users (including physicians, caregivers, families, and friends) in the medical care system can remotely check and monitor physiological data on patients. Users are required to get them registered physically with the trustworthy authority before they can access the system. Following successful registration, the user receives a smart card from the trusted authority, which they can use to access the medical care system together with their mobile devices (such as a laptop, tablet computer, PDA, or smartphone). Within a certain amount of time following successful authentication, the user can access the patient-sensed data obtained from sensor nodes [26].

Gateway Node

Modern IoT gateways frequently facilitate bidirectional data communication between the cloud and IoT devices. An IoT gateway serves as a hub between the clinician and the sensor node, connecting IoT devices and sensors to cloud-based computing and data processing.

IoT Sensor Node

Real-time patient data is collected and transmitted by IoT-enabled sensor nodes [27]. IoT in healthcare includes various sensor devices, including sphygmomanometers (blood pressure monitors), fluid level sensors, thermometers, electrocardiograms, and pulse oximeters, which have a wireless linking to the doctor's devices *via* a gateway [28].

Adversary Model

According to the Dolev-Yao(DY) model, an adversary can intercept, alter, or expunge the exchanged messages to interfere with data being transmitted through an insecure channel and threaten the reliability of data [29]. The DY threat model [30] is commonly used in protocol security analysis. The KGC, MEC servers, and cloud servers can communicate with each other *via* a wired communication channel, while the MEC servers and vehicles can communicate with each other *via* a wireless (public) communication channel.

- The model DY assumes that an opponent may completely control the public channel. Through a public channel, an attacker can intercept, delete, alter, and fabricate the communications that are transmitted [31].
- An attacker might physically seize the vehicle's onboard unit (OBU), which houses the credentials and secrets, in order to use power analysis attacks to retrieve the data that has been saved [32].
- An attacker may attempt to guess the password and identity of a genuine user by using dictionary guessing.
- An adversary can use stolen or falsified information to try a multiplicity of assaults, together with replay attacks, man-in-the-middle attacks, and impersonation.

PROPOSED SCHEME

The phases of the proposed lightweight user authentication for IoT-based healthcare system are as follows: Sensor nodes monitor and sense real-time patient data, and the gateway nodes transmit the sensed data to the user, *i.e.*, healthcare professionals.

Stage 1: User registration phase

Stage 2: Sensor node registration phase

Stage 3: Login and authentication phase

Stage 1: User Registration Phase

During this phase, the healthcare professionals will get themselves registered at the gateway node so that they are allowed to get access to the sensor node data (Fig. 3). The following steps are executed:

Step 1: The user inputs the user identity UID and password PWD. It then produces a random nonce r1, which is used to compute masked password $MPW=h(PWD\|r1)$. It then transmits a registration demand message containing the UID to the node gateway.

Step 2: On getting the message for registration from the user, the node gateway will generate a set of random nonces g1,g2,g3, and compute $TID=h(UID\|g1\|K_{gw})$, $S1=h(UID\|g2\|K_{gw})$, and $S2=h(UID\|g3\|K_{gw})$, and store UID, TID, S1, and S2.

Step 3: This is stored temporarily on the gateway node, and only S2 is kept, which is the secret key of the user between the sensor node and the user. The S2 is transmitted to the sensor node *via* the gateway node. It is deleted by the gateway node after that. Then, the gateway node forwards the message back to the user<TID, S1, S2> over a secure channel.

Step 4: On receiving the message <TID,S1,S2> from the gateway node computes its parameters $A1=TID\oplus MPW$, $A2=S1\oplus MPW$, $A3=S2\oplus MPW$, $A4=h(PWD\|UID)\oplus r1$, $A5=h(TID\|S1\|S2\|r1)$ and stores A1,A2,A3,A4,A5.

User Registration Phase	
Healthcare Professional (U)	**Gateway Node (GWN)**
Inputs UID, PWD Generates random nonce:r1 Computes masked password $MPW=h(PWD\|r1)$	
UID →	
	Generates random nonce: g1,g2,g3 Computes: $TID=h(UID\|g1\|K_{gw})$ $S1=h(UID\|g2\|K_{gw})$ $S2=h(UID\|g3\|K_{gw})$ ***Stores UID,TID,S1,S2***
	← TID,S1,S2
$A1=TID\oplus MPW$ $A2=S1\oplus MPW$ $A3=S2\oplus MPW$ $A4=h(PWD\|UID)\oplus r1$ $A5=h(TID\|S1\|S2\|r1)$ ***Stores A1,A2,A3,A4,A5***	

Fig. (3). User registration phase.

Stage 2: Sensor Node Registration Phase

During this stage, various sensor nodes monitoring the patients are registered with the gateway node (Fig. **4**). The following steps are executed:

Step 1: To get the sensor node registered, the sensor node forwards its unique identity SID as a registration call message on a protected channel to the node gateway.

Step 2: On receiving the registration call message, the gateway node generates a random nonce g4, and computes $TSID=h(SID \| g4 \| K_{gw})$, and then stores SID, TSID, and sends the response message <TSID, TID, S2> back to the sensor node.

Step 3: Sensor node obtains the parameters from the message <TSID, TID, S2> and stores them.

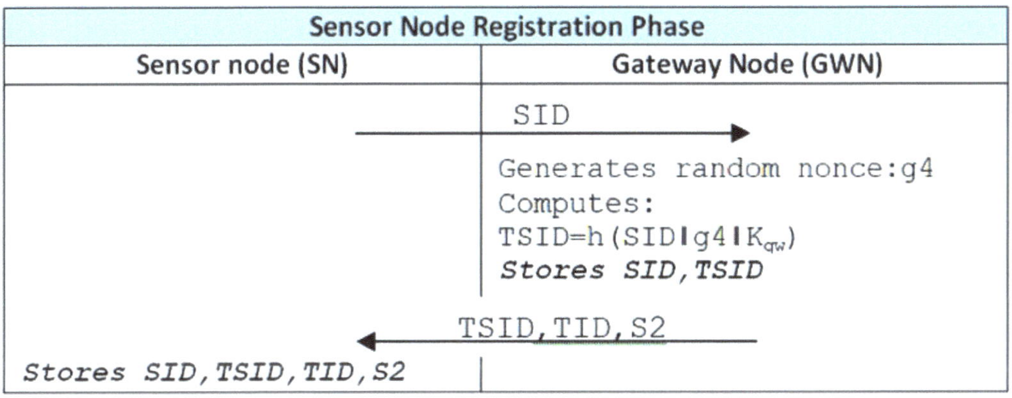

Fig. (4). Sensor node registration phase.

Stage 3: Login and Authentication phase

During this stage, the user, gateway node, and sensor nodes mutually validate each other and generate a session key, which is used by the user and the sensor nodes to exchange messages in an encrypted manner. Every time the user wants to extract the secret sensor data, this stage is executed, and a fresh session key is produced for communication (Fig. **5**). The following steps are executed:

Step 1: The user enters their unique identity UID and password PWD. It then extracts using the parameters stored during the registration phase, $r1=h(PWD \| UID) \oplus A4$, computes the masked password $MPW=h(PWD \| r1)$, and then computes $TID=A1 \oplus MPW$, extracts $S1=A2 \oplus MPW$, $S2=A3 \oplus MPW$ using the computed masked password, and then calculates $A5'=h(TID \| S1 \| S2 \| r1)$. It then checks if the computed value A5' is the same as that stored in its memory, *i.e.*,

A5'=A5? This is done to verify whether the credentials entered by the user are correct or not. If the check fails, then the login request is completed here only; otherwise, the process continues.

Step 2: The user then generates random nonces r2 and r3 and computes A6=r2⊕S1, A7=r2⊕S1, A8=h(r2‖TID‖TS1), where TS1 is the login timestamp value, and it then sends the login request message <A6, A7, A8, TID, TS1> to the node gateway on the open diffident channel.

Step 3: The node gateway, on receiving the login request message <A6, A7, A8, TID, TS1>, will first verify the identity of the user before proceeding further. It will extract r2=A6⊕S1, compute A8'=h(r2‖TID‖TS1), and then check for the correctness of the received parameters A8=A8'?

Step 4: It then generates a random nonce g5 and computes the parameters TID'=h(UID‖g5‖K_{gw}), B1=TSID⊕g5, B2=TID⊕g5, B3=TID'⊕g5, B4=h(g5‖TSID‖TID‖TID'‖TS2) where TS2 is the gateway node's timestamp used to maintain message freshness. It then sends the message <B1,B2,B3,B4,A7,TS2>to sensor node on insecure channel.

Step 5: The sensor node, on receiving the message<B1, B2, B3, B4, A7, TS2>, will first verify the identity of the gateway node. It will extract g5=B1⊕TSID, TID=B2⊕g5, TID'=B3⊕g5, r3=A7⊕S2 and computes B4'=h(g5‖TSID‖TID‖TID'‖TS2). It then checks if B4=B4'? If it matches, then the sensor node validates the gateway node as legitimate and proceeds further; otherwise terminates the process.

Step 6: The sensor node then generates a session key SK, which will be used for messages with the user for sensitive data exchange. It then computes C1=SK⊕S2, C2=h(SK‖TID'‖r3), C3=h(C1‖C2‖TSID‖TS3) where TS3 is the sensor node timestamp. And then the sensor node sends the message <C1, C2, C3, TS3> to the node gateway.

Step 7: On receiving the message <C1, C2, C3, TS3> from the sensor node, the gateway node performs the following actions. Computes C3'=h(C1‖C2‖TSID‖TS3).

Checks if C3'=C3? To check the newness of the message received. If it matches, the process continues; else, the process is terminated.

Step 8: It then computes the parameters which are sent to the user to communicate the session key SK, B5=h(TID‖TID'), B6=TID'⊕S1. It then sends the message <B5,B6,C1,C2,TS4> to the user.

Step 9: On getting the message <B5,B6,C1,C2,TS4> from the gateway node, it then computes TID'=B6⊕S1,B5'=h(TID‖TID') and A1'=TID'⊕MPW. It then checks the validity of the received message using the check if A1=A1'? If equal, the message is valid and the process is carried forward; otherwise rejected.

Step 10: The user then extracts the session key SK from the received parameters. It extracts the session key as SK=C1⊕S2, which is used to exchange the sensor data in an encrypted manner. It then computes C2'=h(SK‖TID'‖r3) and checks if C2'=C2? to confirm the validity of the SK received. If satisfied, the received SK is valid; otherwise invalid.

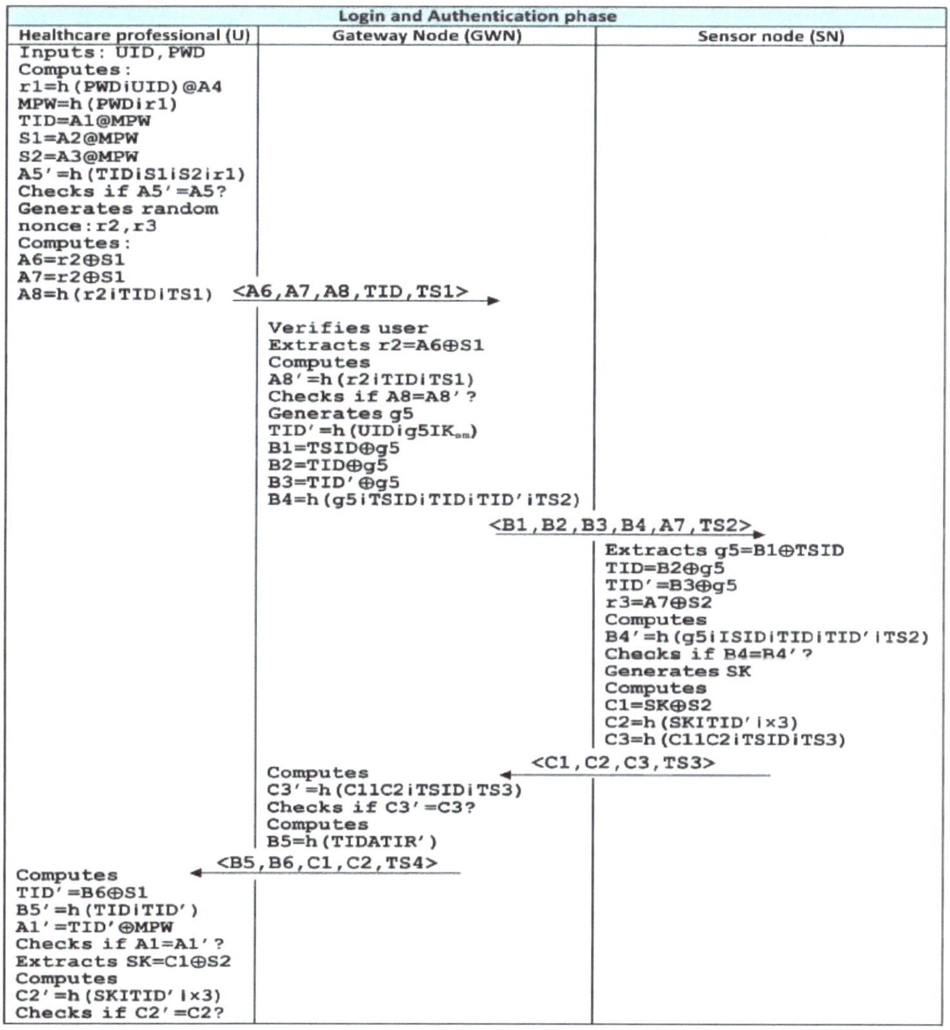

Fig. (5). Login and authentication phase.

INFORMAL SECURITY ANALYSIS

Despite being extremely challenging to accomplish, the security of any key agreement protocol for the Internet of Things environment is of utmost importance [29]. To ensure that the proposed scheme is secure, this part examines and thoroughly analyses the robustness of the proposed system against a variety of current security breaches that are relevant to the proposed framework (Table **1**).

Mutual Authentication

Mutual authentication among the user, gateway node, and sensor node is accomplished using the suggested protocol. Additionally, this feature guarantees that the technique is secure from replay and MITM attacks.

Session Key Agreement and Its Security

Secure communication between the communication partners is the goal of the authentication techniques. The proposed technique provides mutual authentication and establishes a secure session key that is produced independently by the user, node gateway, and sensor node. It is tough for an intruder to calculate the session key from the parameters sent on the open channel. Furthermore, the complexity of solving ECDLP means that an intruder cannot produce the session key even if he manages to gather session-related parameters.

Perfect Forward Secrecy

The SK is calculated from a random nonce and timestamps of the current session. If the session key of any previous session gets compromised, the intruder won't be able to get access to the sensor node data due to the presence of the fresh nonce and timestamps. The new session key cannot be calculated by the hacker using any of the old session keys. This absolute forward secrecy is thus maintained by the proposed framework.

Man-in-the-Middle Attack (MITM)

The secret parameters of user, gateway node, and sensor node are unknown to an attacker; hence, the attacker in the proposed approach cannot create an ECDH-based session key. The key session is computed in an independent manner from each party and is never sent through the insecure channel, but the parameters of the key secret are transmitted through the secure channel.

Denial of Services (DoS)

In the proposed protocol, the users compensate for communications through trusted sensors, and sensors could be installed without the prior permission of the users and therefore, this protocol stops the possibility of DoS attack from attacked or false sensors. There is no danger that a malicious node will try and disrupt by sending repeated messages to the responder.

Replay Attack and Integrity

In order to prevent replay attacks and guarantee message integrity and freshness, the proposed key agreement protocol first verifies message freshness using a nonce between resource-constrained sensors and the distant server. After that, it communicates with the remote server using a timestamp between reliable sensors.

Scalability

To create a shared pairwise key with other sensors, further sensors can be added in the initialization stage of the suggested network model. The protocol is scalable since the new sensor can create a secure connection with a remote server after a successful activation.

Table 1. Security features and defense mechanisms of the proposed protocol.

Security Feature	Defense Mechanism
Mutual Authentication	Prevents MITM and replay attacks *via* challenge-response.
Session Key Security	Uses ECC, Keys derived independently, not shared openly.
Perfect Forward Secrecy	Fresh nonces& timestamps prevent key compromise.
MITM Attack Resistance	ECDH-based session key never transmitted insecurely.
DoS Prevention	Trusted sensors require user approval, blocking attacks.
Replay Attack Prevention	Nonce and timestamps ensure message freshness.
Scalability	New sensors establish secure keys during setup.

SIMULATION RESULTS

We have analyzed the security characteristics of our suggested system and formally verified its security using the widely utilized AVISPA program. This utility checks if an authentication system is secure from MITM and replay attacks. Because it may be used to confirm if a protocol is benign and secure against both active and passive adversaries, the AVISPA tool is frequently used for assessing authentication methods. The tool writes the protocol code for the user, gateway node, and sensor node modules using High-level Protocol Specification Language

(HLPSL). The results of testing the protocol against the commonly used back-ends (i) OFMC and (ii) CL-AtSe are displayed in Figs. (**6** and **7**), respectively. All of the communications have been given to the invader, who can engage with other roles. Its primary objective is to reveal hidden keys and jeopardize the legitimacy of various roles. When putting this method into practice, the OFMC and CL-AtSe back-ends confirm that any attacks may be detected. If the scheme is secure, SAFE will be reported; if not, the security attack will be displayed. The overview of these two back-ends makes it abundantly evident that our plan is secure from intrusions.

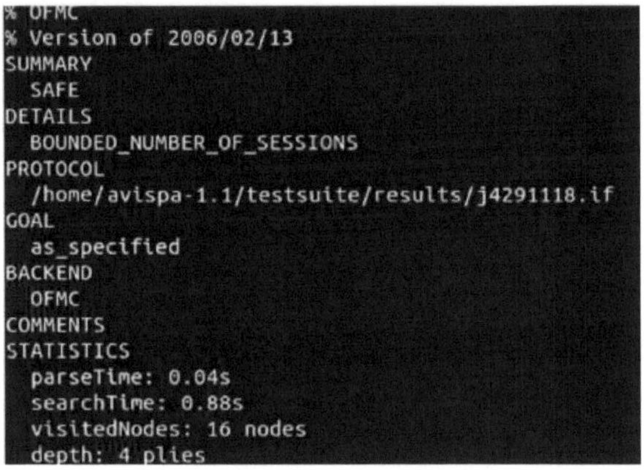

```
% OFMC
% Version of 2006/02/13
SUMMARY
  SAFE
DETAILS
  BOUNDED_NUMBER_OF_SESSIONS
PROTOCOL
  /home/avispa-1.1/testsuite/results/j4291118.if
GOAL
  as_specified
BACKEND
  OFMC
COMMENTS
STATISTICS
  parseTime: 0.04s
  searchTime: 0.88s
  visitedNodes: 16 nodes
  depth: 4 plies
```

Fig. (6). OFMC backend result for the proposed protocol.

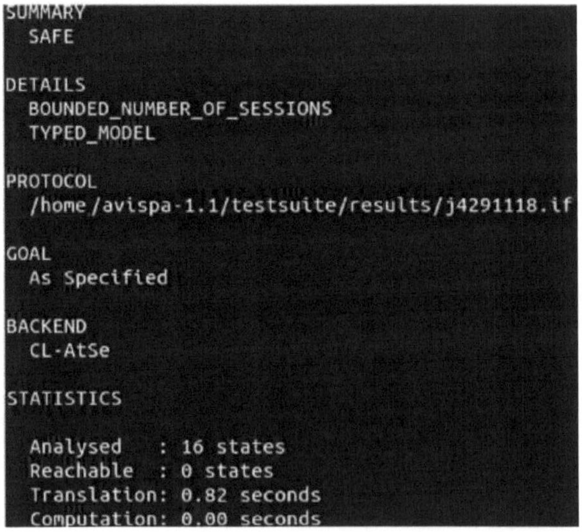

```
SUMMARY
  SAFE

DETAILS
  BOUNDED_NUMBER_OF_SESSIONS
  TYPED_MODEL

PROTOCOL
  /home/avispa-1.1/testsuite/results/j4291118.if

GOAL
  As Specified

BACKEND
  CL-AtSe

STATISTICS

  Analysed    : 16 states
  Reachable   : 0 states
  Translation: 0.82 seconds
  Computation: 0.00 seconds
```

Fig. (7). CL-AtSe backend result for proposed protocol.

CONCLUSION

In order to verify approved individuals and sensing nodes in IoT-based medical systems, this function puts forth an innovative and efficient authentication approach. Research into existing literature uncovered that current plans often fail to satisfy fundamental protection necessities or are unsuitable for asset-constrained environments. To address these holes, the planned convention ensures common validation and session key arrangement between healthcare suppliers and patients' IoT gadgets. It successfully verifies the legitimacy of both clients and sensors, along these lines ensuring basic wellbeing information from approved access and altering. Among the key advantages of the proposed technique is its lightweight plan, which conserves the restricted energy resources of wearable or implanted sensors. Another benefit is that the strategy empowers complex yet steady correspondence between nodes while keeping up multifaceted nature through fluctuating sentence structures. It accomplishes a decent parity, conveying vital subtleties with an engaging, human-like style. Through formal validation with the rigorous AVISPA tool, the protocol withstands an array of security dangers, including replay and man-in-the-middle attacks. Simulation outcomes demonstrate its practicability and effectiveness, validating its applicability in authentic healthcare situations. Furthermore, its distributed design allows for resilient operation even in fragmented network conditions.

FUTURE WORK

While the proposed protocol adequately addresses contemporary security complications, longer term, we will research its integration with post-quantum cryptographic basics to reinforce longstanding security. Additionally, incorporating AI-based anomaly detection would permit real-time monitoring for emerging threats and strengthen adaptive system resilience over time. Broadening the protocol to encourage interoperable, mass user environments - such as smart medical centers and pervasive medical equipment networks - will also be a key concentration. Moreover, the protocol's robustness and adaptability will be validated by real-world deployment and across various IoT platforms under diverse operating conditions.

ACKNOWLEDGEMENTS

The authors of this paper are thankful to GNDU College, Jalandhar, and Guru Nanak Dev University Regional Campus, Jalandhar, for providing infrastructural facilities to complete this research work.

REFERENCES

[1] B. Bera, A. K. Das, and B. Sikdar, "Quantum-Resistant Secure Communication Protocol for Digital Twin-Enabled Context-Aware IoT-Based Healthcare Applications," *IEEE Trans. Netw. Sci. Eng.,* vol. 12, no. 4, pp. 2722–2738, 2025. [http://dx.doi.org/10.1109/TNSE.2025.3553044]

[2] M. Almulhim, and N. Zaman, "Proposing secure and lightweight authentication scheme for IoT based e-health applications", in: *Proc. IEEE Int. Conf. Adv. Commun. Technol. (ICACT)*, Gangwon-do, South Korea, Feb. 11–14, 2018, pp. 481–487.

[3] P. Kumar, S.G. Lee, and H.J. Lee, "E-SAP: efficient-strong authentication protocol for healthcare applications using wireless medical sensor networks", *Sensors (Basel),* vol. 12, no. 2, pp. 1625-1647, 2012. [http://dx.doi.org/10.3390/s120201625] [PMID: 22438729]

[4] M.S. Hossain, "Cloud-supported cyber–physical localization framework for patients monitoring", *IEEE Syst. J.,* vol. 11, no. 1, pp. 118-127, 2017. [http://dx.doi.org/10.1109/JSYST.2015.2470644]

[5] R.K. Pathinarupothi, P. Durga, and E.S. Rangan, "IoT-based smart edge for global health: Remote monitoring with severity detection and alerts transmission", *IEEE Internet Things J.,* vol. 6, no. 2, pp. 2449-2462, 2019. [http://dx.doi.org/10.1109/JIOT.2018.2870068]

[6] M.A. Rahman, M.S. Hossain, M.S. Islam, N.A. Alrajeh, G. Muhammad, and M.A. Jan, "Secure and provenance enhanced internet of health things framework: A blockchain managed federated learning approach", *IEEE Access,* vol. 8, pp. 205071-205087, 2020. [http://dx.doi.org/10.1109/ACCESS.2020.3037474] [PMID: 34192116]

[7] G. Sharma, and S. Kalra, "A novel scheme for data security in cloud computing using quantum cryptography", *Proc. Int. Conf. Adv. Inf. Commun. Technol. Comput.,* pp. 1-6, 2016. [http://dx.doi.org/10.1145/2979779.2979816]

[8] G. Sharma, and S. Kalra, "Identity based secure authentication scheme based on quantum key distribution for cloud computing", *Peer-to-Peer Netw. Appl.,* vol. 11, no. 2, pp. 220-234, 2018. [http://dx.doi.org/10.1007/s12083-016-0528-2]

[9] S. Mishra, B. Mondal, and R.K. Jha, "Lightweight authentication scheme based on ECC for IoT", *SN Comput. Sci.,* vol. 5, no. 7, p. 949, 2024. [http://dx.doi.org/10.1007/s42979-024-03291-5]

[10] H.M. Chen, J.W. Lo, and C.K. Yeh, "An efficient and secure dynamic ID-based authentication scheme for telecare medical information systems", *J. Med. Syst.,* vol. 36, no. 6, pp. 3907-3915, 2012. [http://dx.doi.org/10.1007/s10916-012-9862-y] [PMID: 22673892]

[11] T. Cao, and J. Zhai, "Improved dynamic ID-based authentication scheme for telecare medical information systems", *J. Med. Syst.,* vol. 37, no. 2, p. 9912, 2013. [http://dx.doi.org/10.1007/s10916-012-9912-5] [PMID: 23345091]

[12] Z.Y. Wu, Y.C. Lee, F. Lai, H.C. Lee, and Y. Chung, "A secure authentication scheme for telecare medicine information systems", *J. Med. Syst.,* vol. 36, no. 3, pp. 1529-1535, 2012. [http://dx.doi.org/10.1007/s10916-010-9614-9] [PMID: 20978928]

[13] H. Debiao, C. Jianhua, and Z. Rui, "A more secure authentication scheme for telecare medicine information systems", *J. Med. Syst.,* vol. 36, no. 3, pp. 1989-1995, 2012. [http://dx.doi.org/10.1007/s10916-011-9658-5] [PMID: 21360017]

[14] J. Wei, X. Hu, and W. Liu, "An improved authentication scheme for telecare medicine information systems", *J. Med. Syst.,* vol. 36, no. 6, pp. 3597-3604, 2012. [http://dx.doi.org/10.1007/s10916-012-9835-1] [PMID: 22374237]

[15] S. Challa, M. Wazid, A.K. Das, N. Kumar, A. Goutham Reddy, E.J. Yoon, and K.Y. Yoo, "Secure signature-based authenticated key establishment scheme for future IoT applications", *IEEE Access,* vol. 5, pp. 3028-3043, 2017. [http://dx.doi.org/10.1109/ACCESS.2017.2676119]

[16] X. Jia, D. He, L. Li, and K.K.R. Choo, "Signature-based three-factor authenticated key exchange for internet of things applications", *Multimedia Tools Appl.,* vol. 77, no. 14, pp. 18355-18382, 2018. [http://dx.doi.org/10.1007/s11042-017-5560-6]

[17] L. Zhou, X. Li, K.H. Yeh, C. Su, and W. Chiu, "Lightweight IoT-based authentication scheme in cloud computing circumstance", *Future Gener. Comput. Syst.,* vol. 91, pp. 244-251, 2019. [http://dx.doi.org/10.1016/j.future.2018.08.038]

[18] M. Masud, G.S. Gaba, S. Alqahtani, G. Muhammad, B.B. Gupta, P. Kumar, and A. Ghoneim, "A lightweight and robust secure key establishment protocol for Internet of Medical Things in COVID-19 patients care", *IEEE Internet Things J.,* vol. 8, no. 21, pp. 15694-15703, 2021. [http://dx.doi.org/10.1109/JIOT.2020.3047662] [PMID: 35782176]

[19] M.S. Farash, M. Turkanović, S. Kumari, and M. Hölbl, "An efficient user authentication and key agreement scheme for heterogeneous wireless sensor network tailored for the Internet of Things environment", *Ad Hoc Netw.,* vol. 36, pp. 152-176, 2016. [http://dx.doi.org/10.1016/j.adhoc.2015.05.014]

[20] R. Amin, S.K.H. Islam, G.P. Biswas, M.K. Khan, L. Leng, and N. Kumar, "Design of an anonymity-preserving three-factor authenticated key exchange protocol for wireless sensor networks", *Comput. Netw.,* vol. 101, pp. 42-62, 2016. [http://dx.doi.org/10.1016/j.comnet.2016.01.006]

[21] G. Sharma, and S. Kalra, "A lightweight user authentication scheme for cloud-IoT based healthcare services", *Iran. J. Sci. Technol. Trans. Electr. Eng.,* vol. 43, no. S1, pp. 619-636, 2019. [http://dx.doi.org/10.1007/s40998-018-0146-5]

[22] R. Canetti, and H. Krawczyk, *"Universally composable notions of key exchange and secure channels," in Proc. Adv. Cryptol. — EUROCRYPT 2002.,* L.R. Knudsen, Ed., Springer: Berlin, Heidelberg, 2002, pp. 337-351.

[23] M. Turkanović, B. Brumen, and M. Hölbl, "A novel user authentication and key agreement scheme for heterogeneous ad hoc wireless sensor networks, based on the Internet of Things notion", *Ad Hoc Netw.,* vol. 20, pp. 96-112, 2014. [http://dx.doi.org/10.1016/j.adhoc.2014.03.009]

[24] R. Amin, and G.P. Biswas, "A secure light weight scheme for user authentication and key agreement in multi-gateway based wireless sensor networks", *Ad Hoc Netw.,* vol. 36, pp. 58-80, 2016. [http://dx.doi.org/10.1016/j.adhoc.2015.05.020]

[25] M. Wazid, A.K. Das, S. Shetty, J. J P C Rodrigues, and Y. Park, "LDAKM-EIoT: Lightweight device authentication and key management mechanism for edge-based IoT deployment", *Sensors (Basel),* vol. 19, no. 24, p. 5539, 2019. [http://dx.doi.org/10.3390/s19245539] [PMID: 31847431]

[26] G.S. Gaba, G. Kumar, H. Monga, T.H. Kim, and P. Kumar, "Robust and lightweight mutual authentication scheme in distributed smart environments", *IEEE Access,* vol. 8, pp. 69722-69733, 2020. [http://dx.doi.org/10.1109/ACCESS.2020.2986480]

[27] L. Hu, M. Qiu, J. Song, M.S. Hossain, and A. Ghoneim, "Software defined healthcare networks", *IEEE Wirel. Commun.,* vol. 22, no. 6, pp. 67-75, 2015. [http://dx.doi.org/10.1109/MWC.2015.7368826]

[28] S.U. Amin, M. Alsulaiman, G. Muhammad, M.A. Mekhtiche, and M. Shamim Hossain, "Deep Learning for EEG motor imagery classification based on multi-layer CNNs feature fusion", *Future*

Gener. Comput. Syst., vol. 101, pp. 542-554, 2019.
[http://dx.doi.org/10.1016/j.future.2019.06.027]

[29] A. Rahman, M.S. Hossain, N.A. Alrajeh, F. Alsolami, and M.A. Alrubaian, "Adversarial examples – security threats to COVID-19 deep learning systems in medical IoT devices", *IEEE Internet Things J.,* vol. 8, no. 12, pp. 9603-9610, 2021.
[http://dx.doi.org/10.1109/JIOT.2020.3013710] [PMID: 36811011]

[30] A.K. Sangaiah, D.V. Medhane, G-B. Bian, A. Ghoneim, M. Alrashoud, and M.S. Hossain, "Energy-aware green adversary model for cyber-physical security in industrial system", *IEEE Trans. Industr. Inform.,* vol. 16, no. 5, pp. 3322-3329, 2020.
[http://dx.doi.org/10.1109/TII.2019.2953289]

[31] G.S. Gaba, G. Kumar, H. Monga, T.H. Kim, M. Liyanage, and P. Kumar, "Robust and lightweight key exchange (LKE) protocol for industry 4.0", *IEEE Access,* vol. 8, pp. 132808-132824, 2020.
[http://dx.doi.org/10.1109/ACCESS.2020.3010302]

[32] A. Armando, D. Basin, Y. Boichut, L. Compagna, and J. Cuéllar, P. HankesDrielsma, S. Mödersheim, D. von Oheimb, M. Rusinowitch, J. Santiago, M. Turuani, L. Viganò, and L. Vigneron, "The AVISPA tool for the automated validation of internet security protocols and applications," in *Proc. Int. Conf. Comput.-Aided Verif.*, 2005, pp. 281–285.

CHAPTER 13

Exploring the Role of Quantum AI in Enhancing the Web Accessibility Evaluation Techniques

Suman Devi[1,*], **Jasjit Singh Samagh**[1], **Satinder Kaur**[2], **Gurpreet Singh**[2] and **Kumari Sarita**[3]

[1] *Department of Computer Science and Engineering, Chaudhary Devi Lal University, Sirsa, Haryana, India*

[2] *Department of Computer Engineering and Technology, Guru Nanak Dev University, Amritsar, Punjab, India*

[3] *Department of Computer Science, Guru Nanak Dev University, Amritsar, Punjab, India*

Abstract: In ensuring an inclusive digital environment, web accessibility plays an important role. The existing AI-based techniques face challenges in handling the dynamism of modern web structures. This chapter presents a comparative analysis of Quantum AI and classical AI techniques used for web accessibility evaluation. A comparative analysis approach is applied to examine the key accessibility parameters using a real-world dataset, efficiency, accuracy, and computational overheads of both approaches. The findings indicate that in the structured evaluation tasks, the classical AI performed well. By leveraging the computational advantages of QAI, processing time can be reduced, and the precision can be enhanced. QAI demonstrates superior efficiency in processing complex and large-scale accessibility assessments.

The present research provides important perspectives on the evolving role of QAI in web accessibility evaluation, offering a foundation for future advancements in automated assessment techniques.

Keywords: Accessibility testing, Artificial Intelligence (AI), Automated evaluation, Decoherence, Entanglement, Fidelity, Human-Computer Interaction (HCI), Interference, Machine learning models, Quantum Machine Learning (QML), Quantum optimization, Quantum-enhanced accessibility, Quantum AI, Quantum computing, Qubit, Quantum circuit, Sensor integration, Superposition, User Experience (UX), Web accessibility standards.

* **Corresponding author Suman Devi:** Department of Computer Science and Engineering, Chaudhary Devi Lal University, Sirsa, Haryana, India; E-mail: sumankasnia@gmail.com

Satveer Kour, Harvinder Singh, Anupam Bonkra & Rupinder Singh (Eds.)

INTRODUCTION

To create an inclusive digital environment, it is essential to ensure web accessibility for individuals with disabilities. They can interact with the digital content seamlessly. The existing evaluation techniques face significant challenges in assessing accessibility compliance against the Web Content Accessibility Guidelines (WCAG) framework. WCAG provides guidelines for making digital platforms more accessible. The complex issues, such as semantic ambiguities and dynamic content rendering, are not often detected by the traditional evolution automated and manual methods. The existing evaluation techniques face challenges in adaptation to assistive technologies. These limitations hinder the effectiveness of current accessibility assessment tools, necessitating more advanced solutions.

QAI offers a promising approach for solving these difficulties. The combination of quantum computing technology with AI features produces enhanced processing power alongside improved dataset recognition capabilities. QAI utilizes improved machine learning capabilities and optimization techniques that boost both performance and accuracy, as well as data scale evaluation. Through enhanced accessibility barrier detection, QAI achieves better automation of compliance checks that deliver immediate user experience enhancements.

This document investigates the part QAI plays in changing techniques that evaluate web accessibility. QAI technologies manage to bypass standard procedure restrictions. The enhanced detection accuracy leads to better digital content accessibility through this approach. The evaluation of QAI aims to serve three principal functions beyond its initial purposes. Development of advanced methodologies for accessibility assessment leads to enhanced digital inclusivity and equity [1].

The Current State of Web Accessibility Evaluation

The evaluation is carried out to understand whether the digital content can be used by individuals with disabilities in accordance with the established WCAG guidelines. Current evaluation approaches rely on automated tools that can identify issues such as low color contrast, missing alt text, and improper heading structures. However, despite their potential, these tools have several limitations:

- **Lack of Semantic Understanding:** Traditional tools struggle to interpret the context and meaning of web content, leading to missed issues that require human judgment [2].

- **Dynamic Content Accessibility:** Traditional static evaluation methods face difficulty in addressing accessibility issues. But on the other hand, modern web applications often feature dynamic content that is generated in real-time [3].
- **Real-Time Feedback and Adaptation:** Existing tools often fail to provide real-time feedback and adaptations, limiting the tools' ability to enhance real-time user experience [4].

The Potential of Quantum AI in Web Accessibility

Quantum AI creates solutions through combining quantum computing capabilities with AI strategies to handle problems more efficiently compared to traditional computers. Quantum AI provides several solutions through its synergistic power to overcome existing issues in web accessibility evaluation.

- **Enhanced Semantic Analysis:** Quantum AI utilizes advanced Natural Language Processing (NLP) together with machine learning algorithms to perform semantic content evaluation that detects complex accessibility problems.
- **Real-Time Processing:** Quantum Computing simultaneously processes data so it executes real-time web content evaluation, which enables immediately accessible content resolution after discovery of emerging problems [5].
- **Improved Accuracy:** Quantum AI can analyze large datasets and complex patterns more efficiently, leading to more accurate detection of accessibility violations and reducing false positives and negatives [6].

Key Applications of Quantum AI in Web Accessibility

Automated Accessibility Testing

QAI plays an important role in improving the accuracy and comprehensiveness of automated accessibility testing. For example, quantum-powered machine learning models can analyze web content to detect improper heading structure, inadequate alt text, color contrast, etc. Such kinds of violations can be detected in an adequate way. Evaluation of the entire website rather than just evaluating a single page (case with traditional tools): QAI can process a large volume of data quickly and more efficiently.

Real-Time Accessibility Enhancement

Real-time accessibility enhancement is one of the most promising applications of QAI. By integrating QAI into a content management system or into web browsers, a developer can detect and rectify accessibility issues dynamically. For example, QAI has the potential to adjust color contrast, generate alt text for images, and optimize real-time keyboard navigation with a seamless, inclusive user experience.

Semantic Accessibility Evaluation

To cater to diverse user needs and to create more inclusive digital experiences [7], QAI has a semantic accessibility evaluation capability, which is useful for identifying the kind of uses that traditional tools miss, like ambiguous interpretation of guidelines and complex semantic challenges.

AI-Powered Remediation

AI-powered remediation is another significant application of QAI. It automatically corrects accessibility issues by modifying the DOM in real-time. It provides real-time actionable solutions and reduces the need for manual evaluation [8].

Limitations and Considerations

While QAI has great potential for enhancing web accessibility evaluation, there are several limitations and considerations that must be considered:

- **Technical Limitations:** To realize its full potential, significant technical challenges must be overcome. And the integration of quantum computing with AI is still in its early stages [9 - 12].
- **Ethical Considerations:** The creation and use of quantum AI must be guided by ethical principles, such as openness, responsibility, and inclusion, to make sure that the technology helps everyone [13 - 15].
- **User Feedback and Adaptation:** User feedback is essential to get its full potential. QAI systems must be designed in a way that will incorporate user feedback and adapt to evolving accessibility needs, ensuring that they remain effective and relevant over time [16, 17].

LITERATURE REVIEW

Accessibility evaluation is the essential aspect of digital inclusivity to ensure that disabled users can interact with the digital content effectively. Various researchers have explored the issues associated with the accessibility evaluations and the potential of the emerging technological revolutions to enhance the evaluations. Traditional accessibility assessment methods, automated tools, and manual auditing often fail to detect semantic inconsistencies, real-time content behavior, and dynamic user adaptation. Researchers have investigated the role of AI and QAI to address the issues and improve digital inclusivity.

Huang *et al.* (2024) [18] highlighted the limitations of traditional accessibility evaluation methods and proposed AI-driven solutions to correct real-time accessibility issues automatically. How machine learning algorithms can be used to improve compliance with WCAG by analyzing user interaction.

Othman *et al.* (2023) [19] explored AI-powered assessment tools for accessibility enhancement and to automate remediation processes. Researchers' findings indicate that the integration of AI with accessibility validation significantly improves efficiency and digital inclusivity by reducing evaluation time.

Yadavali (2024) [20] explored the role of natural language processing and the semantic accessibility evaluation in detecting accessibility issues. Through AI models, the contextual relationships within the digital content and the ambiguities that hinder comprehension for users relying on assistive technologies are being addressed in this study. The results indicate that web content aligned with cognitive accessibility principles and semantic evaluation improves inclusivity.

Bajammal and Mesbah (2021) [21]: For analyzing semantic inconsistencies in accessibility, they have investigated machine learning algorithms. How the issues related to ambiguous navigation, ambiguous instructions, and content organization can be detected. This study has the potential to address the issues related to structure and accessibility. The integration of semantic evaluation and accessibility, integrating semantic evaluation into the accessibility assessment framework, is a more holistic approach to digital inclusivity.

Huang *et al.* (2024) [22] have discussed automated evaluation for accessibility enhancement using QAI. The automatic evaluation is powered by the advanced AI-driven models to detect and resolve the issues systematically and efficiently without human intervention. The integrated approach of QAI presents new opportunities for scalability and real-time adaptive solutions.

Comparative Analysis of AI-Driven Web Accessibility Solutions

A comparative analysis of 15 research studies was conducted to gain deeper insights into how AI and quantum AI are integrated in web accessibility. These studies were selected based on their relevance to AI-driven accessibility solutions, assistive technologies, and semantic evaluation frameworks. The analysis examines key aspects such as the objectives of each study, AI techniques employed, major findings, challenges identified, and future research directions.

The following table (Table **1**) presents a structured comparison of these studies, highlighting their contributions to web accessibility improvements and identifying gaps that need to be addressed for the effective implementation of AI in inclusive digital environments.

Table 1. Comparative analysis of web accessibility methods.

Ref. No.	Title	Objectives	Method Used	Limitations	Findings	Results
[3]	AI-Powered Real-Time Accessibility Enhancement: A Solution for Web Content Accessibility Issues	1. Address primary web accessibility issues identified in WCAG. 2. Propose an AI-enabled system for real-time accessibility enhancement.	1. An AI-enabled system enhances web accessibility dynamically. 2. Machine learning algorithms identify and rectify accessibility issues.	1. Developers have limited awareness of accessibility implications. 2. Potential code bugs and API failures.	1. The AI system dynamically enhances web accessibility in real-time. 2. Case studies confirm efficacy.	1. The AI system improves web accessibility in real time. 2. Empirical evaluation shows efficacy across diverse scenarios.
[4]	IrisMath: A Blind-friendly Web-Based Computer Algebra System	1. Develop CAS for blind engineering students 2. Overcome academic limitations faced by visually impaired individuals.	1. Blind-friendly CAS development 2. Assessment of functional, non-functional, and usability requirements.	1. Delay in descriptive audio for key presses 2. Inability to navigate through input elements	1. IrisMath supports blind engineering students in academic activities. 2. Usability requirements met.	1. Enables math operations for the visually impaired 2. Offers various output formats
[5]	A Heuristic Method to Evaluate Web Accessibility for Users With Low Vision	1. Evaluate accessibility for low vision users. 2. Identify primary deficiencies in web accessibility.	1. Heuristic evaluation method based on barrier walkthrough 2. Inspection and observation methods for accessibility assessment.	1. The manual method is time-consuming and costly. 2. High-ranking websites may still lack accessibility.	1. High-ranking websites may not be accessible or inclusive. 2. Manual evaluation methods are time-consuming and costly.	1. Evaluators analyzed the severity of each website and grouped data by categories. 2. Manual methods are still essential.

(Table 1) cont.....

Ref. No.	Title	Objectives	Method Used	Limitations	Findings	Results
[6]	Automatic adaptation of open educational resources: an approach from a multilevel methodology based on students' preferences, educational special needs, artificial intelligence, and accessibility metadata	1. Develop automated support for accessible educational resources. 2. Address challenges in virtual education using artificial intelligence.	1. Multilevel methodological proposal for automatic adaptation 2. Research conducted with students with disabilities	1. Sample selection limitation 2. Quality and context issues with images and audio	1. Automated tool for adapting educational resources with accessibility metadata. 2. Research aims to support AI applications in virtual education.	1. The results of the paper show positive values for the three categories analyzed. 2. The text quality generated by the audio module is comparable to that achieved with external tools.
[7]	Lexical Simplification System to Improve Web Accessibility	1. Improve comprehension of Spanish texts. 2. Provide systematic support for accessibility guidelines compliance.	1. Complex word identification using state-o- -the-art resources. 2. Substitute generation and selection with machine learning techniques.	1. Room for improvement in substitute generation tasks. 2. Comparable results to English, indicating further development is needed.	1. Improved F1-scores in complex word identification 2. Promising results in generating context-aware and simpler definitions.	1. CWI task: Achieved an F1 score of 0.794, outperforming other systems. 2. Comparable results in SG/SS tasks.
[8]	Design of an Intelligent Human-Computer Interaction System for Hard of Hearing and Non-Disabled People	1. Solve communication problems for hard-of-hearing individuals. 2. Integrate AI with wearable devices for effective interaction.	1. Classification of gestures with a BP neural network 2. Combining artificial intelligence with wearable devices	1. Communication inconvenience between hard-of-hearing and non-disabled people 2. Need for artificial intelligence and wearable devices for effective communication	1. An intelligent system combines AI and wearable devices for communication 2. Gestures classified with a BP neural network for effective communication.	1. Designed an intelligent interaction system for communication 2. Utilizes AI and wearable devices for gesture classification.

(Table 1) cont.....

Ref. No.	Title	Objectives	Method Used	Limitations	Findings	Results
[9]	Towards Assisting the Visually Impaired: A Review on Techniques for Decoding the Visual Data From Chart Images	1. Analyze methods for decoding visual data from chart images. 2. Explore existing literature on graph comprehension and extraction techniques.	1. Modality-based approaches, conventional methods, and deep learning-based methods are used. 2. The paper explores methods for extracting visual encoding from chart images.	1. Deep learning needs further improvements in reasoning based on chart images. 2. Recreating data from raster images has unresolved issues.	1. Deep learning excels in localization and classification tasks. 2. More research is needed for reasoning from chart images.	1. Strong results in image classification 2. Research works are still in progress for accessing data from vector images.
[10]	Techniques for the Publication of Accessible Multimedia Content on the Web	1. Propose techniques for accessible multimedia. 2. Evaluate tool compliance.	1. Five-phase methodology based on accessibility standards and guidelines. 2. Comprehensive review of multimedia accessibility principles and techniques.	1. Authoring tools lack required accessibility features. 2. Non-compliance with ATAG 2.0 causes accessibility failures.	1. Proposed 278 techniques for accessible multimedia publication. 2. Identified 80 potential failures in multimedia accessibility compliance.	1. 278 publishing techniques proposed 2. 80 failures outlined
[11]	Web Accessibility Evaluation of Videos Published on YouTube by Worldwide Top-Ranking Universities	1. Evaluate the accessibility of YouTube videos from top universities. 2. Highlight the need for improved video accessibility compliance.	1. Five-phase methodology for evaluating video accessibility. 2. Manual evaluation of 91,421 YouTube videos.	1. No automatic tools for evaluating accessibility requirements exist. 2. Manual evaluation of a large number of videos is required.	1. Only 17 videos had associated captions. 2. Compliance with accessibility criteria has improved over time.	1. Only 17 videos had associated captions. 2. North American universities published the most videos.
[12]	A Framework to Enhance User Experience of Older Adults With Speech-Based Intelligent Personal Assistants	1. Understand the usability of SIPAs from the older adults' perspective. 2. Suggest an improvement framework	1. Interviews with seniors 2. Inductive and deductive coding analysis of collected data	1. Small number of participants 2. Exclusion of special needs personnel	1. Identified usability challenges faced by older adults with SIPAs. 2. Suggested design improvements for better user experience in SIPAs.	1. Identified the key themes. 2. Suggestions for SIPAs: Privacy, interpersonal skills, and contextual awareness improvements

(Table 1) cont.....

Ref. No.	Title	Objectives	Method Used	Limitations	Findings	Results
[13]	Preliminary Evaluation of Interactive Search Engine Interface for Visually Impaired Users	1. Design and improve the search engine interface for VI users. 2. Evaluate usability and accessibility using established guidelines.	1. Formal Concept Analysis for data analysis 2. Nielsen + WCAG 2.0 evaluation	1. Most frequently violated heuristics: consistency, documentation 2. Most frequently violated WCAG guidelines: distinguishable, navigable, and affordance.	1. Most violated Nielsen's heuristics: consistency, documentation. 2. Navigation/documentation lacking	1. Most violated Nielsen's heuristics: consistency, documentation. 2. Affordance issues are critical.
[14]	Development of an Ontology for the Inclusion of App Users With Visual Impairments	1. Develop an ontology-based user profile for app recommendations. 2. Facilitate app selection for users with visual impairments.	1. Test and interviews for user evaluation results. 2. Bravo to the Hoyos and Reyes method for ontology creation.	1. Difficulty in selecting suitable apps for users with impairments. 2. Lack of specified accessibility features in app descriptions.	1. Developed an ontology for personalized app recommendations for visually impaired users. 2. Improved user profile model enhances app search and selection processes.	1. Developed an ontology for personalized app recommendations for visually impaired users. 2. Merged user profile and apps ontology for improved app selection.
[15]	Improving Accessibility in Online Education: Comparative Analysis of Attitudes of Blind and Deaf Students Toward an Adapted Learning Platform	1. Evaluate adaptive platform usability. 2. Compare blind and deaf students' perceptions of adaptations.	1. Survey Analysis 2. Moodle platform adaptation.	1. Problems with accessibility and usability in learning platforms 2. Varying ease of use perception	1. Positive attitude towards adaptation by both groups. 2. Differences in ease of use and content access perception.	1. The majority favored adaptation 2. Usefulness perception varied.
[16]	Assistive Devices Analysis for Visually Impaired Persons: A Review on Taxonomy	1. Comparative analysis of assistive devices for visually impaired persons. 2. Highlight attributes, challenges, and limitations of existing techniques.	1. Sensors: Infrared, ultrasonic, and imagery sensors are used for input. 2. Machine learning: Processes signals and extracts useful information for feedback.	1. Limited functionality 2. Challenges and limitations of assistive devices are highlighted.	1. A comprehensive comparison was done. 2. Highlighted attributes, challenges, and limitations of existing techniques.	1. In-depth review presented 2. The paper highlights the attributes, challenges, and limitations of these devices.

(Table 1) cont.....

Ref. No.	Title	Objectives	Method Used	Limitations	Findings	Results
[17]	Low-Cost Assistive Technologies for Disabled People Using Open-Source Hardware and Software: A Systematic Literature Review	1. Analyze the role of OSHW and OSS in AT development. 2. Inform stakeholders.	1. Systematic literature review (SLR) methodology 2. PRISMA guidelines for review stages	1. Limitation 1: Use of limited databases for the searching process. 2. Limitation 2: Exclusion of specific terms used by researchers.	1. Analyzed 809 studies on low-cost assistive technologies. 2. Identified challenges in accessibility and development of assistive devices.	1. The paper provides a systematic literature review on low-cost assistive technologies. 2. OS tools emphasized in design.

On the basis of the above comparative analysis, the key findings highlight the transformative impact of AI and QAI on web accessibility [23]. AI-driven solutions dynamically enhance accessibility by identifying and rectifying issues in real time, particularly in compliance with WCAG standards. Assistive technologies, such as speech recognition and blind-friendly computer algebra systems, significantly improve task completion rates and inclusivity for users with disabilities. Studies overlook the effectiveness of AI-driven heuristic evaluation approaches in detecting unidentified issues. Automated evaluation methods suffer from delays and inconsistencies [24]. AI-driven approaches have promising results. The studies validating the efficiency of these approaches across diverse scenarios. This integration holds immense potential, but optimization and standardization are necessary to get its maximum impact.

CONCLUSION

QAI has the potential to address the challenges identified by the existing tools. It is a revolution in web accessibility, and it has the potential to evaluate more effectively and efficiently. It is a powerful approach for creating more inclusive digital experiences with the potential to enhance semantic analysis and improve accuracy in real-time processing. By integrating quantum computing with AI, a developer may create more effective, inclusive, and advanced evaluation techniques. That is more beneficial for the users, developers, and the whole society as well.

FUTURE SCOPE

This study sheds light on the potential of QAI in web accessibility evaluation approaches while highlighting areas of future work. Future work should focus on the optimization of QAI algorithms and their practical implementation with the current technical limitations. The focus will be on the computational efficiency enhancement. To improve the performance and scalability, the hybrid model of quantum computing with advanced machine learning and deep learning should be explored. Expanding QAI applications to multimodal content such as images and videos will enhance digital inclusivity. Additionally, incorporating dynamic accessibility monitoring and behavior analysis for better web accessibility assessment can be considered for future work.

ACKNOWLEDGEMENT

The authors of this paper are thankful to Chaudhary Devi Lal University, Sirsa, and Guru Nanak Dev University, Amritsar, for providing infrastructural facilities to complete this research work.

REFERENCES

[1] A. Bajammal, and A. Mesbah, "Machine learning for detecting semantic inconsistencies in web accessibility", *International Journal of Web Accessibility Research,* vol. 14, no. 3, pp. 45-62, 2021.

[2] R. Yadavali, "Enhancing semantic accessibility evaluation using AI-driven natural language processing techniques", *Journal of Digital Inclusion Studies,* vol. 19, no. 2, pp. 78-95, 2024.

[3] S. Dash, "AI-powered real-time accessibility enhancement: A solution for web content accessibility issues," *J. Online Inform.*, vol. 9, no. 1, 2024. [http://dx.doi.org/10.15575/join.v9i1.1310]

[4] A. M. Zambrano, D. I. Pilacuán, M. N. Salvador, F. Grijalva, N. O. Garzón, and H. Carvajal Mora, "IrisMath: A blind-friendly web-based computer algebra system," *IEEE Access*, vol. 11, pp. 71766–71776, 2023. [http://dx.doi.org/10.1109/ACCESS.2023.3281761]

[5] P. Acosta-Vargas, L. Antonio Salvador-Ullauri, and S. Luján-Mora, "A Heuristic Method to Evaluate Web Accessibility for Users With Low Vision", *IEEE Access,* vol. 7, pp. 125634-125648, 2019. [http://dx.doi.org/10.1109/ACCESS.2019.2939068]

[6] P. Ingavélez-Guerra, V. Robles-Bykbaev, A. Perez-Munoz, J. R. Hilera, and S. OtónTortosa, "Automatic adaptation of open educational resources: an approach from a multilevel methodology based on students' preferences, educational special needs, artificial intelligence, and accessibility metadata", *IEEE Access,* 2022. [http://dx.doi.org/10.1109/ACCESS.2021.3139537]

[7] R. Alarcon, L. Moreno, and P. Martínez, "Lexical simplification system to improve web accessibility", *IEEE Access,* vol. 9, pp. 58755-58767, 2021. [http://dx.doi.org/10.1109/ACCESS.2021.3072697]

[8] Q. Fu, J. Fu, S. Zhang, X. Li, J. Guo, and S. Guo, "Design of intelligent human-computer interaction system for hard of hearing and non-disabled people", *IEEE Sens. J.,* vol. 21, no. 20, pp. 23471-23479, 2021. [http://dx.doi.org/10.1109/JSEN.2021.3107949]

[9] K.C. Shahira, and A. Lijiya, "Towards assisting the visually impaired: a review on techniques for decoding the visual data from chart images", *IEEE Access,* vol. 9, pp. 52926-52943, 2021. [http://dx.doi.org/10.1109/ACCESS.2021.3069205]

[10] T. Acosta, J. Zambrano-Miranda, and S. Luján-Mora, "Techniques for the publication of accessible multimedia content on the web", *IEEE Access,* vol. 8, pp. 55300-55322, 2020. [http://dx.doi.org/10.1109/ACCESS.2020.2981326]

[11] T. Acosta, P. Acosta-Vargas, J. Zambrano-Miranda, and S. Luján-Mora, "Web accessibility evaluation of videos published on youtube by worldwide top-ranking universities", *IEEE Access,* vol. 8, pp. 110994-111011, 2020.

[http://dx.doi.org/10.1109/ACCESS.2020.3002175]

[12] M. U. Islam and B. M. Chaudhry, "A framework to enhance user experience of older adults with speech-based intelligent personal assistants," *IEEE Access*, vol. 11, pp. 16683–16699, 2023. [http://dx.doi.org/10.1109/ACCESS.2022.3230151]

[13] A. Aqle, K. Khowaja, and D. Al-Thani, "Preliminary evaluation of interactive search engine interface for visually impaired users", *IEEE Access,* vol. 8, pp. 45061-45070, 2020. [http://dx.doi.org/10.1109/ACCESS.2020.2977593]

[14] M.I. Torres-Carazo, M.J. Rodríguez-Fórtiz, and M.V.H. Torres, "Development of an ontology for the inclusion of app users with visual impairments", *IEEE Access,* vol. 9, pp. 44339-44353, 2021. [http://dx.doi.org/10.1109/ACCESS.2021.3065274]

[15] C. Batanero-Ochaita, L. De-Marcos, L.F. Rivera, J. Holvikivi, J.R. Hilera, and S.O. Tortosa, "Improving accessibility in online education: comparative analysis of attitudes of blind and deaf students toward an adapted learning platform", *IEEE Access,* vol. 9, pp. 99968-99982, 2021. [http://dx.doi.org/10.1109/ACCESS.2021.3095041]

[16] S. Zafar, M. A. Khan, M. A. Khan, M. Imran, M. Shoaib, and M. A. Khan, "Assistive devices analysis for visually impaired persons: A review on taxonomy," *IEEE Access*, vol. 10, pp. 13354–13366, 2022. [http://dx.doi.org/10.1109/ACCESS.2022.3146728]

[17] J. Á. Ariza and J. M. Pearce, "Low-Cost Assistive Technologies for Disabled People Using Open-Source Hardware and Software: A Systematic Literature Review," *IEEE Access*, vol. 10, pp. 124894-124927, 2022. [http://dx.doi.org/10.1109/ACCESS.2022.3221449]

[18] H. Huang, Y. Zhang, M. Liu, and X. Chen, "AI-driven real-time accessibility evaluation for web compliance: Enhancing WCAG adherence through machine learning", *IEEE Access,* vol. 12, pp. 12345-12358, 2024.

[19] M. Othman, L. Rahim, S. Tan, and A. Khalid, "Automated web accessibility testing using artificial intelligence: A step towards inclusive digital environments", *Comput. Electr. Eng.,* vol. 110, p. 108053, 2023.

[20] R. Yadavali, "Semantic accessibility evaluation using AI: Leveraging NLP to enhance cognitive web accessibility", *J. Web Semant.,* vol. 78, p. 102456, 2024.

[21] N. Bajammal, and A. Mesbah, "Analyzing semantic inconsistencies in web accessibility using machine learning", *ACM Trans. Web,* vol. 15, no. 4, pp. 1-25, 2021.

[22] C. Huang, A. Ma, S. Vyasamudri, E. Puype, S. Kamal, J.B. Garcia, S. Cheema, and M. Lutz, "ACCESS: Prompt engineering for automated web accessibility violation corrections", *arXiv preprint arXiv:2401.16450,* 2024.

[23] S. Venkataraajalu, "Quantum computing and machine learning in medical decision-making: A comprehensive review", *MDPI,* 2024.

[24] E.A. Draffan, J.L. Alty, and D. Harris, "The role of artificial intelligence in accessibility: A review", *Univers. Access Inf. Soc.,* vol. 19, no. 1, pp. 1-15, 2020. [http://dx.doi.org/10.1007/s10209-019-00658-5]

CHAPTER 14

A Quantum Intelligence AI-Driven Secure Framework for IoV: QI-CAI Clustering Architecture with FDS-QI Deep Learning Security Model

Sumit Kumar[1,*], **Ishpreet Singh Virk**[2], **Anupam Bonkra**[1], **Ritu**[3], **Sunil Kumar Chawla**[4] and **Omar Mbrouk**[5]

[1] *Department of Computer Science and Engineering, Maharishi Markandeshwar (Deemed to be University), Mullana, Haryana, India*

[2] *Department of Computer Science & Engineering, Chandigarh Engineering College (CEC) Landran, Mohali, Punjab, India*

[3] *Department of Computer Science & Engineering, Chandigarh College of Engineering- CGC Jhanjeri, Mohali, Punjab, India*

[4] *Chitkara University Institute of Engineering and Technology, Chitkara University, Rajpura, Punjab, India*

[5] *Department of Nano-Chemistry and its Environmental Applications, Environmental Studies and Research Institute, University of Sadat City, Sadat City, Menofia, Egypt*

Abstract: This chapter proposes a novel Quantum Intelligence (QI)-based optimized, secure, and intelligent architectures for the IoT-based VANETs, known as Internet of Vehicles (IoV). Such technologies range from general Quantum Intelligence, AI, ML, and DL, through to the specific architectures upon which these solutions may be based, including ANN and the Levenberg Neural Engine as examples. The first proposed architecture, known as Quantum Intelligence-Driven Cluster-Based Adaptive Intelligence (QI-CAI), represents a core contribution in enhancing IoV communication by enabling dynamic and efficient clustering through the integration of Internet of Things (IoT) enabled intelligent services within the combined framework. In continuity, the second proposed architecture, Fine-Tuned Deep Learning Security with Quantum Intelligence (FDS-QI) Model, for improve security and avoid cyber-attacks. Together, these two architectures form a unified framework that addresses both communication efficiency and security in next-generation IoV systems.

[*] **Corresponding author: Sumit Kumar:** Department of Computer Science and Engineering, Maharishi Markandeshwar (Deemed to be University), Mullana, Haryana, India; E-mail: kumarsumit.cse@gmail.com

Satveer Kour, Harvinder Singh, Anupam Bonkra & Rupinder Singh (Eds.)

Keywords: AI-driven security, Clustering architecture, Deep learning models, Internet of vehicles (IoV), Quantum computing, Quantum-enhanced security, Quantum intelligence (QI), Quantum optimization, Real-time security, Secure communication, Security frameworks, Vehicle networks, Vehicle security systems.

INTRODUCTION

The urban transport systems are years ahead in connectivity and intelligence. In this chapter, a secure integrated architecture is proposed by incorporating Quantum Intelligence (QI) supported AI, ML, and DL to improve the traffic efficiency and security in the area of the Internet of Vehicles (IoV). The framework supports the use of IoT sensors to facilitate interoperable data sharing, and QI-enhanced ML methods automate decision-making and communication processes. The solution itself consists of two core architectures. A novel large-scale quantum-enhanced multiple vehicle-routing model called Quantum Intelligence-Driven adaptive clustered-based intelligent (QI-CAI) model to alleviate traffic congestion through a quantum intelligence dynamic programming approach was proposed as the first, and in the second, a large-scale quantum-enhanced multi-vehicle routing algorithm with different features but optimized around better using quantum processing, avoiding congestion source avoidance scheme to prevent such congestion. The limitation of human intelligence procedures by machines particularly includes self-correction mechanisms, reasoning by applying rules to form conclusions, and learning, where machines acquire data and rules for their use. This chapter explores the integration of Artificial Intelligence (AI) and Quantum Intelligence (QI) as a transformative paradigm for enhancing cybersecurity [1]. Specific applications of AI include the development of expert systems that exhibit specialized knowledge, speech recognition enabling machines to understand and interpret human speech, and machine vision allowing systems to interpret visual information similarly to human perception [2]. The objective of Artificial intelligence is to develop intelligent machines that can execute tasks typically requiring human intelligence [3].

- **Quantum Intelligence (QI):** Quantum intelligence uses quantum computing to improve data processing and problem-solving, enabling faster and more efficient analysis of complex tasks [4].
- **Artificial Intelligence (AI):** The Capability to acquire and apply knowledge or simulation of intelligent behaviour. Learn how to solve problems and make intelligent decisions.
- **Machine Learning (ML):** A subclass of AI that uses computer algorithms. It can learn from examples on its own without being explicitly programmed and can be trained with a large set of data.

- **Deep Learning (DL):** A subclass of ML that uses basic layered Artificial Neural Networks (ANN) to simulate human decision-making.
- **Artificial Neural Network (ANN):** The inspiration for Artificial Neural Networks (ANNs) is derived from Biological Neural Networks (BNNs), which are designed to address intricate processes observed in biological systems by employing chemically connected neurons.

Types of Machine Learning (ML)

AI training is required when the learning system has to adapt to and develop precise responses to inputs, particularly when the input's information is restricted or uncertain. The training phase entails exposing the AI system to a variety of instances and settings, allowing it to learn and increase its capacity to handle a wide range of inputs. This adaptive learning is especially useful when dealing with uncertainties or gaps in knowledge, allowing the AI system to make educated judgments and respond accurately even in complicated or new circumstances. Fig. (**1**) depicts the categorization of Machine Learning (ML) methodologies.

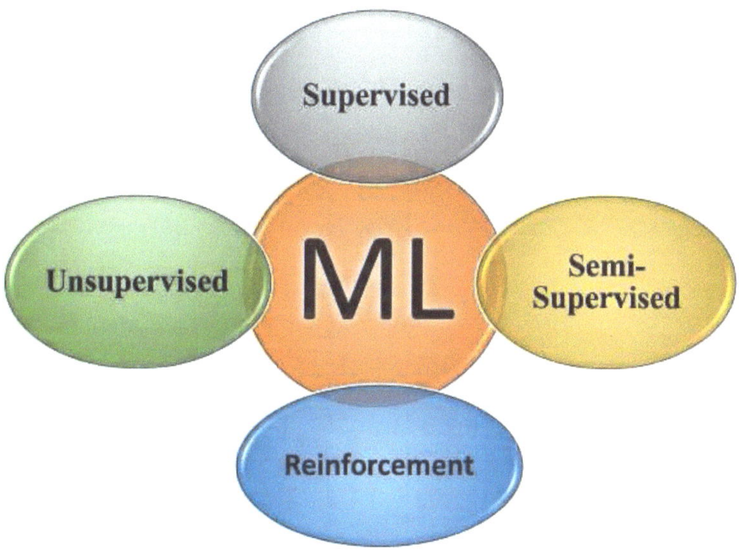

Fig. (1). Classification of machine learning (ML) [5].

Supervised or Task-driven Learning

It makes predictions about the next value based on tagged data. The essential assumption in this model is that the system consistently generates the intended response when the input is applied. The system works by predicting outcomes for known cases and then comparing its predictions to the recognized results. This iterative approach allows the system to identify and learn from its failures, improving its predictive skills and overall performance over time. This continual feedback loop is critical for improving and optimizing the system's capacity to produce accurate and desired replies.

Unsupervised or Data-driven Learning (Identify clusters using unlabelled data)

In this mode, the preferred response is unknown, and therefore, explicit error messages cannot be employed to improve network performance. Since there is no information available regarding the accuracy or inaccuracy of responses, learning is carried out based on measurements of the system's responses to inputs. The system adapts and refines its behaviour through an iterative process of adjusting its responses based on the observed outcomes, aiming to improve performance without explicit knowledge of the desired acknowledgment.

Semi-Supervised Machine Learning (Use both unlabelled data and labelled data)

This learning occupies a position among "supervised and unsupervised" learning in the area of ML. In this technique, the algorithm is given a dataset that includes both labelled and unlabelled data. The algorithm learns from the labelled dataset and generalizes patterns to generate predictions about unlabelled examples. Semi-supervised learning is especially beneficial in situations when obtaining fully labelled datasets is difficult or costly.

Reinforcement Machine Learning (Learn from Mistakes)

This sort of learning is part of the machine learning category that is used to train a model in order to identify an optimal solution to a particular problem by making independent decisions. This strategy has the improvement of the model, promoting good behaviors by rewarding them and, in the same way, reducing the probabilities of the model making bad decisions by penalizing it. This learning paradigm is especially important in situations where the model is able to talk to the environment and has to learn what is best through a process of trial and error.

Feedforward Neural Network

A feedforward neural network is a basic and elementary type of artificial neural network comprising computationally optimized designs. It consists of several layers of nodes, known as neurons, and the flow of information is from the input layer to the output layer through one or more intermediate or concealed layers in a forward direction only. Most of the feedforward Artificial Neural Networks (ANN) are trained using ML approaches like Levenberg neural propagation. This also improves the request and reply (RREQ and RREP) processes; it also comes with an enhanced AODV protocol aimed at making route discovery select the best route, which is beneficial in this system [6]. Some of the parts of a Feedforward Neural Network (FNN) are as follows (Fig. **2**).

- Input Layer
- One or more Hidden Layers
- Output Layer
- Weighted Connections
- Activation Functions

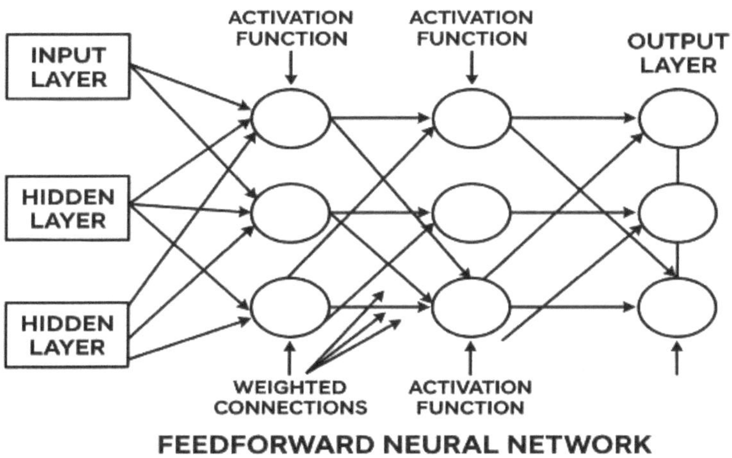

Fig. (2). Components of a feedforward neural network (FNN) [7, 8].

Levenberg Neural Engine

In VANET, using the proposed NN integrating the Levenberg-Marquardt method has the following objectives: Enhancing the current VANET capabilities of data processing, prediction, as well as decision making. In the following, the Levenberg-Marquardt method is employed to solve the nonlinear least squares problems. It is widely applied in such problems as training neural networks. It incorporates the gradient descent and the Gauss-Newton method and is suggested to be robust even if it operates with highly sensitive Jacobian matrices. That is why it has one damping parameter of step size that makes it adaptive for many-run solution problems.

CONTRIBUTION OF THE CHAPTER

- Use Quantum intelligence to fine-tune machine learning models and respond to evolving cyber threats.

- This approach significantly improves cybersecurity by tweaking a quantum intelligence machine learning model for essential data processing.
- Evaluating and improving these algorithms can significantly increase threat detection accuracy and reaction times.
- This work not only improves the security of digital ecosystems but also sheds light on the growth of cybersecurity approaches, paving the way for more robust and proactive defence mechanisms in the face of an ever-changing collection of threats.

These contributions provide a foundation for the development of IoT VANET and present the areas for their further evolution in terms of Quantum computing and machine learning in cybersecurity, communication effectiveness, optimum network architecture, and routing protocols. This chapter briefly discusses the IoT architecture, IoT applications, and the routing protocols for Internet of Vehicles (IoV). It also explores the basics of AI and ML and explains various learning methods, including the Feedforward Neural Networks, the Levenberg Neural Engine, to name a few. This chapter of the book is divided into three large parts. Section 1 includes the literature review that outlines the development of security solutions using ML and routing data. It investigates various machine learning methodologies, such as supervised, semi-supervised, unsupervised, and neural networks, in the context of cybersecurity. Section 2 describes the suggested quantum AI-ML architectures, clustering techniques, tuning, and data transfer. Section 3 examines the important findings of both designs, stressing their relevance, prospective applications, and future research paths, providing significant insights for researchers looking to improve security in IoT-based networks.

LITERATURE SURVEY

After a detailed study of research publications on the topic of Quantum Intelligence-enabled IoV communication and security, the focus is on the routing methods and optimization strategies being used so far. Authors from different backgrounds contribute to these publications, adopting various methodologies and algorithms to overcome the issues associated with VANET communication. This section of the paper delves into a survey of existing work related to secure communication and the minimization of traffic congestion in the IoT-based VANET.

In 2025, AlptugAytekin *et al.* [9] presented Quantum X-Secure E-Eavesdropped T-Colluding Symmetric Private Information Retrieval. This work explores classical and quantum variations of X-secure, E-eavesdropped, and T-colluding SPIR, with a focus on symmetric privacy for both user and database. The quantum extension introduces two schemes for QXSETSPIR, with one achieving super-dense coding gain and the other requiring no extra uploads but not always achieving the same gain.

In 2024, Monika *et al.* [10] explored the current research trend and challenges in the domain of Quantum-Enhanced Intelligent Transportation Systems (QEITS). Using scientometric methods, the study provides a comprehensive analysis of the developmental status, research distribution, and emerging trends in QEITS.

In 2023, the study conducted by Tosunoglu *et al.* [11] revolved around the concept that the detection of network anomalies is essential for spotting hostile activity compromising network security. There were difficulties with their unusual, resource-constrained architecture. There was a demand for adaptable threat detection systems. Conventional techniques required expensive, labelled data. A unique method that combined the K-Means and C5.0 algorithms revealed salient features and achieved a 96% success rate in classifying malicious nodes in VANETs. Though the literature explores the research efforts to mitigate the threats in VANETs, the present research will delve into model tuning to achieve a better threat detection accuracy.

In 2022, Magaia *et al.* [12] introduced a novel routing scheme called 'Group and Route' (GnR) that utilizes edge learning and social power to facilitate effective communication in the Internet of Vehicles (IoV). The Group and Route (GnR) scheme incorporates clustering and efficient routing methods to enhance the output of Vehicular Ad-Hoc Network (VANET) communications. Performance evaluation demonstrates the stability of the clustering algorithm across diverse road scenarios, suggesting it as a viable approach in the context of mobile Internet of Vehicles (IoV) nodes.

In 2022, Sindhwani *et al.* [13] offer a review of soft computing methods applied to clustering-based routing protocols in Vehicular Ad-Hoc Networks. This article systematically examines clustering-based protocols applied in VANETs, with a focus on those integrating soft computing techniques. The classification of various soft computing methodologies, including PCO, k-means, neural networks, ABC, genetic algorithm, and fuzzy logic.

In 2022, G. Kaur *et al.* [14] worked on a Hybrid optimization approach in Vehicular Ad-Hoc Networks for secure routing based on trust, with a deep learning-based system for detecting attacks.A hybrid optimization-based Deep Maxout Network was created by the authors for attack grouping in order to solve these problems. The findings showed enhanced classification and routing performance, with scores of 0.9395, 0.9462, 0.2454J, and 0.4402 for precision, recall, energy, and trust, respectively. The purpose of this strategy was to improve the security, mobility, and efficiency of VANET applications in the Intelligent Transport System.

In 2022, Ferrag, Mohamed Amine *et al.* [15] reviewed and analyzed cybersecurity intrusion detection specifically tailored for Agriculture 4.0. The focus of the analysis includes machine learning-based solutions, datasets employed, and potential future directions in this context. The review aims to examine the challenges and the opportunities existing in the area of VANETs, ML, and threat detection. The survey revolves around the research published to claim the success of ML models for cybersecurity in VANETs.

Offer an extensive categorization of IDS in each developing technology, considering the machine learning techniques employed.

In 2022, H. Bangui *et al.* [16] offered a hybrid ML model for the discovery of intrusions in VANETs.Most of the approaches involved integration of supervised, unsupervised, or deep learning concepts. The results from the experiments reveal that the proposed machine learning model significantly improves attack detection accuracy when compared to the traditional application of ML models.

In 2021, Ali *et al.* [17] concentrated on employing machine learning techniques for ensuring secure vehicular communication in IoT-based VANET. The authors conduct a review focusing on the latest developments and uses of ML in this domain. Their examination encompasses the incorporation of DL, reinforcement learning, and evolutionary algorithms.

In 2021, Turan *et al.* [18] proposed a path loss estimation and detection of traffic congestion for heterogeneous VANETs enhanced with machine learning. According to this scheme, mixed vehicular communications aims to improve vehicle-based communication security, dependability, and delay by combining a variety of communication technologies into a single communication system. The entire spectrum of mobility and jamming scenarios is not fully addressed by traditional fitting-based models for route loss prediction or rule-based models for Radio Frequency (RF) jamming detection of different communication systems. Reliable V2V communications are made possible by technologies like Vehicular Visible Light Communications (V-VLC). Using classifier-based and Random Forest regression techniques using measurement data. These techniques train a large number of diverse learners, and the absolute outcome is calculated by taking the average of the results from all learners. The dynamic nodes and routing issues gave rise to problems, including malicious attacks and unanticipated node misbehaviour.

In 2019, Gyawali *et al.* [19] analysed various attacks, including DoS attacks, sybil attacks, and false alarm generation attacks, which can be launched against vehicular networks. Numerous cryptographic strategies have been suggested for safeguarding vehicle networks from these kinds of assaults. It has been demonstrated, therefore, that cryptographic techniques are less effective in thwarting insider attacks that occur from inside the vehicle setup. A misbehaviour recognition system has been determined to be more efficient in identifying and avoiding attacks from within. Misbehaviour detection system based on machine learning, trained on datasets produced through extensive simulation efforts in an authentic within vehicular networks.

In 2019, Muhammad AsimSaleem *et al.* [20] conducted research on information transmission using IoT-based VANETs with congestion control mechanisms. The key highlights of their study are outlined as follows: Traditionally, researchers have relied on the fundamental routing protocol standards for VANETs. However, the proposed routing mechanism demands a significant amount of energy as it considers routes between vehicles or Roadside Units (RSUs) consecutively. The central point here is to devise a multi-mediator system to enhance the route discovery mechanism in Vehicular Ad-Hoc Networks. The routing mechanism is based on four mediators, which can be intermediate communication vehicles or Roadside Units (RSUs). These mediators collaborate to establish optimal routes and reduce traffic congestion on the VANET. As a result, an effective hybrid cluster-based routing method emerges as a better option for data transmission in IoT-based VANETs, with the goal of minimizing traffic disturbances.

In 2019, Gyawali *et al.* [21] discussed different attacks, such as DoS attacks, sybil attacks, and false alarm generation attacks that may be performed on the vehicular networks. There are numerous cryptographic methods proposed for securing car networks from these types of threats. This means, therefore, the premise that cryptographic techniques are not as effective in preventing inside attacks that originate within the vehicle setting has been proven. It is, therefore, clear that a misbehaviour recognition system is capable of providing better means for the identification and prevention of internal threats. Misbehaviour detection system which uses the machine learning approach and has been trained with the help of datasets that have been developed by performing a large number of simulations in realistic vehicular networks.

In 2018, Lucy Sumi *et al.* [22] created an IoT-based VANET for traffic regulation, with the goal of helping emergency vehicles. The following are some observations presented in their study: The authors provided a platform that combines principles from the IoT and VANET to allow priority emergency vehicles to flow through traffic more smoothly, solving the critical issue of congestion. The proposed system uses real-time traffic data to help emergency vehicles and ambulances find the best route to their destination. The suggested system contributes to minimizing transmission delays for medical assistance during accidents and ensures the timely delivery of medicines to patients.

In 2018, Xiaojie Wang *et al.* [23] provided a practical solution for offloading live traffic control in edge-enabled Internet of Vehicles, aiming to decrease the execution time of the system. The key points related to this study are outlined below: Initially, the study proposes a practical solution that facilitates the offloading of live traffic control in Edge-enabled Internet of Vehicles, targeting to reduce the average execution time of the system. The authors did not explore the utilization of external vehicles for communication with a variety of roadside units (RSUs) to offload data from fog nodes for Traffic Management Systems (TMS).

Zandi *et al.* [24] and Hamdi *et al.* [25] discuss effective route discovery and secure communication in VANETs, respectively. The primary objective of any VANET network model is to maximize the delivery rate of data packets within a network, and IoT-based communications emerges as the optimal solution for this. Using the Firefly optimization strategy, which performs well in dynamic and widely dispersed geographical areas, the suggested method provides a near-optimal solution to the routing problem with the lowest latency. Existing works have tended to overlook crucial aspects such as secure communication and network security. Additionally, vehicular traffic congestion remains a significant challenge for both developed and developing countries. The growing number of connected cars is anticipated to contribute to a substantial increase in data and traffic.Traffic congestion leads to various inconveniences, including road accidents, substantial fuel consumption by vehicles, air and noise pollution, and vehicle damage. Examining specific traffic congestion control techniques is essential to guarantee the effective and advanced operation of a network while maintaining security. IoT plays a vital role in transforming traditional VANETs into intelligent vehicular ad-hoc networks (InVANETs) for device-to-device (D2D) communication [26]. Adopting a cluster-based routing scheme enhances road safety and efficiency in VANETs.

PROPOSED QI-CAI ARCHITECTURE

Based on the conclusions derived from the survey and gap analysis, a novel Quantum Intelligence-Driven Cluster-Based Adaptive Intelligence (QI-CAI) architecture has been developed by integrating IoT-based VANET and intelligent services. Figure **3** visually depicts the conceptual representation of this advanced QI-CAI architecture.

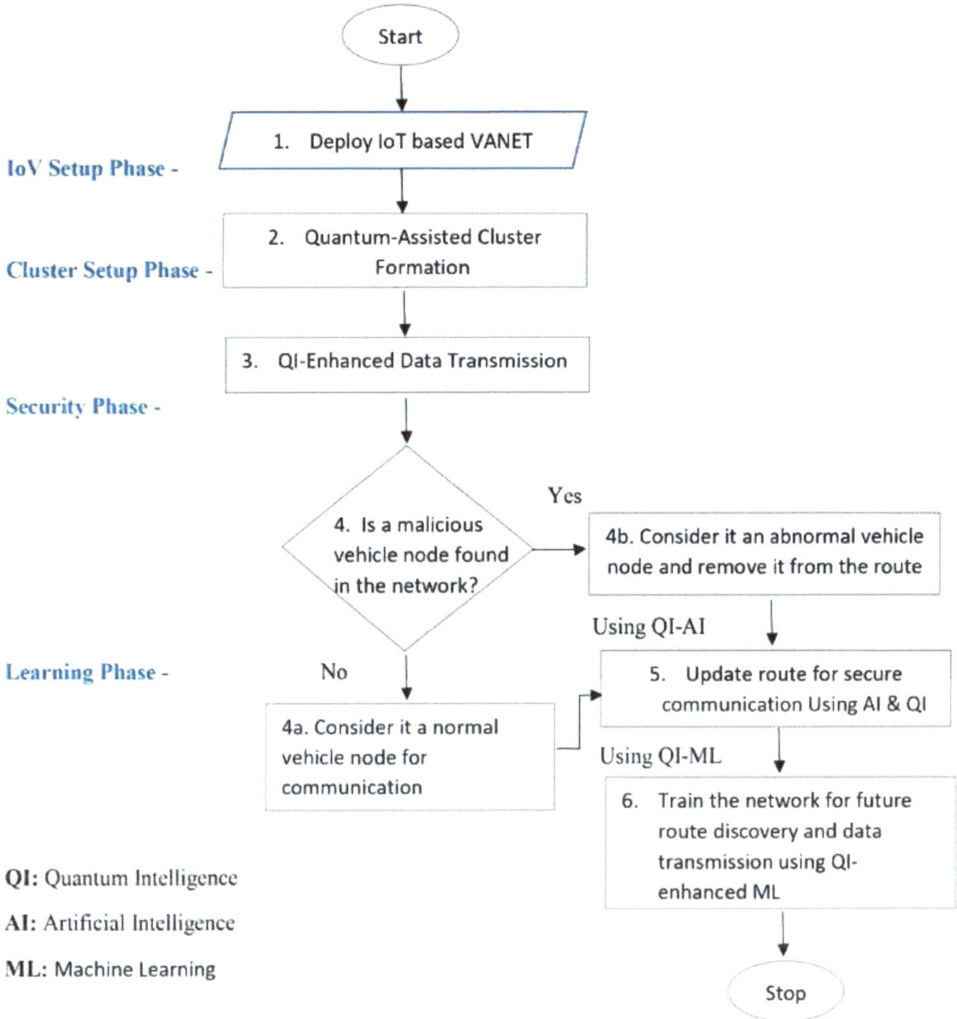

Fig. (3). Proposed quantum intelligence-driven cluster-based adaptive intelligence (QI-CAI) architecture [27].

This innovative architecture is specifically designed to enhance communication intelligence, ensuring both smart and secure communication. The primary goal is to reduce traffic congestion efficiently. Through the incorporation of IoT and intelligent services, the proposed architecture aims to address existing challenges and provide a robust solution for improved vehicular communication in a connected environment.

1. **IoV Setup Phase:** (Design and deploy IoT-based VANET)
    a. Step 1 output: Division of the coverage area into clusters using Quantum Intelligence (QI)-optimized algorithms.

2. **Cluster Setup Phase:** (Clusters formation and Data transmission)
    a. Step 2 output: Selection of Cluster Head (CH) in each area using QI-driven decision-making.
    b. Step 3 output: Cluster-based intelligent quantum-secured routing

3. **Security Phase:** *Malicious node, Update route, and Network training*
    a. Step 4, 5 output: If a malicious vehicle node is found in the network, implement Cluster-Based Intelligent Quantum-Secured Routing.

4. **Learning & Optimization:**
    a. Step 6 output: Train the network for future route discovery and data transmission using Quantum Intelligence-enhanced Machine Learning (QI-ML).

In this work, the first focus is on existing traffic congestion control techniques in Phase-1, and it is considered the first problem. To solve this problem, the selection of CH vehicle nodes is suitable for the VANET environment. In Phase 2, the problem of VANET routing is considered and solved with the help of IoT communication using an intelligent reactive routing protocol concept. In Phases 3 and 4, an intelligent, secure approach for an alternative path selection is considered a better solution to provide secure and fast communication in VANETs.

Outcomes of Proposed QI-CAI Model

Listed below are some significant outcomes derived from the suggested QI-CAI architecture, offering solutions to real-life challenges in existing Internet of Vehicles (IoV) networks:

- Using Quantum-secured routing approaches based on clustering, combined with intelligence services, holds significant promise for the future IoV network.
- The integration of Quantum Intelligence (QI), Artificial Intelligence (AI), and Machine Learning (ML) with cluster-based intelligent routing helps to identify networks blocked by attackers or non-functional vehicles.
- The IoV network incorporates traffic congestion mitigation for faster and more reliable communication.
- This innovative approach aims to improve the overall efficacy and consistency of communication in vehicle networks, eliminating congestion issues and creating a smooth and responsive IoV environment.

Furthermore, our suggested QI-CAI architecture, which incorporates AI, ML, and cluster-based routing, would provide maximal data delivery while maintaining safe and fast communication.

Comparison with Existing Framework

In this section, the Other/S or the current Overall/multi-mediators are compared with the new proposed Quantum Intelligence-Driven Cluster-Based Adaptive Intelligence (QI-CAI). Just like in the case of the Overall framework, our suggested CAI framework is introduced for IoT-based VANET.

- In existing Overall frameworks [20], the first step is data transmission, and the next step is clustering, but in our case, it is the opposite.
- The second step for clustering in the existing framework is for multi-mediator selection. The scheme has a total of four types of mediators to collect data and identify optimal paths for forwarding packets, and maintain connectivity throughout the functioning.
  - **Framework Mediator (FM):** It keeps the maximum number of adjacent nodes. Framework Mediator next selects the Group Head or Group Mediator.
  - **Group Mediator (GM):** Selection of the group head mediator based on higher load. Group mediators are used to reduce transmission expenses. The group mediator next selects the optimal mediator and router mediator.
  - **Optimal Mediator (OM):** The Optimal Mediator is used to minimize routes for transmission based on framework data.
  - **Router Mediator (RM):** Use of the Router Mediator to maintain connectivity. It also makes the path consistent or preserved.
  - The intermediate vehicle routing scheme in the current framework is time-consuming with irregular communication patterns. Additionally, there is no use of AI and ML techniques like in our suggested QI-CAI framework.

TUNING OF QI-ENHANCED MACHINE LEARNING MODEL

In the field of wireless communication, Vehicular Ad hoc Network (VANET) has grown rapidly. Its main goal is to create networks of communication designed especially for automobiles [28]. These networks are carefully engineered to maximize resource sharing among moving cars on the roads, hence improving overall network performance. Identifying the optimal path between a source and destination within the network, commonly known as route discovery, is a critical and fundamental task in Vehicular Ad-hoc Networks (VANETs) [29]. In this chapter, there is an effort to enhance cybersecurity by applied optimization in machine learning. The authors explain a dynamic method that enhances present algorithms in such a way that augments the detection of threats. It helps increase the protection of digital environments and shows trends in the functioning of cyber threats. To achieve this goal, the authors conduct a thorough study of safety concerns in VANETs through the identification of three data models of attack, moderate-attack, and no-attack with the help of MSE. This strategy looks into the probability and the severity of threats that may threaten the achievement of organizations' goals and objectives. This paper offers systematized knowledge on proactive security in VANETs by using MSE as a tagging method. In order to enhance the threat assessment, a vehicle rating system is also incorporated. In this system, the Levenberg algorithm is employed in estimating the behaviour and performance of the vehicle in VANET. Each vehicle is assigned a score referred to as the service measures score, which represents the extent to which the vehicle affects the cybersecurity and the network's performance. This integrated technique enhances contribution to QoS in VANETs, enhances threat recognition, and provides a system-health check.

MACHINE LEARNING AS SECURITY MAINTENANCE

Route data, therefore, marks a new shift in cybersecurity in that advanced algorithms called machine learning based security prevention algorithms have been developed [30]. Traditional security methods involved rule-based and signature-based systems. While these were somewhat effective, they were ultimately insufficient to handle the emerging, advanced-level security threats. To this end, new models of security threats have emerged, and Machine Learning (ML) algorithms as a useful tool to detect and eliminate the threats with efficiency [31]. With the help of routing data in conjunction with machine learning techniques, the nature of cybersecurity has transformed to become predictive in detecting threats and responding to them. Typically, in the early developments of utilizing machine learning in the field of cybersecurity, the main aim was to design the anomaly-detecting mechanisms [32]. These systems utilized the prior routing record as well as the activity flow to determine a normative behavior. The possible security risks were obtained through deviations from the baseline mentioned above. This method was useful for recognizing established attack patterns, but it has drawbacks when dealing with previously unknown or zero-day assaults [33].

In terms of VANET security, the goals of efficient machine learning approaches should be defined as follows: increase the speed and effectiveness, and, simultaneously, reduce the level of negative impact on network performance. The first topic that should be tackled with regard to machine learning approaches is the enhancement of the accuracy and effectiveness of Security risks specific to VANET. The main security threats, on the other hand, Special VANET comprises threats depending on unauthorized access to the vehicle, security threats due to malicious vehicles, and denial of service attacks. Machine learning techniques can help to identify patterns and signs of possible security threats in VANET by considering dynamic and varied information such as car paths, message exchanges, and sensors. The machine learning models can be utilized in either a supervised, unsupervised, or semi-supervised manner to enhance the threat detection in VANETs. Another important field that needs considerable reinforcement of the use of approaches based on machine learning is the optimization of resource use and network performance. The VANETs are characteristically deployed to work in dynamic environments with limited computational capability, bandwidth, and power. Certain algorithms should be developed to work appropriately for these devices with limited resources in terms of power consumption or computational capabilities, and required communications. It is possible to improve resource utilisation and make machine learning-based security solutions practicable and effective to implement in VANET by adopting lightweight machine learning models, feature selection, and distributed learning.

Supervised learning algorithms made a significant advance by allowing security systems to be trained on labeled datasets, allowing them to detect a greater spectrum of threats. These algorithms might categorize network traffic into specified categories, such as harmful or benign, utilizing data metrics as characteristics. Supervised learning facilitated the creation of Intrusion Detection Systems (IDS) that can discriminate between different types of attacks while avoiding false positives. Unsupervised learning methods, such as clustering and autoencoders, have greatly improved the identification of novel threats [34]. These algorithms analyze routing data without previous classifications, identifying anomalies based on statistical departures from the norm.

In general, the advantages are the ability to discover new patterns of attack that the experts were not aware of, and the flexibility to respond to new threats. Routing data can also be helped by the threat intelligence feeds in the security systems. These streams provide continuous information on threats and vulnerabilities familiar to the system and machine learning algorithms to increase the timeliness of the process [35]. The inclusion of route data analysis in the threat intelligence work enhances the quality and speed of threat detection and mitigation.

PROPOSED FDS-QI MODEL

This section describes our approach's methodology, experimental architecture, and results, demonstrating its potential to improve cybersecurity efficacy in the

VANET environment. Fig. (4) shows an architecture flow diagram that may be used to understand the proposed work.

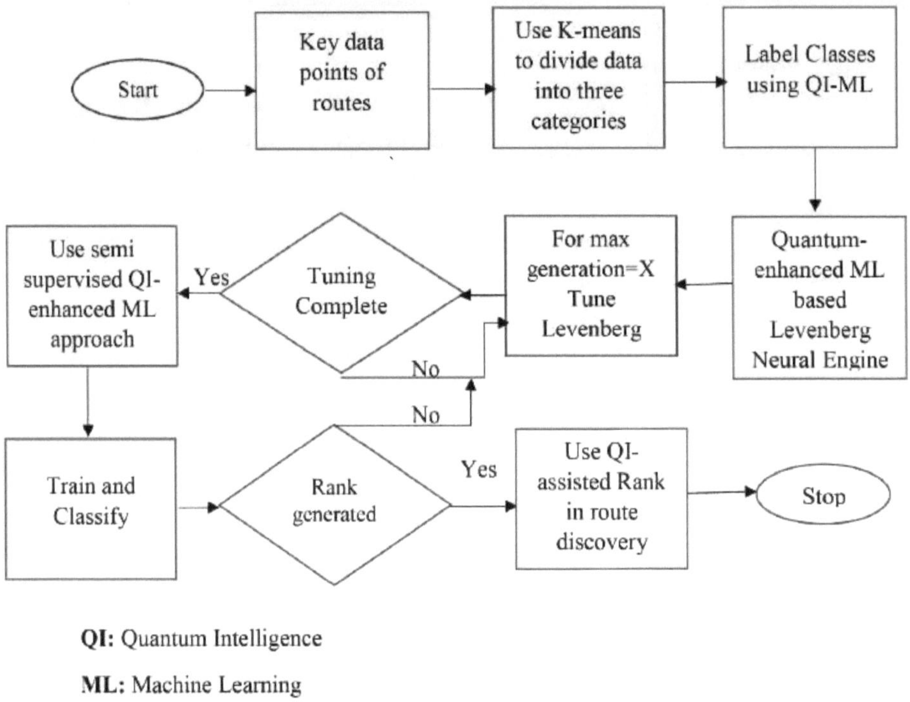

Fig. (4). Proposed fine-tuned deep learning security with quantum intelligence (FDS-QI) model [36].

The proposed study divides the consolidated data from various routes appear three unique parts, where the criterion for their differentiation is the Mean Square Error (MSE), which identifies them as 'attack', 'moderate-attack', and 'no-attack'. This technique is more useful in evaluating the type and degree of security risks in VANETs since it can provide an indication of the vulnerability level. Through MSE as a labelling model, the research presented in this paper presents a detailed and refined depiction of the current state of cybersecurity in VANETs that could be immensely useful for the network administrators and security personnel to take preventive measures for preserving these all-important communication networks. Fig. (4) illustrates the proposed approach, and the following ten steps are described in detail:

1. **Dataset and Pre-processing:** Select characteristics or critical data points from the NSL-KDD dataset for additional clustering before moving on to training and classification.

2. **Optimized Route Discovery:** Apply the K-means algorithm using selected attributes for data clustering.
3. Use QI-ML to analyse security risks in VANETs by categorizing NSL-KDD data into 'attack', 'moderate-attack', and 'no-attack' or 'Safe' using Mean Square Error (MSE) labelling techniques. The data is separated into two sets: training and testing. The training dataset is used to tweak or fit the model, while the testing dataset is used to assess it. Quantum-enhanced Levenberg Neural Engine: The training data provides instructions to the Quantum-enhanced ML-based Levenberg Neural Engine, allowing the model to learn. After training, the model can later be employed for rank generation.
4. **Security Mechanism for Threat Detection:** Tuning algorithms train neural networks based on three attack indices. Route division is a difficult operation since each node participates in several routes, necessitating the deployment of an intelligence algorithm.
5. **Deep Learning Model Tuning and Optimization:** Neural engines train and categorize datasets using input and target data to provide rankings.
6. **Deployment and Real-World Application:** Measuring QoS parameters like as precision, recall, accuracy, and F1-Score may rank vehicles and demonstrate their influence on network performance and cybersecurity.

With this end goal, numerous qualities from the NSL-KDD dataset are selected, and the k-means clustering system is used to cluster comparable data points from the route-based dataset into clusters. The system helps the network to enhance its performance on the identification of "Attack", "Moderate attack", and "No attack" in the given IoT-based VANET context when exposed to a diversified data set for training. In addition, in order to enhance the threat assessment approach, a scoring system for concerns in the car network is introduced according to the performance measures. This ranking method, based on the Levenberg algorithm, is useful for the assessment of individual cars' behavior and performance within the VANET context. A quantitative analysis of such factors of the performance, including precision, recall, and accuracy, will lead to an indexing of the vehicle in terms of the proportion that it contributes to the total network performance, which in effect will determine the degree to which it impacts the overall cybersecurity to the network. This integrated approach is also effective in enhancing the ability of detecting security threats while providing a general view of the overall network's health and the effects individual cars have on VANETs [37].

Proposed QI-CAI Architecture for IoV Communication

The first design applies IoT-based VANET and intelligent technologies in the development of the Quantum Intelligence-Driven Cluster-Based Adaptive Intelligence (QI-CAI) architecture. This can be done through the architecture for sending intelligence securely and, therefore, eliminating traffic congestion. QI-CAI has the following components: Input and Output Vehicle setup, Cluster setup, and the security measures. The first step in the IoV process is to form and implement IoT-based VANETs. The setup work of the cluster includes cluster construction as well as data transfer. Lastly, the security mechanism phase identifies mischievous nodes, reconstructs the paths, and also builds the network. In this phase, AI is employed to identify compromised nodes, which cannot carry out the interaction with other nodes in the network, leading to the buildup of traffic jams. As a subcomponent, ML approaches are an essential feature that is responsible for changing the paths used in future communication and network training.

Proposed FDS-QI Model for Attack Detection

The third architecture enhances the machine learning interventions that are noticeable in enhancing cybersecurity by increasing the chances of identifying threats and responding to them faster. This enhances the security of living spaces of the VANETs and offers information regarding the development of cybersecurity over the years. In this paper, we delve deep into the issue of security in VANETs through classifying it as an attack, moderate attack, or no attack with the help of MSE as the labeling method. Besides, the performance information-based car ranking increases threat level identification and enhances network condition. The suggested architecture may evaluate the network using the QoS parameters such as Precision of the network, recall, and most importantly, Accuracy. Therefore, the calibration of a Quantum-based ML model can enhance the Precision, recall value as well as the threat detection rate fractions. This combined approach will also add extra factors of flexibility and addition proactive defense to VANETs because of the constant development of threats.

CONCLUSION

IoT and VANET are subfields of the Internet of Vehicles (IoV) network. In VANET networks, discovering the most efficient route between a source and a target within the network is a critical task. On the other hand, the V2X communication mode in the IoV environment has given rise to various data security challenges as well as privacy protection. Thus, IoV becomes an easy target for an intruder to launch multiple malicious attacks.

- A review is conducted on related work on IoT-based VANETs using AI and ML approaches in IoV. The literature review revealed that many approaches have been proposed for efficient routing and security of critical data in recent years, but reducing traffic congestion and improving security in IoT-based VANET networks is still a challenge.

- To enable smart city environments using intelligent vehicles, we designed three novel architectures for smart and secure communications in IoV, thereby reducing traffic congestion. To accomplish the goals, two different architectures, *viz*, Proposed QI-CAI Architecture for IoV Communication and Proposed Tuned FDS-QI Model for Attack Detection, within a common framework, are already discussed in the above section.

FUTURE SCOPE AND REAL-WORLD APPLICATIONS

The chapter provides several key contributions that can guide future research and practical implementations in the field of IoV:

- **Quantum-based advancement of IoV Networks:** It suggests that the Internet of Vehicles (IoV) will evolve from VANETs, driven by the growth of IoT-based web services. The integration of artificial intelligence, machine learning, and neural networks as classifiers for training IoV networks will ensure more reliable and efficient routing mechanisms.
- **Enhanced Security and Fast Communication:** The research emphasizes the need for improved security and faster communication to reduce traffic congestion. It suggests further exploration of multi-layered security systems for IoT-based VANETs, utilizing vehicle traffic data from multiple sources.
- **Quantum Intelligence-based Deep Learning:** The study highlights the potential for integrating Quantum Intelligence (QI) and Deep Learning (DL) strategies to calculate and enhance Quality of Service (QoS) parameters, offering a novel approach to improving the performance of IoT-based VANETs.
- **Cybersecurity Enhancements using Quantum Computing:** This chapter makes a key contribution to cybersecurity by fine-tuning quantum-based machine learning algorithms for data analysis. This work leads to substantial improvements in threat detection accuracy and response time, offering a more resilient approach to cybersecurity in evolving digital ecosystems.

Therefore, future research in this domain is necessary to perform comparisons, verify, and validate the proposed framework using QoS metrics like throughput, packet drop ratio, latency, precision, recall, and accuracy.

ACKNOWLEDGEMENT

The authors of this paper are thankful to CGC Landran, CGC Jhanjeri-Mohali, MMDU Mullana, and Chitkara University, Chandigarh, for providing infrastructural facilities to complete this research work.

REFERENCES

[1] S. Paul, N.R. Choudhury, B. Pandit, and A. Dawn, "Integration of AI and quantum computing in cybersecurity: A comprehensive review," in *Advances in Mechatronics and Mechanical Engineering*, K. Mishra, Ed. Hershey, PA, USA: IGI Global, vol. B, 2024, pp. 287–308. [http://dx.doi.org/10.4018/979-8-3693-7076-6.ch014]

[2] S.S. Shadrin, O.O. Varlamov, and A.M. Ivanov, "Experimental autonomous road vehicle with logical artificial intelligence", *J. Adv. Transp.,* vol. 2017, pp. 1-10, 2017. [http://dx.doi.org/10.1155/2017/2492765]

[3] A. Osório, and A. Pinto, "Information, uncertainty and the manipulability of artificial intelligence autonomous vehicles systems", *Int. J. Hum. Comput. Stud.,* vol. 130, pp. 40-46, 2019. [http://dx.doi.org/10.1016/j.ijhcs.2019.05.003]

[4] D. Chauhan, P. Ranka, P. Bahad, and R. Pathak, "Applications of quantum artificial intelligence: A systematic review," in *Advances in Mechatronics and Mechanical Engineering*, K. Mishra, Ed. Hershey, PA, USA: IGI Global, vol. B, 2024, pp. 159–182. [http://dx.doi.org/10.4018/979-8-3693-7076-6.ch008]

[5] J. Prakash, L. Murali, N. Manikandan, N. Nagaprasad, and K. Ramaswamy, "RETRACTED ARTICLE: A vehicular network based intelligent transport system for smart cities using machine learning algorithms", *Sci. Rep.,* vol. 14, no. 1, p. 468, 2024. [http://dx.doi.org/10.1038/s41598-023-50906-7] [PMID: 38172149]

[6] A. Talpur, and M. Gurusamy, "Machine learning for security in vehicular networks: a comprehensive survey", *IEEE Commun. Surv. Tutor.,* vol. 24, no. 1, pp. 346-379, 2022. [http://dx.doi.org/10.1109/COMST.2021.3129079]

[7] K.A.M. Ali, C. Li, W. Han, S. Issa, M.H. Eid, S.F. Mahmoud, and M.A.E. Mohammed, "Performance evaluation and prediction of optimal operational conditions for a compact date seeds milling unit using feedforward neural networks", *Sci. Rep.,* vol. 15, no. 1, p. 4764, 2025. [http://dx.doi.org/10.1038/s41598-025-87508-4] [PMID: 39922878]

[8] S.H. Mahir, M.T.A. Tashrif, M.A. Karim, D. Kundu, A. Rahman, M.A. Hamza, F. Al Farid, A.S.M. Miah, and S. Mansor, "Advanced hydro-informatic modeling through feedforward neural network, federated learning, and explainable ai for enhancing flood prediction", *IEEE Open J. Comput. Soc.,* vol. 6, pp. 726-738, 2025. [http://dx.doi.org/10.1109/OJCS.2025.3556424]

[9] A. Aytekin, M. Nomeir, S. Vithana, and S. Ulukus, "Quantum X -secure E -eavesdropped T -colluding symmetric private information retrieval", *IEEE Trans. Inf. Theory,* vol. 71, no. 5, pp. 3974-3988, 2025. [http://dx.doi.org/10.1109/TIT.2025.3551697]

[10] Monika, and S.K. Sood, "A scientometric analysis of quantum driven innovations in intelligent transportation systems", *Eng. Appl. Artif. Intell.,* vol. 138, p. 109258, 2024. [http://dx.doi.org/10.1016/j.engappai.2024.109258]

[11] B.A. Tosunoglu, and C. Kocak, "Feature selection for clustering and classification based attack detection systems in vehicular ad-hoc networks", *Microprocess. Microsyst.,* no. Feb, p. 104808, 2023. [http://dx.doi.org/10.1016/j.micpro.2023.104808]

[12] N. Magaia, P. Ferreira, P.R. Pereira, K. Muhammad, J.D. Ser, and V.H.C. de Albuquerque, "Group'n route: an edge learning-based clustering and efficient routing scheme leveraging social strength for the internet of vehicles", *IEEE Trans. Intell. Transp. Syst.,* vol. 23, no. 10, pp. 19589-19601, 2022. [http://dx.doi.org/10.1109/TITS.2022.3171978]

[13] M. Sindhwani, S. Sachdeva, K. Arora, T. Yoon, D. Yoo, G.P. Joshi, and W. Cho, "Soft computing techniques aware clustering-based routing protocols in vehicular ad hoc networks: a review", *Appl. Sci. (Basel),* vol. 12, no. 15, p. 7922, 2022. [http://dx.doi.org/10.3390/app12157922]

[14] G. Kaur, and D. Kakkar, "Hybrid optimization enabled trust-based secure routing with deep learning-based attack detection in VANET", *Ad Hoc Netw.,* vol. 136, p. 102961, 2022. [http://dx.doi.org/10.1016/j.adhoc.2022.102961]

[15] M. A. Ferrag, L. Shu, O. Friha, and X. Yang, "Cyber security intrusion detection for Agriculture 4.0: Machine learning-based solutions, datasets, and future directions," *IEEE/CAA J. Autom. Sinica*, vol. 8, no. 4, pp. 664–682, 2021. [http://dx.doi.org/10.1109/JAS.2021.1004344]

[16] H. Bangui, M. Ge, and B. Buhnova, "A hybrid machine learning model for intrusion detection in VANET", *Computing,* vol. 104, no. 3, pp. 503-531, 2022. [http://dx.doi.org/10.1007/s00607-021-01001-0]

[17] E.S. Ali, M.K. Hasan, R. Hassan, R.A. Saeed, M.B. Hassan, S. Islam, N.S. Nafi, and S. Bevinakoppa, "Machine learning technologies for secure vehicular communication in internet of vehicles: recent advances and applications", *Secur. Commun. Netw.,* vol. 2021, pp. 1-23, 2021. [http://dx.doi.org/10.1155/2021/8868355]

[18] B. Turan, A. Uyrus, O.N. Koc, E. Kar, and S. Coleri, "Machine learning aided path loss estimator and jammer detector for heterogeneous vehicular networks," in *Proc. IEEE Global Commun. Conf. (GLOBECOM)*, Madrid, Spain, 2021, pp. 1–6. [http://dx.doi.org/10.1109/GLOBECOM46510.2021.9685428]

[19] S. Gyawali, and Y. Qian, "Misbehavior detection using machine learning in vehicular communication networks", in *Proc. IEEE Int. Conf. Communications (ICC)*, Shanghai, China, May 2019, pp. 1–6. [http://dx.doi.org/10.1109/ICC.2019.8761300]

[20] M.A. Saleem, Z. Shijie, and A. Sharif, "Data transmission using iot in vehicular ad-hoc networks in smart city congestion", *Mob. Netw. Appl.,* vol. 24, no. 1, pp. 248-258, 2019. [http://dx.doi.org/10.1007/s11036-018-1205-x]

[21] A. Tolba, "Content accessibility preference approach for improving service optimality in internet of vehicles", *Comput. Netw.,* vol. 152, pp. 78-86, 2019. [http://dx.doi.org/10.1016/j.comnet.2019.01.038]

[22] L. Sumia, and V. Ranga, "Intelligent traffic management system for prioritizing emergency vehicles in a smart city", *Int. J. Eng., Trans. B: Appl.,* vol. 31, no. 2, pp. 278–283, Feb. 2018. [http://dx.doi.org/10.5829/ije.2018.31.02b.11]

[23] X. Wang, Z. Ning, and L. Wang, "Offloading in internet of vehicles: a fog-enabled real-time traffic management system", *IEEE Trans. Industr. Inform.,* vol. 14, no. 10, pp. 4568-4578, 2018. [http://dx.doi.org/10.1109/TII.2018.2816590]

[24] M. Zandi, M. Jahanshahi, and A.R. Hedayati, "Routing optimization in vehicular social networks using firefly algorithm," *Int. J. Ind. Math.*, vol. 13, no. 4, pp. 1–9, 2021. [Online]. Available: https://civilica.com/doc/1886915

[25] M.M. Hamdi, Y.A. Yussen, and A.S. Mustafa, "Integrity and authentications for service security in vehicular ad hoc networks (VANETs): A review," in *Proc. Int. Conf. Humanitarian Technology (HORA)*, 2021, pp. 1–6. [http://dx.doi.org/10.1109/HORA52670.2021.9461327]

[26] S. Debroy, P. Samanta, A. Bashir, and M. Chatterjee, "SpEED-IoT: Spectrum aware energy efficient routing for device-to-device IoT communication", *Future Gener. Comput. Syst.,* vol. 93, pp. 833-848, 2019. [http://dx.doi.org/10.1016/j.future.2018.01.002]

[27] S. Kumar, and J. Singh, "Internet of vehicles (IOV) over vanets: Smart and secure communication using IOT", *Scalable Computing,* vol. 21, no. 3, pp. 425-440, 2020. [http://dx.doi.org/10.12694:/scpe.v21i3.1741]

[28] H. Hasrouny, A.E. Samhat, C. Bassil, and A. Laouiti, "VANet security challenges and solutions: A

survey", *Veh. Commun.,* vol. 7, pp. 7-20, 2017. [http://dx.doi.org/10.1016/j.vehcom.2017.01.002]

[29] R. Tomar, M. Prateek, and G.H. Sastry, "Vehicular adhoc network (vanet)-an introduction", *International Journal of Control Theory and Applications,* vol. 9, no. 18, pp. 8883-8888, 2016.

[30] R. Geetha, and T. Thilagam, "A review on the effectiveness of machine learning and deep learning algorithms for cyber security", *Arch. Comput. Methods Eng.,* vol. 28, no. 4, pp. 2861-2879, 2021. [http://dx.doi.org/10.1007/s11831-020-09478-2]

[31] R. Gupta, S. Tanwar, S. Tyagi, and N. Kumar, "Machine learning models for secure data analytics: a taxonomy and threat model", *Comput. Commun.,* vol. 153, pp. 406-440, 2020. [http://dx.doi.org/10.1016/j.comcom.2020.02.008]

[32] S. Khatri, H. Vachhani, S. Shah, J. Bhatia, M. Chaturvedi, S. Tanwar, and N. Kumar, "Machine learning models and techniques for VANET based traffic management: Implementation issues and challenges", *Peer-to-Peer Netw. Appl.,* vol. 14, no. 3, pp. 1778-1805, 2021. [http://dx.doi.org/10.1007/s12083-020-00993-4]

[33] M. Ramalingam, and R. Thangarajan, "Mutated k-means algorithm for dynamic clustering to perform effective and intelligent broadcasting in medical surveillance using selective reliable broadcast protocol in VANET", *Comput. Commun.,* vol. 150, pp. 563-568, 2020. [http://dx.doi.org/10.1016/j.comcom.2019.11.023]

[34] V. Belenko, V. Chernenko, M. Kalinin, and V. Krundyshev, "Evaluation of GAN applicability for intrusion detection in self-organizing networks of cyber physical systems", *2018 International Russian Automation Conference, RusAutoCon 2018,* 2018 [http://dx.doi.org/10.1109/RUSAUTOCON.2018.8501783]

[35] X. Cheng, and B. Huang, "A center-based secure and stable clustering algorithm for VANETs on highways", *Wirel. Commun. Mob. Comput.,* vol. 2019, pp. 1-10, 2019. [http://dx.doi.org/10.1155/2019/8415234]

[36] S. Kumar, and J. Singh, "Tuning of machine learning model to strengthen the digital ecosystem of vehicular ad-hoc networks". in *Proc. 11th Int. Conf. Reliability, Infocom Technol. Optim. (Trends Future Directions) (ICRITO)*, Noida, India, 2024, pp. 1–6. [http://dx.doi.org/10.1109/ICRITO61523.2024.10522316]

[37] S. Kumar, and J. Singh, "An improved firefly algorithm for the rank generation to optimize the route discovery process in IoV", *Journal of Autonomous Intelligence,* vol. 6, no. 3, p. 705, 2023. [http://dx.doi.org/10.32629/jai.v6i3.705]

CHAPTER 15

Wireless Sensor Networks in the Age of AI and Quantum Computing

Kirandeep Kaur[1,*], **Satinder Kaur**[1], **Satveer Kour**[1] and **Gurpreet Singh**[1]

[1] *Department of Computer Engineering and Technology, Guru Nanak Dev University, Amritsar, Punjab, India*

Abstract: Wireless Sensor Networks (WSNs) are essential components of modern information systems because they promote efficient gathering and sharing of information across a variety of domains, such as smart cities, healthcare, and environmental monitoring [1]. Yet, the sensor node's resource limitations, such as energy and storage, largely inhibit real-time accuracy, safety, and scalability. To resolve these challenges, this study examines how existing mechanisms of computing, namely, Artificial Intelligence (AI) and Quantum Computing (QC), may be integrated in wireless networks. The present chapter tries to present a detailed analysis of how QC and AI technologies can enhance WSN performance, security, and efficiency. Predictive maintenance and energy-efficient data transmission have all been investigated through Artificial Intelligence (AI) methods such as Machine Learning (ML) and Deep Learning (DL). Through the help of post-quantum cryptography and quantum algorithms in order to achieve resource optimisation and routing, the work also considers how QC can be employed for security issues. The key findings indicate that although AI provides intelligent, low-latency processing, QC gives strong cryptographic frameworks and optimisation facilities. Notwithstanding these improvements, there are still issues of implementation complexity, scalability, and hardware constraints. Besides outlining future areas of research, including Intelligence-based optimisation models, scalable quantum-secure communication protocols, and the design of intelligent, autonomous sensor networks, the current research highlights the revolutionary possibility of combining AI and QC in WSNs. This review focuses on the revolutionary potential of integrating AI and QC in WSNs and proposes future research areas, such as AI-based optimisation models, scalable quantum-secure communication protocols.

Keywords: AI-enhanced sensor networks, Big data analytics, Data privacy, Edge computing, Energy efficiency, Internet of things (IoT), Quantum algorithms, Quantum computing, Quantum machine learning (QML), Real-time data Processing, Sensor nodes, Sensor networks, Smart cities, Wireless communication, Wireless sensor network security.

[*] **Corresponding author Kirandeep Kaur:** Department of Computer Engineering and Technology, Guru Nanak Dev University, Amritsar, Punjab, India; E-mail: kirandeepcet.rsh@gndu.ac.in

Satveer Kour, Harvinder Singh, Anupam Bonkra & Rupinder Singh (Eds.)

INTRODUCTION

WSNs are widely employed in smart cities, healthcare, industrial automation, farming, military use, and environmental monitoring. Energy challenges, computing power limitations, network security flaws, and inefficient data processing are some of the difficulties that conventional WSNs must overcome [2 - 5]. Emergence of QC and AI offers radical AI-driven methods, including machine learning, deep learning, and reinforcement learning show potential in increasing network security, facilitating autonomous decision-making, building data accuracy, and optimizing resource management [6]. In the meantime, QC offers to solve important problems, including data security, node localisation, and energy-efficient routing by providing exponential computational speedups, innovative encryption techniques, and improved optimisation capabilities [7, 8]. Considering the impact, benefits, and challenges of WSNs becomes crucial when they proceed to develop in the era of AI and QC. This comprehensive review investigates the integration of WSNs, AI, and QCM, focusing more on the developments, the present study's (tm)s gaps, and future advances [9, 10]. WSNs have evolved tremendously over the past years, moreover to continuous advances in data handling, energy efficiency, network protocols, and security factors [1, 3, 5]. Nevertheless, various challenges increase the scalability and real-time processing abilities of conventional WSNs. Merging Artificial Intelligence (AI) and QC could make WSNs more effective and adaptive, providing innovative approaches to these challenges [11]. The background study not only determines existing limitations in traditional WSN architectures but also presents a historical overview of WSN advances and considers how AI and quantum computing would assist in order to overcome significant constraints.

Background Study

WSNs have experienced a huge range of growth over the recent past because of constant advances in information processing, energy utility, protocol designs, and safety measures [1, 3, 5]. Nonetheless, the scalability and real-time operating attributes presented by conventional wireless communications have been affected due to multiple constraints. Incorporating AI with QC provides innovative approaches to these limitations, generating WSNs even more efficient, secured, and reliable [11]. The background research highlights an overview of the historical events of WSNs, recognizes existing constraints of traditional WSN architectures, and outlines how AI and QC could assist in resolving the major limitations.

First-Generation WSNs

Wireless network communications and information gathering have been the primary motivations of prior networks. These networks had very limited opportunities in terms of data retention, processing capacity, and energy efficiency, and depended upon fundamental communication protocols. Sensor nodes were mostly located in a static configuration with constraint ability to adapt towards environmental changes [2, 4, 5]. The industrial automation, environmental monitoring, and military intelligence surveillance also contributed to the majority of applications, where complete information was compiled and transmitted further to a central base station for processing [6, 7]. In addition to having complications alongside network congestion, energy limitations, and inadequate data processing, these WSNs proved to be scalable [8, 9].

Second-generation WSNs

In the second generation, WSNs had imposed sensor nodes, spontaneous mechanisms, and energy-efficient routing protocols as a consequence of the huge growth in wireless communication and integrated structures. These enhancements boosted the fault tolerance capacity, flexibility, and increased the lifespan of the network. Since topology and environmental conditions have certain modifications, nodes were also able to interact dynamically [8, 11]. Furthermore, applying data gathering, clustering, and hierarchical routing strategies enhanced scaling and reduced energy consumption. WSN applications have been strengthened by this generation to encompass smart transport systems, precision agriculture, industrial automation, and healthcare systems [9, 10].

Third-Generation WSNs

The most recent advancement in WSNs employs artificial intelligence (AI), cloud-based services, and edge computing for enabling efficient data processing, automated modelling, and real-time decision-making. In order to recognize patterns, observe discontinuity, and provide automated response messages, such neural networks are associated with machine learning algorithms [12, 13]. As cloud integration offers extensible storage and processing capacity for complicated analytics, edge computing reduces latency whilc processing data distantly at sensor nodes. Since applications that are available for autonomous systems, smart cities, precision healthcare, and industrial IoT, third-generation WSNs provide boosted dependability, confidentiality, and efficiency. In order to regularly optimise data privacy and integrity in the current times, WSN deployments, distributed neural networks, and the blockchain have also been under consideration.

Fig. (**1**) presents a timeline that shows key turning points in the early 20th century to 2025 in the development of Wireless Sensor Networks (WSNs), Artificial Intelligence (AI), and quantum computing. It focuses on significant advances, originating with the emergence of the "ouniversal machine" in the 1930s and Max

Planck's quantum theory in 1900. The history includes significant occurrences, including John McCarthy coining the phrase "Artificial Intelligence" in 1958, the effects of the AI winter in the 1980s, and David Deutsch's 1999 concept of quantum computation.

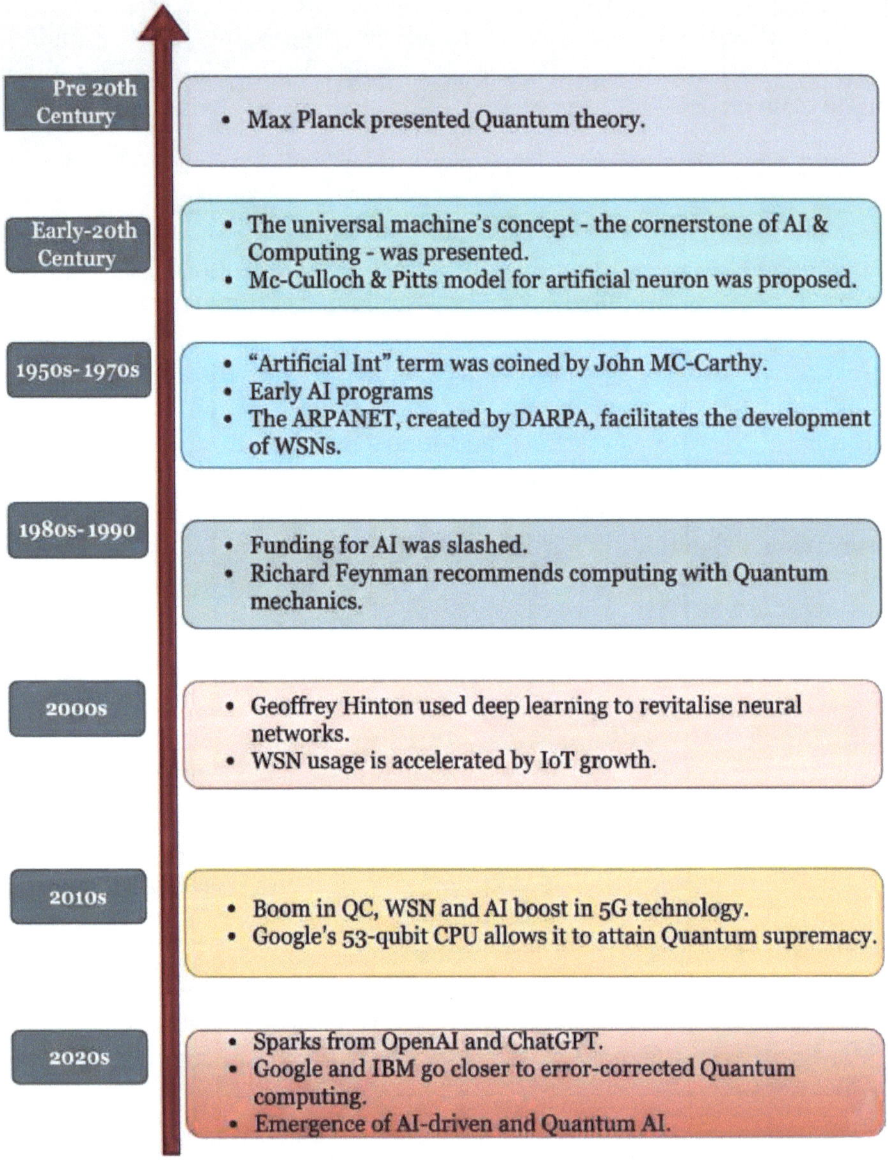

Fig. (1). Timeline and evolution of AI, WSN, and quantum computing.

Prominent developments in the 2000s include Google's progress in driverless vehicles and Geoffrey Hinton's work on deep learning. WSNs and quantum computing advanced rapidly in the 2010s. The 2020s are highlighted in the timeline's conclusion, along with Google and IBM's innovations in error-corrected quantum computing.

Motivation

The rapid growth of smart environments, which include anything from urban infrastructure to industrial automation, has raised the demand for intelligent, secure, and energy-efficient WSNs. However, sensor nodes' inherent limitations—such as their constrained power, computation, and storage capacities—severely impair real-time performance and scalability. Conventional WSN designs are also facing increasing security risks, especially considering the potential of quantum-enabled cyber attacks. Artificial Intelligence (AI) offers powerful tools for edge intelligence, adaptive control, and predictive analytics in this dynamic environment, while QC offers significant methods for network optimisation and encryption. In order to overcome these challenges and enable the development of the next generation of robust, self-governing, and future-proof WSNs, this study is motivated by the necessity to investigate the synergistic integration of AI and QC.

The chapter's structure is set up as follows: The literature survey is demonstrated in Section 2, the applications &innovations are presented in Section 3, and the limitations and challenges are presented in Section 4. Section 6 concludes the chapter, followed by the future scope in Section 6.

RELATED STUDY

Kediri *et al.* [1] in their study represented a comprehensive study, a thorough overview of the advancement of the state-of-the-art in WSN and AI. The authors contributed an in-depth overview of the research findings in a number of academic fields, illustrating how ML approaches could be incorporated to offer novel solutions to the challenges that WSNs inevitably face. Kanchan *et al.* [6] suggested Quantum-inspired PSO for Energy Efficient Clustering (QPSOEEC), a quantum-inspired particle swarm optimisation method. Significantly changing the base station position, the number of sensor nodes and cluster heads, and other factors, the algorithm is validated. The superiority of our algorithm is then shown by comparing our findings to those of other algorithms. Additionally, Khan *et al.* [11], in order to effectively gather data from the deployed sensor nodes, the study indicated an artificial intelligence system that is optimised for healthcare challenges through the use of IoT biosensor networking. Here, an improved tunicate swarm technique is used to optimise the path for data collection and transmission between both the patient and the physician. The recommended approach is recognised for demanding less energy because the best CH was chosen for TSA operation. Furthermore, a number of metrics, including stability period, lifetime, throughput, and clusters per round, are employed to compare the performance of the suggested approach to the current approaches.

Aruchamy *et al.* [2] designed a new AI-based Energy-aware Intrusion Detection and Secure Routing model to create a secure IWSN. To determine different types of attacks, the suggested approach first activates the intrusion detection system. The surveillance model is subsequently combined with a game strategy-based decision-making procedure to establish whether or not protection should be put into existence. In the final stage, an energy-conscious ad-hoc on-demand distance vector algorithm was proposed to offer more authentic and reliable routing across several nodes. The performance results indicated that the proposed system was able to attain a 95% detection accuracy and a 38% reduction in energy consumption when compared to the existing intrusion detection methods. The authors have also suggested an enhanced Optimised Layered Diagnosis Framework (OLDF) to detect, diagnose, and classify sensor node failures [5].

Krishna *et al.* [5] offered an approach that mainly highlighted merging QC into the Internet of Things to maximise the sensor space without compromising the sensor's ability to detect. Moreover, the Rider Optimisation Algorithm (ROA) provided the inspiration for the optimal global search behaviour of the Quantum Computing-based Rider Optimisation (QCRO), which was introduced to optimise the sensor space. Authors [8] implemented a framework for range-based and range-free using the Quantum-based Salp Swarm Algorithm (QBSSA). QBSSA was utilised for comparing and assessing the performance of already existing approaches. By using the Hilbert trajectory, the impact of the Line of Sight propagation was reduced. The simulation results illustrated that the suggested method can localise the mobile target with a 1.5-fold reduction in error compared to HPSO and a 2-fold reduction compared to PSO, while also experiencing a significant reduction in computational time. Table **1** highlights the various existing studies along with their contributions and challenges.

COMBINING WSN, AI, AND QC: A NECESSITY FOR THE FUTURE

The requirement for increased efficiency, security, and real-time decision-making is what motivates the integration of AI and quantum computing into WSNs [14]. Nowadays, WSNs are employed in fields where traditional sensor networks have constraints, such as smart cities, healthcare, defence, and industrial automation. The integration of Artificial Intelligence (AI) and Quantum Computing into Wireless Sensor Networks (WSNs) is transforming the ways in which we work, as well as inhabit and engage with the outside world [15]. These technologies (Fig. **2**) are addressing some of the most pressing challenges faced by the current generation, offering solutions that improve healthcare, enhance environmental sustainability, create safer cities, and empower individuals through data-driven insights. By making systems smarter, more efficient, and more secure, AI and Quantum-enhanced WSNs are not only enhancing quality of life but also paving the way for a more sustainable and equitable future [16]. Table **2** clearly illustrates the future-based comparison of these three technologies.

Table 1. Literature review of the previous studies.

Author/Year	Technology used	Major Contributions	Challenges Noticed
Khediri *et al.***/2022 [1]**	ML, DL, AIoT	Reviews and classifies AI strategies for WSNs (2007-"2023), organizing existing literature. Assesses ML effectiveness in clustering, routing, localization, and more. Identifies key integration challenges and open research issues. Provides guidelines to improve AI scalability and efficiency in WSNs.	AI integration increases energy consumption, especially during training. WSNs' constraints restrict complex ML processing. Protecting sensitive data is crucial in AI-driven WSNs. Selecting the right ML approach depends on the application.
Kanchan *et al.***/2018 [6]**	Quantum Computing, PSO	Introduces a Quantum-inspired PSO for energy-efficient clustering in WSNs. Enhances particle (node) position updates using quantum principles. Improves cluster head selection for better data aggregation and energy conservation. Outperforms LEACH and PSOECHS in energy efficiency through simulations.	Practical testing is limited due to the lack of fully operational quantum computers. CH selection based on distance may cause energy inefficiencies. Optimization challenges persist across different deployment scenarios.
Khan *et al.***/2022 [11]**	AI, WSN, IoT	Enhances healthcare monitoring with optimized data transmission. Uses the Tunicate Swarm Algorithm to reduce energy consumption and boost stability. Increases stability period by 28.27% over OptiGACHS-StSS and 37.84% over GAOC. Supports timely medical intervention for acute conditions.	Limited battery life necessitates advancements in energy harvesting. High data transmission overhead requires optimization. Managing diverse sensor nodes complicates data collection. Patient data protection needs further exploration.

(Table 1) cont.....

Author/Year	Technology used	Major Contributions	Challenges Noticed
Aruchamy *et al.*/2023 [2]	AI, WSN, IoT	Detects DoS and NC attacks in IWSNs using distance, energy, and attack count. Evaluates target and attacker actions to determine protective measures. Merges intrusion detection with energy-efficient routing for enhanced security. Achieves 95% detection accuracy and 38% lower energy consumption than existing models.	Limited battery life challenges efficiency and security. Node mobility and network variability impact performance. Continuous adaptation is needed for robust security. An AI model must balance computation with limited node resources.
Babu *et al.*/ 2024 [22]	WSN, Quantum Computing	OLDF improves fault detection accuracy and reduces false alarms. Combines DBN and CQ-PSO for better fault identification. Tested in NS3 with FDA, FCA, latency, FPR, and AEC metrics. Diagnoses faults using energy, battery status, and packet drop rates.	**Computational Complexity:** High energy use challenges optimization. Addressing multiple fault types while maintaining stability is difficult. Needs further development for practical deployment and self-healing enhancements.
Mengash *et al.*/2022 [3]	AI, WSN, and Quantum Computing	**QBMA-NL Approach:** Uses quantum bird migration optimization for node localization in WSNs. Determines unknown node positions *via* anchor nodes. Modelled on bird mating behaviour for enhanced accuracy. Utilizes RSSI and Euclidean distance for precise localization.	The method excludes protocols for resource planning and data consolidation. Very few parameters have been exploited.
Karishna *et al.*/2022 [5]	Quantum Computing, IoT, WSN	Focuses on maximizing sensor efficiency without reducing sensing capability. Uses SIV, CP, and CI for optimal sensor spacing. Combines quantum computing with the rider optimization algorithm for improved sensor placement. Enables efficient communication using continuous quantum walks. Extensive simulations confirm superiority over baseline methods.	The study compares the proposed algorithm with only a few existing methods, limiting insight into its relative strengths and weaknesses. High **complexity and Cost.** Constraints like SIV, CP, and CI may not generalize well across diverse real-world conditions, affecting model applicability.

Table 2. Feature-based comparison of WSN, AI, and quantum computing.

Features	WSN	AI	Quantum Computing
Definition	Network of spatially distributed sensors to monitor and collect data	Simulation of human intelligence by machines	Computing using quantum-mechanical phenomena like superposition and entanglement
Primary Purposes	Environmental monitoring, data collection, and transmission	Decision-making, prediction, automation	Solve complex problems exponentially faster than classical computers
Core Components	Sensors, nodes, communication protocols, energy sources	Algorithms, data, models, learning frameworks	Qubits, quantum gates, quantum circuits
Computational Model	Embedded, low-power computing	Classical computing with learning models	Quantum mechanics-based computation
Power Consumption	Low power, energy-efficient (battery-dependent)	Moderate to high, depending on model complexity	High (currently requires cryogenic cooling and special hardware)
Data Handling	Collects and transmits raw data	Analyses and makes decisions based on data	Processes complex data with quantum parallelism
Communication	Wireless protocols (Zigbee, Bluetooth, *etc.*)	May include cloud-based or edge communication	Not communication-focused, primarily computational
Scalability	Can scale with increased nodes	Scalable, but training cost grows with data/model size	Limited scalability currently due to hardware constraints
Maturity Level	Mature and widely deployed	Rapidly evolving and widely adopted	Nascent and experimental
Application Examples	Smart agriculture, environmental monitoring, IoT	Image recognition, NLP, autonomous systems	Cryptography, optimization, and drug discovery
Real-time Capabilities	Good for real-time sensing and reporting	Possible with edge AI, depending on model size	Currently not real-time
Security Concerns	Vulnerable to physical and wireless attacks	Susceptible to adversarial attacks and data privacy issues	Potential to break classical encryption systems
Interdisciplinary Links	Embedded systems, networking, electronics	Mathematics, computer science, neuroscience	Physics, computer science, mathematics

Fig. (2). Application areas: WSN, AI, and quantum computing.

Applications and Innovations: WSN, AI, and Quantum Computing

Revolutionizing Healthcare

One of the most significant impacts of AI and Quantum-enhanced WSNs is in the field of healthcare. Wearable gadgets with sensors, such as smart watches, can track vital signs, including blood pressure, oxygen saturation, and heart rate in real time. With the aim to detect the anomalies and offer prior warning signals for illnesses like heart diseases or strokes, AI systems emphasises this data. As an example, a smart watch that continuously tracks heart rate can be worn by an individual with a history of cardiovascular ailments. AI might be able to protect a life if it recognises abnormal patterns and promptly sends alert messages to the user and their physician [16]. Moreover, individuals with chronic ailments like diabetes or hypertension could also manage their symptoms just from the comfort of their homes, owing to remote health surveillance systems. Sensors would monitor their health metrics, and AI approaches provide personalized recommendations, reducing the frequency of visits to the hospitals and enhancing overall well-being [17 - 19].

Enhancing Environmental Sustainability

Addressing environmental challenges is aided by AI and quantum-enhanced WSNs on a large scale. Specifically, air quality sensors in metropolitan areas might record pollution levels while providing AI systems with real-time data. Following data analysis, these systems may pinpoint the sources of pollution and suggest ways to reduce them. For instance, Beijing has installed a network of air quality sensors around the city. AI systems analyse the data to forecast pollution levels and recommend actions to enhance air quality, including limiting traffic or enforcing industrial rules. In a similar vein, WSNs in agriculture enable precision farming by monitoring soil temperature, moisture content, and nutrient levels [20]. AI uses this information to optimise fertilisation and irrigation, saving water and increasing crop yields. In addition to helping farmers, this also promotes environmental preservation and global prosperity [21, 22].

Creating Safer and Smarter Cities

Urban areas are becoming more secure as well as efficient when AI and quantum-enhanced WSNs are combined [23]. In particular, intelligent modes of transportation use AI to optimise traffic light timings and sensors to track traffic flow, which improves commute times and minimises congestion [24, 25]. A 15% reduction in travel time has been attained in Singapore thanks to the implementation of an AI-powered traffic management system that analyses real-time traffic data and adapts signal timings. Furthermore, the arrival of surveillance cameras and sensors that identify suspicious behaviour improves public safety [26]. Law enforcement may take preventative action by using AI algorithms to examine the data and forecast crime hotspots. In the event of natural disasters, such as earthquakes or floods, WSNs provide real-time data to emergency services, helping them respond more effectively and save lives.

Empowering Individuals Through Data

WSNs with AI and quantum advances enable people by offering useful insights from data. For instance, wearable fitness trackers help users reach their fitness objectives by monitoring physical activity while offering them customised suggestions [27]. A wearable device that tracks heart rate, steps, and calories burned is a renowned weight-loss tool. The AI identifies the data to recommend individualized diets and exercise routines. In the same way, AI-driven learning platforms in universities utilize sensor data to deliver individualized education and training. For instance, a student who struggles with maths can utilize AI-based software that adapts to their learning patterns and provides tailored exercises to assist them in improving [28]. This enhances the efficiency and accessibility, learning, particularly for people residing in rural or underdeveloped areas.

Improving Security and Privacy

With an increasingly interconnected world, safety and secrecy are major concerns. Quantum-improved WSNs, which utilize Quantum Key Distribution (QKD) to provide more secure communication, address both of these issues. As an illustration, a bank can utilize quantum encryption to protect the financial information details of its customers against attacks and guarantee secure transactions. AI systems further monitor networks for criminal activity as well as prevent data violations. Smart home WSNs with AI functionalities could possibly detect problems such as gas leaks or explosions and immediately alert people. It not only enhances prudence but also acts as people's and families' peace of mind.

Disaster Preparedness and Response

AI and quantum-enhanced WSNs are preserving lives by enhancing disaster responses and prediction. In regions susceptible to earthquakes like Japan, for instance, a network of seismic sensors gathers up tremors and transmits the data to artificial intelligence devices [29]. These technologies offer communities advance warning *via* data analysis to predict the location and magnitude of earthquakes. In a comparable manner, during floods, WSNs monitor the flow of rivers and rainfall, permitting officials to quickly issue orders for evacuation. Following a disaster, quantum-enhanced optimisation algorithms effectively allocate resources, especially healthcare products and rescue employees, ensuring that support reaches those in need as soon as possible [30].

Economic and Social Benefits

AI and quantum-enhanced WSNs have been working collectively to enhance the quality of existence while generating fresh possibilities for business. Jobs in the IT, medical care, agricultural, and environmental sectors, for instance, have been generated by the advancement and application of these technologies. Precision farming techniques can improve farmers' livelihoods by lowering costs and increasing yields [31]. Furthermore, AI-powered systems enable remote work and education, boosting individuals' access to education and employment possibilities regardless of their location [32]. Since they can participate in the digital economy and upgrade their standard of living, individuals living in underserved or rural areas stand to gain the most from this.

Why is it used Instead of other Technologies?

Unmatched Data Processing Capabilities

Applications like healthcare, environmental monitoring, and smart cities depend on AI and quantum computing's ability to handle and analyse enormous volumes of data in real-time. The enormous quantity and complexity of data produced by WSNs often overwhelm traditional systems, generating latencies and inefficiencies. AI algorithms, on the other hand, have the ability to interpret this data in real-time, spotting trends and forecasting outcomes immediately. Optimisation difficulties that are unsolved for conventional machines can be addressed by quantum computing, which may perform complexities computations tenfold faster [33].

Example: In a smart city, thousands of sensors monitor traffic flow, air quality, and energy usage. Traditional systems might take hours to analyse this data, leading to outdated insights. However, an AI-powered system can process this data in real-time, dynamically adjusting traffic light timings to reduce congestion or optimizing energy distribution to prevent blackouts. This may be enhanced further by quantum computing, which may resolve troublesome routing difficulties, promise more pleasant journeys, and use fewer resources [34].

Enhanced Energy Efficiency

Wireless sensor networks face major issues of energy consumption. This issue primarily grows in remote areas with limited resources [35 - 38]. The conventional WSN protocols often rely on constant protocols for their processing, which results in the wastage of energy. For instance, even when the changes are not taking place, sensors may send signals on a regular basis. On the other hand, AI and quantum computing provide novel approaches to preserving energy [39]. AI may optimise energy levels by dynamically altering sensors' functioning modes by analysing real-time data, while quantum algorithms are capable of handling complex energy optimisation problems, such as finding the most efficient data transmission paths. As an illustration, in precision agriculture, WSNs monitor soil moisture levels for optimal irrigation. By stimulating irrigation at specified intervals, standard methods could waste water as well as electricity. However, by analysing real-time soil data and simply activating irrigation when necessary, AI-powered WSNs safeguard resources. By incorporating quantum algorithms to additionally optimise sensor placement for the greatest coverage with the least amount of energy, farmers may decrease operating expenses.

Superior Security and Privacy

WSN security has become an important consideration, specifically for applications like smart cities, medical care, and defence. Since quantum computers have the ability to break conventional cryptographic techniques in a matter of seconds, they present a threat to traditional encryption algorithms. Modern security features, which are challenging to achieve with conventional technologies, are offered by AI and QC. Ultra-secure communication has become possible by Quantum Key Distribution (QKD), thus making it almost impossible for invaders to intercept data. AI enhances security by directly recognizing and preventing cyber threats.

Consider an instance: In healthcare, patient-transmitted information *via* WSNs needs to be secure in order to meet regulations like HIPAA. Conventional encryption techniques are no longer effective against advanced cyberattacks.

Quantum encryption makes sure that patient data remains protected, even in the case of future quantum-powered threats. In addition, AI techniques can also monitor network traffic for malicious activities, preventing data breaches and ensuring the privacy of sensitive information.

Real-time Decision-making

A vast array of applications, including disaster management and industrial automation, demand real-time decision-making. Traditional approaches are mostly based on pre-programmed rules and are not able to adapt to dynamic environmental changes. For instance, a prior disaster response system might not account for real-time variations in weather conditions or the availability of resources. AI and Quantum Computing enable quicker and more accurate decisions through analysing real-time sensor data and adjusting to new, changing conditions instantly. Quantum computing can resolve complex optimization problems in real-time, which would allow faster decision-making.

Example: During a natural disaster, such as an earthquake, WSNs can offer real-time information on seismic activities, structural damage, and meteorological condition changes. Traditional methods might take longer time intervals for analysing this data, which in turn would slow down the response time. AI systems, on the other hand, could process the data instantly, predicting the impact of the disaster and allocating resources efficiently. Quantum algorithms could be utilized to plan and optimize evacuation routes to ensure that the assistance reaches affected areas as soon as possible, to save lives and minimize the damage.

Scalability and Adaptability

WSNs are often implemented in large-scale settings, for example, smart cities or industrial automation in IoT. Scalability is an issue, especially in traditional systems, due to limitations like data processing constraints, energy inefficiency, and network management issues. AI and Quantum Computing, on the other hand, provide scalability and flexibility that traditional technologies cannot match. AI enables self-organizing networks that can adapt to changes in the environment or network topologies, while quantum computing can handle the huge amounts of information produced by large-scale WSNs, ensuring scalability. Example: In a smart city, thousands of sensors are there to monitor everything from traffic to air quality. Traditional systems might struggle to manage such a vast network, leading to inefficiencies. AI-powered WSNs, however, can autonomously configure and adapt to changes, such as the addition of new sensors or the failure of already existing ones. Quantum computing is capable of processing data from millions of sensors, enabling real-time insights and decision-making, so that the city operates smoothly and efficiently [40, 41].

Solving Intractable Problems

Several problems in WSNs, like resource allocation and network optimisation, are computationally complicated and ineffectively resolved with conventional techniques. Such challenges are particularly well-suited for quantum computing. Large-variable problems or those requiring exponential computational resources are difficult for classical computers to handle, but quantum computers can do so much faster.

For instance, it might be challenging to optimise the position of sensors in industrial IoT to track the condition of equipment. Finding the best solution using traditional methods might require days, which would result in inefficiencies. However, this concern could be addressed in a matter of moments by quantum-enhanced WSNs, which guarantee optimal coverage while *via* a minimum amount of energy. The collected information may be analysed by AI to forecast equipment breakdowns and plan maintenance, which minimises expenses.

Future-Proofing Technology

AI and quantum computing are projected to become the foundations of next-generation systems as technology advances. WSNs are going to be helpful and significant in the future if these technologies are invested in. As AI and quantum computing develop, traditional technologies can become outdated, which would ultimately result in increased expenses and inefficiencies. On the other hand, these technologies are at the vanguard of innovation, providing solutions that are both efficient now and flexible enough to meet new difficulties in the future. For example, Quantum-enhanced WSNs may provide extremely secure communication channels in security and defence that are resistant to potential cyber threats. Long-term security is guaranteed by the AI system's capacity to continuously learn and adjust to diverse kinds of assaults. As technology evolves, this sturdiness guarantees that investments in WSNs shall continue to be worthwhile.

LIMITATIONS AND CHALLENGES

Data transmission, hardware, energy consumption, security, consistency, and cost are only some of the common challenges brought about by the convergence of Quantum Computing (QC), Artificial Intelligence (AI), and Wireless Sensor Networks (WSN). Although WSNs' poor computing capability, energy, and storage capacity do not facilitate the emerging of AI and QC quantum computers require dedicated hardware and pristine environments. In addition, with traditional WSNs and quantum systems, hybrid solutions must deal with variations in computational models. The high latency of quantum communication and the susceptibility of quantum entanglement create synchronisation problems. Additionally, research into quantum AI algorithms is in its infancy, and AI models take a significant or large amount of computing power, which cannot be provided by WSNs.

Whereas AI and QC require high processing resources and call for energy-efficient executions, WSNs are based on low-energy sources, making power management another major concern. Integration is complicated by security threats, including the potential that quantum computers might break traditional cryptography techniques, leaving WSNs vulnerable, and the potential for AI-based cyberattacks. Data protection mandates the use of quantum-secured encryption, *e.g.*, Quantum Key Distribution (QKD). In addition, due to heterogeneous communication protocols and paradigms of computing, non-standardization and incompatibility render integration challenging. Additionally, due to the requirement for a lot of infrastructure by AI-based WSNs and quantum hardware being still expensive, massive deployment is not possible because of high costs and scalability issues. Even with these constraints, if energy, security, and interoperability challenges are addressed, effective integration would revolutionize high-performance computing, effective sensing, and secure networking.

CONCLUSION

A revolutionary paradigm that speeds up data processing, decision-making, and computational power is provided by the combination of Wireless Sensor Networks (WSNs), Artificial Intelligence (AI), and quantum computing. The systems capable of solving difficult real-world problems are made intelligent, adaptable, as well as secure through this synergy. This research brought out the promise of the integration in various fields by pointing out significant applications like cybersecurity, smart healthcare, industrial automation, and environmental monitoring. Given its promise, a range of challenges remain to be addressed, including the energy hurdles of WSNs, the computational complexity of AI models, and the nascent state of quantum hardware development. Widespread adoption is also inhibited by interoperability challenges and security issues. These limitations can be reduced, however, with further advances in secure communication protocols, quantum algorithms, and low-power AI models. Future work should aim to create quantum-AI algorithms that are specially optimized for WSNs, enhancing resource efficiency and ensuring the sustainability of real-world deployment. It is expected that with further development of such technologies, their convergence will transform data-driven decision-making and enable systems to become smarter, more secure, and more effective. The smart and interconnected world can be expected as a result of this multi-disciplinary approach, and it will unveil the potential for revolutionary technologies.

FUTURE SCOPE

The forthcoming research should focus on creating portable and self-learning AI models that can be accomplished on sensor nodes with finite resources. This will allow for anomaly detection in real-time at the edge and dynamic routing. Executing quantum-related assisted collaborative learning for decentralized intelligence that protects confidentiality in distributive WSNs is facilitated through the integration of Quantum computing. Additionally, the reliability of decision-making could be crucially increased with the execution of Quantum Neural Networks (QNNs) to make sophisticated pattern recognition and predictions. More advanced solidarity strategies based on new quantum paradigms could, in due course, increase distributed WSN schemes even more. Finally, developing an overarching simulation and deployment platform enabling the support for AIQC combined models would expedite innovation and real-world problems related to market infrastructures, self-driving cars, and precision farming.

ACKNOWLEDGEMENTS

The authors of this paper are thankful to Guru Nanak Dev University, Amritsar, for providing infrastructural facilities to complete this research work.

REFERENCES

[1] A. Benfradj, A. Thaljaoui, T. Moulahi, R.U. Khan, A. Alabdulatif, and P. Lorenz, "Integration of artificial intelligence (AI) with sensor networks: Trends, challenges, and future directions," *J. King Saud Univ. Comput. Inf. Sci.*, vol. 36, no. 1, 2024.

[2] S.J. Nawaz, S.K. Sharma, S. Wyne, M.N. Patwary, and M. Asaduzzaman, "Quantum machine learning for 6G communication networks: State-of-the-art and vision for the future", *IEEE Access,* vol. 7, pp. 46317-46350, 2019.
[http://dx.doi.org/10.1109/ACCESS.2019.2909490]

[3] W. Osamy, A.M. Khedr, A. Salim, A.I. AlAli, and A.A. El-Sawy, "Recent studies utilizing artificial intelligence techniques for solving data collection, aggregation and dissemination challenges in wireless sensor networks: a review", *Electronics (Basel),* vol. 11, no. 3, p. 313, 2022.
[http://dx.doi.org/10.3390/electronics11030313]

[4] R. Priyadarshi, "Energy-efficient routing in wireless sensor networks: a meta-heuristic and artificial intelligence-based approach: a comprehensive review", *Arch. Comput. Methods Eng.,* vol. 31, no. 4, pp. 2109-2137, 2024.
[http://dx.doi.org/10.1007/s11831-023-10039-6]

[5] K.P. Seng, L.M. Ang, and E. Ngharamike, "Artificial intelligence Internet of Things: A new paradigm of distributed sensor networks", *Int. J. Distrib. Sens. Netw.,* vol. 18, no. 3, 2022.
[http://dx.doi.org/10.1177/15501477211062835]

[6] L. Manman, P. Goswami, P. Mukherjee, A. Mukherjee, L. Yang, U. Ghosh, V.G. Menon, Y. Qi, and L. Nkenyereye, "Distributed artificial intelligence empowered sustainable cognitive radio sensor networks: A smart city on-demand perspective", *Sustain Cities Soc.,* vol. 75, p. 103265, 2021.
[http://dx.doi.org/10.1016/j.scs.2021.103265]

[7] N. Charef, A. Ben Mnaouer, M. Aloqaily, O. Bouachir, and M. Guizani, "Artificial intelligence implication on energy sustainability in Internet of Things: A survey", *Inf. Process. Manage.,* vol. 60, no. 2, p. 103212, 2023. [http://dx.doi.org/10.1016/j.ipm.2022.103212]

[8] C.Y. Liu, H.Y. Yu, and I.C. Tsai, "Applying AI analysis-based IoT system control to the individualized learning field", *Proc. IEEE Int. Conf. Eng., Technol. Educ. (TALE),* pp. 1-7, 2019. [http://dx.doi.org/10.1109/TALE48000.2019.9225908]

[9] J. Qu, Q. Yuan, Z. Li, Z. Wang, F. Xu, Q. Fan, M. Zhang, X. Qian, X. Wang, X. Wang, and M. Xu, "All-in-one strain-triboelectric sensors based on environment-friendly ionic hydrogel for wearable sensing and underwater soft robotic grasping", *Nano Energy,* vol. 111, p. 108387, 2023. [http://dx.doi.org/10.1016/j.nanoen.2023.108387]

[10] Z. Lv, L. Qiao, and R. Nowak, "Energy-efficient resource allocation of wireless energy transfer for the internet of everything in digital twins", *IEEE Commun. Mag.,* vol. 60, no. 8, pp. 68-73, 2022. [http://dx.doi.org/10.1109/MCOM.004.2100990]

[11] P. Danzi, A.E. Kalor, R.B. Sorensen, A.K. Hagelskjaer, L.D. Nguyen, C. Stefanovic, and P. Popovski, "Communication aspects of the integration of wireless IoT devices with distributed ledger technology", *IEEE Netw.,* vol. 34, no. 1, pp. 47-53, 2020. [http://dx.doi.org/10.1109/MNET.001.1900180]

[12] L. Sun, X. Jiang, H. Ren, and Y. Guo, "Edge-cloud computing and artificial intelligence in internet of medical things: architecture, technology and application", *IEEE Access,* vol. 8, pp. 101079-101092, 2020. [http://dx.doi.org/10.1109/ACCESS.2020.2997831]

[13] N. Babu, and S.V.N. Santhosh Kumar, "Chaos quantum optimization□??based layered diagnosis framework for faulty sensor node diagnosis and classification in wireless sensor networks", *Int. J. Commun. Syst.,* vol. 37, no. 11, p. e5793, 2024. [http://dx.doi.org/10.1002/dac.5793]

[14] A.M. Bongale, and C.R. Nirmala, "Firefly algorithm inspired energy aware clustering protocol for wireless sensor network", *Int. J. Commun. Netw. Distrib. Syst.,* vol. 23, no. 3, pp. 380-411, 2019. [http://dx.doi.org/10.1504/IJCNDS.2019.101916]

[15] G. Lăzăroiu, M. Andronie, M. Iatagan, M. Geamănu, R. Ştefănescu, and I. Dijmărescu, "Deep learning-assisted smart process planning, robotic wireless sensor networks, and geospatial big data management algorithms in the Internet of Manufacturing Things," *ISPRS Int. J. Geo-Inf.*, vol. 11, no. 5, 2022. [http://dx.doi.org/10.3390/ijgi11050277]

[16] M.R. Mahmood, M.A. Matin, P. Sarigiannidis, and S.K. Goudos, "A comprehensive review on artificial intelligence/machine learning algorithms for empowering the future IoT toward 6G era", *IEEE Access,* vol. 10, pp. 87535-87562, 2022. [http://dx.doi.org/10.1109/ACCESS.2022.3199689]

[17] M. A. Khan, S. Ullah, M. A. Khan, A. Alazab, and M. Imran, "Convergence of blockchain, IoT, and AI for enhanced traceability systems: A comprehensive review," *IEEE Access*, vol. 13, pp. 152470–152495, 2025.

[18] L. Gashi, A. Luma, and Y. Januzaj, "The integration of Wireless Sensor Networks, Mobile Networks and Cloud Engineering for a decision support system—A Systematic Literature Review", *Proc. Int. Congr. Hum.-Comput. Interact., Optim. Robot. Appl. (HORA),* pp. 1-8, 2022. [http://dx.doi.org/10.1109/HORA55278.2022.9799924]

[19] R. Blake, L. Michalkova, and Y. Bilan, "Robotic wireless sensor networks, industrial artificial intelligence, and deep learning-assisted smart process planning in sustainable cyber-physical manufacturing systems, J. Self-Gov", *Manag. Econ.,* vol. 9, no. 4, pp. 48-61, 2021.

[20] M.S. Basingab, H. Bukhari, S.H. Serbaya, G. Fotis, V. Vita, S. Pappas, and A. Rizwan, "AI-based decision support system optimizing wireless sensor networks for consumer electronics in e-commerce", *Appl. Sci. (Basel),* vol. 14, no. 12, p. 4960, 2024. [http://dx.doi.org/10.3390/app14124960]

[21] M. Hanif, H. Ashraf, Z. Jalil, N.Z. Jhanjhi, M. Humayun, S. Saeed, and A.M. Almuhaideb, "AI-based wormhole attack detection techniques in wireless sensor networks", *Electronics (Basel),* vol. 11, no. 15, p. 2324, 2022. [http://dx.doi.org/10.3390/electronics11152324]

[22] A. Tazhiyeva, "Challenges and opportunities of introducing Internet of Things and artificial intelligence applications into supply chain management," M.S. thesis, School of Technology and Innovations, Univ. Vaasa, Vaasa, Finland, 2018.

[23] S.B. Junaid, A.A. Imam, A.N. Shuaibu, S. Basri, G. Kumar, Y.A. Surakat, A.O. Balogun, M. Abdulkarim, A. Garba, Y. Sahalu, A. Mohammed, Y.T. Mohammed, B.A. Abdulkadir, A.A. Abba, N.A.I. Kakumi, and A.K. Alazzawi, "Artificial intelligence, sensors and vital health signs: a review", *Appl. Sci. (Basel),* vol. 12, no. 22, p. 11475, 2022. [http://dx.doi.org/10.3390/app122211475]

[24] T.S. Delwar, U. Aras, S. Mukhopadhyay, A. Kumar, U. Kshirsagar, Y. Lee, M. Singh, and J.Y. Ryu, "The intersection of machine learning and wireless sensor network security for cyber-attack detection: a detailed analysis", *Sensors (Basel),* vol. 24, no. 19, p. 6377, 2024. [http://dx.doi.org/10.3390/s24196377] [PMID: 39409417]

[25] P. Bhambri and S. Rani, "Challenges, opportunities, and the future of industrial engineering with IoT and AI," in *Integration of AI-Based Manufacturing and Industrial Engineering Systems with the Internet of Things*, R. Rana, Ed. Boca Raton, FL, USA: CRC Press, 1st ed., 2023, pp. 1–18.

[26] S. Shajari, K. Kuruvinashetti, A. Komeili, and U. Sundararaj, "The emergence of AI-based wearable sensors for digital health technology: a review", *Sensors (Basel),* vol. 23, no. 23, p. 9498, 2023. [http://dx.doi.org/10.3390/s23239498] [PMID: 38067871]

[27] A. Massaro, "Advanced electronic and optoelectronic sensors, applications, modelling and industry 5.0 perspectives", *Appl. Sci. (Basel),* vol. 13, no. 7, p. 4582, 2023. [http://dx.doi.org/10.3390/app13074582]

[28] A. Ikram, H. Mehmood, M.T. Arshad, A. Rasheed, S. Noreen, and K.T. Gnedeka, "Applications of artificial intelligence (AI) in managing food quality and ensuring global food security", *CYTA J. Food,* vol. 22, no. 1, p. 2393287, 2024. [http://dx.doi.org/10.1080/19476337.2024.2393287]

[29] S. Zhang, S. Wei, Z. Liu, T. Li, C. Li, X.L. Huang, C. Wang, Z. Xie, O.A. Al-Hartomy, A.A. Al-Ghamdi, S. Wageh, J. Gao, Y. Tang, H. Wang, Q. Wang, and H. Zhang, "The rise of AI optoelectronic sensors: From nanomaterial synthesis, device design to practical application", *Mater. Today Phys.,* vol. 27, p. 100812, 2022. [http://dx.doi.org/10.1016/j.mtphys.2022.100812]

[30] P. Dini, L. Diana, A. Elhanashi, and S. Saponara, "Overview of AI-models and tools in embedded IIoT applications", *Electronics (Basel),* vol. 13, no. 12, p. 2322, 2024. [http://dx.doi.org/10.3390/electronics13122322]

[31] E. Rojas, D. Carrascal, D. Lopez-Pajares, J. Alvarez-Horcajo, J.A. Carral, J.M. Arco, and I. Martinez-Yelmo, "A Survey on AI-Empowered Softwarized Industrial IoT Networks", *Electronics (Basel),* vol. 13, no. 10, p. 1979, 2024. [http://dx.doi.org/10.3390/electronics13101979]

[32] S.M. Popescu, S. Mansoor, O.A. Wani, S.S. Kumar, V. Sharma, A. Sharma, V.M. Arya, M.B. Kirkham, D. Hou, N. Bolan, and Y.S. Chung, "Artificial intelligence and IoT driven technologies for environmental pollution monitoring and management", *Front. Environ. Sci.,* vol. 12, p. 1336088, 2024.

[http://dx.doi.org/10.3389/fenvs.2024.1336088]

[33] B. Mao, F. Tang, Y. Kawamoto, and N. Kato, "AI models for green communications towards 6G", *IEEE Commun. Surv. Tutor.,* vol. 24, no. 1, pp. 210-247, 2022. [http://dx.doi.org/10.1109/COMST.2021.3130901]

[34] D. Alsadie, "Artificial intelligence techniques for securing fog computing environments: trends, challenges, and future directions", *IEEE Access,* vol. 12, pp. 151598-151648, 2024. [http://dx.doi.org/10.1109/ACCESS.2024.3463791]

[35] V. Thakare, G. Khire, and M. Kumbhar, "Artificial intelligence (AI) and internet of things (IoT) in healthcare: Opportunities and challenges", *ECS Trans.,* vol. 107, no. 1, pp. 7941-7951, 2022. [http://dx.doi.org/10.1149/10701.7941ecst]

[36] S.I. Ali, "Consideration of web technology and cloud computing inspiration for AI and IoT role in sustainable decision-making for enterprise systems", *J. Inf. Technol. Informatics,* vol. 3, no. 2, p. 4, 2024.

[37] P. Aruchamy, S. Gnanaselvi, D. Sowndarya, and P. Naveenkumar, "An artificial intelligence approach for energy□??aware intrusion detection and secure routing in internet of things□??enabled wireless sensor networks", *Concurr. Comput.,* vol. 35, no. 23, p. e7818, 2023. [http://dx.doi.org/10.1002/cpe.7818]

[38] H.A. Mengash, R. Marzouk, S.B.H. Hassine, A.M. Hilal, I. Yaseen, and A. Motwakel, "Quantum Artificial Intelligence Based Node Localization Technique for Wireless Networks", *Comput. Mater. Continua,* vol. 73, no. 1, 2022.

[39] P. Kanchan, and S.D. Pushparaj, "A quantum inspired PSO algorithm for energy efficient clustering in wireless sensor networks", *Cogent Eng.,* vol. 5, no. 1, p. 1522086, 2018. [http://dx.doi.org/10.1080/23311916.2018.1522086]

[40] Salim El khediri, Awatef Benfradj, Adel Thaljaoui, Tarek Moulahi, Rehan Ullah Khan, Abdullatif Alabdulatif, Pascal Lorenz, "Integration of artificial intelligence (AI) with sensor networks: Trends, challenges, and future directions", *Journal of King Saud University - Computer and Information Sciences*, vol. 36, no. 1, p. 101892, 2024. [http://dx.doi.org/10.1016/j.jksuci.2023.101892]

[41] P. Liao, X. Wang, Y. Shan, L. An and S. Mao, "Wireless Sensing in Artificial Intelligence of Things: A General Quantum Machine Learning Framework," in *IEEE Network*, vol. 39, no. 3, pp. 207-214, 2025. [http://dx.doi.org/10.1109/MNET.2025.3536925]

SUBJECT INDEX

A

Abnormal patterns 267
Academia 29, 45, 47, 48
  pilot projects linking 47
Accessibility assessment 225
Accessibility compliance 225, 231
  improved video 231
  multimedia 231
Accuracy improvements 41
Accurate market predictions 197
Acid phosphatase 117
Activation functions 240
Activity flow 249
Acute conditions 264
Acute respiratory distress syndrome (ARDS) 122, 128
Adaptability 115, 209, 220, 271
  intelligent 209
  workhorse's 115
Adaptations 137, 140, 170, 225, 226, 227, 230, 232
  dynamic user 227
  favored 232
Adaptive robotic systems 109
Advanced analytics 207
Advanced pattern recognition techniques 196
Advanced simulation capabilities 190
Advancements 2, 3, 12, 35, 40, 41, 42, 43, 44, 45, 75, 76, 93, 107, 108, 123, 145, 166, 196, 202,
  key 123, 196
  quantum computing technology 44
  revolutionary 202
  technological 145
  theoretical 40
Adversary model 212
AEC metrics 265
Aerospace 25, 158
Agglomerative clustering 177, 178, 179, 183, 185
Artificial general intelligence (AGI) 104, 109, 110
AI-accelerated hardware 154
AI-asa-Service (AIaaS) 22
AI-assisted optimization 54
AI-based cyberattacks 273
Algorithm complexity 8, 9, 33, 41, 45, 57, 86, 101, 107, 143, 160, 199
  design 9, 41
  designers 47
  development 8, 33, 45, 57, 199
  efficiency 33, 101
  stability 41
  validation 86
challenges 143
Allocation 65, 67, 160, 184
  asset 67
  optimized task 160
Alzheimer's disease 66
Amazon web services (AWS) 5, 22, 57
Ambiguities 140, 225, 228
  semantic 225
Analog data 207
Analysis scalability 186
Analytical technique 81
Analytics 5, 22, 23, 52, 53, 147, 154, 196, 200, 209, 260, 262
  cloud-based 209
  complicated 260
  predictive 22, 52, 53, 200, 262
  prescriptive 200
  real-time 5, 23, 147, 154
Artificial neural networks (ANN) 97, 133, 134, 236, 238, 239
Acute respiratory distress syndrome (ARDS) 122, 128

B

Behavior analysis 234
Behavioral response 34
Big data processing 199

Satveer Kour, Harvinder Singh, Anupam Bonkra & Rupinder Singh (Eds.)

Bio-computational techniques 121
Biochemical interactions 195
Bioinformatics techniques 120
Biological data 104, 165
  complex 165
Biological neural networks (BNNs) 238
Biopharmaceutical research 66
Bitwise XOR 210
Block decimation, time-evolving 85
Blockchain 71, 260
Blockchain-based banking systems 71
Boston consulting group 1
Branching node splitting processes 115

C

CAGR forecast 2
Carbon footprint 171
Calinski-Harabasz 179, 185
Cluster Head (CH) 247, 262
Chord networks 39, 40
Classical machine learning (CML) 8, 97, 159, 160
Classifiers 112, 113, 114, 115, 116, 118, 122, 123, 125, 126, 127, 128, 129
  random DT 115
  variational quantum 122
Cloud services 5, 10, 22, 24, 69, 70, 71, 201
  commercial quantum 10
  quantum-secured 71
Clusters 173, 176, 177, 178, 179, 180, 181, 182, 183, 184, 185, 186, 247, 252, 253
  detected 182
  indicated betterdefined 184
  non-globular 173, 182
  optimal 178
  spherical 170, 173, 178, 185
  time-dependent 186
Convolutional neural networks (CNNs) 144

D

D-wave 68, 75, 157, 193
Data clustering 184, 252
Defense advanced research projects agency (DARPA) 71, 76
Dolev-Yao (DY) 212

E

Elliptic curve cryptography (ECC) 36, 68, 207, 208, 209, 210, 218
Efficient matrix operations 141
Eigenvalues 24, 103, 177
  approximate 24
  calculating 103
Encryption algorithms 41, 70, 108, 270
  adopted block 41
  novel 70
  traditional 270

F

Fault-tolerant quantum computing (FTQC) 25, 144
Feedforward neural network (FNN) 239, 240, 241
Framework mediator (FM) 248
Fraud detection 12, 17, 33, 35, 38, 41, 42, 65, 67, 76, 147, 149, 164, 165
  financial 33
  instantaneous 67
  physics-based 38
  real-time 164
  reshape 165
Fundamentals of quantum computing 18, 83, 99, 135, 136, 191

G

Gauss-newton method 240
Gaussian-kernel-non-linear approach 121
Gene encoding (GE) 127
Goldman Sachs 67, 105
  financial behemoths 105
Grover's algorithm 4, 133, 137, 192

H

Hadamard gates 84, 100
Hamiltonian-manifested systems 88
Harrow-hassidim-lloyd (HHL) 141
Hash-based cryptography 70
Hasten 38, 110
Human-computer interaction (HCI) 224
High-frequency trading (HFT) 12, 36, 38, 68
HPRD 112, 113, 116, 117, 121, 123, 127
  data set 116
  database 116
  hybrid 113
Hyperparameter adjustments 115
Hyperspectral imaging 172

I

IBM 34, 37, 40, 67, 69, 70, 75, 106, 108, 110, 157, 158, 193
Improved drug matching 64
Improved energy efficiency 152
Improving qubit coherence 9
Integration 10, 16, 17, 22, 23, 27, 28, 144, 154, 156, 173, 205, 209, 210, 228, 224, 236, 237, 262, 263, 264, 273
  cloud-edge 154
  effective 273
  gradual 144
  sensor 224
  smart city 156
  smooth 28
  synergistic 262
  t-SNE 173
Interactive search engine interface 232
IoT-based VANETs 236, 241, 243, 244, 245, 248, 253, 254

J

Jacobian matrices, sensitive 240

K

k-means 170, 172, 173, 176, 177, 178, 179, 180, 183, 184, 185, 242
K-statistics 123
Knapsack Problem 87

L

Laboratory analysis 174
Latent failure patterns 163
Lattice-based cryptography 70
Learning models 4, 43, 46, 54, 56, 69, 89, 98, 103, 127, 134, 141, 144, 159, 164, 166, 170, 226, 240, 250
  classical machine 159
  enhancing machine 4
  fine-tune machine 240
  lightweight machine 250
  quantum-enhanced machine 69, 164
  quantum machine 46, 89
  quantum-powered machine 226
  statistical 127
Levenberg neural engine 236, 240, 241
Lightweight user authentication 212

M

Machine learning 34, 37, 42, 53, 75, 97, 140, 160, 233, 202
  advanced 233
  amplifying 34
  classical 97, 160
  quantum-assisted 37
  quantum-enhanced 42, 202
  statistical 140
  traditional 75
  transform 53
Mass-producing quantum computing chips 42
Matrix 177
  covariance 177
Microsoft azure quantum 7, 70, 71
Metal-organic frameworks (MOFs) 26

Molecular dynamics 75, 104
Monte carlo simulations 67
Mean Square Error (MSE) 249, 251, 252, 253
Mutation prediction 113
Myopic framework 11

N

Naïve Bayes 121
Noisy intermediate-scale quantum (NISQ) 8, 9, 12, 19, 20, 97, 139, 141, 143,
Natural language processing (NLP) 143, 144
  large-scale 143
  real-world 144
Noise mitigation 54
NOT-type gates 98

O

Operational efficiency 24, 84, 149, 156, 172
Operational principle, basic 82
Operationalization 40
Operations 160, 245
  advanced 245
  independent 160
Optimized risk mitigation strategies 197
Optimizing radiation dosage 65
Optimizing routes 72
Outliers 170, 173, 178, 182, 183, 185
  identifying 182

P

Principal component analysis (PCA) 96, 97, 98, 102, 103, 170, 172, 173, 175, 177, 180, 185, 186
Performance evaluation 86, 242
Pfizer 104
Pharmaceutical R&D 26
Post-quantum cryptography (PQCs) 8, 10, 12, 33, 35, 41, 42, 46, 47, 70, 71, 106, 108, 109, 110
PRISMA guidelines 233
Protein folding 47, 66, 104

Q

Q-ai integration 149
Quantum associative memory (QAM) 137
Quantum approximate optimization algorithm (QAOA) 10, 24, 25, 47, 67, 80, 85, 87, 88, 99, 103, 141
Quantum-assisted reinforcement learning (QARL) 56
Quantum-based salp swarm algorithm (QBSSA) 263
Qubit count 60, 86
  limited 60
Quantum optimization techniques 85
Quantum's processors 54

R

R-squared values 176
Reliable V2V communications 243
RF-based algorithm 121
Rider optimisation algorithm (ROA) 263
Risk assessment 12, 17, 41, 45, 52, 105, 197
  credit 67
  efficient 38
  enhancing 196
  financial 67
Routing chord networks 40

S

SEER database 122
Shor's algorithm 4, 35, 41, 42, 47, 68, 192
Support vector machines (SVM) 6, 7, 53, 56, 88, 102, 120, 121, 126, 127, 133, 160, 161, 170

T

TensorFlow quantum (TFQ) 123, 139
Time-evolving block decimation (TEBD) 85

Two-factor authentication 205

U

UAV and machine learning capabilities 172
Ultra-secure communication 270
low vision 229

V

Variational quantum algorithms (VQAs) 85, 102, 103
Variational quantum circuits (VQCs) 10, 56
Variational quantum eigensolver (VQE) 24, 47, 80, 86, 88, 99, 141
Vehicular Ad hoc Network (VANETs) 242, 244, 245, 247, 248, 249, 250, 251, 252, 253, 254

W

Web content accessibility guidelines (WCAG) 225, 228, 229, 232, 233, 235

X

X-ray images 64

Y

Yeast Genome 12

www.ingramcontent.com/pod-product-compliance
Lightning Source LLC
LaVergne TN
LVHW070947210926
848482LV00002B/126